A LEVEL BIOLOGY for OCR A

  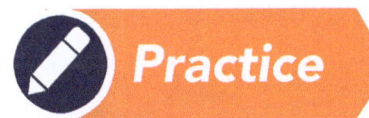

Deborah Shah-Smith
Andrew Chandler-Grevatt
Robert Brooks
Michael Fisher
Rachel Wong

3 steps to access your free online copy of this book

1. Visit Education Bookshelf (http://bookshelf.oxfordsecondary.co.uk).
2. Create an account by clicking the *register* button or *sign in* if you already have an account.
3. Click on the *Activate Your Publication* button and enter your unique access code (printed on the inside cover).

Contents

 Shade in each level of the circle as you feel more confident and ready for your exam.

How to use this book — iv

1 Practical activity groups	2
2 Cell structure	10
3 Biological molecules	22
4 Nucleotides and nucleic acids	38
5 Enzymes	50
6 Biological membranes	60
7 Cell division, diversity, and organisation	72
8 Exchange surfaces	84
9 Transport in animals	96
10 Transport in plants	110
11 Communicable diseases	122
12 Biodiversity	136
13 Classification and evolution	146
14 Communication and homeostasis	156
15 Excretion	168
16 Neuronal communication	180
17 Hormones	192
18 Plant and animal responses	202
19 Photosynthesis	216

20 Respiration 230

21 Cellular control 244

22 Patterns of inheritance 254

23 Manipulating genomes 266

24 Cloning and biotechnology 278

25 Ecosystems, populations, and sustainability 292

26 Unifying concepts 306

Multiple-choice questions 308

How to use this book

This book uses a three-step approach to revision: **Knowledge**, **Retrieval**, and **Practice**. It is important that you do all three; they work together to make your revision effective.

1 Knowledge

Knowledge comes first. Each chapter starts with a **Knowledge Organiser**. These are clear, easy-to-understand, concise summaries of the content that you need to know for your exam. The information is organised to show how concepts relate to each other so you can understand how the knowledge fits together, rather than learning lots of disconnected facts.

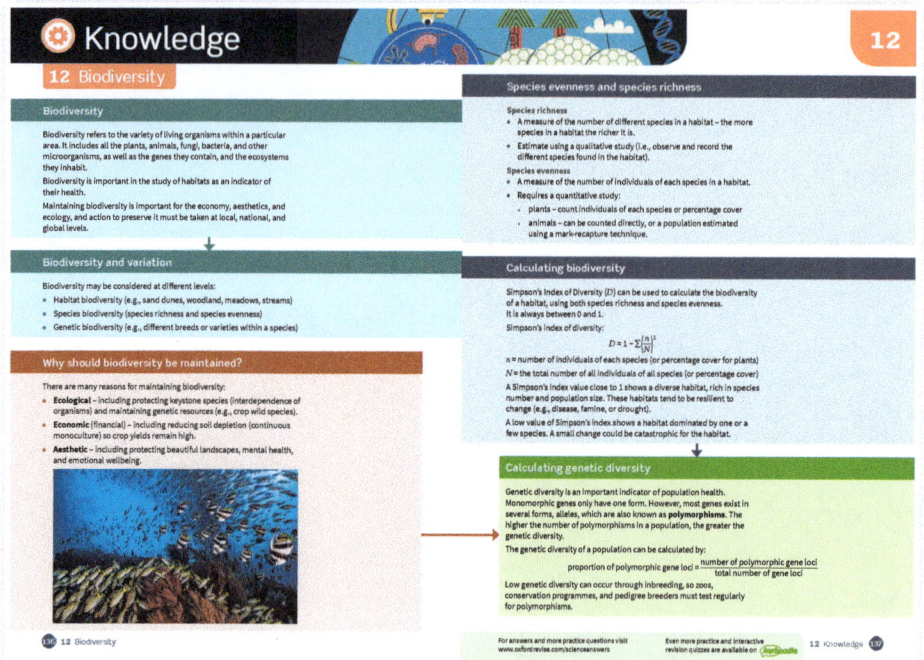

2 Retrieval

The **Retrieval questions** help you learn and quickly recall the information you've acquired. Memorise the short questions and answers about the content in the Knowledge Organiser, then cover the answers with some paper and write as many as you can from memory. Check back to the Knowledge Organiser for any you got wrong, then attempt the questions again until you can answer all the of them correctly.

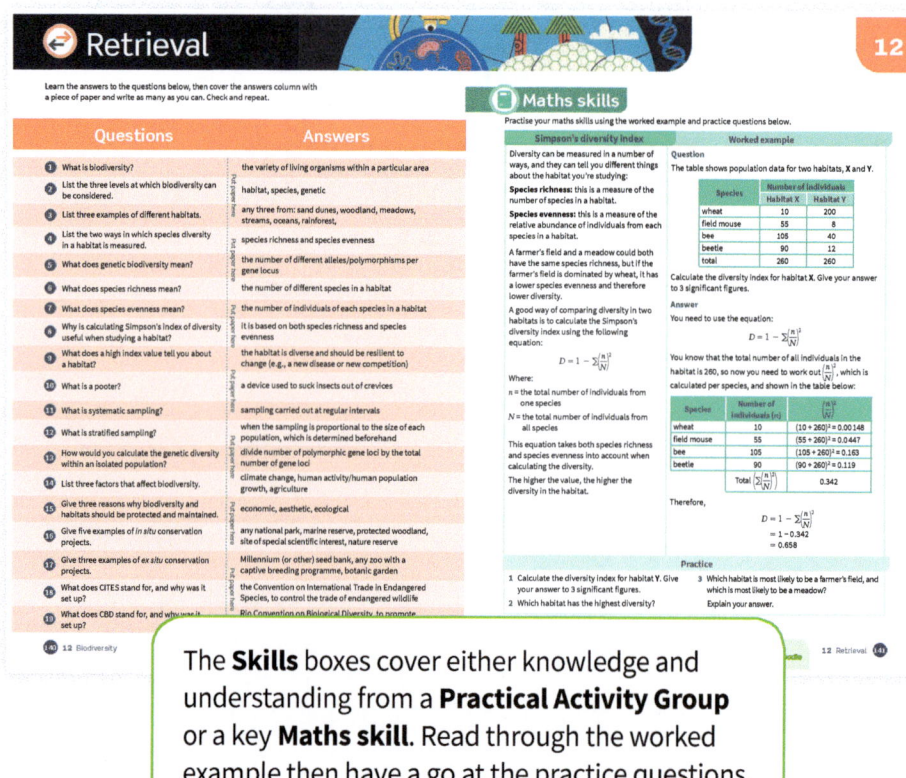

The **Skills** boxes cover either knowledge and understanding from a **Practical Activity Group** or a key **Maths skill**. Read through the worked example then have a go at the practice questions.

Storing these basic facts in your long-term memory through regular retrieval practice will mean you will find it easier to apply them to complex situations and difficult questions.

3 Practice

Once you think you know the Knowledge Organiser and Retrieval answers really well you can move on to the final stage: **Practice**.

Each chapter has lots of **exam-style questions**, that test your ability to:

- apply your knowledge and understanding, including from the Practical Activity Groups
- analyse and evaluate information
- combine knowledge from different parts of the course (synoptic questions).

Questions with the link icon will have **synoptic links**. This means that they will assess the content from the current chapter along with knowledge from elsewhere in the course.

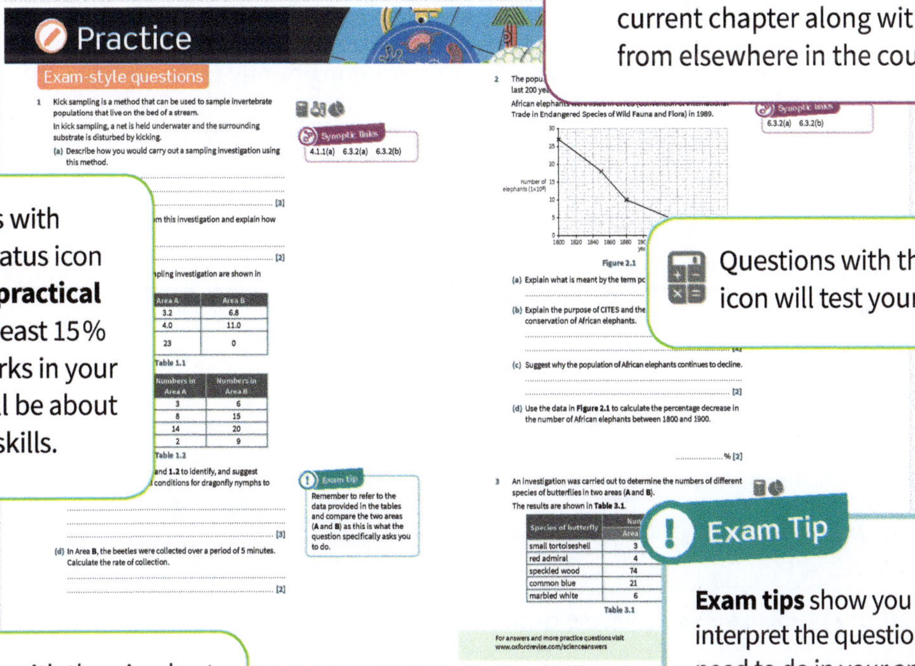

Questions with the apparatus icon test your **practical skills**. At least 15% of the marks in your exams will be about practical skills.

Questions with the calculator icon will test your **maths skills**.

Questions with the pie-chart icon will test your skills in **analysis and evaluation** of data and information.

Exam tips show you how to interpret the questions, what you need to do in your answers, and advice on how to secure as many marks as possible.

kerboodle

All the **answers** are on Kerboodle and the website.
www.oxfordrevise.com/scienceanswers

⚙ Knowledge

1 Practical activity groups

Assessment of Practicals

At least 15% of the total Biology assessment is based on 'indirect assessment of practical skills', which includes the 12 Practical Activity Groups (PAGs). These practical-based questions are the practical endorsement of your A-level qualification. They can be found in all three papers, assessing your planning, implementing, analysis, and evaluation skills. You may be required to draw graphs, calculate results, describe and explain data trends, and evaluate the experiment, suggesting improvements to it.

These practical questions are written to test whether you can apply your understanding and knowledge of these experiments and the scientific concepts behind them. Therefore, it is important to have completed the practicals before your examinations.

Practical skills and knowledge assessed in written papers

Keep track of your confidence in each skill that may be assessed in your exams.

- ☐ Plan experiments to investigate a scientific concept, including selecting suitable apparatus, equipment, and techniques
- ☐ Identify controlled variables
- ☐ Evaluate if the experimental method is appropriate to meet the expected outcomes
- ☐ Use a wide range of practical apparatus and techniques correctly
- ☐ Use appropriate units for measurements
- ☐ Present observations and data in an appropriate format
- ☐ Process, analyse, and interpret qualitative and quantitative experimental results
- ☐ Use appropriate maths skills to analyse quantitative data
- ☐ Use appropriate significant figures when presenting quantitative data
- ☐ Plot and interpret graphs from experimental results, including labelling axes and using appropriate scales, quantities, and units, and measuring gradients and intercepts
- ☐ Evaluate results and draw conclusions
- ☐ Identify anomalies in experimental measurements
- ☐ Describe limitations in experimental procedures
- ☐ Evaluate precision and accuracy of measurements and data, including error margins, percentage errors, and uncertainties in apparatus
- ☐ Suggest improvements to procedures and apparatus to refine experimental design

Apparatus and techniques

You will have used a range of apparatus and techniques when carrying out your practical activities. In your written examinations, you might be asked about the following skills.

a	Use appropriate apparatus to record a range of quantitative measurements (to include mass, time, volume, temperature, length, and pH)
b	Use appropriate instrumentation to record quantitative measurements, such as a colorimeter or potometer
c	Use laboratory glassware apparatus (such as beakers, test tubes, conical flasks) for a variety of experimental techniques, including serial dilutions
d	Use a light microscope at high power and low power, including use of a graticule
e	Produce annotated scientific drawings from observation
f	Use qualitative reagents to identify biological molecules, such as Benedict's and biuret solutions
g	Separate biological compounds using thin layer/paper chromatography or electrophoresis (e.g., amino acids, DNA fragments)
h	Safely and ethically use organisms to measure plant or animal responses and physiological functions
i	Use microbiological aseptic techniques, including the use of agar plates and broth
j	Safely use instruments for dissection of an animal organ or plant organ
k	Use sampling techniques in fieldwork
l	Use ICT, such as computer modelling or a data logger, to collect data, or use software to process data

Additional skills assessed in the practical endorsement (spec 1.2.1)

- Apply investigative approaches and methods to practical work (in PAG 10–12)
- Keep appropriate records of experimental activities
- Present information and data in a scientific way
- Use appropriate software and tools to process data, carry out research, and report findings
- Use online and offline research sources (PAG 12)
- Correctly cite sources of information (PAG 12)

PAG 1 – Microscopy

In this practical, you will use a light microscope to observe and identify the stages of mitosis, and use an eyepiece graticule to find the length of chromosomes. You will also need to calibrate the eyepiece graticule using the stage micrometer for each lens. You also need to draw annotated diagrams of the cells at different stages of mitosis.

Key knowledge and skills

- [ ] Use a light microscope at high power and low power, including use of a graticule
- [ ] Produce scientific drawings from observations with annotations

Example practical

The eyepiece graticule is placed in the eyepiece and calibrated using a stage micrometer with each objective lens. This allows you to know how big each graticule division is at each magnification power, which enables you to measure the size of the specimen. Then view the prepared slide under the microscope to identify cells at different stages of mitosis and to measure the length of chromosomes.

Tips
- Be familiar and careful with the conversion of units when calibrating the microscope, especially between cm, mm, and μm in this case. Show your working when doing calculations to avoid confusion.
- Remind yourself of the rules of scientific drawings, such as smooth, non-feathery lines, making sure all ends meet, etc.

PAG 2 – Dissection

The purpose of this practical is for you to carry out a detailed examination of the external and internal structures of an animal or plant organ, relating them to their function. You are expected to draw annotated scientific diagrams of the dissected structures.

Key knowledge and skills

- [ ] Safely use instruments for dissection of an animal organ or plant organ
- [ ] Use a light microscope at high power and low power, including use of a graticule
- [ ] Produce scientific drawings from observations with annotations

Example practical

A mammalian heart is typically used. Examine its external features before cutting it, particularly identifying the coronary arteries. Then cut down each side of the heart to open up the atria and ventricles and examine the valves between the chambers, before drawing a labelled diagram of the heart.

Tips
- Observe the structures of the different parts of the organ to explain their functions, for example, compare and explain the difference in thickness of the ventricular walls.
- For a heart dissection, feel either side of the heart to identify its left and right sides. The tougher, harder side should be the left of the heart, which is on your right as you look at it.

1 Practical activity groups

PAG 3 – Sampling techniques

This practical involves using sampling techniques on two separate sites to calculate species diversity using Simpson's index of diversity.

Key knowledge and skills

☐ Use sampling techniques in fieldwork

☐ Produce scientific drawings from observations with annotations

Example practical
The experiment is done on two lawns, which may have different conditions. Ten random coordinates must be generated beforehand to reduce the effect of bias. Placing a square quadrat at each coordinate, identify different species using a key and count their numbers. Calculate species diversity, using the data generated.

Tips
- It is crucial to use random coordinates from a random number generator, and not just pick coordinates when you are at the field. This is to reduce the effect of bias as much as possible.
- Do not discard a data point if there are none of your selected species present. Keep in mind that there may be an uneven distribution even if your results are all recorded from the same area with the same environmental factors.

PAG 4 – Rates of enzyme-controlled reactions

This practical focuses on changing a particular variable to measure its effect on the rate of an enzyme-controlled reaction. Different factors can be altered, for example, temperature.

Key knowledge and skills

☐ Use appropriate apparatus to record a range of quantitative measurements (to include mass, time, volume, temperature, length, and pH)

☐ Use laboratory glassware apparatus for a variety of experimental techniques to include serial dilutions

☐ Use ICT such as computer modelling or a data logger to collect data, or use software to process data

Example practical
Change the concentration of hydrogen peroxide (substrate) to see the effect of substrate concentration on the rate of catalase. The rate of reaction can be calculated by measuring the volume of oxygen produced in a minute.

Tips
- Ensure control variables are kept constant for a fair test.
- 'Iodine' alone cannot test for the presence of starch, only 'iodine solution' or 'iodide in potassium iodide solution' can.
- The rate of reaction can be measured in different ways. It can be the time taken for a product to be made, or for all substrate to react. Alternatively, it can be measured as the amount of product produced in a set time period.

PAG 5 – Colorimeter or potometer

This PAG focuses on the use of a colorimeter or potometer. Colorimeters measure the absorbance or transmittance of light through coloured test samples. They provide information on concentrations of chemicals. Potometers measure a plant's water uptake over a period of time.

Key knowledge and skills

- [ ] Use appropriate apparatus to record quantitative measurements, such as a colorimeter or potometer
- [ ] Use laboratory glassware apparatus for a variety of experimental techniques to include serial dilutions.

Example practical

A colorimeter can be used to investigate the effect of temperature on beetroot membrane permeability. It can also be used to determine glucose concentration in a test sample with the use of Benedict's solution, after generating a calibration curve with known concentrations. Potometers with young shoots can be set up under different conditions. This allows us to investigate how different factors affect a plant's transpiration rate.

Tips

- Keep in mind the potometer only estimates the transpiration rate – it is not an exact measurement. This is because the water absorbed by the plant can be used for different purposes, such as photosynthesis and maintaining cells' turgidity. We cannot assume that the water taken up in the potometer is all lost via transpiration.
- Higher glucose concentrations form more precipitate with Benedict's solution, which will absorb more light, leading to higher absorbance values. The colorimeter can measure transmittance as well, which shows the opposite trend – higher transmittance values mean more light is passing through the test sample, which indicates that less precipitate is formed due to a lower glucose concentration.

PAG 6 – Chromatography or electrophoresis

This PAG focuses on the use of chromatography or electrophoresis to separate biological molecules. Chromatography is used to separate substances by size and solubility. It is typically used to isolate amino acids and photosynthetic pigments. Electrophoresis separates charged substances by their size, such as DNA fragments.

Key knowledge and skills

- [ ] Separate biological compounds using thin layer/paper chromatography or electrophoresis

Example practical

A grass extract is made using propanone, which dissolves the photosynthetic pigments in the grass. The extract is added to the chromatography paper as a dot. The paper is then placed into a chromatography chamber to let it run, stopping it before the solvent front reaches the top. Then the retention values of each separated pigment are calculated to identify them.

Tips

- Avoid touching the chromatography paper as any sebum transferred from your fingers onto the paper will also be separated in the process, affecting your results.
- Be careful to not let the original dot submerge under the solvent, as it will be dissolved in the liquid rather than being separated on the chromatography paper.
- The chromatograms of photosynthetic pigments will fade very quickly in the light, as the pigments will react under sunlight. Therefore, it is better to mark the spots and complete measurements as quickly as possible.
- Keep in mind that DNA is negatively charged, so the fragments should be placed at the cathode (negative) end. As the electric current passes through the gel, the fragments are then attracted towards the anode (positive) end, separating out by length and size of charge.

PAG 7 – Microbiological techniques

This PAG requires you to use aseptic techniques to carry out microbiological studies. Population density of microbes can be determined through dilution plating. The effect of antibiotics on bacterial growth can also be investigated. Genetic engineering of bacterial plasmids can also be done.

resulting plates. *E. coli* plates can be prepared with antibiotic multi-test rings to investigate which antibiotic is most effective by measuring the zones of inhibition. The Green Fluorescent Protein gene can be inserted into plasmid DNA to make transformed bacteria glow under UV light.

Key knowledge and skills

- [ ] Use laboratory glassware apparatus for a variety of experimental techniques to include serial dilutions
- [ ] Use microbiological aseptic techniques, including the use of agar plates and broth

Example practical
Dilution plating involves a serial dilution of bacterial broth cultures, which are then added to agar plates. The population density can be estimated in the

Tips
- When counting the colonies in dilution plating, an assumption is made that each colony was formed from one initial bacterium. It is important to estimate how many colonies there are in overlapping colony patches.
- If equipment is passed through the Bunsen flame to be sterilised, it must be allowed to cool before use, otherwise the heat will kill the microbes, affecting your results.

PAG 8 – Transport in and out of cells

This PAG focuses on investigating the movement of substances by diffusion and osmosis across membranes. The most common practical is determining the water potential of potatoes. Effects of various factors on diffusion and osmosis can also be investigated in this PAG.

Key knowledge and skills

- [ ] Use appropriate apparatus to record a range of quantitative measurements (to include mass, time, volume, temperature, length, and pH)
- [ ] Use laboratory glassware apparatus for a variety of experimental techniques to include serial dilutions
- [ ] Use ICT such as computer modelling or a data logger to collect data, or use software to process data

Example practical
Several sucrose solutions of different concentrations are prepared by serial dilution. Identical potato cylinders are placed into each of them for a set time period. A graph can then be plotted based on their percentage change in mass to determine the sucrose concentration of the potato. Then a calibration curve is used to determine the relevant water potential.

Tips
- Make sure to remove the skin on the potato cylinders, as the skin affects how much water can move into and out of the potato tissue, producing invalid results.
- Ensure you blot the plant tissues dry in the same way each time, without squeezing them.
- Remember the maximum water potential is 0 kPa in pure water only.
- When plotting the graph of percentage change in mass against sucrose concentration, the x-intercept marks zero change in mass (y-variable), which means there is no net water movement, indicating that the water potential in the potato is the same as the surrounding solution. This allows us to find out what the sucrose concentration of the potato is.

PAG 9 – Qualitative testing

A qualitative test produces a positive or negative result to show if a particular substance is present or not, without measuring its quantity or concentration. Qualitative testing of different biological molecules using various reagents is typically shown by a colour change.

Key knowledge and skills

- [ ] Use laboratory glassware apparatus for a variety of experimental techniques to include serial dilutions
- [ ] Use qualitative reagents to identify biological molecules

Example practicals
Biuret solution changes from blue to purple in the presence of proteins. The addition of ethanol and water to lipids produces a white emulsion layer. When reducing sugars mix with Benedict's solution in a hot water bath, red precipitates are formed.

Tips
- When describing the procedures of testing reducing sugars with Benedict's reagent, make sure to include the step of heating the mixture in a hot water bath. Without this step, results would not be generated.
- The colour of precipitates made in the Benedict's test gives an indication of the sugar concentration. High concentrations make red precipitates, whereas orange and green precipitates indicate medium and low sugar concentrations respectively.
- The Benedict's test can be quantified with the use of a colorimeter.

PAG 10 – Investigation using a data logger or computer modelling

Molecular modelling software can be used to look at different biological molecules in more detail. Probes and sensors can be connected to a data logger to monitor the change of conditions, such as temperature and pH, over time.

Key knowledge and skills

- [ ] Use ICT such as computer modelling or a data logger to collect data, or use software to process data
- [ ] Apply investigative approaches

Example practical
The structure of DNA can be examined in more detail with the use of RasMol, a molecular modelling software. Different atoms can be colour-coded for a better understanding of their chemical structure. The length of hydrogen bonds between the bases can also be measured with the software.

Tips
- Purines have two carbon rings, whereas pyrimidines have one. This is why they always pair up with each other to ensure their atoms are close enough to form hydrogen bonds.
- Consider the benefits of using data loggers rather than experimental measurements. Be prepared to evaluate the accuracy of different approaches.

PAG 11 – Investigation into the measurement of plant or animal responses

Physiological responses of animals and plants can be affected by various factors and changes in the environment. This PAG allows you to explore how animals' heart rate may be affected under different situations and how tropism works in plants.

Key knowledge and skills

☐ Safely and ethically use organisms to measure plant or animal responses and physiological functions

☐ Apply investigative approaches

Example practical
The investigation is to see if low- and moderate-intensity exercise causes a change in heart rate. Null hypotheses are made in both cases and young adult volunteers first record their resting heart rate. A standardised exercise at different intensities should be carried out, with their heart rates recorded immediately after each exercise. A *t*-test should then be used to determine if there is significant difference in heart rate before and after the different intensities of exercise.

Tips
- Try to keep other variables as controlled and constant as possible for a fair test.
- Evaluate the reliability of results generated by a small sample size and consider how the experiment can be improved.
- Consider the accuracy of your method of measuring heart rate. Measuring pulse rate using your fingers on your wrist or neck may not be as reliable as using a heart rate monitor.

PAG 12 – Research skills

This PAG provides an opportunity to develop your research skills. This may involve designing and carrying out a practical investigation, doing a literature review and case studies, and correctly citing information sources. The final write-up should include an introduction, aim, hypothesis, procedure, results, conclusion, evaluation, and references.

Key knowledge and skills

☐ Apply investigative approaches

☐ Use online and offline research skills

☐ Correctly cite sources of information

Example practical
An example is to investigate how a factor affects the rate of photosynthesis in pondweed. The first step may be to use a range of different sources to research how abiotic factors affect the process. Then plan and conduct an experiment to investigate one particular factor. Record and process your results, then draw a conclusion based on your findings. An evaluation should be done to consider how the experimental procedure can be improved.

Tips
- It is important to evaluate the validity and reliability of your sources, especially those found online.
- When evaluating a method, consider any steps that may increase the error size. Consider what can be done to improve the accuracy, precision, validity, and repeatability of the results, such as doing repeats, increasing sample size, using equipment with smaller intervals, etc.

Knowledge

2 Cell structure

Cell structure and microscopes

Understanding the structure of cells is a fundamental concept in biology, as every living thing is made up of cells. There are eukaryotic cells (i.e., animal, plant, and fungal cells) and prokaryotic cells (i.e., bacteria). In complex, multicellular organisms, eukaryotic cells become specialised for specific functions.

Microscopes are instruments that have allowed us to observe cell structure and provide evidence to support hypotheses about the roles of cells and organelles.

Magnification and resolution

Magnification	the number of times greater the size of the image is than the size of the real object	$\text{magnification} = \dfrac{\text{image size}}{\text{size of real object}}$
Resolution	the ability to distinguish between two objects that are very close together – higher resolution means more detail	ribosomes are 25 nm in diameter, so do not interfere with light waves (wavelength of about 400 nm). Therefore they cannot be seen using an optical microscope because its resolution is too low

Staining

Stains are used in microscopy to:
- make cells more visible
- increase contrast
- identify different cell components.

Stains for specific biochemicals are used.

For example, iodine solution stains starch granules blue and black; methylene blue stains genetic material in animal cells blue.

In confocal microscopy, fluorescent dyes can be used to tag specific molecules.

Measuring cells

When using a light microscope, specimens can be measured using two steps:

1. A **stage micrometer** is a slide that has actual scales etched onto it. It is used to calibrate an **eye piece graticule**.
2. An **eye piece graticule** has arbitrary units as a scale for measurement. The scale is used to measure the specimen. The actual measurement of the specimen is calculated using the calibration data (from the stage micrometer).

Microscope images

Plant cells viewed using a light microscope

Chloroplast viewed using a SEM

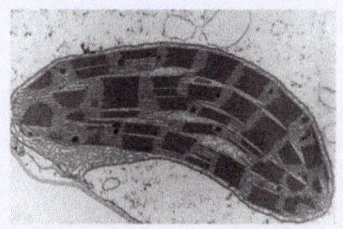

2

Microscopes

Microscope	light microscope	transmission electron microscope (TEM)	scanning electron microscope (SEM)	laser scanning confocal microscope (LSCM)
Principles	• uses light to form an image • light that passes through or reflects from the surface of the specimen is seen	• uses electrons to form an image • electrons that pass through the specimen are detected	• uses electrons to form an image • electrons that are reflected from the surface on the specimen are detected	• uses a laser beam to scan an object pixel by pixel, creating a 3D image of the reflected photons. 2D images of higher resolution can also be produced
Functionality	• magnification to 2000× • resolution to 200 nm • living and non-living specimens can be observed	• magnification to 1 000 000× • resolution to 0.2 nm • only dead or non-living specimens can be used	• magnification to 1 000 000× • resolution to 3–20 nm • only dead or non-living specimens can be used	• requires a compromise between resolution, scan time, and photodestruction of the specimen

Main organelles in a prokaryotic cell

Prokaryotic cells are much smaller than eukaryotic cells, and differ from them by having:

- a cytoplasm that lacks membrane-bound organelles
- smaller ribosomes (70S instead of 80S)
- no nucleus, instead they have a single loop of DNA that:
  - is free in the cytoplasm
  - has no associated proteins
- a cell wall that contains **peptidoglycan**, a **glycoprotein**.

In addition, many prokaryotic cells have:

- one or more **plasmids**
- a **capsule** surrounding the cell
- one or more **flagella**.

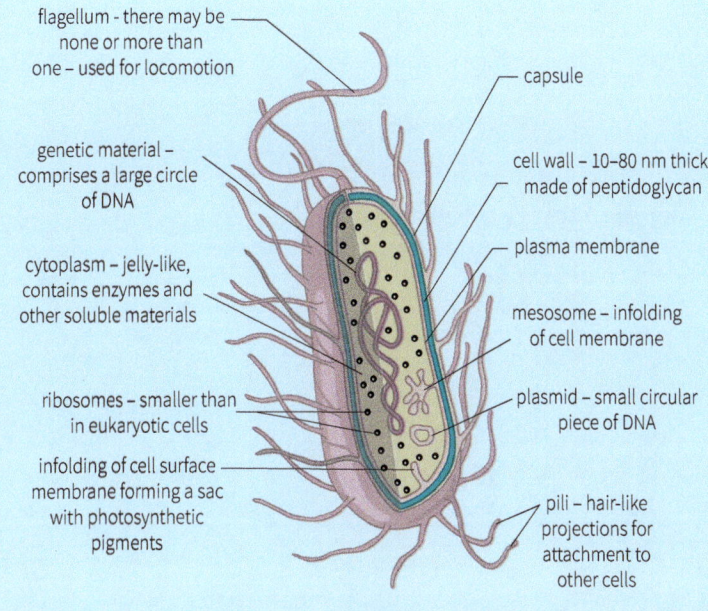

2 Knowledge 11

Cell structure and ultrastructure

The light microscope has limitations in magnification and resolution. The use of other types of microscope, using electrons instead of light, has revealed the ultrastructure of cells.

Main organelles in an animal cell

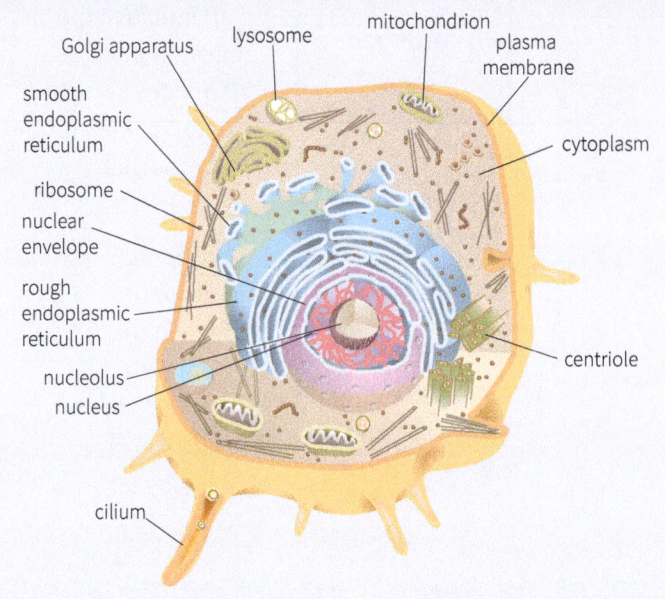

Main organelles in a plant cell

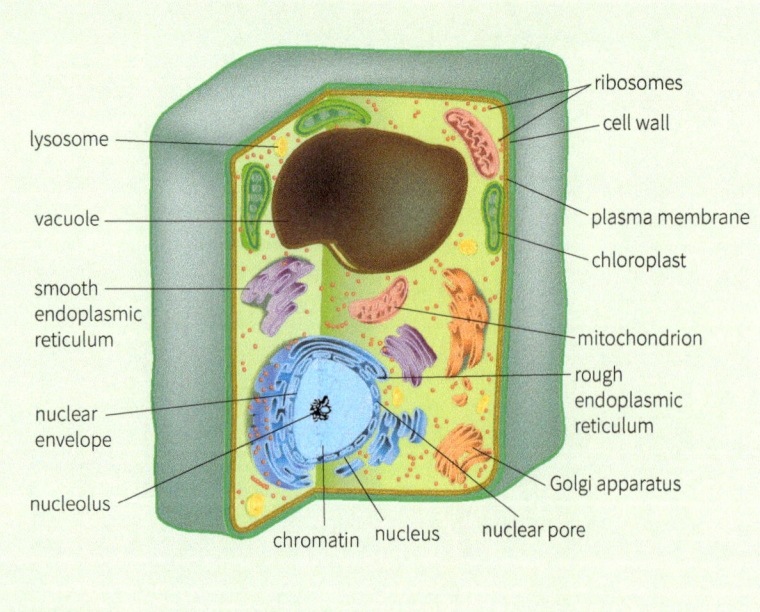

Organelles common to plant and animal cells

Plasma membrane:
- very thin phospholipid bilayer (~ 7 nm) surrounding the cell
- controls exchange between the cell and its environment

Nucleus:
- stores DNA and coordinates the cell's activities, which include growth, intermediary metabolism, protein synthesis, and reproduction
- contains chromosomes (linear DNA strands and associated histone proteins) and one or more nucleoli
- the nuclear envelope has nuclear pores to control exchange between the nucleus and cytoplasm

Mitochondrion:
- ~ 1–10 μm long rod-shaped organelle
- has a smooth outer membrane and an inner membrane highly folded into cristae
- carries out aerobic respiration which takes place in the matrix and on the cristae, producing ATP

Cytoskeleton

The cytoskeleton has three main functions:

1. Giving **mechanical strength** to the cell, to reduce squashing
2. **Aiding transport** within cells including whole organelles
3. **Enabling cell movement**.

2 Cell structure

Additional organelles

Smooth endoplasmic reticulum (SER) (in plants and animals):
- similar structure to RER, but no ribosomes
- synthesises lipids, steroids, and some hormones (e.g., testosterone and oestrogen).
- synthesises, stores, and transports carbohydrates

Permanent vacuoles (in plants):
- contains sap and helps support the plant

Cell wall (plants, algae, and fungi):
- composed mainly of cellulose in plants
- composed of chitin and cellulose in fungi
- composed of glycoproteins in algae
- provides mechanical strength whilst remaining permeable
- maintains the cell shape and may have pores to connect cells

Chloroplasts (in plants and algae):
- oval-shaped organelles (3–10 μm long)
- surrounded by two membranes
- disc-like thylakoids arranged in stacks called grana
- internal fluid is called the stroma
- the light-dependent reactions of photosynthesis take place on the thylakoid membranes
- light-independent reactions take place in the stroma

Flagella (mostly animal cells and bacteria):
- long, whip-like structures
- involved in motility of the cell

Cilia (mostly animal cells):
- short, hair-like structures
- involved in moving substances past the cell

Centrioles (mostly in animal cells):
- only visible using TEM/SEM
- form spindle fibres involved in mitosis and meiosis
- found at the base of cilia and flagella

Protein production in plant and animal cells

Ribosome
- tiny granules 25 nm in diameter
- site of protein synthesis
- 80S in eukaryotic cells

Rough endoplasmic reticulum (RER)
- an extended system of membrane sacs that runs throughout the cell
- site of protein modification
- encrusted with ribosomes

Golgi apparatus and Golgi vesicles
- stacks of flattened membranes
- collects, processes, and sorts molecules that are then transported in Golgi vesicles to other parts of the cell or secreted out of the cell
- modifies proteins
- makes lysosomes

Lysosome
- a Golgi vesicle that releases lysozyme and contains other hydrolytic enzymes for variety of functions

Retrieval

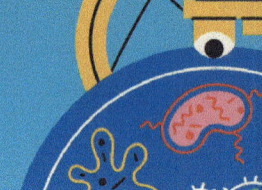

Learn the answers to the questions below, then cover the answers column with a piece of paper and write as many as you can. Check and repeat.

	Questions	Answers
1	What is the name of the cell organelle that synthesises proteins?	ribosomes/rough endoplasmic reticulum
2	What is the name of the cell organelles that release lysozyme?	lysosomes
3	What is the name of the cell organelle that makes lipids, steroids, and some hormones?	smooth endoplasmic reticulum
4	Which organelles are involved with protein synthesis?	nucleus, rough endoplasmic reticulum (RER), ribosomes, Golgi apparatus and vesicles
5	What is the name of the cell organelle that carries out photosynthesis?	chloroplasts
6	What is the function of flagella?	locomotion
7	Describe the structure of a chloroplast.	oval-shaped organelle, 3–10 µm long surrounded by two membranes, with disc-like thylakoids arranged in stacks called grana; the internal fluid is called the stroma
8	What is the structure and function of cilia?	made of microtubules, cilia are short, hair-like structures involved in moving substances past the cell
9	What type of cells are animal, fungal, and plant cells?	eukaryotic
10	What type of cells are bacteria?	prokaryotic
11	Which three organelles do plant cells have that are not present in animal cells?	permanent vacuole, cell wall, and chloroplasts
12	What is the difference in chemical composition between a eukaryotic plant cell wall and a prokaryotic cell wall?	plant cell walls contain cellulose; bacterial cell walls contain peptidoglycan, a glycoprotein
13	What is the difference between the organelles in a prokaryotic cell and a eukaryotic cell?	prokaryotic cells lack membrane-bound organelles
14	What is the difference between the ribosomes in a prokaryotic cell and in a eukaryotic cell?	prokaryotic cells have smaller 70S ribosomes; eukaryotic ribosomes are 80S
15	Define magnification.	the number of times greater the size of the image is than the size of the real object
16	How can you calculate the magnification of an object?	magnification = image size ÷ actual size of object
17	What is the limitation of light microscopy?	magnification to 2000×, resolution to 200 nm

14 2 Cell structure

18	Define resolution	the ability to see 2 objects as separate entities; it is the level of detail seen in an image
19	What are the three functions of the cytoskeleton?	1 mechanical strength 2 aiding transport within cells 3 enabling cell movement (e.g., phagocytes and amoebae)

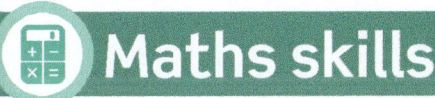

Maths skills

Practise your maths skills using the worked example and practice questions below.

Using standard form

In Biology, it's common to come across extremely large or extremely small numbers that you'll need to work with. To make these more manageable, scientists often convert these numbers into standard form, which presents these numbers in a more concise way.

Standard form is written as:

$$x \times 10^y$$

Where:

x = a number between 1 and 10

y = any positive or negative whole number.

If y is positive, then standard form represents a very big number. If it is negative, it represents a very small number.

For example,

$3 \times 10^4 = 3 \times (10 \times 10 \times 10 \times 10)$
$ = 30\,000$

$6 \times 10^{-3} = \dfrac{6}{10^3} = \dfrac{6}{1000}$
$\phantom{6 \times 10^{-3}} = 0.006$

Worked example

Question

A leaf has 50 000 000 cells on its surface. Give this number in standard form.

Answer

First, you need to break this equation down to find both x and y of:

$$x \times 10^y$$

$50\,000\,000 = 5 \times 10\,000\,000$

So, $x = 5$

Then, you need to find y:

$10\,000\,000 = 10^7$ (there are 7 zeros)

$y = 7$

Therefore, $50\,000\,000 = 5 \times 10^7$

Question

The diameter of the SARS-CoV-2 viral particle is 0.000 2 mm. Give this number in standard form.

Answer

$0.000\,2 = 2 \div 10\,000$

So, $x = 2$

As there are 4 zeros in 10 000, the power (y) is 4. But, because you had to divide by 10 000, you need to put a minus before our power to convey that it's a small number.

So, $y = -4$.

Therefore, $0.000\,2 = 2 \times 10^{-4}$

Practice

Express these values in standard form:

1. 25 000
2. 675 000 000
3. 0.000 078

Express these values in normal form:

4. 4.28×10^{-5}
5. 9.7×10^{12}
6. 2.473×10^{-8}

For answers and more practice questions visit www.oxfordrevise.com/scienceanswers

Even more practice and interactive revision quizzes are available on kerboodle

2 Retrieval 15

Exam-style questions

1 **Figure 1.1** shows an animal cell.

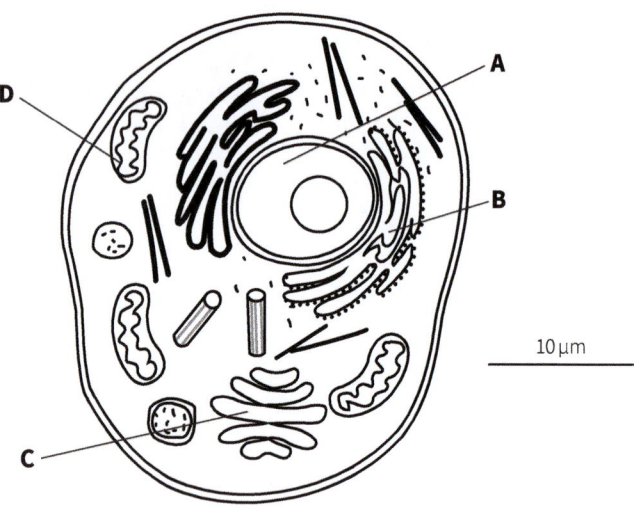

Figure 1.1

(a) (i) Name the cell components **A** and **B**.

A ....

B .... [2]

(ii) State the function of organelles **C** and **D**.

C ....

D .... [2]

(b) Name two components in plant cells that are not present in animal cells.

.... [2]

(c) Using the scale bar, calculate the magnification of the diagram. Show your working.

.... [2]

> ⚠ **Exam tip**
>
> When calculating magnification, make sure that the units for the sizes are the same before doing the calculation.

2 (a) In **Table 2.1**, tick the box if the organelle is found in that cell type. This includes **specialised cells** as well.

Organelle	Animal cell	Plant cell	Prokaryotic cell
cell wall			
nucleus			
centrioles			
rough ER			
mitochondria			
chloroplasts			

Table 2.1

[6]

2 Cell structure

(b) The cytoskeleton in cells is made up of microtubules and microfilaments.

Outline the different roles of cytoskeleton with examples.

....
....
....
....
....
....
....
....
....
.... [5]

> **! Exam tip**
> Think about how the cytoskeleton can affect the whole cell and the individual organelles within the cell.

3 (a) Complete **Table 3.1** to compare the ultrastructure of prokaryotic and eukaryotic cells.

Feature	Prokaryotic cell	Eukaryotic cell
DNA structure		
chemical that makes up the cell wall		
size of ribosomes		

Table 3.1

[6]

(b) The digestion of starch starts in the mouth, where salivary glands produce amylase.

Outline how different organelles within a salivary gland cell produce and release amylase out of the cell.

Quality of writing is assessed in this question.

....
....
....
....
....
....
....
....
....
....
.... [6]

> **! Exam tip**
> Enzymes are proteins. Think about the organelles that are involved in protein synthesis and how proteins can be packaged, modified, and transported out of the cells.

4   An experiment was carried out to investigate the function of different organelles.
    Some animal and plant cells were broken apart, releasing all of their cellular contents within test tubes **A** and **B**. The test tubes were then centrifuged to separate different components within the mixtures based on their mass difference. The more mass a component has, the lower its band.

    Figure 4.1 shows the results of the two test tubes after centrifugation.

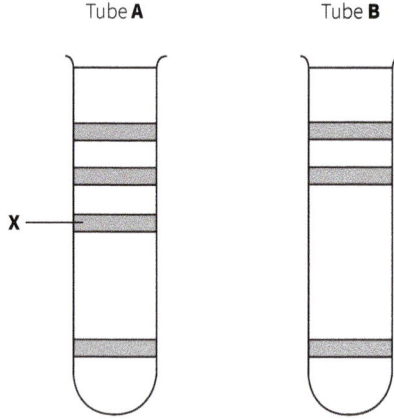

Figure 4.1

Each test tube was then tested to identify the cellular components.
Table 4.1 shows the results.

Test	Test tube A	Test tube B
ability to make glucose	glucose is made	no glucose is made
ability to make proteins	proteins are made	proteins are made
ability to make ATP	ATP is produced	ATP is produced
presence of DNA	DNA is present	DNA is present

Table 4.1

(a) (i) Identify which test tube contains animal cells and explain your answer.

....

....

....

.... [2]

(ii) Identify which component makes up the the band labelled **X** in test tube **A**.

.... [1]

(iii) Suggest which three components are separated in test tube **B**.

....

....

.... [3]

> **! Exam tip**
>
> You are not expected to know the process of centrifugation, but you are expected to be able to analyse unfamiliar data and answer questions based on the information you're given and your biological knowledge.

2 Cell structure

A test tube containing components within prokaryotic cells was also centrifuged (test tube **C**). It was then compared with test tube **B**, as shown in **Figure 4.2**.

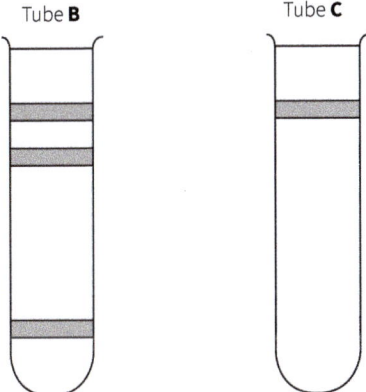

Figure 4.2

> **! Exam tip**
>
> Comparing tubes **A** and **B**, you can identify what the three organelles are in test tube **B** based on your understanding of animal and plant cells. Now compare that to a prokaryotic cell in test tube **C**, which does not have any membrane-bound organelles within: what is the one organelle in test tube **B** that is not membrane-bound?

(b) (i) Assuming each component has their unique banding within centrifugation, suggest the organelle component shown in test tube **C**.

.... [1]

(ii) Some people suggested that the band result in test tube **C** is inaccurate.

Suggest why.

....
.... [2]

5   Prokaryotic and eukaryotic cells have slightly different mechanisms of protein synthesis.

Figure 5.1 shows how prokaryotic cells produce proteins.

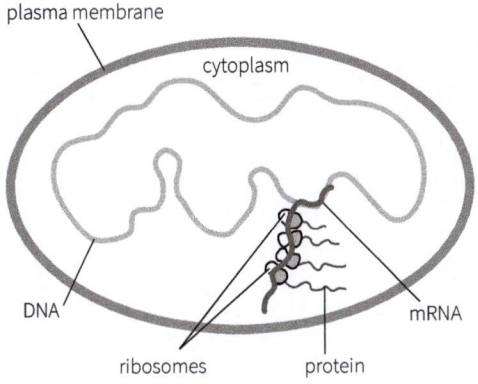

Figure 5.1

(a) Using information in **Figure 5.1**, describe similarities and differences between protein synthesis in prokaryotic and eukaryotic cells.

....
....
....
.... [4]

(b) (i) Staining is often an essential step in microscopy.
Give two reasons to explain why.

....

....

....

.... [2]

A student has prepared a slide with cheek cells. Before they placed the slide under the light microscope, the student used a stage micrometer to calibrate the eyepiece graticule.

Figure 5.2 shows what the student saw on high power (×400).

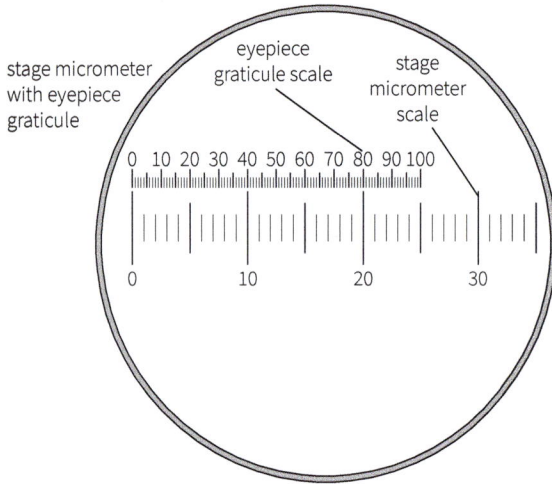

Figure 5.2

After calibration, the student looked at the cheek cell slide under the light microscope at high power (×400) again.

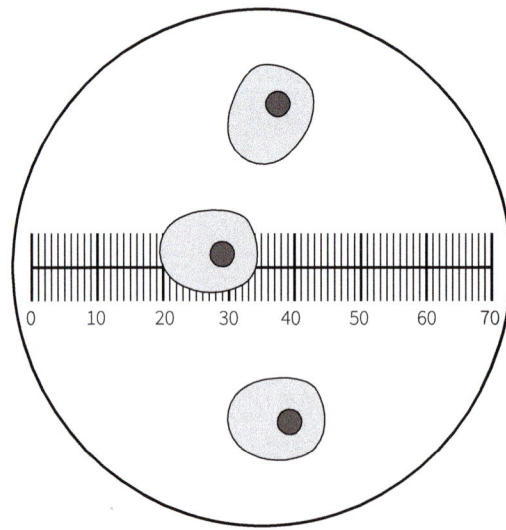

Figure 5.3

(ii) Calculate the size of the cheek cell shown in **Figure 5.3**. Present your answer in µm.

.... µm [3]

> ! **Exam tip**
>
> Make sure that you show your working clearly in separate steps when doing calculations. Correct working steps would score some marks even if your final answer is wrong.

20 2 Cell structure

6 Cells rely on their DNA to code for proteins.

(a) (i) Describe how DNA is packaged within the nucleus in eukaryotic cells.

....
....
....
....
....
.... [2]

Synoptic link

2.1.2m

(ii) State a difference between the structure of bacterial DNA and animal chromosomes.

....
.... [1]

There are several levels of protein structure. **Table 6.1** shows some of their descriptions.

Letters	Descriptions
A	disulfide bonds are formed
B	bonding with other subunits
C	hydrogen bonds are involved
D	sequence of amino acids
E	further 3D folding of the polypeptide
F	peptide bonds are involved
G	α helices and/or β pleated sheets are formed

Table 6.1

(b) Answer the following questions using the letters **A–G**. Some letters may be used twice.

(i) Select the letter(s) that represent the primary structure of a protein.

.... [1]

Exam tip

You will need to use your knowledge of protein structure from Chapter 3 *Biological molecules*.

(ii) Select the letter(s) that represent the secondary structure of a protein.

.... [1]

(iii) Select the letter(s) that represent the tertiary structure of a protein.

.... [1]

(iv) Select the letter(s) that represent the quaternary structure of a protein.

.... [1]

Knowledge

3 Biological molecules

Properties of water

Water is a molecule that has unusual properties due to the hydrogen bonds that form between its molecules. Many of these properties make it essential for life processes.

Six important properties of water in biology are:

Property	Examples
1 it is a **metabolite** in many metabolic reactions	condensation and hydrolysis reactions, and photosynthesis
2 it is the **solvent** where metabolic reactions occur	the cytoplasm (70–95% water)
3 relatively high **heat capacity**	buffers temperature changes – a large amount of energy is needed to raise the temperature of large bodies of water a small amount, so oceans, seas, and lakes maintain a relatively stable temperature
4 relatively large **latent heat of vaporisation**	losing small amounts of water through evaporation has a cooling effect (e.g., sweating, panting, transpiration)
5 strong **cohesion** between water molecules	supports columns of water in xylem for the transpiration stream and produces surface tension where water meets air
6 ice is less **dense** than water	lakes do not freeze completely so aquatic organisms are not killed as temperatures fall

The role of inorganic ions

Inorganic ions are charged atoms or molecules that do not contain carbon. They occur in a range of concentrations within cells and body fluids. Cations are positively charged and anions are negatively charged.

Ion	Biological function
calcium (Ca^{2+})	involved in transmission of nervous impulses, regulation of protein channels, muscle contraction, hardening teeth and bones
sodium (Na^+)	involved in transmission of nervous impulses, active transport Na^+ pump, co-transport of glucose and amino acids across membranes
potassium (K^+)	involved in transmission of nervous impulses, active transport, and plant cell turgidity
hydrogen (H^+)	the higher the concentration, the lower the pH of bodily fluids
ammonium (NH_4^+)	source of nitrogen used to make organic molecules
nitrate (NO_3^-)	source of nitrogen for organic molecules
hydrogencarbonate (HCO_3^-)	involved in the regulation of blood pH and transport of carbon dioxide in the blood
chloride (Cl^-)	involved in transport of carbon dioxide in the blood through the chloride shift
phosphate (PO_4^{3-})	components of biological molecules such as nucleotides, ATP, and the formation of the phospholipid bilayer
hydroxide (OH^-)	the higher the concentration, the higher the pH of bodily fluids

Monomers and polymers

Monomers are small units that make up larger molecules.

Polymers are large molecules made up of a large number of monomers.

For carbohydrates and proteins, monomers are joined by **condensation reactions**, with the elimination of a water molecule.

Bonds between polymers can be broken down through **hydrolysis**, using a water molecule.

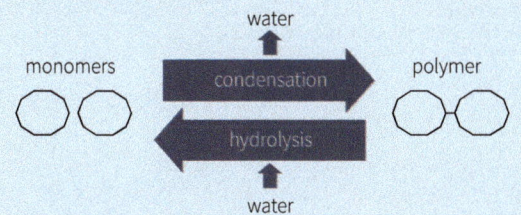

Organic substances

All life on Earth shares a common chemistry. Just a few groups of **carbon-based** compounds make up the cells of all living organisms.

Four carbon-based compounds common to all living organisms:

Molecule	Elements	Example functions
carbohydrates	C, H, O	energy store and source in cells, structural components in plasma membranes and cell walls
lipids	C, H, O	forms bilayer of plasma membranes, some hormones, energy store
proteins	C, H, O, N, S	cell structure, enzymes, chemical messengers, blood components
nucleic acids	C, H, O, N, P	genetic code for protein production

Hexose and pentose monosaccharides

The glucose molecule has a ring structure and is a hexose (6-carbon) monosaccharide. Glucose has two isomers, **α-glucose** and **β-glucose**.

Glycogen and **starch** are formed by polymerisation of α-glucose molecules.
Cellulose is formed by polymerisation of β-glucose molecules.

Ribose sugars are pentose (5-carbon) monosaccharides that occur in ribonucleic acid (RNA), ATP, and NAD.

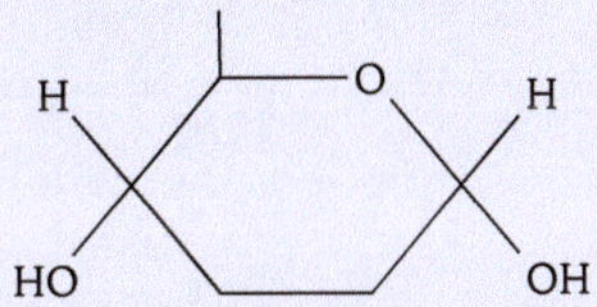

α-glucose 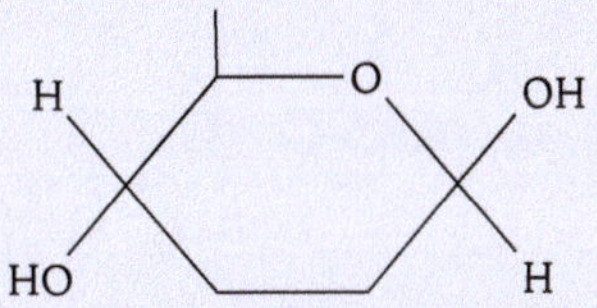   β-glucose 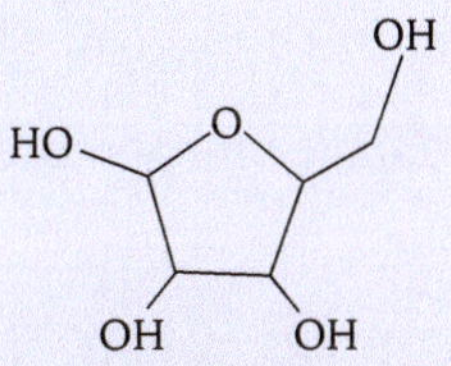   ribose sugars

Formation of disaccharides and polysaccharides

Disaccharides are formed by joining **two** monosaccharides with a **glycosidic bond**. Polysaccharides are formed by connecting **many** monosaccharides with this bond.

Examples of disaccharides:

glucose + glucose = maltose

glucose + fructose = sucrose

glucose + galactose = lactose

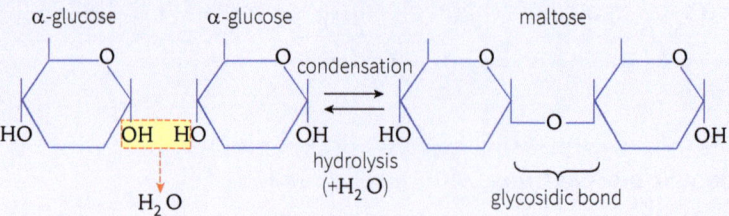

Structure and function of polysaccharides

Molecule	Structure	Function
glucose	• hexose monosaccharide with a ring structure • two isomers, α-glucose and β-glucose	• soluble molecule that is used for respiration, stored as glycogen or starch as energy reserves, or used in structural molecules
amylose	• a helical, unbranched polysaccharide made of α-glucose molecules • glycosidic bond linking the α-glucose molecules is an α-1,4 glycosidic bond	• stores energy (see starch)
amylopectin	• a branched polysaccharide • bonds linking the α-glucose molecules are α-1,4 and α-1,6 glycosidic bonds	• stores energy (see starch)
starch	• spiral molecule composed of amylose and amylopectin	• water-insoluble molecule that stores energy in plant cells without affecting water potential
glycogen	• highly branched polysaccharide • the glycosidic bonds are readily hydrolysed, releasing the α-glucose molecules	• energy store in animals • stores excess glucose in muscle and liver cells. • the branching structure allows rapid hydrolysis to release glucose
cellulose	• long (unbranched) polysaccharide chains made of β-glucose • chains held by hydrogen bonds	• provides structural support in plants • prevents lysis during osmosis

Saturated or unsaturated?

The R-group of a fatty acid may be saturated or unsaturated.

Unsaturated lipids have one or more double bonds (−C=C−).

Saturated   **Unsaturated**

3 Biological molecules

Properties of lipids

Triglycerides

Triglycerides are not water soluble. Saturated molecules are usually solid at room temperature.

Triglycerides are synthesised by the formation of three **ester bonds** between one glycerol molecule and three fatty acids – this is called **esterification**.

Phospholipids

Phospholipids have a hydrophilic head and a hydrophobic tail, and form phospholipid bilayer membranes.

The image below is an example of a phospholipid.

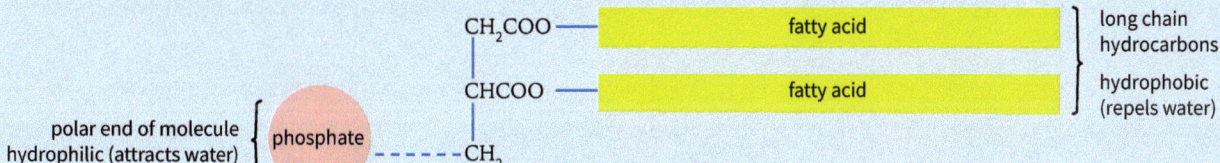

Properties and functions of lipids

- **Triglycerides** have a long hydrocarbon tails that **stores energy**. Breakdown products can be used as a respiratory substrate. They can be stored in cells without affecting the water potential.
- The **hydrophobic properties** of lipids are utilised in waterproofing in biological organisms such as the cuticle of leaves, exoskeletons of some insects, and bird feathers.
- **Cholesterol** is a lipid that functions as a steroid, is an essential component of prokaryotic and eukaryotic plasma membranes, and is used to make steroid hormones, vitamin D, and bile.

Chemical tests for biological molecules

Biological molecule	Chemical test	Results
proteins	**Biuret test** is added to the sample in solution. Leave for 5 minutes and observe for colour change.	• positive result is purple • usually uses a control of distilled water and a sample with egg albumen
reducing sugars	**Benedict's reagent** is heated to 80°C with a solution of the sample. **Reagent test strips** can be used for semi-quantitative results.	• on heating, if a reducing sugar is present, there will be a red or orange precipitate • use colorimetry and a calibration curve to quantify reducing sugars in a sample
non-reducing sugars (e.g., sucrose)	If a reducing sugar is not present, heat with hydrochloric acid to reduce the non-reducing sugar. Sodium hydrogen carbonate solution is added to neutralise the acid. Then **Benedict's reagent** is added before heating to 80°C.	• on heating, if a non-reducing sugar is present, there will be a red or orange precipitate
starch	Iodine (known as **iodine solution**) is dripped on to a sample (solid or liquid).	• positive test turns solution from yellow to blue/black
lipids	Known as the **emulsion test**, the sample is dissolved first in ethanol and then water is added, then the sample is shaken.	• if lipids are present, the solution goes milky white

Structure of amino acids

The **general structure** of an amino acid is:

H₂N—C(R)(H)—COOH

Symbol	Label
NH₂	amine group
COOH	carboxyl group
R	side chain

The **twenty amino acids** that are common to all organisms differ from each other only in their side chain (R group).

Peptides and polypeptides

Amino acids are the **monomers** of proteins.

Amino acids can join together, via a **condensation** reaction, forming a **peptide bond**, with water as a by-product.

A **dipeptide** molecule is formed by the condensation of **two** amino acids.

A **polypeptide** is formed by the condensation of **many** amino acids.

A **functional protein** can contain one or more polypeptides (e.g., one molecule of haemoglobin contains four polypeptide chains).

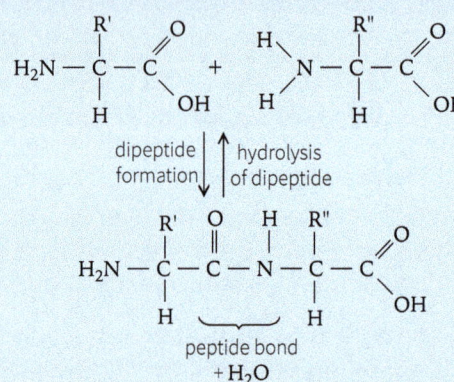

Globular and fibrous proteins

Globular proteins	Fibrous proteins
• spherical shape • water soluble because they have R groups on the inside that are hydrophobic, and ones on the outside that are hydrophilic • involved in metabolic processes	• usually made of long polypeptide chains that form fibres • insoluble because they have amino acids with hydrophobic R groups • very strong, yet flexible
Haemoglobin is a protein that carries oxygen. Known as a conjugated protein, it is made of four polypeptide chains and four haem prosthetic groups that contain an iron (Fe^{2+}) ion.	**Collagen** is a fibrous protein found in bones and tendons, allowing them to withstand large pulling forces. It is also is found in artery walls to allow them to cope with high pressures.
Insulin is a protein involved in controlling blood glucose levels. It is made of two polypeptide chains, which are joined by disulfide bonds. It is specific to the shape of cell membrane receptors.	**Keratin** is a strong molecule that has a large number of cysteine amino acids and therefore many disulfide bonds. It is found in hooves, horns, and fingernails.
Pepsin is an enzyme that functions in the acidic environment of the stomach. It has a few basic R groups, hydrogen bonds, and a disulfide bond.	**Elastin** is an elastic fibrous protein found in the walls of blood vessels, the lungs, and the bladder.

Protein structures

Protein structure	Diagram	Description	Function and examples
primary		The number and sequence of amino acids in the polypeptide chain. Encoded by DNA and then mRNA.	Determines the structure of the polypeptide, and the 3D shape of proteins and their active sites.
secondary	alpha helix; beta-pleated sheet	**Hydrogen bonds** form between some amino acids to either pleat or twist a polypeptide. A single hydrogen bond is weak but many hydrogen bonds give these structures stability.	Beta-pleated sheets are structural, like silk. Alpha helices make up DNA-binding and transmembrane proteins.
tertiary	hydrophobic interaction; polypeptide backbone; hydrogen bond; disulfide bridge; ionic bond	The final 3D specific shape of the polypeptide is held in place by **ionic bonds, disulfide bonds,** and **hydrogen bonds** between **R groups**. It is also determined by the hydrophobic and hydrophilic interactions.	Globular proteins (e.g., enzymes), or fibrous proteins (e.g., collagen).
quaternary		Separate twisted or folded polypeptides linked together. Non-protein, or **prosthetic**, groups may be associated with proteins having a quaternary structure.	Haemoglobin is made of four polypeptide chains, each with the prosthetic group haem.

Retrieval

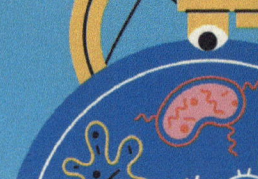

Learn the answers to the questions below, then cover the answers column with a piece of paper and write as many as you can. Check and repeat.

	Questions	Answers
1	What are the four main carbon-based molecules common to all life?	carbohydrates, lipids, proteins, nucleic acids
2	Which two types of biological molecules act as the main stores of energy?	carbohydrates and lipids
3	What are the units of a polymer called?	monomers
4	What is the name of the reaction that builds polymers?	condensation reaction
5	What is the name of the reaction that breaks down polymers?	hydrolysis reaction
6	What are the monomers of the disaccharide sucrose?	glucose and fructose
7	What type of bond forms between two monosaccharides?	glycosidic bond
8	What is an anion? Give an example.	negatively charged ion, such as nitrate ions (NO_3^-)
9	Which type of biological molecule forms the major part of plasma membranes?	lipids / phospholipid
10	Give three named examples of globular proteins.	haemoglobin, insulin, enzymes (pepsin)
11	How can the presence of reducing sugars be measured quantitively?	reagent test strips and colorimetry
12	Which isomer of glucose makes up glycogen?	α-glucose
13	What are the three groups of lipids?	triglycerides, phospholipids, cholesterol
14	Which bonds form between glycerol and fatty acids?	ester
15	What is the test for lipids?	emulsion test
16	Which molecules are triglycerides made of?	glycerol and three fatty acids
17	Which type of lipid is common in plasma membranes?	phospholipids
18	Which three elements are common to biological molecules?	carbon, hydrogen, oxygen
19	What makes a lipid unsaturated?	carbon–carbon double bonds
20	Which chemical is used in the biochemical test for starch?	iodine/potassium iodide

28 3 Biological molecules

Maths skills

Practise your maths skills using the worked example and practice questions below.

Producing a dilution series

There are a number of biological investigations that use a **dilution series**. A dilution series is used in laboratories to progressively dilute a concentrated solution into a dilute one.

Examples of the use of dilution series in biology experiments include:

1. Making a calibration curve with Benedict's reagent and a dilution series of glucose.
2. Investigating osmosis – the effect of a sucrose or sodium chloride solution on plant tissues.

When creating a dilution series, you must know the volumes of stock solution (such as glucose solution) and distilled water needed to create the final concentration for each dilution.

This can be calculated by:

$$V_1 \times C_1 = V_2 \times C_2$$

where:

- V_1 = volume of stock solution needed
- C_1 = concentration of the stock solution
- V_2 = volume of the dilution
- C_2 = concentration of the dilution (this forms the dilution series)

Worked example

Question

Create a glucose dilution series containing the following concentrations: 0.00, 0.25, 0.50, 0.75, and 1.00 mol dm⁻³, using a stock glucose solution of 1 mol dm⁻³. The final volume of each solution should be 10 cm³.

Answer

1. Find the volume (V_1) of 1 mol dm⁻³ stock glucose solution (C_1) required to produce a 10 cm³ dilution (V_2) with a final concentration of 0.25 mol dm⁻³ (C_2):

   If $$V_1 \times C_1 = V_2 \times C_2$$

   then $$V_1 = \frac{V_2 \times C_2}{C_1}$$

2. Substitute your known values into the equation:

   V_2 = 10 cm³, C_2 = 0.25 mol dm⁻³, and C_1 = 1.00 mol dm⁻³

   $$V_1 = \frac{10 \times 0.25}{1.00} = 2.5$$, therefore you will need to use 2.5 cm³ stock solution.

3. As the final volume must be 10 cm³, you subtract 2.5 from 10 to calculate how much distilled water is needed, which is 7.5 cm³. This will create a 10 cm³ dilution with a concentration of 0.25 mol dm⁻³.

4. Repeat this method to fill out the rest of the table, as shown below.

Test tube	Final concentration of glucose (mol dm⁻³)	Volume distilled water (cm³)	Volume 1 mol dm⁻³ glucose solution (cm³)	Final volume (cm³)
A	0.00	10.0	0.0	10.0
B	0.25	7.5	2.5	10.0
C	0.50	5.0	5.0	10.0
D	0.75	2.5	7.5	10.0
E	1.00	0.0	10.0	10.0

Practice

1. A student is creating a sodium chloride dilution series to investigate osmosis in potato tubers. They will need the following concentrations: 0.00, 0.25, 0.50, 0.75, and 1.00 mol dm⁻³ from a sodium chloride stock solution of 1 mol dm⁻³. Draw the dilution series table that they will need in order to carry out this experiment.

2. A student is creating a glucose dilution series to produce a standard curve of absorbance against glucose concentration. They will need the following concentrations: 0.1, 0.3, 0.5, 0.7, 0.9, and 1.0 mol dm⁻³ from a stock solution of glucose with a concentration of 2.0 mol dm⁻³. Draw the dilution series table that they will need in order to carry out this experiment.

Practice

Exam-style questions

1   The structure of the amino acid alanine is shown in **Figure 1.1**.

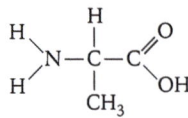

Figure 1.1

(a) Draw a circle around the R group of alanine. [1]

(b) A student separated a mixture of amino acids, including alanine, using thin layer chromatography.

Figure 1.2 shows the chromatogram produced by the student.

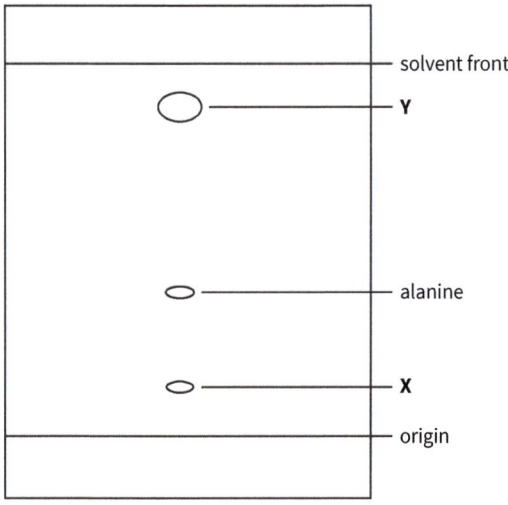

Figure 1.2

(i) Calculate the R_f value of alanine.

.... [2]

> **Exam tip**
>
> When asked to perform a calculation, show your working. You may gain a mark or two even if your final answer is incorrect.

(ii) Name the amino acid labelled **X** using the R_f values in **Table 1.1**.

Show your working.

Amino acid	R_f value
glutamine	0.13
arginine	0.20
tryptophan	0.66

Table 1.1

.... [2]

30   3 Biological molecules

(iii) The spot labelled **Y** contained two amino acids: leucine and isoleucine.

Suggest why these two amino acids were not separated by thin layer chromatography.

....
....
.... [2]

(iv) Another student wrote a method for conducting thin layer chromatography:

(1) Hold the TLC plate by the edges and avoid damage to the surface of the plate.

(2) Draw a pencil line across the TLC plate, 0.5 cm from the bottom edge.

(3) Place the sample on the pencil line using a pipette, allowing the spot to dry before adding the next drop.

(4) Place the chromatography solvent in a jar so that it is no more than 0.4 cm deep.

(5) Lower the TLC plate into the jar.

(6) Allow the solvent to soak up the plate.

(7) After 20 minutes, remove the plate from the jar and mark the position of the solvent front with a pencil.

Suggest two improvements to the student's method.

....
....
....
.... [2]

2 Many of the properties of water that benefit organisms are caused by hydrogen bonding.

Synoptic links

3.1.2d   3.1.3d

(a) Draw a diagram to show a hydrogen bond between two water molecules.

Include any relevant partial charges in the water molecules.

[3]

(b) Explain why glucose and amino acids dissolve in the blood.

....
....
....
.... [3]

(c) Complete the following passage, which outlines how the properties of water allow transport in plants, by writing the correct words in the gaps.

Water evaporates from openings called .... in plant leaves. This creates a .... stream. Hydrogen bonds between water molecules produce ...., which maintains a continuous chain of water molecules in the xylem vessel. Water molecules also form hydrogen bonds with molecules in the xylem wall. This is called .... [4]

(d) Biological molecules can be hydrolysed in the presence of water.

Complete **Table 2.1**, which shows some molecules that can be hydrolysed, the bonds that are broken and the molecules that are formed.

Molecule being hydrolysed	Bond broken	Molecule(s) formed
starch		maltose
sucrose		
triglyceride		
		amino acids

Table 2.1 [4]

> **Exam tip**
>
> Remember that a disaccharide is formed from two monosaccharides. You need to know the names of three disaccharides (maltose, sucrose, and lactose) and the monosaccharides from which they are formed.

3 The biuret test is used to identify proteins.

(a) Complete the following passage, which describes the biuret test, by writing the most appropriate words in the gaps.

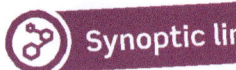

3.1.3f

.... is added to a liquid sample, using equal .... Drops of copper sulfate are added to the sample solution. After mixing, a .... colour indicates the presence of protein. [3]

(b) (i) A student thought a solution contained a reducing sugar.

The solution colour changed to green when it was heated with Benedict's solution.

The student concluded that the solution contained small amounts of glucose.

Evaluate the student's conclusion.

....
....
....
.... [3]

> **Exam tip**
>
> When you are asked to evaluate a conclusion, try to include at least one point that supports the conclusion and at least one point that does not support the conclusion.

(ii) Describe how the student could test for a non-reducing sugar.

....
....
....
.... [3]

3 Biological molecules

(c) A student conducted tests on three biological samples, **A**, **B**, and **C**. **Table 3.1** shows the results of the tests.

Sample	Colour after iodine test	Colour after Benedict's test	Colour after treatment with HCl and Benedict's test
A	black	orange	red
B	yellow	red	red
C	yellow	blue	red

Table 3.1

One of the samples contained blood plasma and one of the samples contained fluid from a phloem sieve tube.

Use evidence from **Table 3** to identify which sample contained blood plasma and which sample contained fluid from a sieve tube. Explain your answer.

....

....

....

.... [4]

(d) A student tried to identify the presence of a lipid using the emulsion test. The student used the following method.

(1) Mix the sample with water.

(2) Pour the water and sample into a test tube of ethanol.

(3) Heat the mixture.

Describe two errors made by the student.

....

....

.... [2]

4   Proteins have a range of structures, which are adapted to their roles.

> **Synoptic links**
> 2.1.3f 2.1.4c 2.1.4di

(a) Titin is the largest protein to be discovered. One form of titin contains 34 350 amino acids in total, including all 20 of the different amino acids found in humans.

(i) State the chemical elements that are found in titin.

.... [2]

(ii) Calculate the minimum length of mRNA required for the translation of titin.

.... [1]

(b) Rhodopsin is a light-sensitive protein that is found in the eye. **Figure 4.1** shows the structure of rhodopsin.

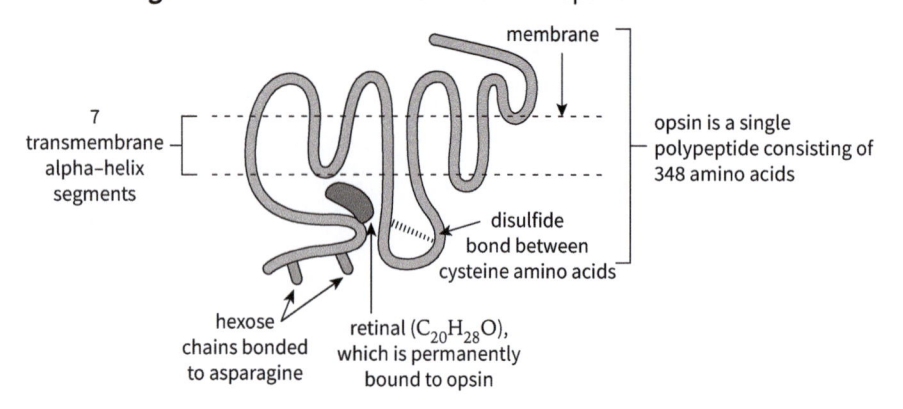

Figure 4.1

Labels on figure:
- membrane
- 7 transmembrane alpha–helix segments
- opsin is a single polypeptide consisting of 348 amino acids
- disulfide bond between cysteine amino acids
- hexose chains bonded to asparagine
- retinal ($C_{20}H_{28}O$), which is permanently bound to opsin

> **! Exam tip**
>
> This is an example of a question that requires you to apply your knowledge in an unfamiliar context. In this example, consider what you have learned about the features of each level of protein structure and pick out the information that is relevant to each level.

Use the information in **Figure 4.1** to describe the structural features of rhodopsin.

In your answer, you should refer to the different levels of protein structure.

....
....
....
....
.... [5]

(c) ATP synthase is an enzyme that catalyses the formation of ATP. The ATP synthase protein has the following structure.
- A hydrophilic F_1 region consisting of five different subunits.
- A hydrophobic F_0 region consisting of three different subunits.

(i) Suggest whether ATP synthase is a globular or fibrous protein. Explain your answer.

....
....
....
.... [3]

(ii) State which level of protein structure is responsible for the active site of ATP synthase.

.... [1]

(iii) Explain why the active site of ATP synthase may change shape and stop functioning when temperature is increased beyond an optimum value.

....
....
....
....
.... [3]

3 Biological molecules

5   Glycogen, amylopectin, and cellulose are three examples of polysaccharides.

Exam tip
The presence of two different types of glycosidic bond (e.g., 1,4 and 1,6 links) in a polysaccharide indicates that it will be branched.

(a) (i) Complete **Table 5.1**, which compares the structures of glycogen and amylopectin.

Molecule	glycogen	amylopectin
Type of glycosidic bonds	1,4 and 1,6 links	
Helical?		yes
Branched?	yes	

[3]

Table 5.1

(ii) Explain how the structures and properties of glycogen and amylopectin are suited to their function as storage polymers.

....
....
....[2]

(b) Cellulose is a polysaccharide formed from β-glucose.

(i) State the difference in structure between α-glucose and β-glucose.

....
....[1]

(ii) Explain how the structure of cellulose is suited to its function.

....
....
....
....[3]

6   A scientist planned to analyse the rate of protein hydrolysis using colorimetry.

The scientist first constructed a calibration curve using the following method:

(1) Using a syringe and distilled water, dilute a stock protein solution to form 5 cm³ of the following protein solutions in test tubes: 1%, 0.8%, 0.6%, 0.4%, 0.2%, and 0%.

(2) Add 5 cm³ of biuret solution to each tube and incubate for 10 minutes at 35 °C.

(3) Using a dropping pipette, fill a colorimeter cuvette with each of the solutions in order.

(4) Add a green filter (520 nm) to the colorimeter and then use the 0% tube to zero the cuvette.

(5) Find the absorbance in arbitrary units for each protein dilution by placing the cuvette into the colorimeter.

(6) Plot a calibration curve of absorbance against % protein.

(a) (i) Describe how the scientist would produce the 1% protein solution from a starting solution of 5% protein.

....

....[1]

(ii) Describe one precaution the scientist should take in step iii to increase the validity of their results.

....

....[1]

(iii) Explain why the scientist used a green filter.

....

....

....

....[2]

(iv) Sketch the expected appearance of the calibration curve.

> **Exam tip**
>
> When asked to sketch or complete a graph, include labelled axes with appropriate units.

[2]

(b) The scientist planned to analyse the effect of varying protease concentration on the rate of protein hydrolysis.

State two variables that the scientist needs to ensure are controlled.

....

....[2]

3 Biological molecules

7 Explain how the properties of the molecules in plasma membranes allow the membranes to perform their roles.

....
....
....
....
....
....
....
....
....
....
....
....
....
.... [6]

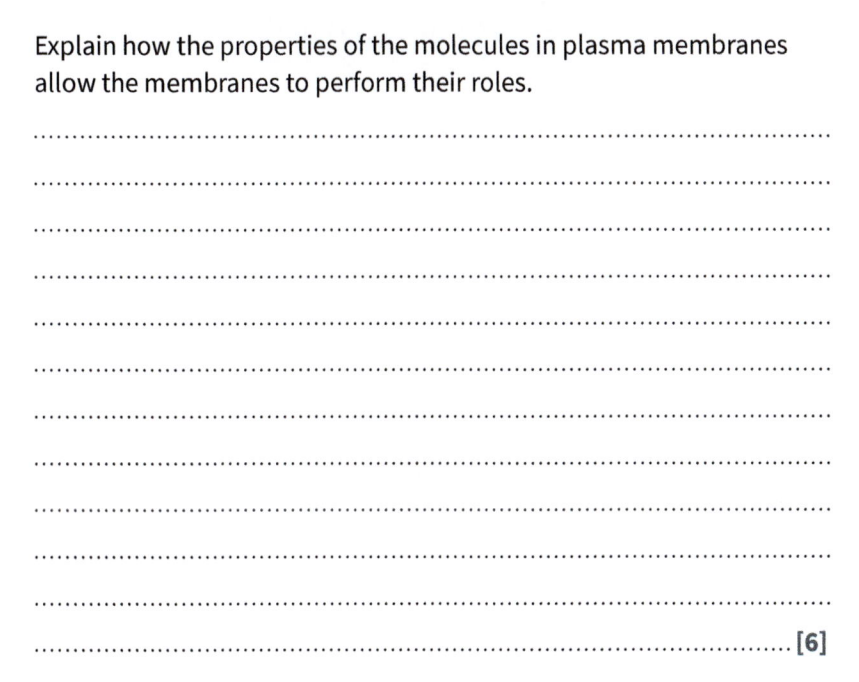

Synoptic link
2.1.5b

8 Chitin is a polysaccharide found in insects and fungi. Arabinoxylan is a polysaccharide found in plants. The structural features of these two polysaccharides are shown in **Table 8.1**.

Polysaccharide	chitin	arabinoxylan
Monomer(s)	2-(acetylamino)-2-deoxy-D-glucose	arabinose and xylose
Type of glycosidic bonds	1,4 links	1,4 and 2,3 links
Helical?	no	sometimes
Branched?	no	yes
Cross links between polymer chains?	yes	no

Table 8.1

Outline the similarities and differences between the structures of:
- chitin and cellulose
- arabinoxylan and amylopectin.

....
....
....
....
....
....
....
....
....
....
.... [6]

Knowledge

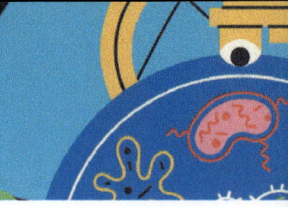

4 Nucleotides and nucleic acids

Structure of a nucleotide

A nucleotide is the monomer from which nucleic acids are made. Each nucleotide is formed from a pentose sugar, a nitrogen-containing organic base, and a phosphate group.

Both DNA and RNA are polymers of nucleotides.

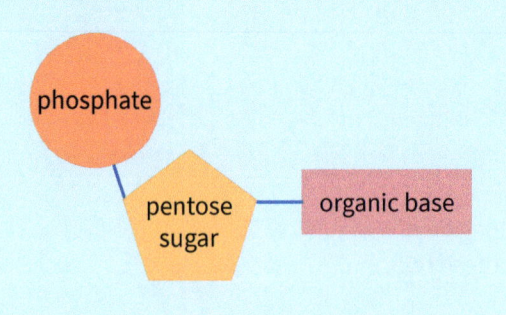

Structure of ATP

Adenosine triphosphate (ATP) is a **nucleotide** and is formed from a molecule of **ribose**, a molecule of **adenine**, and **three phosphate groups**.

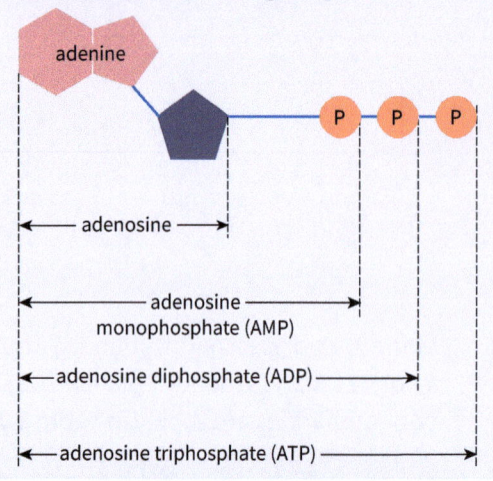

A DNA nucleotide

Deoxyribonucleic acid (DNA) is a nucleotide that holds genetic information. The components of a DNA nucleotide are:
- deoxyribose sugar
- a phosphate group
- one of the organic bases:
  - the purines – adenine (A) and guanine (G)
  - the pyrimidines – cytosine (C) and thymine (T)

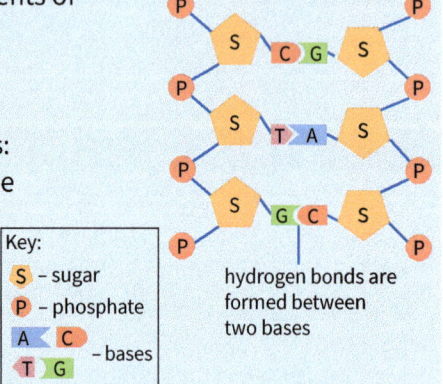

Key:
- S – sugar
- P – phosphate
- A, C, T, G – bases

DNA is a **double-stranded** molecule with a ladder-like structure, that twists into a double helix.

The two sugar-phosphate backbones are held in place by pairs of complementary bases joined by hydrogen bonds.

The two DNA strands are **anti-parallel**, running in opposite directions.

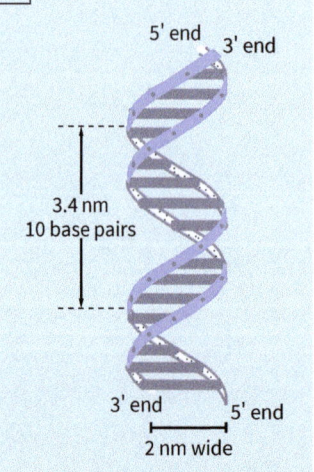

3.4 nm
10 base pairs

2 nm wide

An RNA nucleotide

The components of an RNA nucleotide are:
- a ribose sugar
- a phosphate group
- one of the organic bases:
  - adenine
  - cytosine
  - guanine
  - uracil (replaces thymine)

RNA is a relatively short, **single-stranded** molecule.

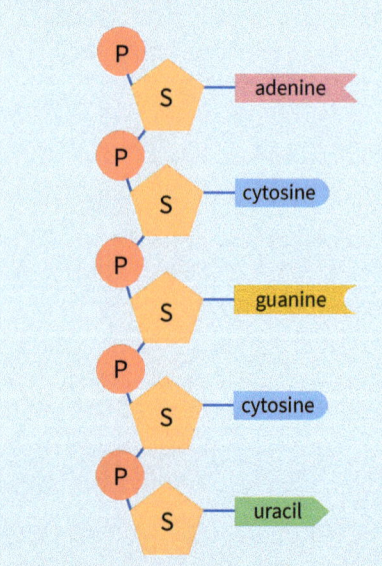

DNA and RNA

A **condensation** reaction between two nucleotides forms a **phosphodiester bond** to form a polynucleotide.

A **hydrolysis** reaction breaks the phosphodiester bonds between two nucleotides.

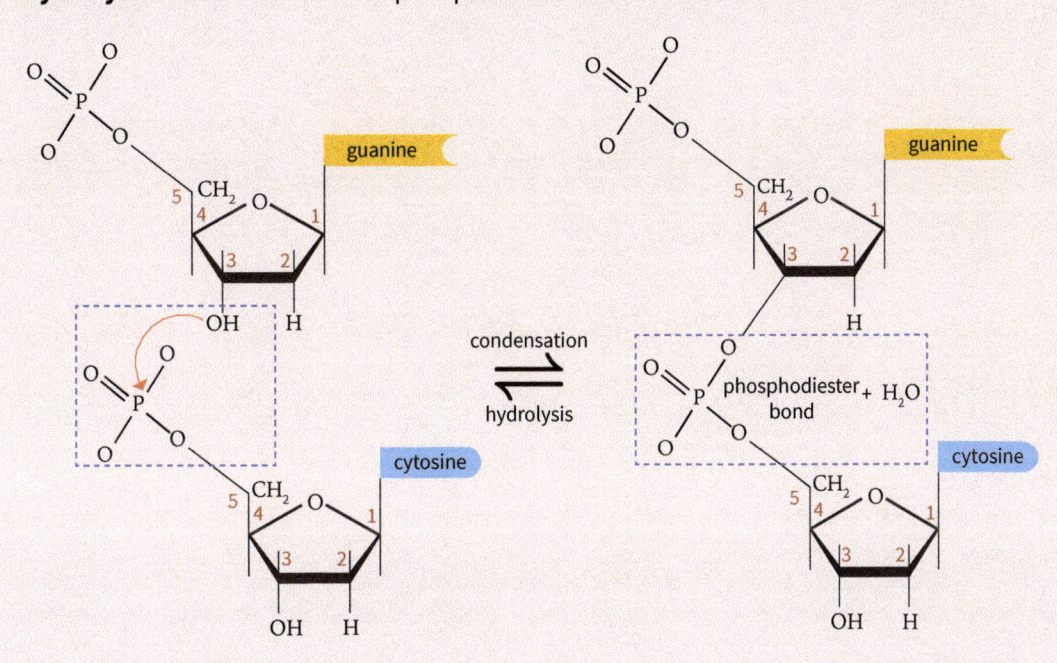

DNA replication

The semi-conservative replication of DNA ensures genetic continuity between generations of cells.

1. **DNA helicase** breaks the hydrogen bonds between the complementary base pairs.

2. The double helix unwinds and separates the two DNA strands.

3. New DNA nucleotides bind to exposed bases on the DNA template strand.

4. **DNA polymerase** catalyses the condensation reaction that joins adjacent nucleotides.

Replication needs to be done with accuracy although random, spontaneous mutations do occur.

DNA semi-conservative replication

Stage 1
Helicase unwinds the double helix and separates the two strands by breaking hydrogen bonds.

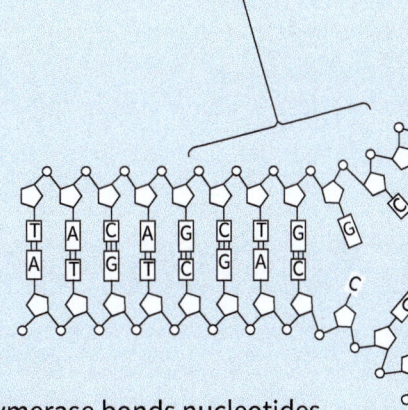

Stage 2
DNA polymerase bonds nucleotides together to form new strands, using the pre-existing strands as templates.

Stage 3
The daughter DNA molecules each rewind into a double helix.

4 Knowledge

Protein synthesis

Protein synthesis is the mechanism in cells whereby:

- a DNA template is transcribed into a **messenger RNA (mRNA)** molecule in the nucleus

- the mRNA is then translated into an amino acid sequence in association with **transfer RNA** (**tRNA**) on ribosomes in the cytoplasm.

Transcription

Transcription is the production of mRNA from DNA. In eukaryotes, pre-mRNA is made as an intermediate step:

1. **DNA helicase** breaks hydrogen bonds between bases, causing DNA to unzip and expose about 12 bases at a time.

2. The enzyme **RNA polymerase** moves along the DNA template strand and attaches free nucleotides to their complementary bases on the DNA. (Remember: in mRNA, thymine is replaced by **uracil**.)

3. RNA polymerase continues making a strand of mRNA until it comes to a STOP codon.

In prokaryotes, transcription results directly in the production of mRNA from DNA.

The image on the right refers to the mRNA being 'spliced'. 'Splicing' is where introns, the non-coding regions of genes, are removed from the pre-RNA molecule, and the exons, the coding regions, are joined together to form the mature mRNA.

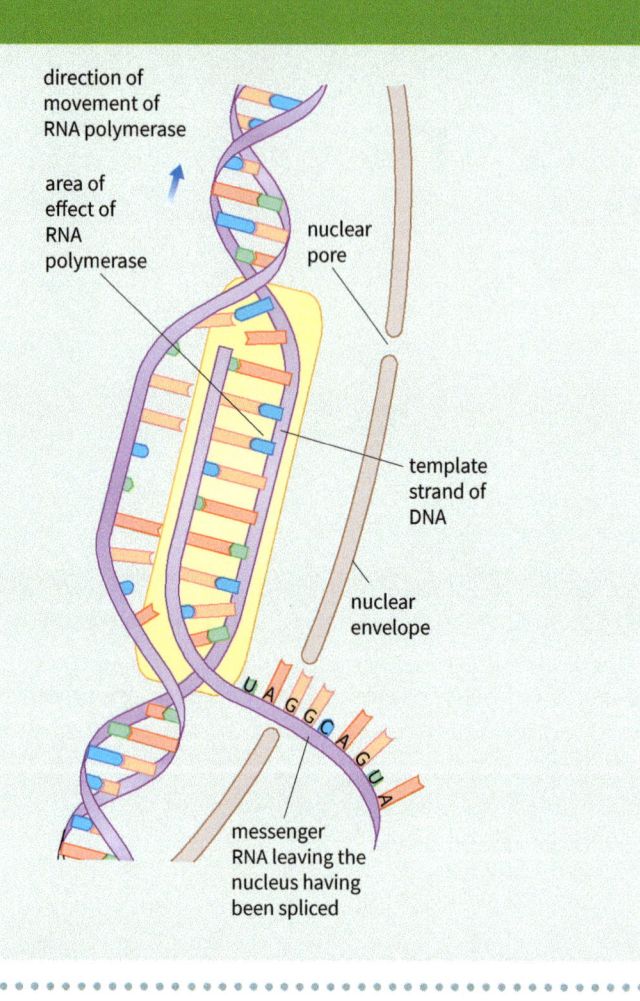

DNA purification

DNA can be purified from cells.

Method:
1. Use a fruit or vegetable, such as peas, onion, kiwi fruit, or strawberries.
2. Blend the DNA source into a 'soup', then add salt and ice-cold water.
3. Pass through a mesh and collect the liquid.
4. Add detergent and mix.
5. Add protease enzymes.
6. Pour solution into a test tube.
7. Add ice-cold ethanol to the solution, at a 45° angle.
8. DNA strands will precipitate between the ethanol and mixture layer.

This method works because:
- salt helps remove DNA bound proteins
- proteases hydrolyse the proteins
- detergent helps disrupt the cell membranes
- ethanol causes the DNA to precipitate.

4 Nucleotides and nucleic acids

The genetic code

The **genetic code** is carried as a sequence of three DNA bases, called a **triplet**, or **codon**. Most triplets code for a specific amino acid, but some code for STOP during transcription. A **gene** is a sequence of triplets, specifying the order of amino acids of a polypeptide or protein.

The genetic code is:
- **universal**
- **non-overlapping**
- **degenerate** (most amino acids are coded for by more than one triplet code).

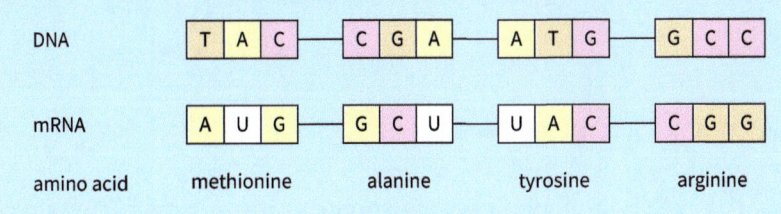

DNA	T A C	C G A	A T G	G C C
mRNA	A U G	G C U	U A C	C G G
amino acid	methionine	alanine	tyrosine	arginine

Translation

Translation is the production of polypeptides from the sequence of codons carried by mRNA:

1. rRNA (ribosomal RNA) makes up the ribosome that moves along the mRNA strand.
2. mRNA moves from the nucleus through a nuclear pore to the cytoplasm and one end (AUG) attaches to a ribosome.
3. A tRNA with a complementary anticodon (UAC), carrying a **specific** amino acid (methionine), moves to the ribosome and pairs with the first mRNA codon.
4. The ribosome moves along the mRNA to the next codon and again pairs up with a complementary tRNA, to bring the two amino acid-carrying tRNAs together.
5. Energy released from ATP is used to form a peptide bond between the amino acids.
6. The ribosome moves to the third mRNA codon, releasing the first tRNA and pairing up a third.
7. When the ribosome reaches a stop codon, the polypeptide is complete and the mRNA and tRNAs are released from the ribosome.
8. The tRNA molecules released from the ribosome can be reused.

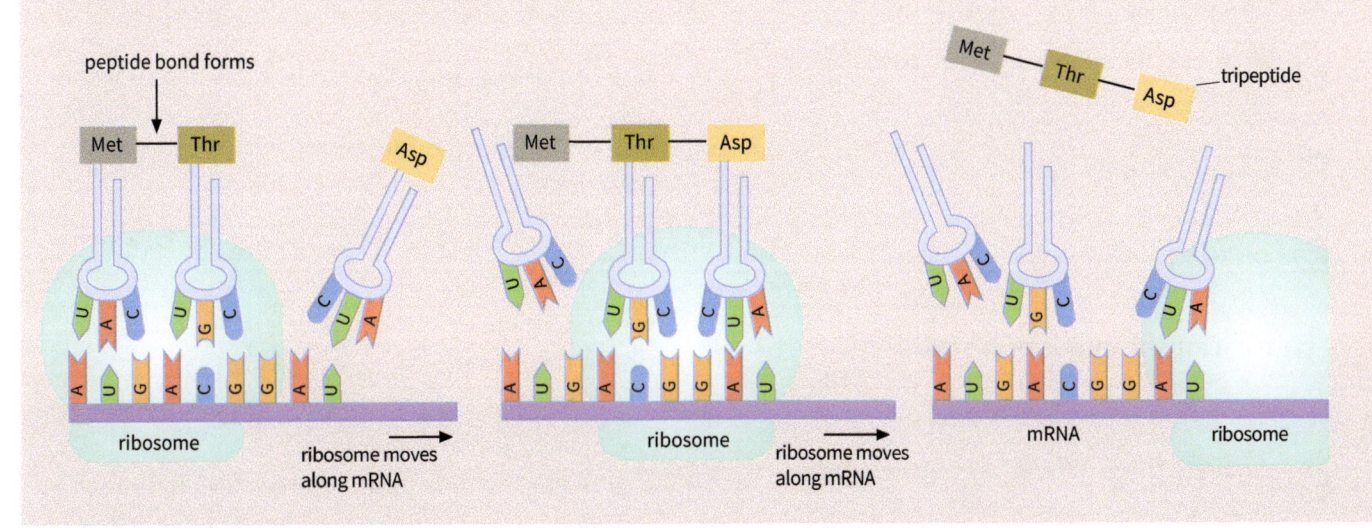

4 Knowledge 41

Retrieval

Learn the answers to the questions below, then cover the answers column with a piece of paper and write as many as you can. Check and repeat.

Questions | Answers

#	Question	Answer
1	What does DNA stand for?	deoxyribonucleic acid
2	What does RNA stand for?	ribonucleic acid
3	What are the monomers of DNA and RNA?	nucleotides
4	What are three general components of a nucleotide?	pentose, phosphate group, nitrogen-containing base
5	What are the four organic bases that occur in DNA?	adenine, cytosine, guanine, and thymine
6	What are the four organic bases that occur in RNA?	adenine, cytosine, guanine, and uracil
7	What type of bond is formed by the condensation of two adjacent nucleotides?	phosphodiester
8	What shape is a DNA molecule?	a double-stranded double helix
9	Which bonds keep the DNA strands together?	hydrogen bonds (between the complementary base pairs)
10	Describe the structure of an RNA molecule.	relatively short polynucleotide chain, single stranded
11	What is the structure of ATP?	one molecule of ribose, one molecule of adenine, and three phosphate groups
12	What is the first stage of semi-conservative DNA replication?	unwinding the double helix
13	What is the role of DNA helicase in DNA replication?	breaking hydrogen bonds between the base pairs
14	What happens at the exposed bases on the template strand of DNA?	free complementary DNA nucleotides are attached
15	What does antiparallel mean?	the two polynucleotide strands run in opposite directions
16	Why is ATP required in translation?	to release energy to form peptide bonds between amino acids
17	What are the three forms of RNA?	messenger RNA (mRNA), transfer RNA (tRNA), and ribosomal RNA (rRNA)
18	What are three differences between DNA and RNA?	• DNA is a long, double strand, RNA is a shorter, single-stranded molecule • DNA has thymine base, whereas RNA has uracil • DNA has the pentose sugar deoxyribose, RNA's pentose sugar is ribose

4 Nucleotides and nucleic acids

19	Why is the genetic code described as degenerate?	most amino acids are coded for by more than one triplet
20	What are the two steps in protein synthesis (in the correct order)?	transcription followed by translation
21	In a sentence, describe what happens during transcription.	a gene is copied in the form of mRNA
22	Where does transcription take place?	in the nucleus
23	What is the role of the enzyme DNA helicase in transcription?	it breaks the hydrogen bonds between complementary base pairs in DNA to unwind the DNA and expose the bases
24	What is the role of the enzyme RNA polymerase in transcription?	it matches up free RNA nucleotides to complementary bases on the unzipped DNA, and joins the RNA nucleotides to form mRNA
25	What would the base sequence in mRNA be for the following DNA nucleotide sequence? A T T G T G C A T C A A	U A A C A C G U A G U U

Maths skills

Practise your maths skills using the worked example and practice questions below.

Predicting base proportions

In DNA, bases always pair with their complementary base:

Adenine (A) – Thymine (T)
Cytosine (C) – Guanine (G)

This means the proportion of bases can be calculated if the proportion of one base is known.

For example, if you know that the proportion of A nucleotides in a strand of DNA is 20%, you know that this must also be true for T. Therefore, the proportion of C and G nucleotides must be 60% (30% for C, and 30% for G).

Worked example

Question
Calculate the proportions of A, C, and G if the proportion of T is 42%.

Answer
T = 42%,
If T = A, A = 42%
T + A = 42 + 42 = 84%
So, G + C = 100 − 84 = 16%
As G = C, $\frac{16}{2} = 8$
Therefore, if T = 42%,
A = 42%
G = 8%
C = 8%

Practice

1 Calculate the proportions of C, A, and T if the proportion of G is 32%.

2 Calculate the proportion of A if C = 31%.

3 The proportion of G in a particular single-stranded DNA template is 17%. Calculate the proportions of bases in a complementary strand of mRNA.

4 Retrieval

Practice

Exam-style questions

1   The structure of ATP is shown in **Figure 1.1**.

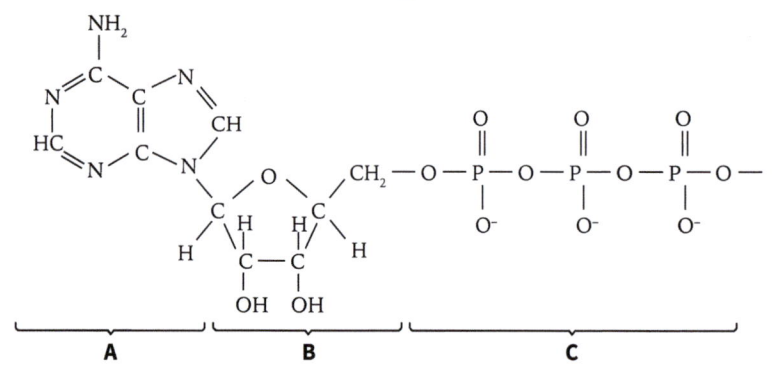

Figure 1.1

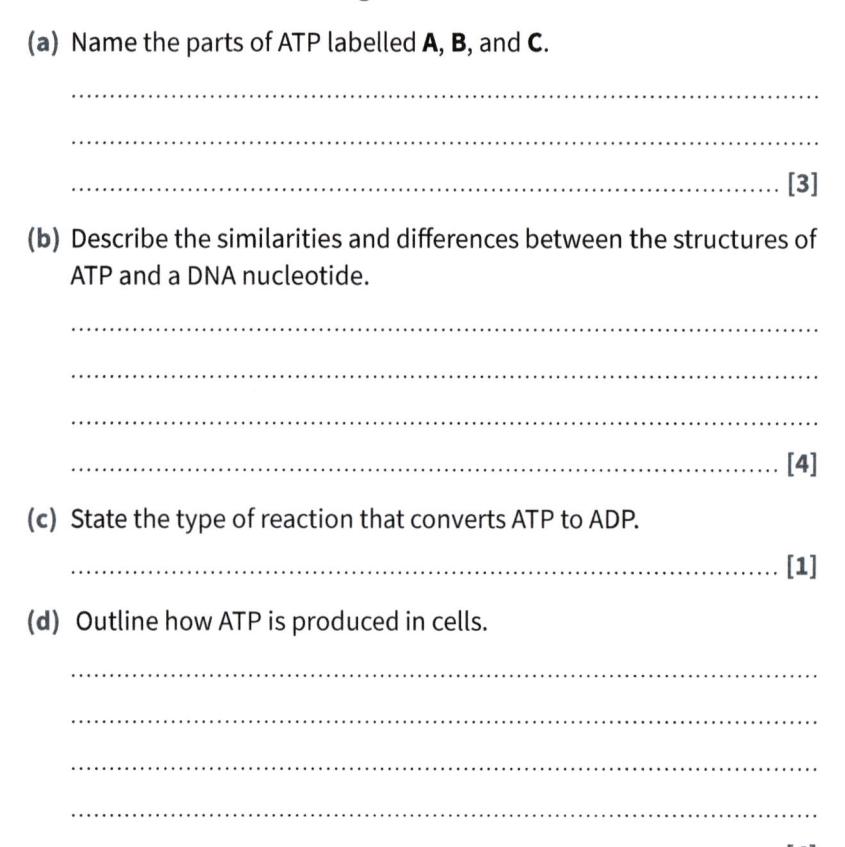

(a) Name the parts of ATP labelled **A**, **B**, and **C**.

....

....

.... [3]

(b) Describe the similarities and differences between the structures of ATP and a DNA nucleotide.

....

....

....

.... [4]

(c) State the type of reaction that converts ATP to ADP.

.... [1]

(d) Outline how ATP is produced in cells.

....

....

....

....

.... [4]

Synoptic links

5.2.1d   5.2.2c   5.2.2e
5.2.2g   5.2.2h

Exam tip

The command word 'outline' indicates that you should give a brief answer, giving essential details only. You can look at mark schemes, including this one, to understand the level of detail expected.

2   DNA replication is often described as semi-conservative.

(a) Matthew Meselson and Franklin Stahl conducted an experiment to show that DNA replication is semi-conservative.

Meselson and Stahl cultured *E. coli* bacteria in a medium containing ^{15}N, an isotope of nitrogen.

DNA containing ^{15}N has a higher density than normal DNA.

The two scientists transferred the ^{15}N *E. coli* to a medium containing ^{14}N. They analysed the density of DNA molecules in each generation of *E. coli*.

4 Nucleotides and nucleic acids

The results of the experiment are shown in **Table 2.1**, where generation 0 is the original ^{15}N population.

Generation	Percentage of DNA molecules (%)		
	High density	Intermediate density	Low density
0	100	0	0
1	0	100	0
2	0	50	50
3	0	25	75

Table 2.1

(i) State where the ^{15}N would be located in a DNA molecule.
.... [1]

(ii) Explain the results for generation **1**.
....
....
....
.... [2]

(iii) Explain the results for generation **2**.
....
....
....
.... [2]

(iv) Conservative replication was an alternative theory of DNA replication that was disproved by Meselson and Stahl's experiment.

The theory of conservative replication suggested that a DNA molecule would replicate to produce two molecules:
- one molecule composed of two template strands
- one molecule composed of two newly synthesised strands

Suggest how the results for generation 1 would differ if conservative DNA replication occurred.
....
.... [2]

> **Exam tip**
>
> You are not expected to learn the details of experiments such as the one conducted by Meselson and Stahl. However, you may be given experimental results in an exam, and you will be expected to apply your knowledge to analyse and interpret the data.

(b) Enzymes need to be transported into the nucleus for DNA replication.

(i) Describe the roles of two enzymes in DNA replication.
....
....
....
.... [2]

(ii) State one other molecule that needs to be transported into the nucleus for DNA replication.

.... [1]

3   Two examples of polynucleotides are RNA and DNA.

(a) (i) State three differences in the structures of RNA polynucleotides and DNA polynucleotides.

....
....
....
....
....
.... [3]

(ii) Complete **Table 3.1** to show the properties of the DNA mononucleotides adenine and cytosine.

Nitrogenous base	Purine or pyrimidine?	Complementary base	Number of hydrogen bonds formed with complementary base
adenine			
cytosine			

Table 3.1

[4]

(b) Scientists have developed synthetic DNA in laboratories. This synthetic DNA contains the natural bases (A, T, C, and G) and new bases, including the complementary bases **P** and **Z**.

The hydrogen bonds between **P** and **Z** are shown in **Figure 3.1**.

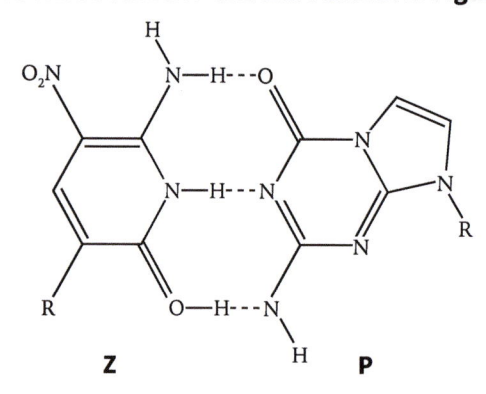

Figure 3.1

> **Exam tip**
>
> Mnemonic memory tools may help you remember the relative size of DNA pyrimidine and purine bases. For example, small pyramid CiTies = the smaller pyrimidines, C and T; big, pure GArdens = the larger purines, A and G.

Suggest which two natural bases are most similar to **P** and **Z**. Explain your answer.

....
....
....
....
....
.... [3]

4 Nucleotides and nucleic acids

4 DNA can be extracted and purified from plant tissue.

(a) (i) Complete the following passage, which describes how DNA can be purified, using the most appropriate words.

Plant tissue is ground to break down cell .... After grinding, the tissue is mixed with .... to break down membranes. Salt and .... enzymes are added to the mixture. Once alcohol has been added, DNA can be visualised and removed. [3]

(ii) Complete **Table 4.1** to explain the importance of three steps in DNA purification.

Step in DNA purification	Why is it added?
addition of salt	
addition of enzymes	
addition of alcohol	

Table 4.1

[3]

> **Exam tip**
> As well as learning the steps in a practical technique, it is important to understand the purpose of each step.

(iii) State the name of laboratory equipment that could be used to grind plant tissue.

.... [1]

5 DNA replication and transcription are two processes that occur in the nucleus.

(a) Complete **Table 5.1** to show some of the features of DNA replication and transcription.

Process	DNA replication	transcription
Which sections of DNA need to be unzipped?		
Enzyme that catalyses the formation of the polynucleotide product		
Polynucleotide product		
Names of the four nitrogenous bases in the product		

Table 5.1

> **Exam tip**
> A polynucleotide is an example of a polymer. DNA polynucleotides are formed from DNA mononucleotides (deoxyribonucleotides), and RNA polynucleotides are formed from RNA mononucleotides (ribonucleotides).

[4]

4 Practice 47

(b) Outline the roles in protein synthesis of the three forms of RNA: mRNA, rRNA, and tRNA.

mRNA ....

....

rRNA ....

....

tRNA ....

.... [3]

6 A gene determines the sequence of amino acids in a polypeptide using a triplet code.

(a) A DNA base sequence is shown below.

T T A T G T A G C

(i) Identify the mRNA base sequence transcribed from this DNA base sequence.

....

.... [1]

(ii) Identify the three anticodons on tRNA molecules that are needed in the translation of these base sequences?

....

....

.... [1]

(b) Several different mRNA codons can code for one amino acid. For example, valine is associated with four mRNA codons: GUU, GUC, GUA, and GUG.

(i) State the name used to describe this characteristic of the genetic code.

.... [1]

(ii) Explain why this characteristic of the genetic code can result in silent mutations.

....

....

....

.... [2]

(c) The DNA triplets TAA, TAG, and TGA do not code for amino acids, but they are crucial in the transcription of a gene.

Suggest the role of these DNA triplets in transcription.

....

....

....

.... [1]

> **Synoptic links**
> 6.1.1a

> **! Exam tip**
> Remember that mRNA and tRNA contain a different base to DNA.

4 Nucleotides and nucleic acids

7 Describe the roles of enzymes in DNA replication in cell nuclei and the uses of enzymes in genetic manipulation in laboratories.

....

....

....

....

....

....

....

....

....

....

....

....

....

....

....

.... **[6]**

> **Synoptic links**
> 6.1.3d   6.1.3e   6.1.3fii

> **Exam tip**
> A level of response question may be composed of two parts. For example, you may be asked to describe two different processes or methods. If possible, divide your answer evenly between the two parts. In this case, to gain 6 marks you should aim to include at least two enzymes from DNA replication and at least two from genetic manipulations.

8 Describe the process of DNA replication and explain why it is described as semi-conservative.

....

....

....

....

....

....

....

....

....

....

....

....

....

....

....

.... **[6]**

> **Exam tip**
> Spend some time planning the structure of your answers to level of response questions. Communication marks within each level can be determined by the order in which you write your answer and whether the answer has a logical structure.

Knowledge

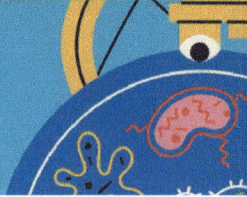

5 Enzymes

What are enzymes?

Enzymes are biological **catalysts** – they speed up rates of reaction but remain unchanged and can be used repeatedly. They catalyse a wide range of **intracellular** (e.g., catalase) and **extracellular reactions** (e.g., amylase and trypsin).

Enzymes are **specific** to a particular substrate. Only a small part of an enzyme, the active site, is functional. The active site has a **tertiary structure**, which is complementary to the substrate.

When an enzyme binds with its substrate(s), an enzyme-substrate complex is formed. The reaction takes place, making an enzyme-product complex. After the reaction, the products leave the active site and the enzyme is free to bind with more substrate.

Each enzyme catalyses the reaction by lowering its **activation energy**, but the rate of reaction is at its highest when it takes place in the optimal conditions for the enzyme.

Models of enzyme action

The **lock and key model** was originally used to explain how enzymes worked. Over time, evidence showed that enzyme molecules are not static and that they adjust their shape. This is now accepted and is called the induced-fit model.

Lock and key model	Induced-fit model
• the shape of the **active site** on an enzyme is complementary to the substrate molecule • the substrate fits into the active site exactly on collision • an **enzyme-substrate complex** is formed • the reaction occurs	• the shape of the **active site** of an enzyme is **not** fully complementary to the substrate molecule • when the substrate molecule collides with the active site, the enzyme molecule changes shape slightly to fit the active site around the substrate • an **enzyme-substrate complex** is formed • the reaction occurs

Induced-fit model of enzyme action

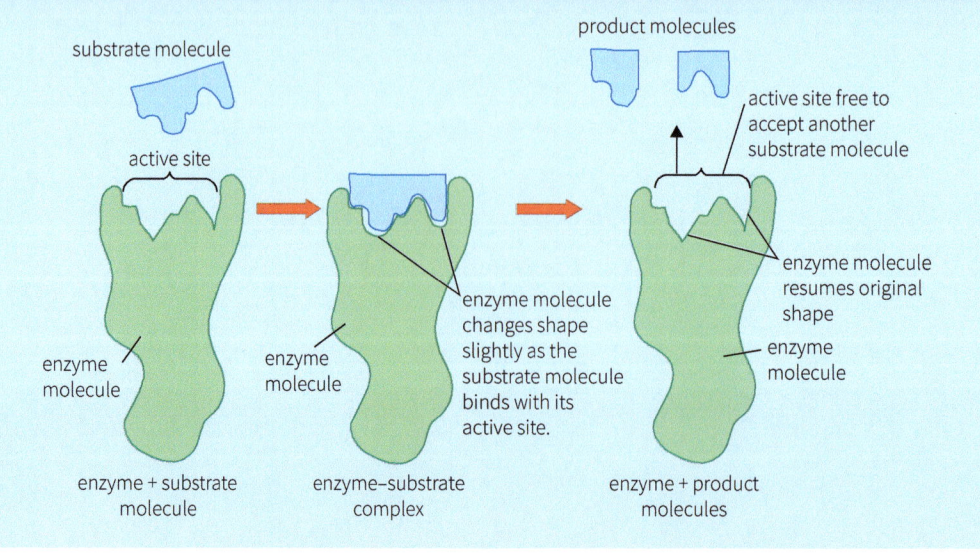

Activation energy

Many biological substrates require a certain amount of activation energy in order to react.

Enzymes are biological catalysts, so they enable reactions by lowering the activation energy that is required for the reaction to occur.

This can be shown on a graph that outlines the energy levels during a reaction, as shown on the right.

Although both the substrate and products have the same energy levels, the energy needed to carry out the reaction is much lower with an enzyme.

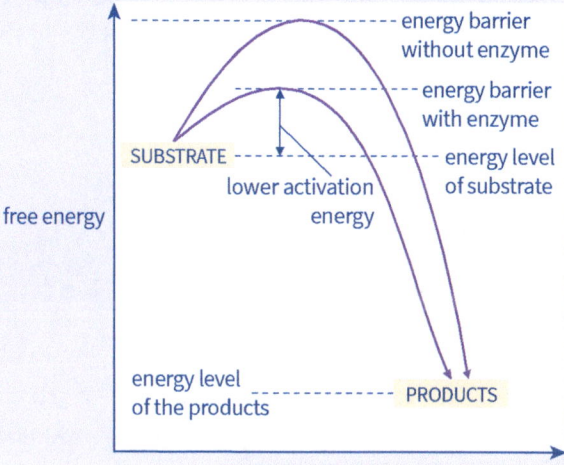

Co-enzymes, cofactors, and prosthetic groups

In some reactions, additional molecules or ions are required.

Role	Description	Example
co-enzyme	an organic molecule that, when present, increases the activity of an enzyme	nicotinamide adenine dinucleotide (NAD) assist electron transport enzymes
cofactor	an inorganic ion	chloride ions assist amylase reactions
prosthetic group	a tightly bound non-amino acid component necessary for enzyme activity	Zn^{2+} on carbonic anhydrase

Investigating the effects of variables on enzyme activity

We can measure the progress of a reaction in various ways.

When a reaction produces a gas (e.g., catalase produces oxygen from the breakdown of hydrogen peroxide), the volume of gas per unit time can be measured to estimate the rate of reaction under different conditions, such as temperature, pH, or enzyme or substrate concentrations.

Some products can be identified using an indicator or chemical test. These reactions can be set up and samples of the reaction can be tested at time intervals (e.g., using iodine solution as an indicator for the breakdown of starch by amylase).

Inactive precursors

Inactive precursors are non-working enzymes that are synthesised to prevent cell damage.

A precursor molecule inhibits proteases to stop them damaging the cell. Only when the proteases are needed is the precursor removed by chemical reactions and the proteases become active.

Enzyme concentration

- Higher enzyme concentration increases the number of active sites.
- More enzyme-substrate complexes form. The reaction rate increases until substrate concentration becomes the limiting factor.

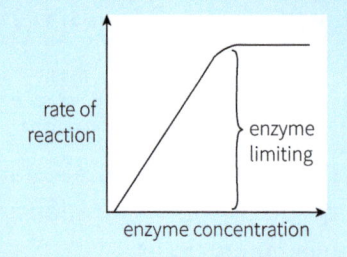

Substrate concentration

- Higher substrate concentration increases the number of enzyme-substrate complexes formed, so the rate of reaction increases.
- When all of the enzyme active sites are working, enzyme concentration will become the rate limiting factor.

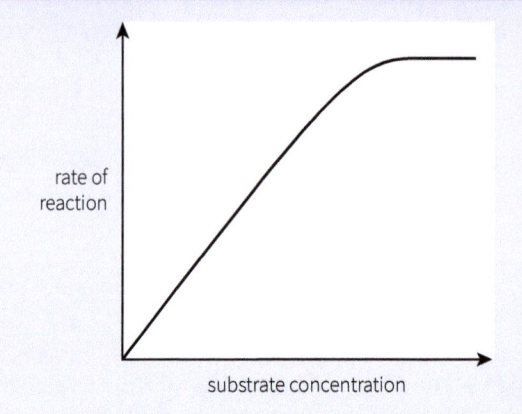

Temperature

- Enzymes have different **optimum temperatures**, which are the temperatures at which the enzymes can work at their maximum rate.
- Raising the temperature increases the rate of reaction following the **temperature coefficient** (Q_{10}).
- The temperature coefficient (Q_{10}) for a specific reaction is the effect of a 10 °C rise in temperature on the rate of the reaction.
- Above the optimum temperature, the rate of reaction slows. If the enzyme becomes **denatured**, and the reaction stops.

$$Q_{10} = \frac{\text{rate of reaction at } (T + 10)°C}{\text{rate of reaction at } T°C}$$

pH

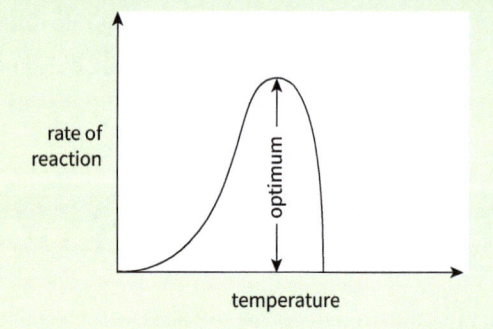

- Different enzymes have different **optimum pHs**, which are the temperatures at which the enzymes can work at their maximum rate.
- Above and below the optimum pH, the rate of reaction decreases.
- pH affects hydrogen bonds and ionic bonds holding the active site in its 3D shape.

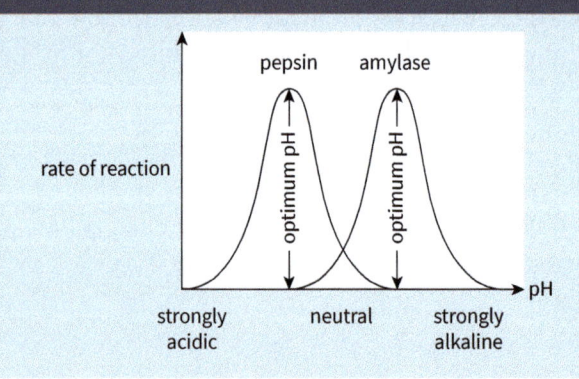

5 Enzymes

Competitive inhibitors

- Compete for the active site of the enzyme.
- An active site blocked by the competitive inhibitor is not able to catalyse a reaction – the rate of the reaction slows.

Non-competitive inhibitors

- Bind to a non-functional part of the enzyme and change the specific shape of the active site.
- The substrate cannot fit into the active site, enzyme-substrate complexes do not form, and the rate of the reaction decreases.

Inhibitors

Enzyme inhibitors control metabolic reactions. This allows product to be **produced** in **very specific amounts**.

There are two types:
- **competitive inhibitors**
- **non-competitive inhibitors**

Binding between both these types of inhibitor and the enzyme can be:
- **irreversible** and **permanent**, or
- **reversible** and **non-permanent**.

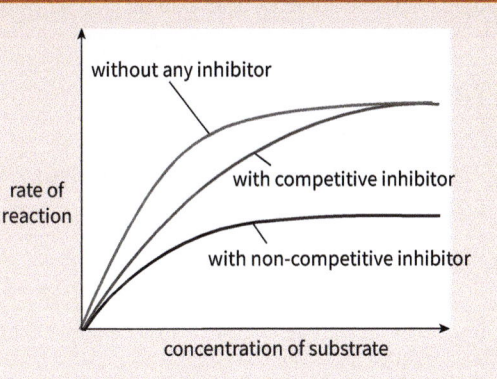

Graph: rate of reaction vs concentration of substrate, showing curves for without any inhibitor, with competitive inhibitor, and with non-competitive inhibitor.

Enzymes in metabolic pathways

Metabolic pathways such as photosynthesis and respiration are made up of a **chain of reactions**, each controlled by enzymes.

Enzyme inhibitors play a role in **controlling** these reactions.

For example, the final product of a pathway acts as an inhibitor of an enzyme earlier in that pathway, creating a negative feedback loop.

Inhibitors as metabolic poisons

Some enzymes involved in **metabolic processes** can be inhibited by **poisons**, leading to illness or even fatality.

For example, potassium cyanide is an irreversible competitive inhibitor of the enzyme cytochrome C oxidase, which is part of the electron transport chain of respiration.

Carbon monoxide is a competitive inhibitor with oxygen for haemoglobin, which is what makes it potentially fatal.

Medicinal use of enzyme inhibitors

Enzyme inhibitors can be used in medicine to treat diseases.

For example:
- Methotrexate is used in **chemotherapy** to inhibit the enzyme dihydrofolate reductase, blocking DNA replication.
- Penicillin is an enzyme inhibitor that interferes with cell wall production, causing bacterial cells to burst.

Retrieval

Learn the answers to the questions below, then cover the answers column with a piece of paper and write as many as you can. Check and repeat.

Questions / Answers

#	Question	Answer
1	What is an enzyme?	a biological catalyst (a protein)
2	What does an enzyme do?	lowers the activation energy of a reaction
3	Which three bonds can form between polypeptides in a tertiary protein structure, creating its shape?	hydrogen, ionic, disulfide bonds
4	What will happen to the rate of an enzyme-controlled reaction if the concentration of enzyme is increased?	it will increase, provided there is enough substrate
5	What will happen to the rate of an enzyme-controlled reaction if the temperature is increased?	it will increase, until the temperature increases kinetic energy so much that hydrogen bonds break, denaturing the enzyme
6	What is a competitive inhibitor?	a non-substrate molecule that fits in the active site of an enzyme
7	What is the coefficient called that predicts the effect of an increase in temperature on enzyme activity?	Q_{10}
8	Where does the reaction take place in an enzyme?	active site
9	What is formed when the substrate has attached to an enzyme?	enzyme-substrate complex
10	What is the accepted model of enzyme action called?	induced-fit model
11	Give an example of an extracellular enzyme.	amylase/trypsin
12	What is the role of some vitamins in enzyme reactions?	to form a co-enzyme
13	What is the name of a molecule that is permanently bound to an enzyme?	prosthetic group
14	What is the limitation of the lock and key model?	it doesn't explain why the activation energy gets lower
15	What is a co-factor in an enzyme reaction?	an inorganic ion that increases the enzyme's activity
16	What are the six factors that can affect enzyme activity?	temperature, pH, enzyme concentration, substrate concentration, competitive inhibitors, non-competitive inhibitors.
17	Why can't an enzyme be used for a different reaction?	the active site is specific to specific substrates

5 Enzymes

Maths skills

Practise your maths skills using the worked example and practice questions below.

Plotting a graph

When plotting a graph, you must ensure that you are displaying your results accurately and in a way that others can easily interpret. Poor graph drawing can lose you a lot of marks in an exam.

Tips for drawing a neat, accurate graph:

1. Use a sharp HB pencil and a ruler; ink should only be used to write titles of the axes and the graph.
2. Make sure all the data fits onto the graph.
3. Use linear scales that use regular intervals, such as 0, 2, 4, 6.
4. Include any units using the accepted scientific form.
5. Data points should be neat, small crosses.
6. Make sure you draw the correct type of graph, such as a line graph, scatter graph, bar chart, or histogram.
7. If drawing a line graph, usual convention requires a line/curve of best fit.
8. Remember, the independent variable is plotted on the x-axis, and the dependent variable is plotted on the y-axis
9. If the graph has more than one set of data, label them at the end of each line.

Worked example

Pectinase is an enzyme often used to help break fruits down into fruit juices. Apple slices were placed in a solution containing pectinase, and the time taken for 10 cm³ of apple juice to be produced was recorded at different concentrations. The results are presented below:

Concentration of pectinase solution (mol dm⁻³)	Time taken for 10 cm³ of apple juice to be produced (minutes)
0.2	18
0.4	13
0.6	10
0.8	8
1.0	11

Question

Draw a graph showing the data in the table.

Answer

First, you need to identify which graph to use. Because concentration is continuous, you need to use a line graph.

Remember to organise your data clearly, with clear axis labels, units, and appropriate intervals.

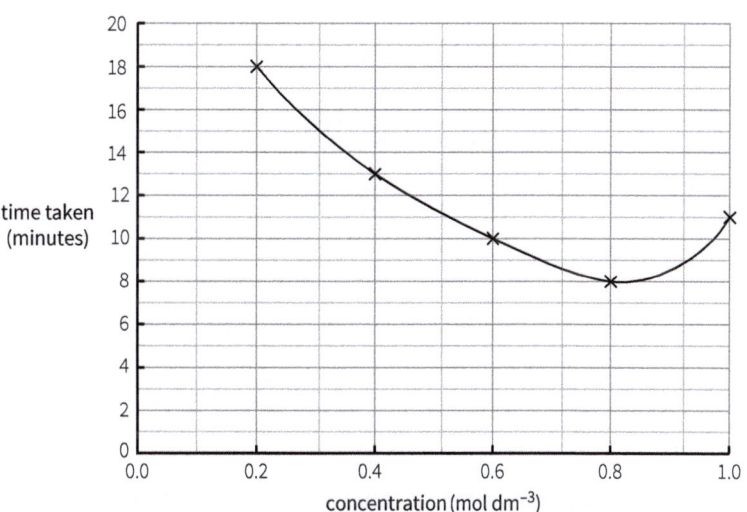

Practice

Using the same concentrations as above, a repeat of the experiment produced the following timings (from low to high):

20, 12, 7, 9, 12

1. Draw a graph using the results of the repeat experiment.
2. Use your graph to determine the optimum pH of the pectinase.

Practice

Exam-style questions

1   The rate of enzyme-controlled reactions can be affected by cofactors and enzyme inhibitors.

   Synoptic link
   5.2.2f

   (a) (i) State the definition of a cofactor.

   ....

   ....

   ....

   ....[2]

   (ii) Complete **Table 1.1** to show the properties and roles of three cofactors.

   Exam tip

   Cofactors can be organic (i.e., contain C–H bonds) or inorganic. Ions are often inorganic cofactors.

Cofactor	Enzyme with which it is associated	Is the cofactor organic or inorganic?	Is the cofactor a prosthetic group?
Zn^{2+}		inorganic	
Cl^-			no
coenzyme A	pyruvate dehydrogenase		

   Table 1.1 [3]

   (b) The synthesis of the amino acid lysine involves several reactions.

   Lysine inhibits enzymes that catalyse two of the reactions in the synthesis pathway.

   Figure 1.1 shows an outline of the reactions in the synthesis of lysine.

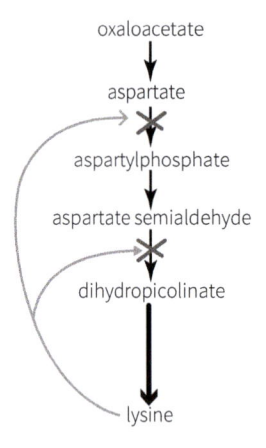

   oxaloacetate
   ↓
   aspartate
   ⇥
   aspartylphosphate
   ↓
   aspartate semialdehyde
   ⇥
   dihydropicolinate
   ↓
   lysine

   Figure 1.1

   (i) State the term used to describe the form of enzyme inhibition shown by lysine.

   .... [1]

   (ii) Suggest one benefit to organisms of this form of enzyme inhibition.

   ....

   .... [1]

56 5 Enzymes

2   Amylase is an enzyme that catalyses the hydrolysis of starch.

(a) Describe the mechanism by which amylase catalyses the hydrolysis of starch.

....

....

....

....

.... [5]

(b) A student tested the effect of pH on the activity of amylase.

The student prepared solutions of amylase that were buffered at different pH values.

The student added starch solution to each amylase solution and recorded the time taken for the starch to be hydrolysed.

(i) State two variables that the student should have controlled to produce valid results.

....

.... [2]

(ii) Suggest how the student would have detected the point at which all the starch had been hydrolysed.

....

....

.... [2]

(iii) The student's results are shown in **Table 2.1**.

pH	Time taken for no starch to be detected (s)
5.0	435
5.5	266
6.0	183
6.5	110
7.0	110
7.5	113
8.0	145

Table 2.1

The student concluded that the optimum pH for amylase activity is 6.75.

Suggest why this conclusion is not valid.

....

....

.... [2]

(iv) Explain why the rate of amylase activity was slowest at pH 5.0.

....

.... [1]

> **Synoptic link**
>
> 2.1.2q

> **Exam tip**
>
> When evaluating the validity of a conclusion, ask yourself three questions: Is the experimental method correct? Has the data been interpreted correctly? Is additional information needed to reach the conclusion?

3   Inulinase is an enzyme that breaks down the carbohydrate inulin in fungal species.

A student tested the effect of temperature on the activity of inulinase.

(a) Describe how the student could produce a 0.1% test solution of inulinase from a 1% stock solution.

....

....

.... [3]

(b) The student's results are shown in **Table 3.1**.

Temperature (°C)	Rate of inulinase activity (a.u.)
20	0.20
30	0.39
40	0.66
50	0.75
60	0.18

Table 3.1

(i) Calculate the temperature coefficient (Q_{10}) between 20 and 40 °C.

Give your answer to two significant figures.

.... [4]

> **Exam tip**
> The rate of enzyme activity tends to double (approximately) for every 10 °C increase in temperature, until the optimum temperature is reached.

(ii) Explain why the rate of inulinase activity increased between 20 and 50 °C.

....

....

....

.... [3]

4   Several factors, including pH, temperature and inhibitors, can affect the rate of enzyme-controlled reactions.

(a) The optimum pH for salivary amylase is 6.8.

Calculate the optimum H^+ concentration for salivary amylase using the formula:

$$H^+ \text{ concentration (mol dm}^{-3}) = 10^{-pH}$$

Express your answer in standard form.

> **Exam tip**
> You are required to be able to use power and logarithmic functions. Practise using the log and 10^x buttons on your calculator.

.... [2]

(b) Explain how high temperatures and extreme changes in pH can denature an enzyme

....

....

....

.... [4]

58   5 Enzymes

(c) Describe three differences between competitive enzyme inhibition and non-competitive enzyme inhibition.

....

....

.... [3]

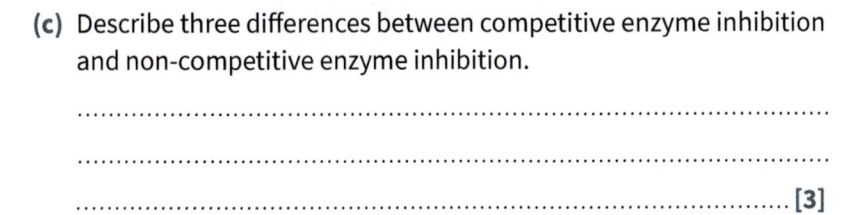

5 Enzymes increase the rate of biochemical reactions by providing an alternative reaction pathway.

(a) The graph in **Figure 5.1** shows energy changes during a reaction without an enzyme.

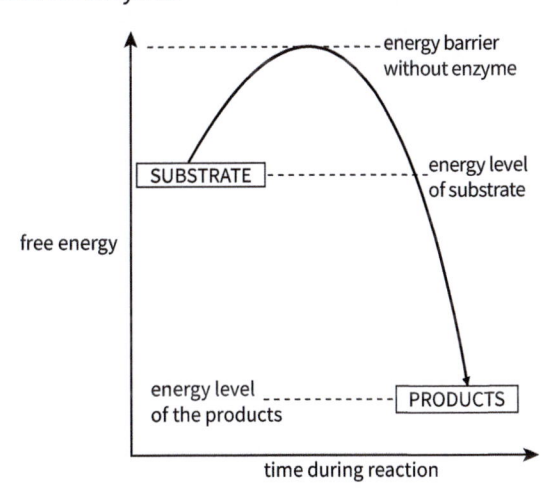

Figure 5.1

Sketch and annotate a new line on the graph to show the effect of an enzyme on the energetics of this reaction. [2]

(b) Describe how models of enzyme action have changed over time.

....

....

....

....

.... [4]

> **Exam tip**
>
> The values and position of a sketched graph do not need to be precise because you are not plotting data. However, the general trend of the curve or line that you sketch should be clear.

6 Outline the reactions catalysed by the following enzymes:
- amylase
- carbonic anhydrase
- ATP synthase

....

....

....

....

....

....

....

....

.... [6]

> **Synoptic links**
>
> 3.1.2i   5.2.2h

> **Exam tip**
>
> In your answer, you should include relevant details of the location of the reactions and any conditions necessary for the enzymes to function.

Knowledge

6 Biological membranes

Membrane structure

Membranes are made up of a **phospholipid bilayer**. The fatty acids form a **hydrophobic** layer sandwiched between the **hydrophilic** phosphate heads. Various proteins are associated with the bilayer.

Carbohydrates are found attached to some lipids (glycolipids) and some proteins (glycoproteins). Cholesterol is found between the fatty acids.

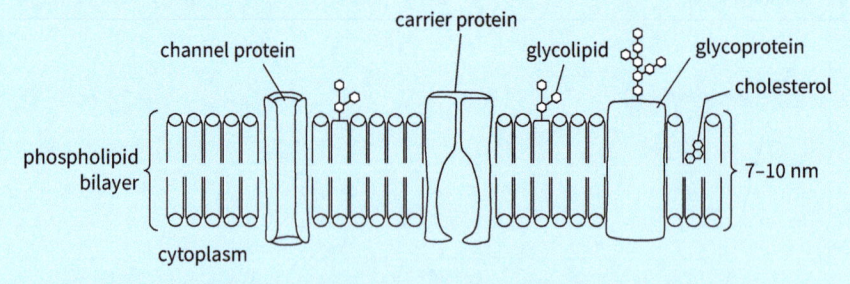

The arrangement of phospholipids and proteins is known as the **fluid-mosaic model**:

- Fluid – the phospholipids move relative to each other
- Mosaic – the proteins, dotted between the phospholipids, are of various shapes and sizes, like a mosaic.

Types of membrane transport

Transport	Movement of molecules	Proteins in membrane	Energy from ATP required	Examples
simple diffusion	higher to lower concentration	none required	no	lipid-based hormones, carbon dioxide, oxygen
facilitated diffusion	higher to lower concentration	channel proteins and carrier proteins	no	glucose, insulin, ions
osmosis	higher water potential to lower water potential	none required but aquaporins will increase osmosis	no	water only
active transport	lower concentration to higher concentration	carrier proteins	yes	magnesium ions into root hair cells from soil
endocytosis	from outside to the inside of the cell	none required	yes	phagocytosis and pinocytosis
exocytosis	from inside of the cell to outside the cell	none required	yes	secretion from cells (e.g., neurotransmitters)

Membrane components

Membrane component	Function
phospholipids	- form the basic structure of a bilayer membrane, which is a partially permeable barrier - make the membrane flexible - prevent the passage of water-soluble molecules - allow the passage of lipid-soluble molecules
intrinsic proteins	- span the bilayer - are enzymes, carrier proteins, and channel proteins
extrinsic proteins	- are found on the surface or embedded in one layer of the membrane - provide mechanical support - in conjunction with glycolipids, act as cell receptors for hormones and other molecules
glycoproteins	- are receptors for chemical signals such as peptide hormones and neurotransmitters - act as receptors for toxins and drugs - role in cell adhesion in some tissues
glycolipids	- have a role in cell recognition, acting as cell markers or antigens
cholesterol	- may be present; restricts movement of other membrane components, making membranes less fluid, providing mechanical stability

Factors affecting membrane structure and permeability

A number of factors increase the permeability of a phospholipid bilayer.

For example, an increase in temperature increases the permeability of, and therefore the rate of transport across, a membrane.

The phospholipids have more kinetic energy, increasing their relative movement and making the membrane 'leaky'.

If the temperature reaches the point at which membrane proteins start to denature, a further increase in membrane permeability will occur.

Organic solvents, such as ethanol, dissolve phospholipids and so will degrade the membrane, eventually destroying it, which allows substances to cross the membrane freely.

Simple diffusion

Simple diffusion is the net movement of molecules in a liquid (or gas) from an area of higher concentration to an area of lower concentration.

It is a passive, random process that uses the kinetic energy of molecules.

The rate of diffusion can be affected by factors such as **surface area** and **temperature**.

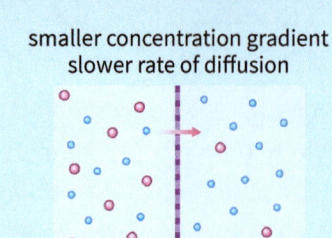

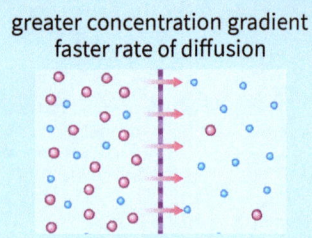

smaller concentration gradient
slower rate of diffusion

greater concentration gradient
faster rate of diffusion

Facilitated diffusion

Large, water-soluble molecules and charged ions cannot pass through the phospholipid bilayer by simple diffusion. They move by **facilitated diffusion** which requires:

Channel proteins – these form pores in the membrane; often specific to an ion or a molecule.

Carrier proteins – these change shape once an ion or a molecule is attached to allow the molecule through the membrane.

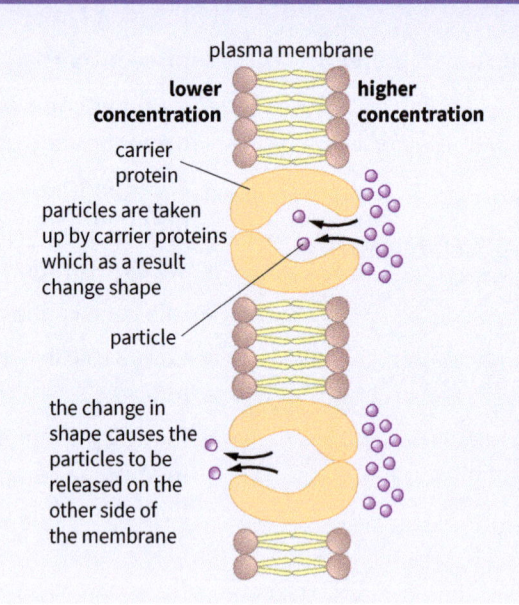

plasma membrane

lower concentration

higher concentration

carrier protein

particles are taken up by carrier proteins which as a result change shape

particle

the change in shape causes the particles to be released on the other side of the membrane

Endocytosis and exocytosis

Endocytosis and exocytosis transport **large quantities** of material into, or out of, the cell. Both require ATP as a source of energy.

Endocytosis
The cell surface membrane wraps itself around the material and brings it into the cell into a vesicle. There are two main forms:
- **phagocytosis**, for solid material
- **pinocytosis**, for liquid material

Exocytosis
The reverse of endocytosis, where a vesicle containing enzymes, mucus, or hormones fuses with the cell surface membrane to release the materials out of the cell.

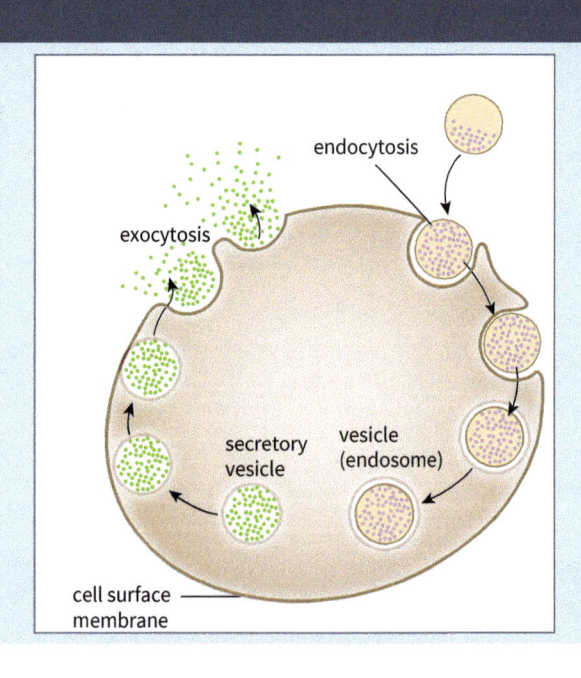

endocytosis

exocytosis

secretory vesicle

vesicle (endosome)

cell surface membrane

6 Biological membranes

Osmosis

Osmosis is the net movement of water molecules by diffusion from a region of higher water potential to an area of lower water potential across a partially permeable membrane.

Water potential is a measure of the ability of water molecules to diffuse; pure water has the highest water potential of 0 kPa.

Pure water
0 kPa

Dilute solution
−10 kPa

Concentrated solution
−100 kPa

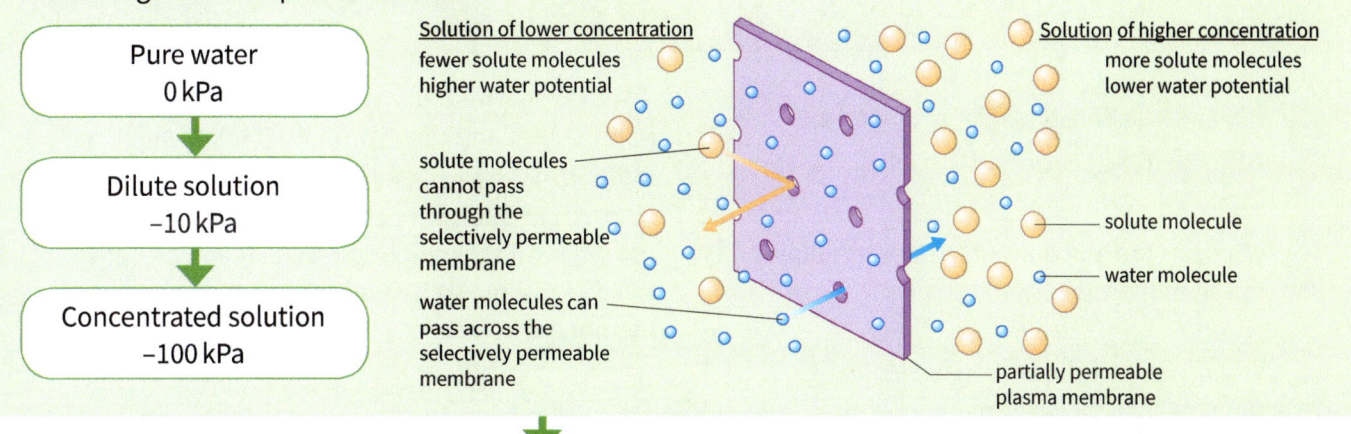

Solution of lower concentration
fewer solute molecules
higher water potential

Solution of higher concentration
more solute molecules
lower water potential

solute molecules cannot pass through the selectively permeable membrane

water molecules can pass across the selectively permeable membrane

solute molecule
water molecule
partially permeable plasma membrane

Osmosis in different concentrations of solution

The diagrams show osmosis in plant cells and animal cells that are in solutions of different concentrations.

protoplast pushed against cell wall
nucleus
cellulose cell wall
protoplast
hypotonic

protoplast beginning to pull away from the cell wall
isotonic

protoplast completely pulled away from the cell wall
hypertonic

contents, including haemoglobin, are released
remains of cell surface membrane
hypotonic

normal red blood cell
isotonic

haemoglobin is more concentrated, giving cell a darker appearance
cell shrunken and shrivelled
hypertonic

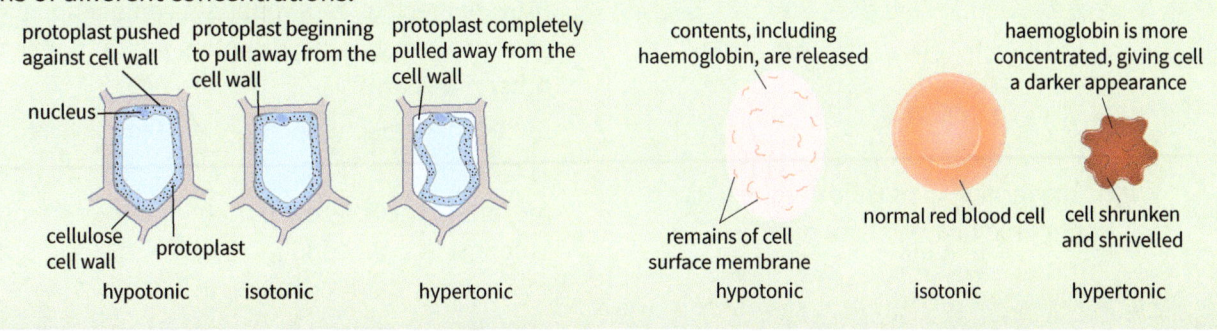

Active transport

Active transport is the movement of substances across a membrane against the concentration gradient, using energy from the hydrolysis of ATP.

Active transport requires **carrier proteins**, called **pumps**, which:

- act as one-way carriers for specific molecules and ions across a membrane
- require energy from the hydrolysis of ATP to ADP and inorganic phosphate
- carry molecules and ions against a concentration gradient
- transport molecules and ions much faster than by diffusion.

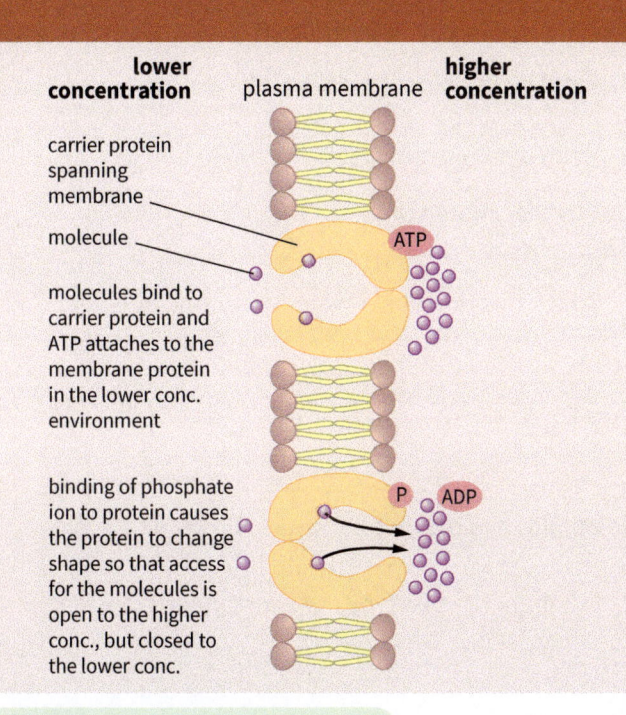

lower concentration
plasma membrane
higher concentration

carrier protein spanning membrane
molecule

molecules bind to carrier protein and ATP attaches to the membrane protein in the lower conc. environment

binding of phosphate ion to protein causes the protein to change shape so that access for the molecules is open to the higher conc., but closed to the lower conc.

Retrieval

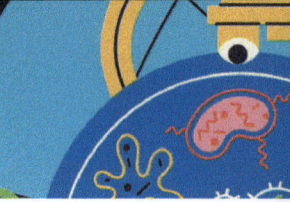

Learn the answers to the questions below, then cover the answers column with a piece of paper and write as many as you can. Check and repeat.

Questions | Answers

#	Question	Answer
1	How are the phospholipids arranged in a membrane?	in a bilayer, with the hydrophobic fatty acid tails in the centre and the hydrophilic phosphate heads pointing towards the outside
2	What are the functions of the phospholipids in a membrane?	to be a partially permeable barrier, to allow the passage of lipid-soluble substances and prevent the passage of water-soluble ones, to make the membrane flexible
3	Where are intrinsic proteins positioned in a phospholipid bilayer?	they span the entire bilayer
4	Where are extrinsic proteins found in a phospholipid bilayer?	they are found on the surface or embedded in one layer
5	What are the roles of intrinsic proteins?	span the bilayer, are enzymes, carrier proteins, and channel proteins
6	What are the roles of extrinsic proteins?	provide mechanical support; in conjunction with glycolipids, act as cell receptors for hormones and other molecules
7	Why is the term fluid mosaic used to describe a phospholipid bilayer membrane?	fluid – the phospholipids are able to move relative to one another mosaic – describes the pattern of proteins scattered amongst the phospholipids so the role is to provide mechanical stability and regulate fluidity
8	What is the role of cholesterol in a membrane?	restricts movement of other membrane components, making membranes less fluid and providing mechanical stability
9	What is the role of glycolipids?	cell recognition / act as antigens
10	What are the roles of glycoproteins?	receptor sites, cell adhesion in some tissues
11	Does facilitated diffusion require energy from ATP?	no
12	Which has the higher water potential: pure water or a concentrated salt solution?	pure water, 0 kPa
13	What is active transport?	the movement of a substance across a membrane against its concentration gradient by a carrier protein, using energy from ATP
14	What is exocytosis?	the movement of a large amount of material out of a cell, requires ATP
15	What are the two types of endocytosis?	phagocytosis (for solids) and pinocytosis (for liquids)

6 Biological membranes

Practical skills

Practise your practical skills using the worked example and practice questions below.

Describe and explain

Beetroot cells have red pigments, called betalains, in their cell vacuoles. The rate at which betalains diffuse out of the vacuole and cell surface membrane can be used to investigate the effect of various factors on the permeability of membranes. The amount of betalains released can be measured using a colorimeter with a green filter (550 nm).

A typical experiment involves looking at the effect of temperature on membrane permeability.

You might be expected to describe and explain the results from the same experiment or a similar investigation using your own data or data that has been provided.

Describe means writing what you see in the data – any trends and patterns or correlations (positive or negative). Examples in the data should be used to highlight an observable change. For example, calculating a percentage change may be desirable.

Explain means demonstrating that you understand the scientific principles underlying the results. You should be able to use and apply your knowledge and understanding to explain the results.

Worked example

An experiment into the effect of temperature on the rate of betalain diffusion from beetroot cells has produced the following graph:

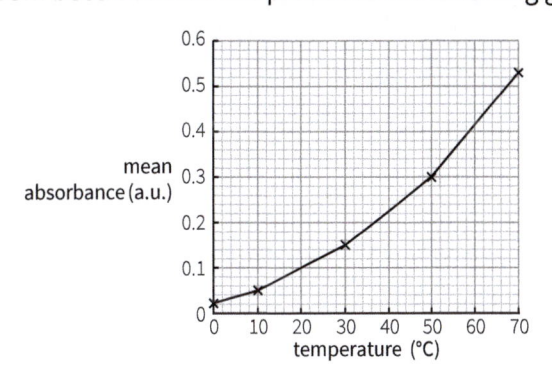

Question
Describe and explain the results in the graph.

Answer
You're being asked to do two things: describe your results (describing the pattern you see), and then explain them (using your knowledge to explain the pattern).

So first describe what you see:

'As temperature increases, the absorbance measured increases. The results show a positive, non-linear relationship, where the increase in absorbance between 50–70 °C (roughly 0.23) is almost 8 times the increase between 0–10 °C (roughly 0.03).'

Then, explain the results using your knowledge of diffusion and proteins:

'The increase in temperature increases the kinetic energy of the phospholipid membrane. This allows betalain to leave the cell through the gaps generated by the movement of the phospholipid membrane. As the temperature increases past 40 °C, the cell membrane is damaged, and the protein channels denature, allowing more betalain to leave the cell. This increases the absorbance measured during the experiment.'

Practice

The effect of temperature on the permeability of beetroot cell membranes is shown below.

1. Plot a graph of the results.
2. Describe and explain any trends in the data.
3. The absorbency result of 0 °C is sometimes higher than expected. Suggest a reason for this.

Temperature (°C)	Mean absorbance of betalain solution (a.u.)
0	0.04
20	0.07
40	0.14
60	0.32
80	0.68

For answers and more practice questions visit www.oxfordrevise.com/scienceanswers

Even more practice and interactive revision quizzes are available on kerboodle

6 Retrieval

Practice

Exam-style questions

1 **Figure 1.1** shows the structure of a plasma membrane.

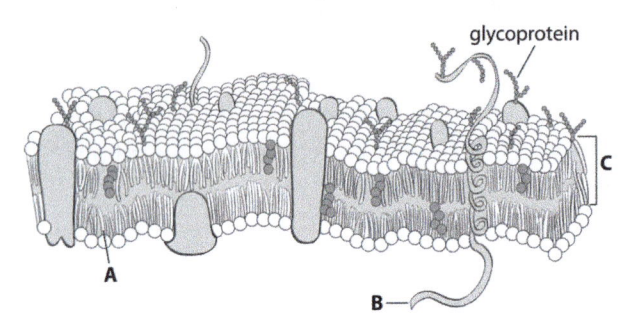

Figure 1.1

(a) (i) Give the names of components **A**, **B**, and **C**.
.... [3]

(ii) State the function of components **A**, **B**, and **C**.
....
....
....
.... [3]

(b) Explain why a bilayer arrangement is formed in cells as seen in **Figure 1.1**.
....
....
....
.... [3]

(c) State three roles of membranes within cells. For each role, name one component that is involved in coordinating that function.
....
....
....
.... [3]

> **Exam tip**
>
> Think about the membrane-bound organelles inside cells. Consider what functions these membranes have and what events occur across those membranes.

2 A student placed a piece of beetroot into a beaker of water and noticed that the water turned red.

(a) Explain why the water turned red.
....
....
....
.... [2]

66 6 Biological membranes

The student then planned an experiment to investigate whether the intensity of red coloration in the water depends on the water temperature. The method is shown below.

(1) Prepare four beetroot cylinders using cork borers.

(2) Remove the skin on the edges of the beetroot cylinders.

(3) Gently rinse the cylinders under running water.

(4) Roll each cylinder on paper towel three times.

(5) Pour water of different temperatures into four boiling tubes: 20 °C, 40 °C, 60 °C, 80 °C

(6) Place a beetroot cylinder into each boiling tube at the same time.

(7) Remove the beetroot cylinders from the water after 10 minutes.

(8) Compare the intensity of the colour in the different boiling tubes of water.

(b) (i) State the independent variable of this experiment.
.... [1]

(ii) State two variables that should be controlled in this experiment.
....
.... [2]

(iii) State the purpose of steps **2**, **3**, and **4**.

Step **2**: ....

Step **3**: ....

Step **4**: .... [3]

(c) A more objective measurement can be done using a colorimeter – a machine that measures the amount of light that can pass through a solution. The transmission of light is plotted against the temperature of the water on a line graph, shown in **Figure 2.1**.

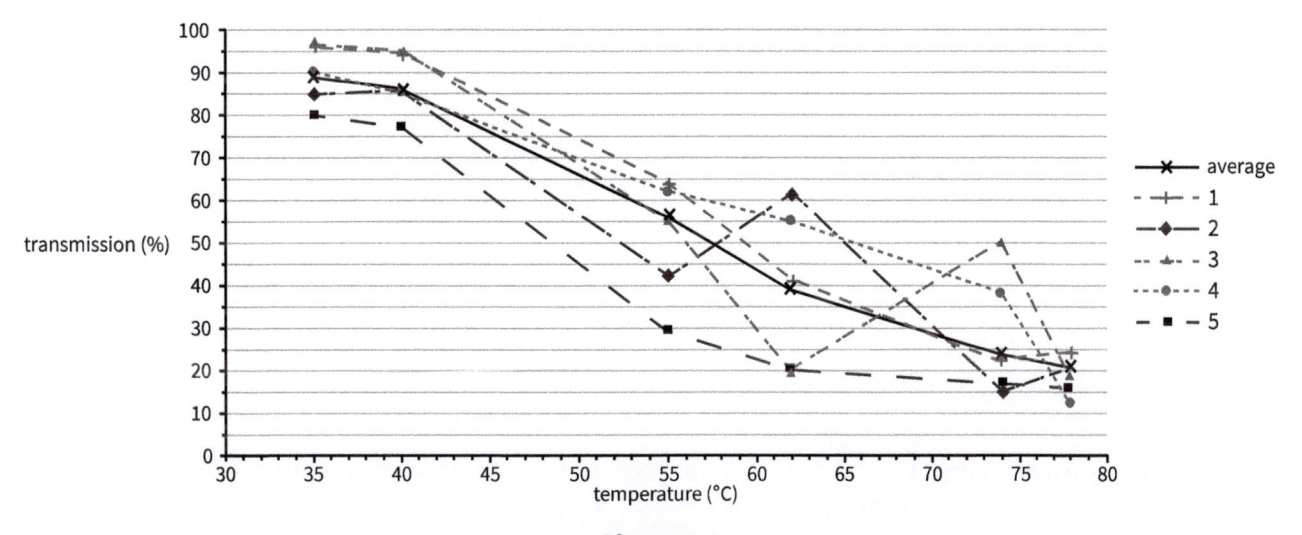

Figure 2.1

Describe and explain the trend shown on the graph in **Figure 2.1**.

....
....
....
....
....
....
.... [5]

> **Exam tip**
>
> The more red pigments that are released into the water, the less light can pass through it, hence the lower the light transmission.

3 Plants need various chemicals in order to grow.

(a) Outline how water and mineral ions are absorbed from the roots and transported throughout the plant.

> **Synoptic link**
>
> 2.1.1.i

....
....
....
....
....
....
.... [5]

(b) Apart from a larger surface area, describe and explain two adaptations of root hair cells that allow efficient absorption of water and mineral ions.

....
....
....
....
.... [4]

> **Exam tip**
>
> Remember to make your answers comparative! An adaptation of a specialised cell can simply be the fact that they have more of a certain organelle which allows them to do their specific function.

(c) When animal and plant cells are placed in distilled water, animal cells burst whereas plant cells become turgid.

Explain why.

....
....
....
....
....
....
.... [5]

4 There are different transport mechanisms of substances across cell membranes.

(a) (i) Define active transport.

....
....
.... [3]

6 Biological membranes

(ii) Give one similarity and one difference between active transport and bulk transport.

....
....
....
.... [3]

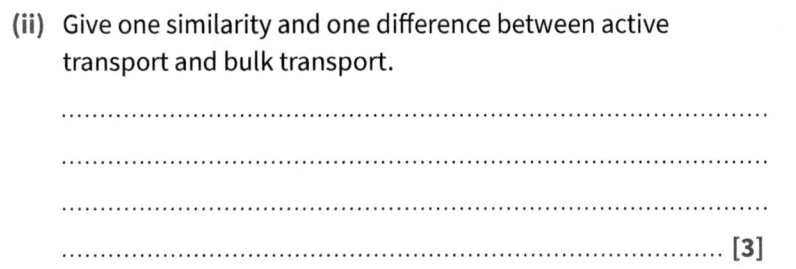

(iii) Tick the correct box in **Table 4.1** to show which mechanism(s) is/are used to transport each substance across cell surface membranes.

Substance	Diffusion	Facilitated diffusion	Active transport	Bulk transport
oxygen				
glucose				
sodium ions				
bacterial cell				

Table 4.1 [4]

(b) The mitochondrion is a double-membrane organelle inside eukaryotic cells. The inner membrane is highly folded, forming the cristae, and contains many intrinsic proteins within. This part of the organelle is crucial to the production of ATP.

(i) Suggest an advantage of the highly folded structure of the inner membrane.

....
....
.... [1]

Figure 4.1 shows a summary of the production of ATP in the mitochondrion.

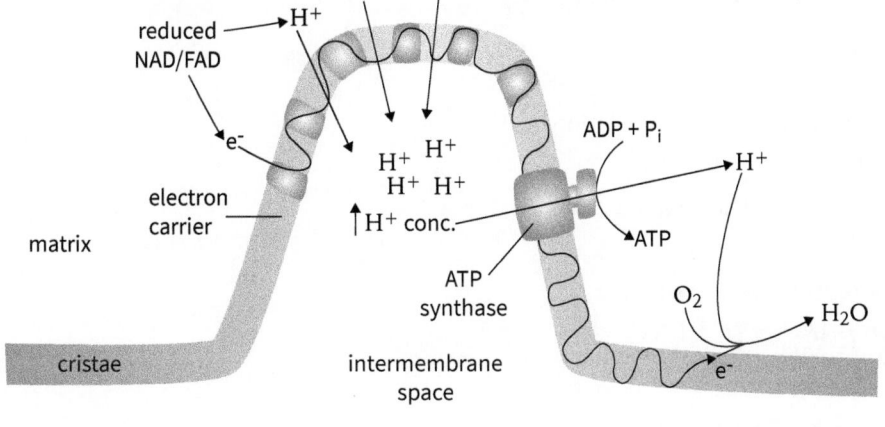

Figure 4.1

(ii) State which mechanism of transport moves the hydrogen ions from the matrix into the intermembrane space.

Explain your answer.

....

....

.... [2]

(iii) State which mechanism of transport moves the hydrogen ions back into the matrix.

Explain your answer.

....

....

....

....

.... [3]

Exam tip

Consider what is needed for each transport mechanism. Then read the information carefully and decide what mechanism is used to move these ions into and out of the intermembrane space.

5 (a) For each of the following components, describe its structure and function within the cell surface membrane.

   (i) Glycoprotein [2]
   (ii) Phospholipid [3]
   (iii) Channel protein [3]

Synoptic link

2.1.4.c

(b) Hydrogen peroxide is a harmful chemical that is produced though cell metabolism. It is broken down by catalase, an intracellular enzyme found in liver cells, into water and oxygen.

An experiment on catalase was conducted using the following method:

(1) Three identical sized cubes were cut from a fresh liver and labelled as cubes **A**, **B**, and **C**.

(2) Cube **A** was stored in the refrigerator.

(3) Cube **B** was stored in the freezer overnight and then defrosted.

(4) Cube **C** was boiled in hot water for 5 minutes.

(5) When all three cubes of liver had returned to room temperature, they were placed in separate beakers containing equal volumes and concentrations of hydrogen peroxide solution.

(i) Describe the mechanism of how catalase breaks down hydrogen peroxide. [3]

Observations were recorded in **Table 5.1**.

Liver cube	Observations
A	some gas bubbles were released
B	a lot of gas bubbles were released
C	no bubbles were released

Table 5.1

6 Biological membranes

(ii) Suggest an explanation for:

Liver cube **A** [3]

Liver cube **B** [3]

Liver cube **C** [3]

> **Exam tip**
> Think about how different temperatures affect membrane structure, enzyme structure and activity.

6 The carbohydrates in our food can be broken down into glucose to be transported and absorbed by our body cells.

The pancreas releases insulin to help our body cells take in glucose.

Insulin binds to receptors of body cells, which triggers glucose transporter proteins to be deposited onto the cell surface membrane.

(a) (i) Suggest which component of the plasma membrane of a body cell would bind to insulin. [1]

(ii) By the binding of insulin to the plasma membrane, a chemical is produced within the cell that triggers the embedding of glucose transporters into the plasma membrane.

Illustrate the steps in which glucose transporters are produced and transported to the cell surface membrane. [5]

(iii) Complete the paragraph by filling in the gaps with the most appropriate words.

There may be more than one word in the blank spaces.

Glucose transporters are embedded within the plasma membrane. They are used to move glucose into cells, down the concentration gradient. They are an example of ...., a component of the plasma membrane. It allows glucose to enter the cell by the mechanism known as .... However, in situations where glucose is absorbed up the concentration gradient, the cells may use sodium–glucose co-transporters, which are a type of membrane protein that change their shape to move glucose and sodium ions into cells simultaneously. For this to happen, sodium ions are first moved up their concentration gradient across the membrane. This requires .... to work and this mechanism of transport is called .... The co-transporters then move both sodium ions and glucose across the membrane. [4]

> **Synoptic link**
> 2.1.1 2.1.2 2.1.4
> 2.1.5 3.1.1

> **Exam tip**
> Glucose transporters are protein channels. Think about which organelles are involved in protein synthesis and transport onto the plasma (cell surface) membrane.

(b) Type 2 diabetes is a disease where the body cells can no longer respond to insulin, hence the amount of glucose taken into cells from the bloodstream is reduced.

Explain why the body cells of a person with type 2 diabetes would lose water easily. [5]

Knowledge

7 Cell division, diversity, and organisation

The cell cycle

Cells have a **cell cycle**, a regular pattern of division followed by a period of growth.

Interphase occupies most of the cell cycle and is a three step process:

- G_1 – proteins required for organelles are synthesised.
- S – DNA replication takes place, resulting in a doubling of the mass of DNA in the cell (2n → 4n)
- G_2 – organelles grow and divide, and energy reserves are increased.

Interphase is sometimes known as the resting phase but the cell is metabolically very active (e.g., replicating DNA and synthesising proteins, which require ATP).

Mitosis – the nucleus divides into two.

Cytokinesis – the cytoplasm divides to form two smaller, genetically identical daughter cells.

Regulation of the cell cycle

It is important that regular checks, **checkpoints**, are made throughout the cell cycle to ensure that each stage is fully completed before progressing to the next one.

Checkpoints occur at:

- the end of G_1 before DNA replication is triggered
- the end of G_2 before mitosis begins
- spindle assembly (or metaphase), to ensure chromosomes are aligned on the spindle.

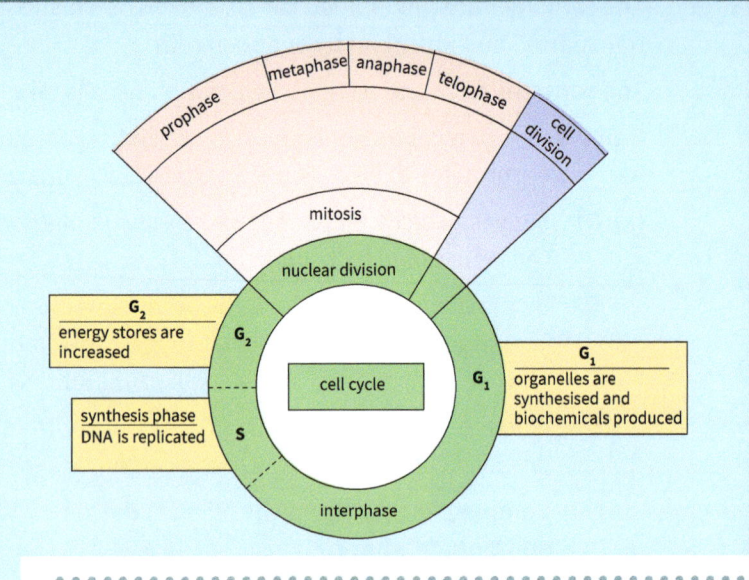

Variations in cell mass and DNA mass during the cell cycle

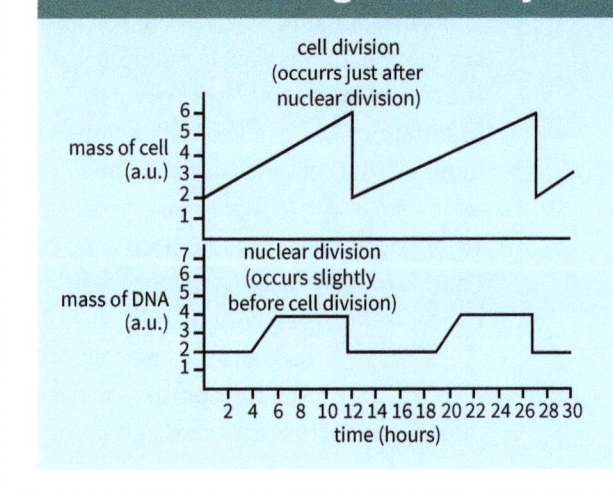

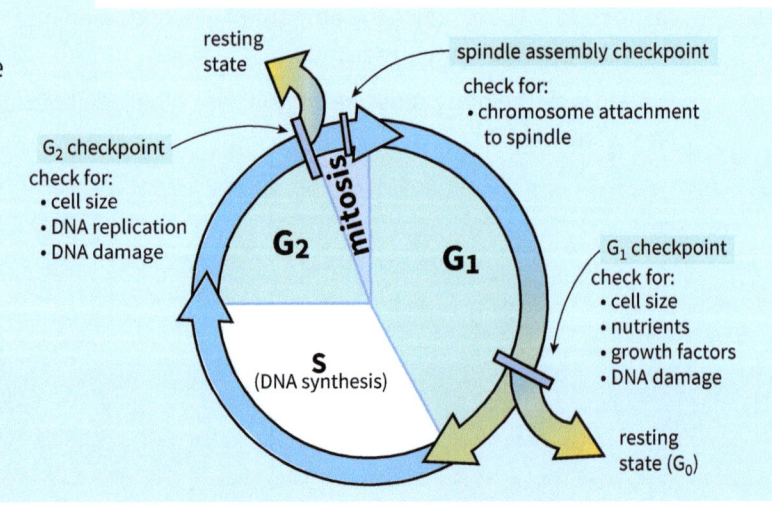

The main stages in mitosis

Using a light microscope, four stages of mitosis can be seen:

Stage of mitosis	Appearance of organelles	Diagram
prophase	• Chromosomes comprise two genetically identical threads called sister chromatids, joined by a centromere. • The chromosomes shorten and thicken by supercoiling and become visible under a microscope when stained. • The nuclear envelope disappears. • The centrioles move to the poles of the cell, producing a network of spindle fibres between them.	
metaphase	• The chromosomes move to the equator of the cell. • Each one becomes attached to a spindle fibre by its centromere.	
anaphase	• The spindle fibres contract, which separates the sister chromatids. • The spindle fibres pull the chromatids towards opposite poles of the cell centromere first (so they make a V shape); each chromatid is essentially a chromosome.	
telophase	• As the two sets of chromosomes reach each of the cell poles, a nuclear envelope forms around each one to form two new nuclei. • The chromosomes start to uncoil. • The spindle fibres break down and disappear. • After telophase, the plasma membrane starts to invaginate to divide the parent cell into two daughter cells (cytokinesis).	

The significance of mitosis in life cycles

Mitosis gives rise to daughter cells that are genetically identical to the parent cell, both in terms of chromosome number and DNA. Organisms need to produce genetically identical daughter cells for:

Asexual reproduction
- Single-celled fungi (e.g., yeasts) divide to produce two genetically identical daughter cells through repeated budding and separation.
- Plants are also able to reproduce via asexual reproduction.
- Some plants and animals (such as insects like aphids) can also use parthenogenesis to reproduce.

Growth
- Multicellular organisms grow by making new, extra cells. It is essential that new cells are genetically identical to the parent cells so they can continue to carry out the same function.

Tissue repair
- Damaged cells need to be replaced with genetically identical ones that will carry out the same function.

The main stages in meiosis

Stage in Meiosis I	Diagram	Stage in Meiosis II (occurs at 90° to plane of meiosis I)	Diagram
Prophase I: chromatids condense, homologous chromosomes form bivalents, crossing over occurs	centriole pairs moving to opposite ends of the cell and spindle forming; point of crossing over; chromosomes seen to comprise two sister chromatids; nuclear envelope disassembling	**Prophase II:** chromosomes condense, spindle re-forms, nuclear envelope breaks down again	spindle fibres re-forming; replicated centrioles and move to poles
Metaphase I: bivalents line up at the equator, independent assortment occurs	spindle fibres; spindle equator; centriole	**Metaphase II:** chromosomes randomly arrange themselves on spindle fibres at equator by centromeres, so independent assortment occurs	chromosomes lying on the equator of the cell
Anaphase I: spindle fibres pull homologous chromosomes to opposite poles of cell	piece of sister chromatid exchanged during crossover in prophase 1; one of the homologous chromosomes being pulled to a pole	**Anaphase II:** chromatids are pulled apart by contracting spindle fibres to poles of cell	chromatid moving towards the pole
Telophase I followed by cytokinesis: nuclear envelope forms around new nuclei	cell divided by constriction	**Telophase II** followed by cytokinesis: nuclear envelope forms around new **haploid** nuclei	nuclear envelope re-forming

Erythrocytes and neutrophils

Not all body cells can undergo mitosis to produce more of themselves. Some cells must be produced from the division and differentiation of stem cells. Genetically identical stem cells in bone marrow differentiate into erythrocytes (red blood cells) and neutrophils (a type of white blood cell).

A stem cell differentiating into an **erythrocyte** loses its nucleus, rough ER, mitochondria, and Golgi apparatus, and becomes packed with haemoglobin. Its shape forms a biconcave disc.

A stem cell differentiating into a **neutrophil** retains its nucleus, which becomes lobed, and the cytoplasm fills with lysosomes.

The significance of meiosis in life cycles

Cell division by meiosis results in the production of four daughter cells, called gametes. Each daughter cell is:
- **haploid** – it has half the chromosome number of the diploid parent cell.
- **genetically unique** – it will have a unique set of alleles due to **independent assortment and crossing over**.

Homologous chromosomes are a pair of chromosomes that have the same genes at the same loci.

Crossing over
During prophase I, homologous chromosomes form bivalents so that non-sister chromatids (i.e., maternal and paternal chromatids) can cross over at locations called chiasmata and exchange sections of chromosome holding the same genes but potentially different alleles.

Independent assortment
This is caused by the random distribution and separation of homologous chromosomes during metaphase I and the random distribution and segregation of sister chromatids at metaphase II.

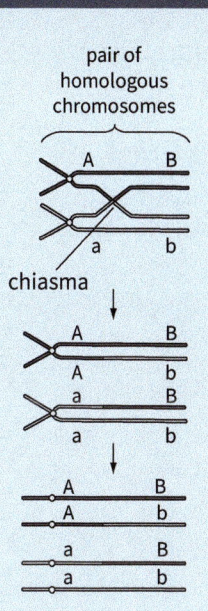

Organisation of cells

Cell – the fundamental unit of life.

↓

Tissue – a collection of similar cells working together with a common function. For example, a muscle is a type of tissue.

↓

Organ – a collection of tissues working together to perform a particular function. For example, the heart is composed of muscle and nerve tissue.

↓

Organ system – a collection of organs working together in a specific role. For example, the heart and lungs are organs included in the pulmonary system.

Viewing mitosis

Plant tissue from growing root tips can be stained, squashed, and examined under a light microscope to reveal stages in the cell cycle, which can then be drawn.

When looking at cells under a microscope, ask yourself what the nucleus is doing and see what stages of mitosis you can identify.

When drawing what you see, keep referring to the image so you include all the detail of the different stages you can see.

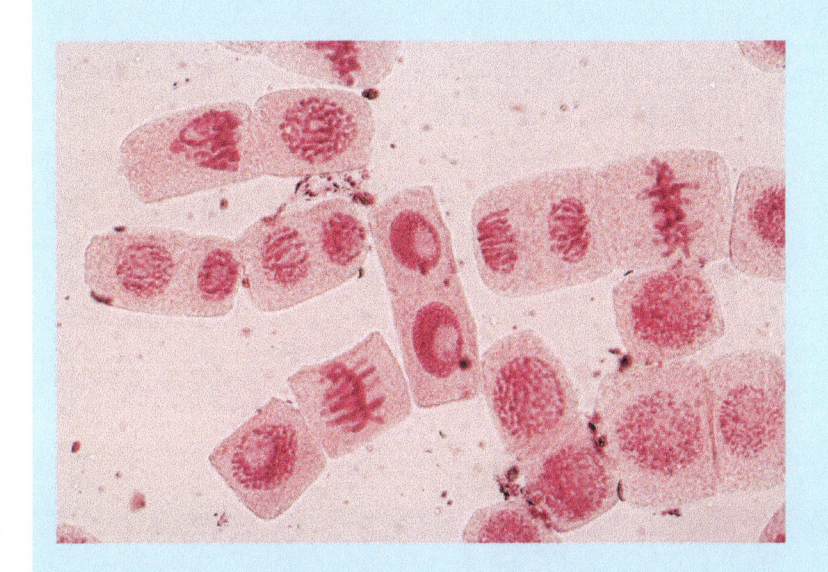

Specialised cells

The cells of multicellular organisms are specialised (differentiated) to carry out specialised functions.

Erythrocyte (red blood cell)
Contains haemoglobin to transport oxygen from lungs to body tissues.

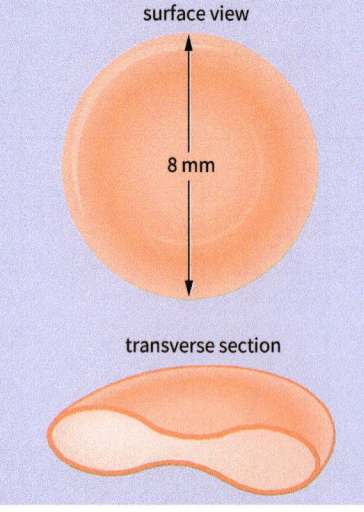

surface view
8 mm
transverse section

Neutrophil
A type of white blood cell involved in phagocytosis, with a cytoplasm filled with lysosomes to break down phagocytosed material.

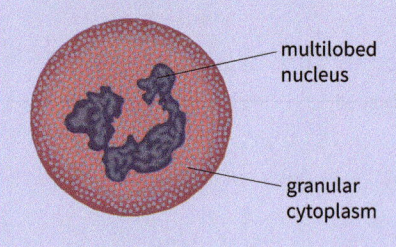

multilobed nucleus
granular cytoplasm

Squamous epithelial cell
Found lining surfaces such as the lungs, blood vessels, and the oesophagus. Has a flat, thin shape to facilitate diffusion of materials across it.

Ciliated epithelial cell
Has tiny extensions called cilia to move mucus along mucous membranes (e.g., in the respiratory tract) or ova along the Fallopian tubes.

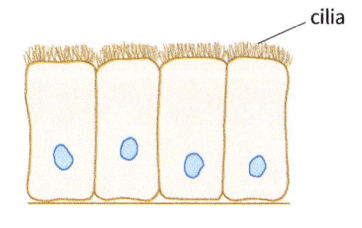

cilia

Sperm cell
Flagellum used to swim to ovum using energy released by the hydrolysis of ATP in the mitochondria in middle section

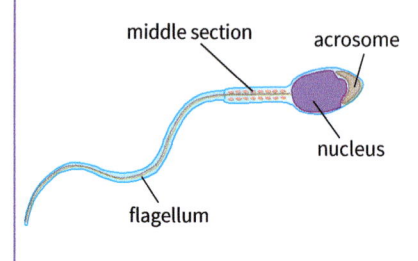

middle section
acrosome
nucleus
flagellum

Root hair cell
Long 'hair' maximises surface area in contact with soil for uptake of water and mineral ions.

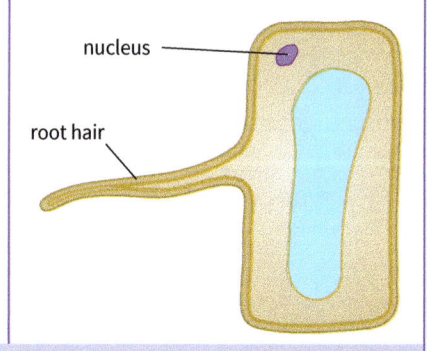

nucleus
root hair

Palisade cell
Long and thin so that the many chloroplasts can absorb maximum sunlight.

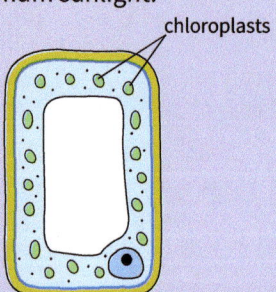

chloroplasts

Guard cell
Arranged in pairs around stomata to control water vapour loss from plant. Guard cells have a thickened cell wall surrounding the pore which causes the bending of the cell when it is turgid.

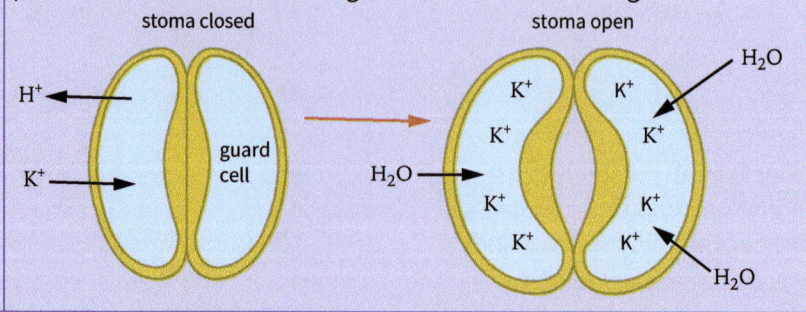

stoma closed
H^+
K^+
guard cell

stoma open
H_2O
K^+
H_2O
H_2O

7 Cell division, diversity, and organisation

Stem cells

Stem cells are cells that have not yet differentiated into specialised cells. Stem cells can divide an unlimited number of times, and are a renewing source of undifferentiated cells.

There are three types of stem cells:

Totipotent cells
- Occur only for a limited time in early mammalian embryos.
- Can differentiate to produce **any** type of body cell, including placental cells.

Pluripotent cells
- Found in embryos.
- Can differentiate into **all** tissue types, except placental cells.

Multipotent cells
- Found in many tissues at any post-embryonic life stage.
- Can differentiate to form a **limited** number of different cell types.

To help you remember the roles of these stem cells, remember that 'toti-' means 'whole', 'pluri-' means 'many', 'multi-' means 'several', and '-potent' means 'ability'.

Xylem and phloem

Xylem vessels and phloem sieve tubes differentiate from plant meristems. Like stem cells, meristems are totipotent and can differentiate into many different cells.

Meristem cells that are destined to become **xylem** vessels elongate. Lignin is deposited in the cell walls to strengthen and waterproof them, and the cell dies. The end cell walls break down to form long, continuous tubes.

Meristem cells forming **phloem** differentiate into companion cells and sieve tube elements.

Potential uses of stem cells in research and medicine

Stem cells are potential treatments for some human neurological disorders, such as **Parkinson's** and **Alzheimer's**. They also have the potential to be used to **repair damaged** tissue, such as breaks in spinal cords causing paralysis, or injured heart muscle after a heart attack.

Stem cells are also being used for research into **developmental biology** to help scientists understand how a fertilised egg cell develops into a multicellular organism, and how and why the process can go wrong.

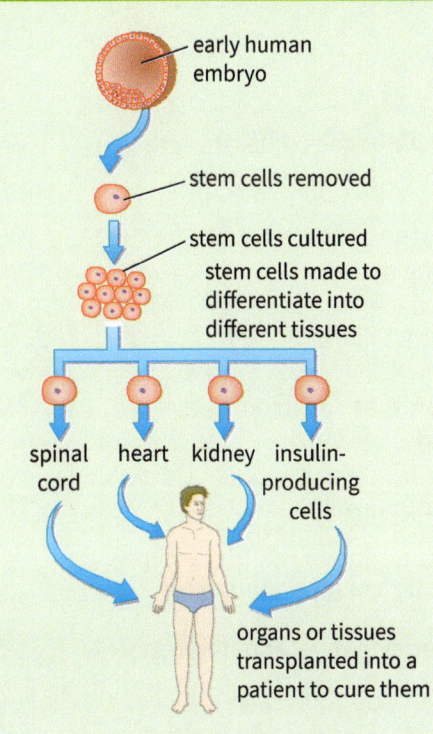

For answers and more practice questions visit www.oxfordrevise.com/scienceanswers

Even more practice and interactive revision quizzes are available on kerboodle

Retrieval

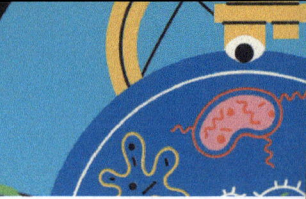

Learn the answers to the questions below, then cover the answers column with a piece of paper and write as many as you can. Check and repeat.

Questions / Answers

#	Question	Answer
1	What are the main stages in the cell cycle?	interphase (G_1, S, G_2), mitosis, cytokinesis
2	What happens during the S stage of the cell cycle?	DNA is replicated
3	Why does the cell cycle need to be controlled?	so that growth is regulated and controlled, otherwise tumours may form
4	What are the three roles of mitosis?	tissue repair, growth, asexual reproduction
5	What are the products of mitosis?	two daughter cells that carry the same number of chromosomes as the parent cell and identical copies of their DNA
6	List the four stages of mitosis in the correct order.	prophase, metaphase, anaphase, telophase
7	Why is a cell in interphase not resting?	the cell is actively synthesising biochemical molecules and organelles, increasing energy reserves, replicating DNA, and growing
8	Describe the appearance of a cell during metaphase.	nuclear envelope is not present, chromosomes align at the equator of the cell
9	What happens during anaphase II of meiosis?	the sister chromatids are pulled apart towards the poles of the cell as the spindle fibres contract
10	What are homologous chromosomes?	a pair of chromosomes – one maternal, one paternal – that have the same genes at particular loci, but possibly different alleles
11	How do the daughter cells differ from the parent cell as a result of meiosis?	the daughter cells are haploid, the parent cell is diploid; they are genetically different
12	How many daughter cells arise from a single parent cell during meiosis?	four
13	What is a bivalent?	a pair of homologous chromosomes aligned next to each other
14	What are the points at which non-sister chromatids join?	chiasmata
15	What is a specialised cell?	a cell that has differentiated, so it can carry out a particular function
16	What is the function of an erythrocyte?	to transport oxygen from the lungs to respiring tissues
17	How is an erythrocyte differentiated to carry out its function?	biconcave disc shape, packed full of haemoglobin (no nucleus, mitochondria, Golgi apparatus, or RER)
18	What is a tissue?	a group of similar cells working to carry out a particular function

7 Cell division, diversity, and organisation

#	Question	Answer
19	Place these in the correct order of complexity: tissue, organ, cell, organ system	cell, tissue, organ, organ system
20	What is a meristem?	an area where cells rapidly divide into differentiated cells in plants
21	What is a stem cell?	an undifferentiated cell (that can divide an unlimited number of times)
22	Where are the stem cells found that differentiate into erythrocytes and neutrophils?	bone marrow
23	How does a meristem cell become part of a xylem vessel?	elongates and aligns with other cells, end to end, and the cell wall becomes lignified, the cell dies and the end walls break down to form a continuous tube
24	What types of disease can potentially be treated by stem cells?	neurological, heart
25	Why is the study of developmental biology important?	helps scientists understand how multicellular organisms develop and how/why processes can go wrong

Practical skills

Practise your practical skills using the worked example and practice questions below.

Calculating actual size from a micrograph

The actual size of an object can be calculated from an image (a drawing or a micrograph) using the equation:

$$\text{actual size (A)} = \frac{\text{image size (I)}}{\text{magnification (M)}}$$

The key part of the calculation is to convert the image size from millimetres (mm) to micrometers (μm) after measuring the image, (i.e., multiply the value by 1000).

Worked example

Question
If the image size is 100 mm and the magnification is 400×, what is the actual size of the object?

Convert 100 mm into μm:

$100 \times 1000 = 100\,000$ μm

Divide the image size by the magnification:

$$\frac{100\,000}{400} = 250\,\mu m$$

Therefore, the actual size of the object is 250 μm.

Practice

1. If the image size of a cell measures 30 mm long at a magnification of 400×, what is the actual length of the cell?

2. At a magnification of 240×, a cell structure has a diameter of 1.2 mm.

   Calculate the actual diameter of the structure.

3. A ribosome measures 10 mm at a magnification of 400 000×.

   Calculate the actual diameter of the ribosome.

Practice

Exam-style questions

1   (a) Complete **Table 1.1** to show the events that happen at different stages of the cell cycle.

Letter	Phase	Event
A		nuclear envelope disappears
B	anaphase	
C	interphase	
D		cytoplasm splits by cleavage furrow
E	telophase	
F		chromosomes line up along the equator

Table 1.1 [6]

(b) Using the letters **A**–**F**, rearrange the order of events in the cell cycle, starting at **C**.

C → ...... → ...... → ...... → ...... → ......   [3]

(c) From the events listed above, suggest whether the information in **Table 1.1** is describing the cell cycle of an animal cell or a plant cell.

Explain your choice.

....

.... [2]

> **Exam tip**
> Make sure you know the difference between cytokinesis in animal cells and plant cells (i.e. the presence of a cell wall in plant cells).

2   **Figure 2.1** shows two cells undergoing cell division.

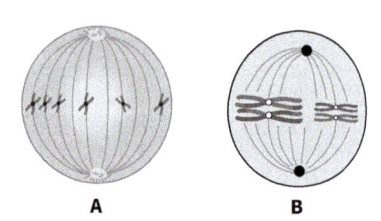

A   B

Figure 2.1

(a) (i) State which cell is undergoing meiosis.

Explain your answer.

....

....

....

.... [2]

(ii) State which cell is in metaphase.

.... [1]

(b) Give one difference between the daughter cells made by cell **A** and cell **B**.

....

.... [2]

> **Exam tip**
> One way to tell the difference between mitosis and meiosis is by looking at how the chromosomes are arranged at the equator. This shows how the DNA is segregated during anaphase – and if there would be an even split of chromosomes or half the number of chromosomes.

80   7 Cell division, diversity, and organisation

(c) (i) There are three checkpoints throughout the cell cycle, one of which occurs during metaphase.

Describe what is being checked during this checkpoint.

....

.... [1]

(ii) State when the other two checkpoints occur and give one thing that is being checked at each checkpoint.

....

....

....

....

.... [4]

(iii) If an error was detected within the cell during checkpoints, the cell exits the cell cycle.
Briefly describe what happens to the cell then.

....

....

....

.... [2]

(iv) Apart from **2 (c) (iii)**, state one other reason why a cell would exit the cell cycle.

....

.... [1]

3 (a) Define the term tissue.

....

....

.... [2]

(b) (i) Explain the difference between totipotent, pluripotent, and multipotent stem cells.

....

....

....

.... [3]

(ii) Give an example of each type of stem cell in humans.

....

....

....

.... [3]

> **Exam tip**
>
> A human develops from a zygote to an embryo and then to a fetus. Consider at which stage the cells just divide to grow, and when they start to differentiate to form different tissues and organs.

(iii) The stem cells found in human bone marrow can differentiate into different types of blood cells, including erythrocytes and neutrophils.

Describe and explain one adaptation for each of these two blood cells.

....
....
....
....
.... [4]

4 Describe and explain three events of meiosis that lead to genetic variation.

1 ....
.... [3]

2 ....
.... [3]

3 ....
.... [3]

> **Exam tip**
>
> Make sure to state clearly what is being separated in the dividing stages of meiosis. Also include the stages of meiosis where these events occur.

5 **Table 5.1** shows the events of meiosis and mitosis. Place a tick in the correct box to identify which process each event occurs in.

Event	Mitosis	Meiosis 1	Meiosis 2
crossing over occurs			
diploid cells are made			
two daughter cells are made			
chromosomes condense			
centromeres split			

Table 5.1 [5]

> **Synoptic link**
>
> 2.1.1.k

> **Exam tip**
>
> Think carefully of the different stages of mitosis and meiosis and consider the purpose of each stage.

(a) *Thermus aquaticus* is a bacterial species that is thermophilic. It is found in hot springs, typically at around 65–70 °C.

(i) Name one cell component that is present in both *Thermus aquaticus* and plant cells but is absent from animal cells.

.... [1]

(ii) Suggest two differences in the genetic material found in *Thermus aquaticus* and in human cells.

....
....
....
....
.... [4]

> **Exam tip**
>
> You will need to draw on knowledge from the chapter on cell structure to answer this question.

82 7 Cell division, diversity, and organisation

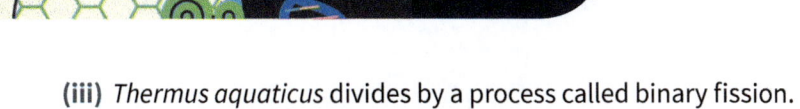

(iii) *Thermus aquaticus* divides by a process called binary fission. **Figure 5.1** shows the process of binary fission.

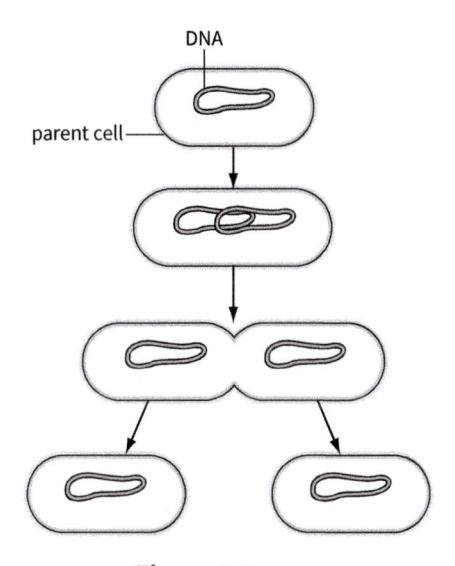

Figure 5.1

Using your own knowledge and **Figure 5.1**, describe and explain one difference in the process of binary fission compared to mitosis.

....
....
....
....
....
.... [2]

6 (a) (i) Name the plant tissue that contains stem cells. [1]
    (ii) Explain what is meant by differentiation. [1]
    (iii) Compare the plasma membranes of a palisade mesophyll cell and a root hair cell. Suggest one similarity and one difference and explain why this difference is important. [3]
  (b) (i) Erythrocytes contain specific proteins that bind to oxygen molecules.

Name the protein and describe how its structure allows it to perform its function. [4]
    (ii) State the type of stem cells that can produce erythrocytes and where they are found within the body. [2]

> **Synoptic links**
> 2.1.2.n   2.1.5.b   2.1.5.d

> **Exam tip**
> For **6 (a) (iii)**, think about the chemicals they need to absorb in order to carry out their functions. How can they absorb these substances? What sort of structures would they need on their plasma membrane in order to do this?

Knowledge

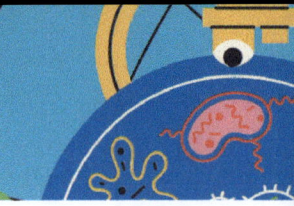

8 Exchange Surfaces

Substance exchange

Most substances – gases, nutrients, ions and so on – cross **cell surface membranes** to enter or leave an organism. In single-celled organisms, simple **diffusion** is adequate for substance exchange.

As animals become larger and more active, their cells are too far from the exchange membranes or surfaces for substances to simply diffuse to them, so they need gas exchange systems to supply oxygen and remove carbon dioxide.

Surface area to volume ratio

The larger the organism's size, the smaller its surface area to volume (SA:V) ratio. The rate of diffusion into and out of an organism increases with surface area.

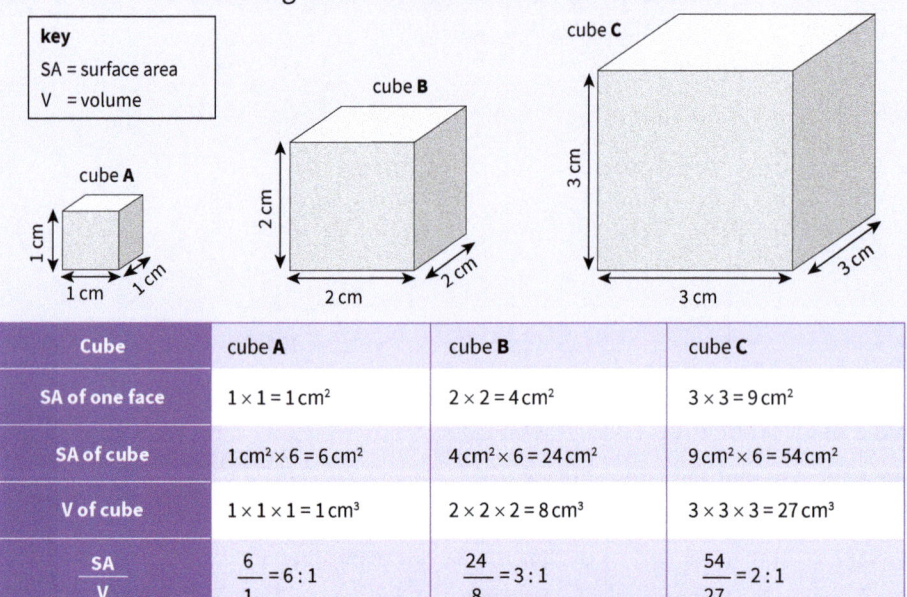

key
SA = surface area
V = volume

Cube	cube A	cube B	cube C
SA of one face	$1 \times 1 = 1\,cm^2$	$2 \times 2 = 4\,cm^2$	$3 \times 3 = 9\,cm^2$
SA of cube	$1\,cm^2 \times 6 = 6\,cm^2$	$4\,cm^2 \times 6 = 24\,cm^2$	$9\,cm^2 \times 6 = 54\,cm^2$
V of cube	$1 \times 1 \times 1 = 1\,cm^3$	$2 \times 2 \times 2 = 8\,cm^3$	$3 \times 3 \times 3 = 27\,cm^3$
$\frac{SA}{V}$	$\frac{6}{1} = 6:1$	$\frac{24}{8} = 3:1$	$\frac{54}{27} = 2:1$

In single-celled organisms, the SA:V ratio is very large, so **simple diffusion** is adequate for substance exchange. The smaller the organism, the larger the SA:V ratio, and the higher the metabolic rate of an organism.

Features of gas exchange systems

To be efficient, gas exchange surfaces have specialised features.

An increased surface area – root hair cells in plants have protrusions to absorb water; the lungs have numerous alveoli that allow oxygen to diffuse across the surface rapidly.

A thin layer – alveoli walls and capillary walls are only one cell thick, to provide a short diffusion pathway.

Maintain a good concentration gradient by a rich blood supply and ventilation.

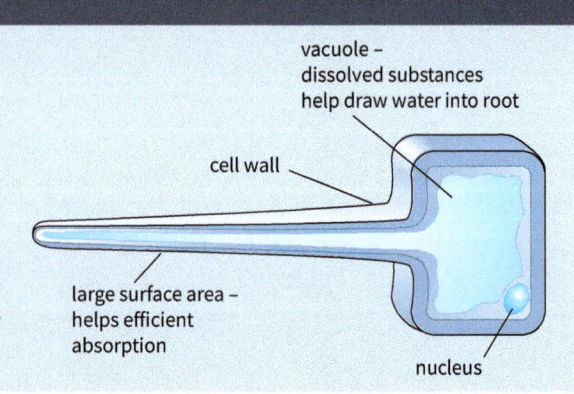

84   8 Exchange Surfaces

Structure of the human gas exchange system

Human gas exchange occurs in the lungs.

Air is drawn into the lungs through the **trachea**. The trachea divides into two **bronchi**, which further divide into **bronchioles**, until they terminate in millions of sacs, the **alveoli**.

Gas exchange between the blood (in capillaries) and the air takes place at the alveoli.

The trachea is supported by **C-shaped cartilage** to keep it open. Cartilage, **smooth muscle**, and **elastic tissue** continue into the bronchi.

The bronchioles have bands of smooth muscle and elastic tissue surrounding them.

Elastic tissue allows the lungs to recoil back into shape after expanding.

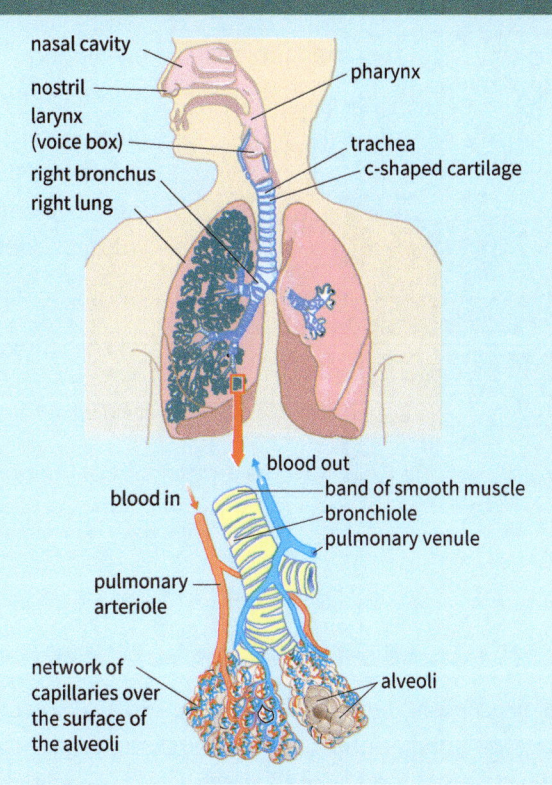

The trachea lining

The trachea has a lining with specific adaptations to prevent particles and microorganisms entering the lungs.

Ciliated epithelial cells and **goblet cells** line the trachea.

The goblet cells produce **mucus**. The ciliated cells move the mucus (and any trapped particles) up the trachea, until it can be swallowed.

Features of the alveolus

Alveoli maximise gas exchange by:
- having a very large surface area
- being moist to aid diffusion of gases
- having a rich blood supply to maintain a concentration gradient
- having very thin walls, like the capillaries, so the diffusion distance between air in alveoli and red blood cells in capillaries is short.

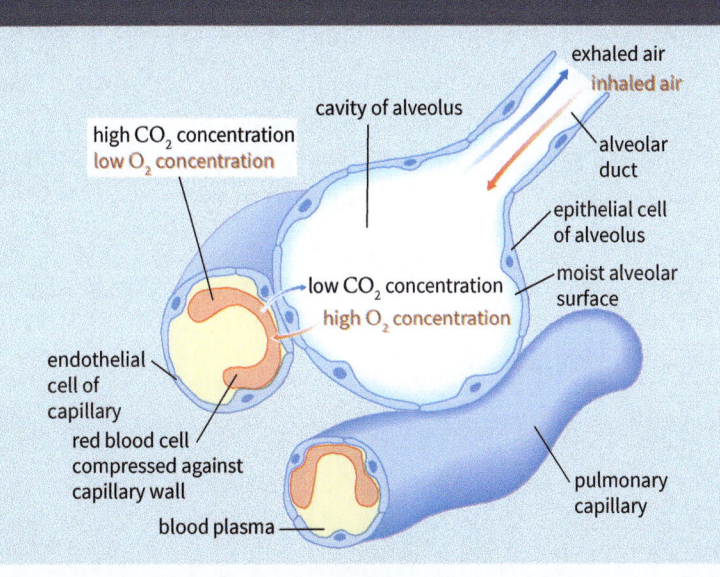

For answers and more practice questions visit www.oxfordrevise.com/scienceanswers

Even more practice and interactive revision quizzes are available on kerboodle

8 Knowledge

Human ventilation

The external and internal intercostal muscles work in antagonistic pairs.

Process	inhalation	exhalation
Intercostal muscles	external intercostal muscles contract, move ribs up	external intercostal muscles relax; when exercising, internal intercostal muscles contract, move ribs down
Diaphragm	contracts, flattens	relaxes, moves up
Volume of lungs	increases	decreases
Movement of air	into the lungs	out of the lungs

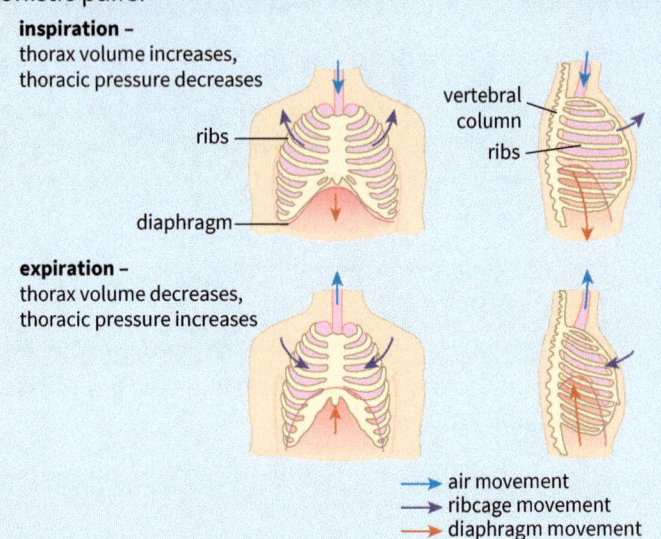

inspiration – thorax volume increases, thoracic pressure decreases

expiration – thorax volume decreases, thoracic pressure increases

Breathing rate and oxygen uptake

Spirometers measure the volume and function of the lungs as well as oxygen uptake. Inhalation and exhalation move the lid of the spirometer, which is recorded by the datalogger. Carbon dioxide from exhaled air is absorbed by soda lime so that the volume of oxygen used can be measured.

Tidal volume – normal volume of air displaced by the lungs at rest per breath (dm^3)

Breathing rate – the number of breaths taken per minute (breaths per minute)

Vital capacity – maximum volume of air that can be exhaled after a maximum inhalation (dm^3)

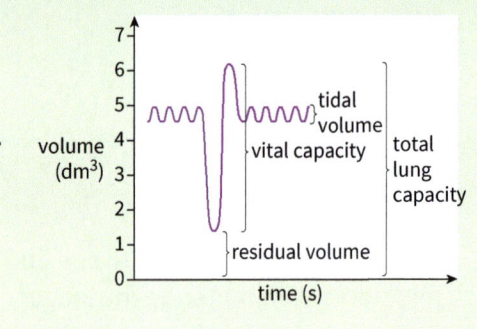

Gas exchange in insects

Many insects have **spiracles** along their thorax and abdomen.

Insects use the movement of the thorax and abdomen to change body volume and move air in and out (ventilation).

Inside, the **tracheae** (tubes) divide until they reach the cells as **tracheoles**. The tracheoles are lined with **tracheal fluid**.

Diffusion of oxygen and carbon dioxide occurs between body cells and the thin walls of the tracheoles. Oxygen and carbon dioxide dissolve in the tracheal fluid and diffuse through the thin walls of the tracheoles and into the body cells.

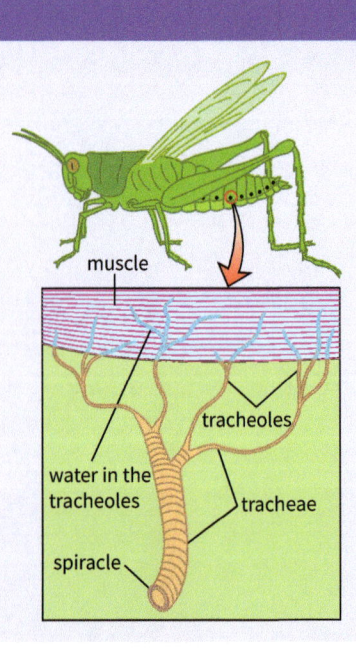

8 Exchange Surfaces

Adaptations of gills

- Gills have several adaptations to maximise efficient gas exchange across them:
  - Each gill filament is covered in many **gill lamellae** to increase surface area.
  - They have a rich blood supply to the gills, to maximise the amount of blood that can be oxygenated via diffusion.
  - The blood and water flow past each other in a **countercurrent system**, so the concentration of oxygen in the water is always higher than in the blood. This maintains a concentration gradient between the water and the blood supply along the whole gill.
  - Ventilation is used to increase water flow over the gills and increase the rate of diffusion.
- Ventilation occurs through the increasing and decreasing volume of the **buccal cavity** and the opening and closing of the **operculum**.
  - The fish opens its mouth, lowering the floor of the buccal cavity, and increasing the volume of the buccal cavity.
  - This lowers the pressure inside the buccal cavity, which forces water into it.
  - The operculum is shut.
  - The fish closes its mouth, reducing the volume in the buccal cavity.
  - Pressure inside the buccal cavity increases, forcing the water across the gill filaments.
  - The operculum opens, and the water flows out of the gills.

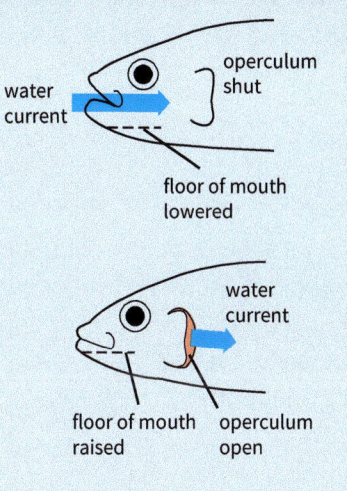

Countercurrent principle

Blood in the capillaries flows in the opposite direction to the water flowing over them, so the oxygen concentration in the water is always higher than the oxygen concentration in the blood along the whole of the gill.

This maximizes the gas exchange compared with a parallel system, as it maintains a concentration gradient for the whole length of the gill lamellae.

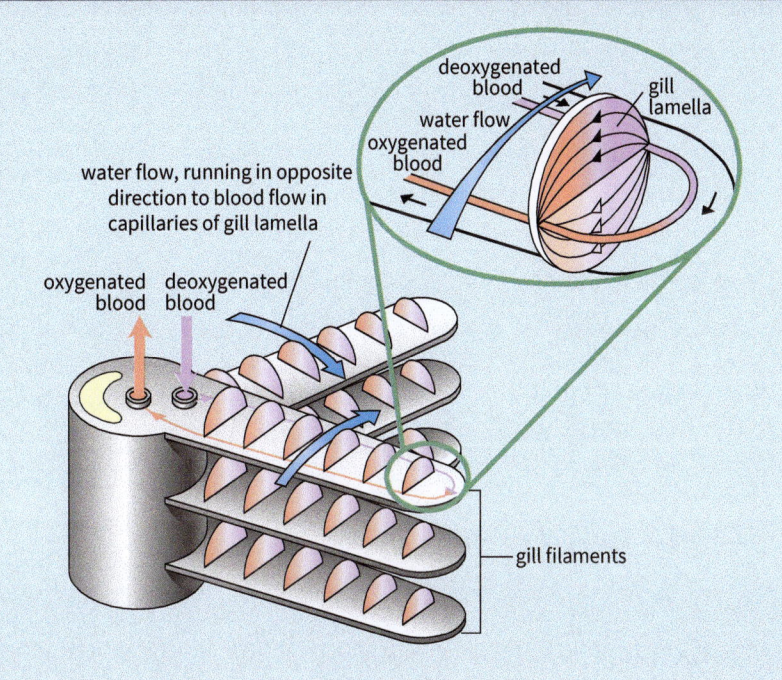

Retrieval

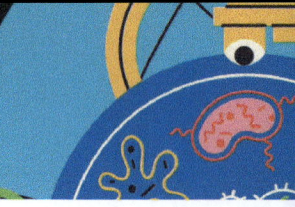

Learn the answers to the questions below, then cover the answers column with a piece of paper and write as many as you can. Check and repeat.

	Questions	Answers
1	How is surface area to volume ratio calculated?	surface area to volume ratio = $\dfrac{\text{surface area}}{\text{volume}}$
2	Which muscles are involved in human ventilation?	external and internal intercostal muscles; diaphragm
3	Describe what happens when a human inhales.	• external intercostal muscles contract, move ribs up • diaphragm contracts, flattens • pressure in thoracic cavity decreases • volume of lungs increases • movement of air into the lungs
4	What is vital capacity?	maximum volume that can be exhaled after a maximum inhalation (dm^3)
5	What does a spirometer measure?	the volume and function of the lungs
6	Describe the function of cartilage in the trachea.	supported by C-shaped cartilage to keep it open, so that air can flow in and out of the lungs
7	What is a concentration gradient?	the difference between the concentration of a substance in two different areas; the larger the concentration gradient, the faster the substance diffuses towards the lower concentration
8	How do insects such as crickets exchange gases?	• air moves into the tracheae (tubes), which divide until they reach the cells as tracheoles • diffusion occurs between body cells and the tracheoles, exchanging gases via the tracheal fluid
9	How do fish ventilate the gills?	increase and decrease in volume of the buccal cavity and opening and closing of the operculum
10	Describe the countercurrent system in fish.	• blood in the capillaries flows in the opposite direction to the water flowing over them • this maximizes the gas exchange compared with a parallel system
11	What are the adaptations of root hair cells to maximise water absorption?	root hair protrusion greatly increases surface area
12	List three features of gas exchange surfaces.	• increased surface area • thin, for a short diffusion pathway • good concentration gradient due to rich blood supply and ventilation
13	What is the function of elastic tissue in bronchi and bronchioles?	allows the lungs to recoil back into shape after expanding

8 Exchange surfaces

Maths skills

Practise your maths skills using the worked example and practice questions below.

Calculating surface area : volume ratios

The surface area to volume (SA:V) ratio is an important factor in an organism's ability to exchange materials. It can be calculated by:

$$SA:V = \frac{\text{surface area}}{\text{volume}}$$

A large surface area provides a large site to exchange materials at a high rate of diffusion, but it can also risk materials diffusing out as well (such as heat or water).

This is why it is important that organisms in cold environments have a small SA:V ratio to conserve heat, and organisms in hot environments have a large SA:V ratio to prevent overheating (though they risk dehydration).

As well as surface area, the rate of diffusion is also affected by:

- length of diffusion pathway, as materials will travel more slowly through a thick membrane
- steepness of concentration gradients, as the rate of diffusion will slow if the concentration gradient across a membrane approaches equilibrium
- size of diffusion molecule, as larger molecules will move more slowly through a membrane

Materials that are too large or must travel against a concentration gradient can use methods such as active transport, which requires energy.

Worked example

Question
An adult has a volume of 0.05 m³ and a surface area of 1.62 m².

Calculate the surface area to volume ratio for this person.

Answer
To do this, you should first work out what the numerical value of the answer is, by substituting your known values into your equation.

$$\frac{\text{surface area}}{\text{volume}} = \frac{1.62}{0.05}$$
$$= 32.4$$

Now, you need to work out the units. It's important your units are consistent when answering this question, so make sure your starting values are all in the same units (i.e., metres or centimetres).

$$\frac{\text{surface area}}{\text{volume}} = \frac{m^2}{m^3}$$

This is the same as writing $m^2 \, m^{-3}$, so all you need to do now is cancel the powers:

$$m^{2-3} = m^{-1}$$

Therefore, the person has a SA:V ratio of 32.4 m^{-1}.

Practice

1. Calculate the SA:V ratio for these organisms:

   Organism **A**: surface area = 24 m²
   volume = 3.8 m³

   Organism **B**: surface area = 0.01 m²
   volume = 2.5×10⁻⁵ m³

   Organism **C**: surface area = 6×10⁻⁸ m²
   volume = 1×10⁻¹¹ m³

2. How many times greater is the SA:V ratio of an amoeba (organism **C**) than that of an elephant (organism **A**)?

3. What adaptations does an elephant have in order to overcome its low intrinsic SA:V?

Practice

Exam-style questions

1. Flukes are a type of parasitic flatworm, as shown in **Figure 1.1**. Once inside the human body, flukes can live within a human's blood vessels.

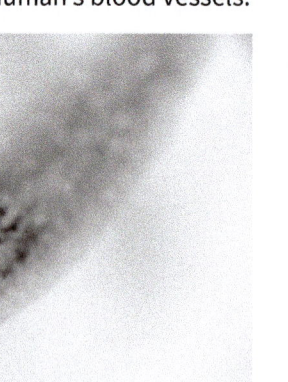

Synoptic links

2.1.5   3.1.2

Figure 1.1

(a) Explain how the structure of a fluke enables effective gas exchange.

....
....
....
.... [2]

Table 1.1 below shows the solubility of oxygen in a blood sample in the lab at varying temperatures.

Temperature of blood (°C)	Solubility of oxygen in blood (cm³ kPa⁻¹ dm⁻³)
0	0.0062
10	0.0056
20	0.0048
30	0.0037
40	0.0028

Table 1.1

!) **Exam tip**

Remember to quote paired data sets with units to support any trends and, where possible, process the data in support of a trend or pattern observed.

(b) Describe the relationship between the temperature of the blood and the solubility of oxygen in the blood.

....
....
....
.... [2]

90   8 Exchange surfaces

(c) The partial pressure of oxygen in the lungs is 100 mm Hg. 98.5% of oxygen is bound to haemoglobin in the blood in the lungs at 37 °C. The volume of oxygen in the lungs is 1.3 dm³.

Calculate the volume of dissolved oxygen at 37 °C that is not bound to haemoglobin in the blood.

Give your answer in standard form.

.... [2]

(d) Flukes can rapidly decrease the blood supply to the chambers of the heart if they are present in the capillaries leading to the pulmonary vein.

State the specific name of another blood vessel where flukes could be present to cause such a decrease.

.... [1]

(e) Suggest and explain the impact a decreased supply of blood through the pulmonary vein could have on the circulatory system.

....
....
....
....
....
....
.... [6]

(f) A flatworm measures 1 mm in width and 20 mm in length. The surface area to volume ratio is 17.48 : 1.

Calculate the volume of the flatworm, giving your answer to 3 significant figures.

.... [3]

2   A cat is a mammal.

(a) Explain how the alveoli are adapted to increase the rate of diffusion of gases in the lungs of cats.

....
....
....
.... [4]

Table 2.1 below shows how a cat's breathing rate changes when it chases a rodent across a field.

Time (s)	Breathing rate (breaths min⁻¹)	Tidal volume (cm³ kg⁻¹)
0	20	15
5	28	16
10	33	18
15	48	20
20	57	23
25	60	25

Table 2.1

(b) Calculate the percentage increase in tidal volume for this cat between 10 and 20 seconds.

.... % [2]

(c) A cat's diaphragm becomes damaged during a fight with another cat.

Suggest what impact this would have on the cat's gas exchange system.

....
....
.... [3]

> **Exam tip**
> Remember that a cat is a mammal so try not to be thrown by a question that may be in an unfamiliar context. Try to explain how the mammalian gas exchange system works in the context of this question (i.e., damaged diaphragm).

3 Tiger barbs are fish that are native to Indonesia.

(a) The binomial name for a tiger barb is *Puntigrus tetrazona*.

State the name of its genus.

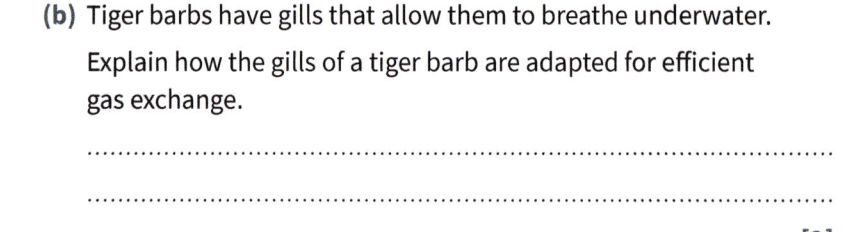

.... [1]

(b) Tiger barbs have gills that allow them to breathe underwater.

Explain how the gills of a tiger barb are adapted for efficient gas exchange.

....
....
.... [2]

> **Synoptic link**
> 4.2.2

(c) Heavy metal ions can occasionally get into the moderately flowing streams inhabited by tiger barbs.

Tiger barb's lamellae and gill filaments can be damaged by water polluted with heavy metal ions. As a consequence, the surface area of lamellae can be reduced.

Suggest why tiger barbs die in areas of heavy metal ion pollution.

....
....
.... [3]

> **Exam tip**
> The key piece of information in the question is that the surface area of lamellae is reduced. Using this, you will need to suggest what the impact will be on the tiger barbs, causing them to die.

8 Exchange surfaces

(d) Explain the function of the operculum in the tiger barb.

....

.... [2]

4 Table 4.1 shows data for a house mouse, *Mus musculus*, and an Asian elephant, *Elephas maximus*.

Animal	Surface area (cm²)	Volume (cm³)	Surface area: volume ratio	Metabolic rate (mm³ O₂ g⁻¹ h⁻¹)
mouse	1279	13.2		1.5
Asian elephant	3.7×10^5	2.4×10^6		0.3

Table 4.1

Synoptic link

3.1.2

(a) Calculate the surface area to volume (SA:V) ratios of the mouse and the elephant in **Table 4.1**.

.... [2]

(b) Describe and explain the relationship between SA:V ratio and metabolic rate shown in **Table 4.1**.

....

....

.... [2]

(c) Elephants can run up to speeds of 11 m s⁻¹. The sympathetic nervous system signals to the elephant's heart to increase its heart rate as more oxygen is required.

Describe how the wave of electrical activity is transmitted in the elephant's heart to facilitate this.

....

....

....

....

....

....

....

.... [6]

Exam tip

Remember that the elephant is a mammal and therefore this is the mammalian heart the question is referring to.

5   *Dytiscus marginicollis* is a giant green water beetle that has the ability to dive underwater. It traps air bubbles beneath its wings to gain food and can be found in North America.

Dytiscus marginicollis comes from the class Insecta.

The air bubble is linked to the giant green water beetle's spiracles and the concentration of oxygen is greater in the bubble than in the water when the giant green water beetle first dives.

Synoptic link

2.1.5

(a) Suggest why giant green water beetles are only able to remain underwater for a short period of time.

....

....

....

.... [4]

Exam tip

Remember to refer to any information given with the question. For this question, refer to the information given at the start about the air bubble, and link this to diffusion.

Figure 5.1 shows how the metabolic rate of giant green water beetles is affected by temperature.

y-axis: metabolic rate (mm³ O₂⁻¹ g⁻¹ hour⁻¹); x-axis: temperature (°C)

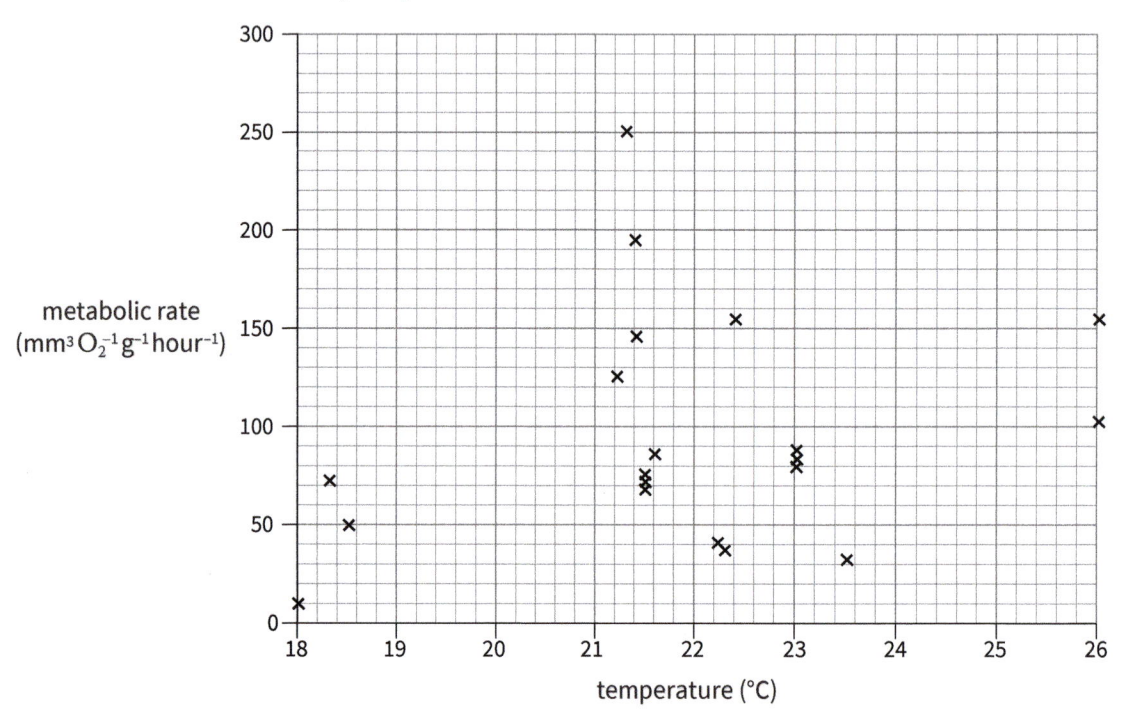

Figure 5.1

A student draws a conclusion from **Figure 5.1**. They state that:

'As the temperature increases, the metabolic rate of the giant green water beetle increases.'

(b) Evaluate the student's conclusion.

....

....

.... [3]

(c) Suggest two other factors that could affect metabolic rate.

....

.... [2]

94   8 Exchange surfaces

6 **Figure 6.1** shows the percentage of Forced Expiratory Volume in 1 second (FEV1) in four different groups of people in relation to smoking cigarettes.

An FEV1 value of 80% or above is considered normal.

Smoking cigarettes can damage the alveoli in the lungs.

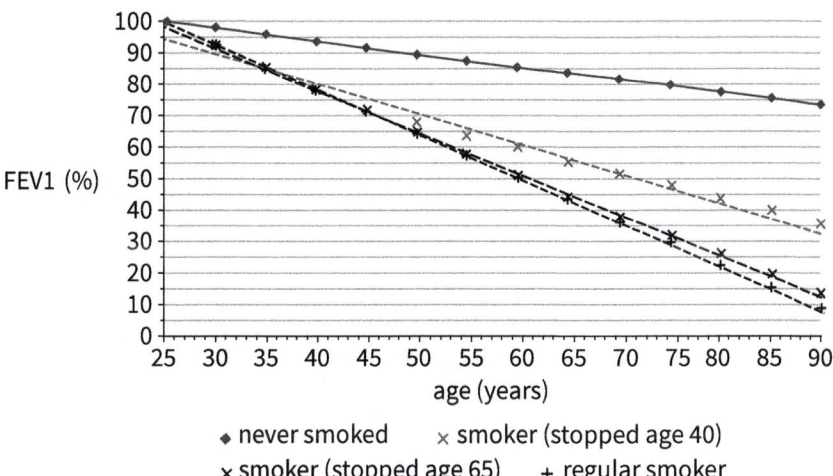

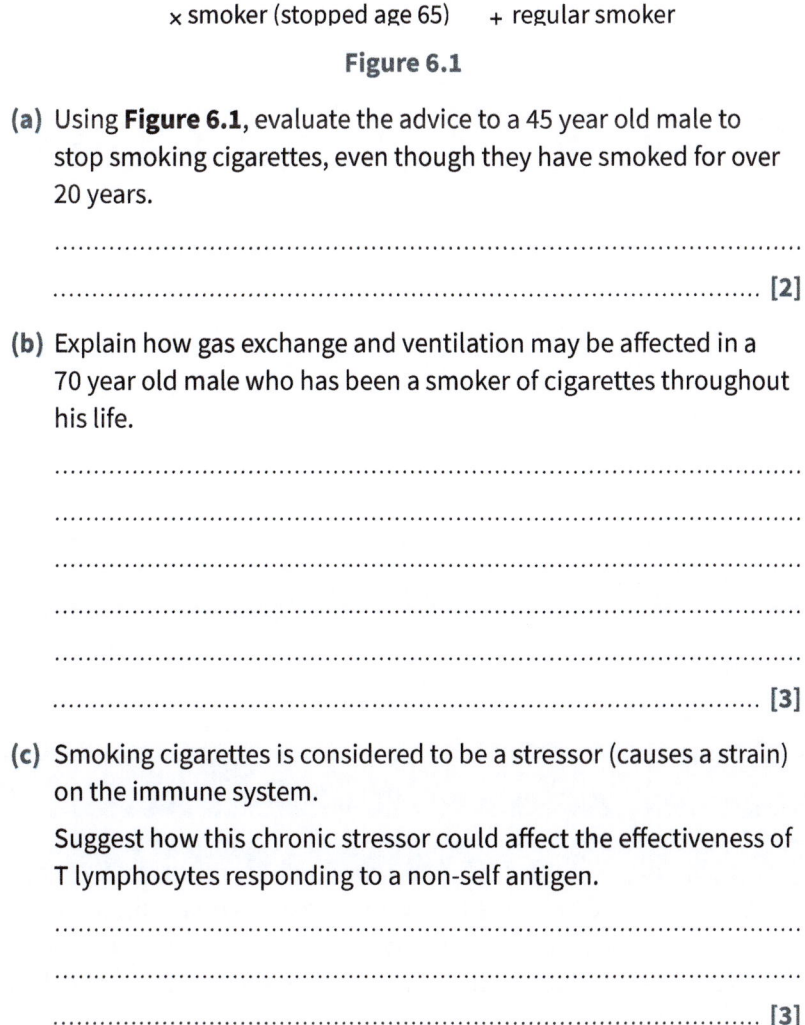

Synoptic link
3.2.4

[Graph showing FEV1 (%) vs age (years) from 25 to 90, with four lines: never smoked, smoker (stopped age 40), smoker (stopped age 65), regular smoker]

Figure 6.1

(a) Using **Figure 6.1**, evaluate the advice to a 45 year old male to stop smoking cigarettes, even though they have smoked for over 20 years.

....
.... [2]

Exam tip

When data are provided, as in **Figure 6.1**, make sure you use the data to inform your answer. When evaluation is required make sure you give pros and cons.

(b) Explain how gas exchange and ventilation may be affected in a 70 year old male who has been a smoker of cigarettes throughout his life.

....
....
....
....
.... [3]

(c) Smoking cigarettes is considered to be a stressor (causes a strain) on the immune system.

Suggest how this chronic stressor could affect the effectiveness of T lymphocytes responding to a non-self antigen.

....
....
.... [3]

Knowledge

9 Transport in animals

Circulatory systems

As organisms get larger, their surface area to volume ratio decreases, and diffusion is no longer sufficient to provide for these needs, so they need a circulatory system.

Open circulatory systems (found in insects and arthropods):
- bathe all the cells in a fluid called **haemolymph**, where substance exchange takes place.

Closed circulatory systems:
- involve a pump (heart) and vessels through which blood is circulated between the gas exchange surface and the body cells.

- Fish have a **single closed circulatory system**: blood is pumped by the heart, through the gills, to the body, and back to the heart.
- Mammals, birds, amphibians, and reptiles have a **double closed circulatory system** where the blood visits the heart twice in every complete circuit.

Human circulatory system

The heart has two main arteries:
- **pulmonary artery** – transports deoxygenated blood to the lungs
- **aorta** – transports oxygenated blood to the body.

The heart has two main veins:
- **pulmonary vein** – receives oxygenated blood from the lungs
- **vena cava** – receives deoxygenated blood from the body.

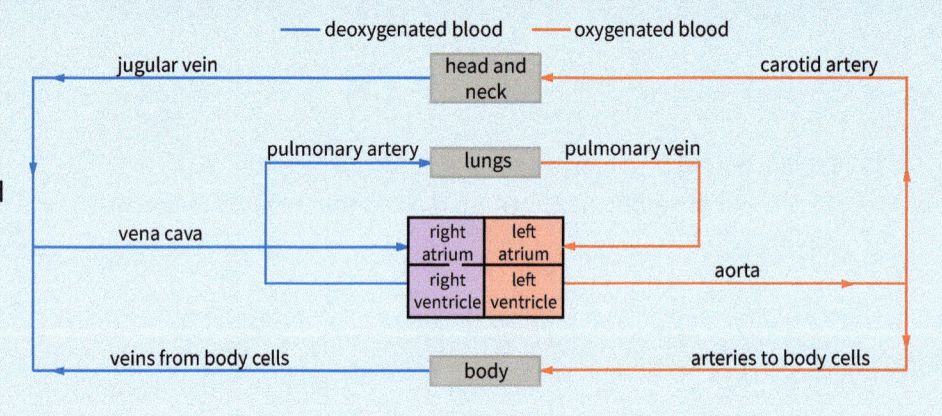

Comparing blood, tissue fluid, and lymph

Blood	Tissue fluid	Lymph
• Contains plasma with dissolved glucose, amino acids, mineral ions, hormones, large proteins (e.g., albumin, globulins). • Contains red blood cells, platelets, and white blood cells. • Erythrocytes carry oxygen, carbon dioxide, and antigens	• Same as blood but no red blood cells, leucocytes (type of white blood cell), or large proteins.	• Lymph vessels are sac-like and some tissue fluid drains into them. They have valves and the lymph circulates when skeletal muscles contract • Contains less oxygen, glucose, and amino acids but more carbon dioxide, fatty acids, lymphocytes, and antibodies than blood.

9

Structure of blood vessels

Arteries can withstand high pressures due to their thick walls containing elastic tissue and smooth muscle tissue.

Arterioles are much smaller arteries that deliver blood to capillaries. Arterioles have thinner walls than arteries and less elastic tissue.

Veins and **venules** contain some elastic and muscle tissue, but have thinner walls and a larger lumen compared to arteries. They can contain valves.
Venules have much thinner walls than veins.

Blood from arterioles flows into **capillaries** and then back into venules.

Capillaries are very small blood vessels, 4–10 μm in diameter. They allow only one red blood cell through at a time. They are made of a single layer of endothelial cells.

Water and solutes pass across the capillary walls to and from the tissues.

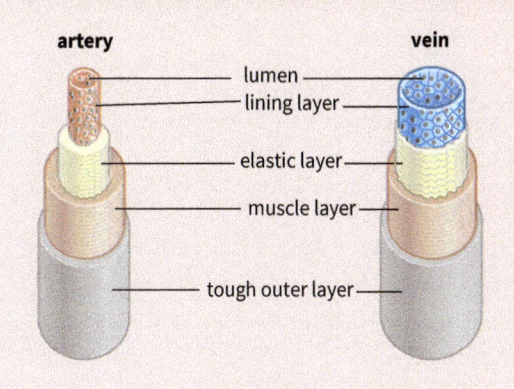

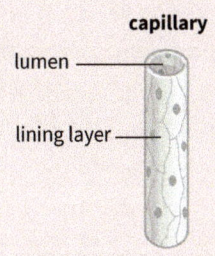

Tissue fluid formation

Tissue fluid is formed around the body cells, bathing them in solutes. It then drains into lymphatic vessels, and eventually back into the bloodstream.

Two different kinds of pressure are involved in the formation and draining of tissue fluid:

- **Hydrostatic pressure** – the pressure from fluid on the walls of the capillary, usually forcing plasma out of the circulatory system.

- **Oncotic pressure** – osmotic pressure from proteins in the blood plasma that draws water into the circulatory system.

Plasma leaves the capillary at the arteriole end because the hydrostatic pressure is greater than the oncotic pressure.

Towards the venous end, most of the tissue fluid moves back into the capillary because the oncotic pressure is greater than the hydrostatic pressure.

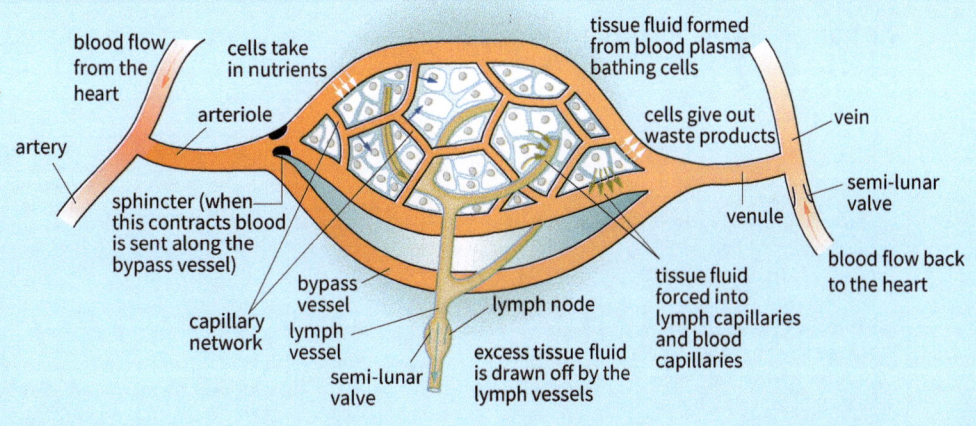

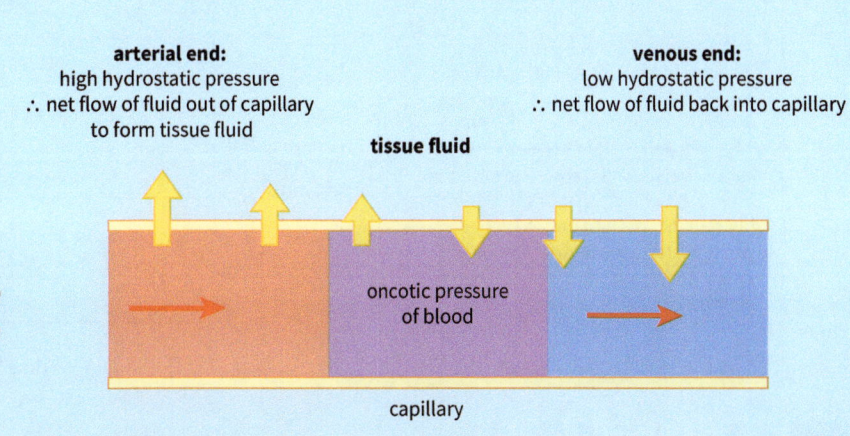

arterial end:
high hydrostatic pressure
∴ net flow of fluid out of capillary to form tissue fluid

venous end:
low hydrostatic pressure
∴ net flow of fluid back into capillary

For answers and more practice questions visit www.oxfordrevise.com/scienceanswers

Even more practice and interactive revision quizzes are available on kerboodle

9 Knowledge 97

The structure of the human heart

The human heart is made of cardiac muscle, and has four chambers – two **atria** and two **ventricles**.

Each atrium and ventricle is separated by **valves** to keep a unidirectional flow of blood.

Oxygenated blood is collected in the left atrium, pushed into the left ventricle (which has a thicker muscular wall), and then pushed through the aorta to the whole body.

At the same time, deoxygenated blood returns from the body into the right atrium and is pushed into the right ventricle, which contracts, pumping the blood to the lungs via the pulmonary artery.

On the outside of the heart, there are visible blood vessels, the coronary arteries and veins. The heart can be dissected to reveal the internal structure.

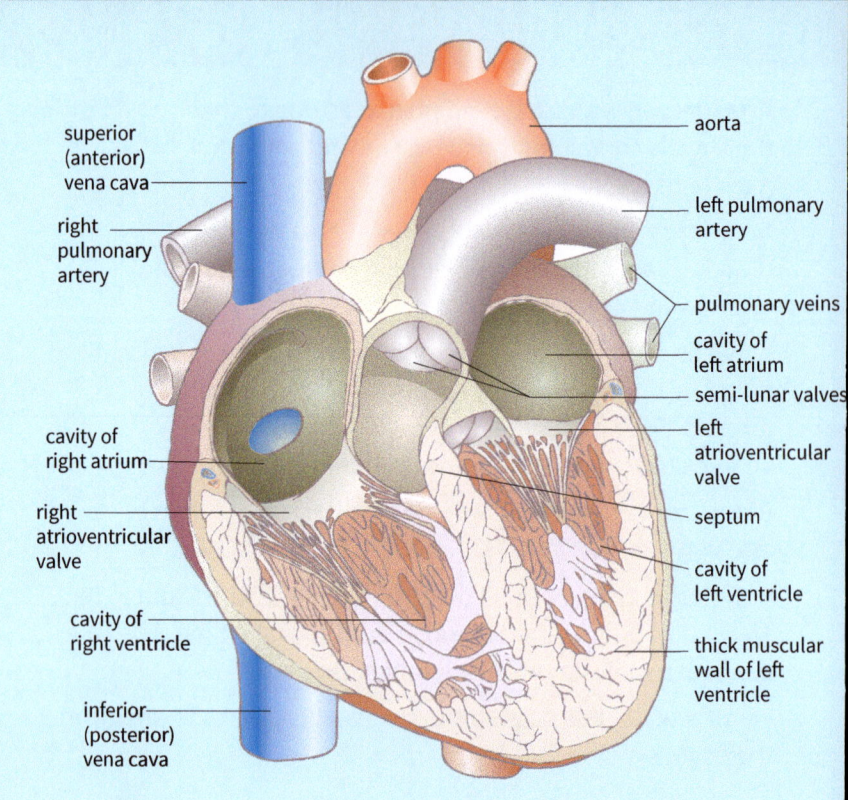

Labels on heart diagram: superior (anterior) vena cava, right pulmonary artery, cavity of right atrium, right atrioventricular valve, cavity of right ventricle, inferior (posterior) vena cava, aorta, left pulmonary artery, pulmonary veins, cavity of left atrium, semi-lunar valves, left atrioventricular valve, septum, cavity of left ventricle, thick muscular wall of left ventricle.

Pressure and volume changes during the cardiac cycle

The human circulation system is closed and so the pressure can be regulated.

Aortic pressure rises when **ventricles** contract as blood is forced into the **aorta**. It then gradually falls, but never below around 12 kPa, because of the elasticity of its wall, which creates a recoil action – essential if blood is to be constantly delivered to the tissues. The recoil produces a temporary rise in pressure at the start of the relaxation phase.

Atrial pressure is always relatively low because the thin walls of the **atrium** cannot create much force. It is highest when they are contracting, but drops when the **left atrioventricular valve** closes and its walls relax. The atria then fill with blood, which leads to a gradual build-up of pressure until a slight drop when the left atrioventricular valve opens and some blood moves into the ventricle.

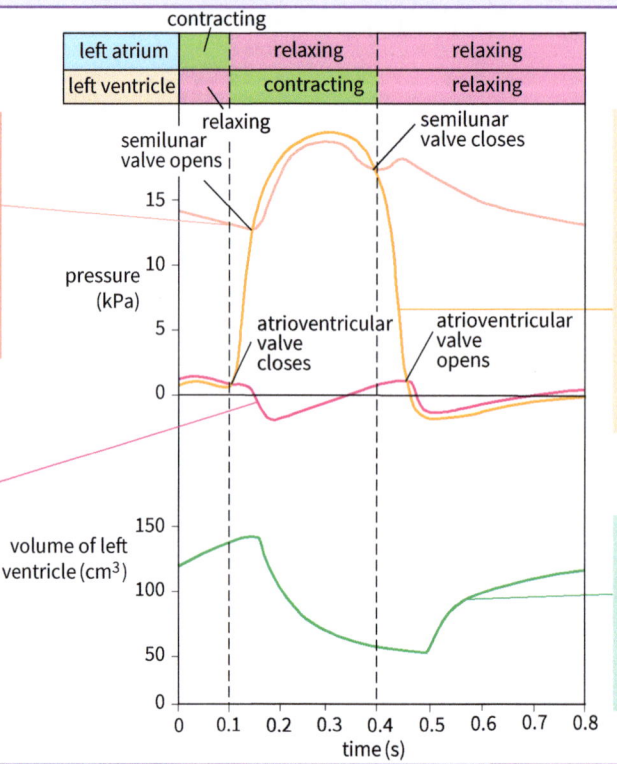

Ventricular pressure is low at first, but gradually increases as the ventricles fill with blood as the **atria** contract. The **left atrioventricular valves** close and pressure rises dramatically as the thick muscular walls of the **ventricle contract**. As pressure rises above that of the aorta, blood is forced into the aorta past the **semilunar valves**. Pressure falls as the **ventricles** empty and the walls relax.

Ventricular volume rises as the atria contract and the ventricles fill with blood, and then drops suddenly as blood is forced out into the aorta when the **semilunar valve opens**. Volume increases again as the ventricles fill with blood.

Graph labels: left atrium contracting / relaxing / relaxing; left ventricle relaxing / contracting / relaxing; semilunar valve opens; semilunar valve closes; atrioventricular valve closes; atrioventricular valve opens; pressure (kPa) 0, 5, 10, 15; volume of left ventricle (cm³) 0, 50, 100, 150; time (s) 0, 0.1, 0.2, 0.3, 0.4, 0.5, 0.6, 0.7, 0.8.

9 Transport in animals

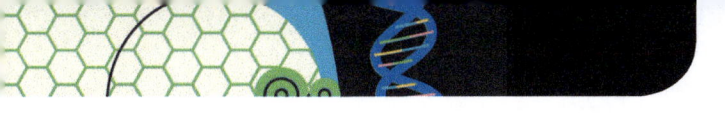

Haemoglobin and oxygen transport

Haemoglobin is a **protein** with **quaternary structure**, and it is made up of four polypeptide chains which each have a prosthetic haem group.

Red blood cells contain haemoglobin to **transport oxygen** from the lungs to the respiring cells.

Carbon dioxide transport

Carbon dioxide, produced from respiration, is transported in the blood in several ways.

- Most carbon dioxide diffuses into the red blood cells (RBCs).
  - It forms carbonic acid (H_2CO_3) by reacting with water, catalysed by carbonic anhydrase.
  - The carbonic acid dissociates into hydrogen carbonate (HCO_3^-) ions and hydrogen ions (H^+). The hydrogen carbonate ions diffuse out of the RBC into the plasma.
  - This leaves the inside of the RBC with a deficit of negative ions, causing chloride ions to diffuse into the RBC from the plasma.
  - This exchange of ions (HCO_3^- for Cl^-) is known as the **chloride shift**.
- A small number of carbon dioxide molecules dissolve in the blood plasma.

Some carbon dioxide molecules also attach directly.

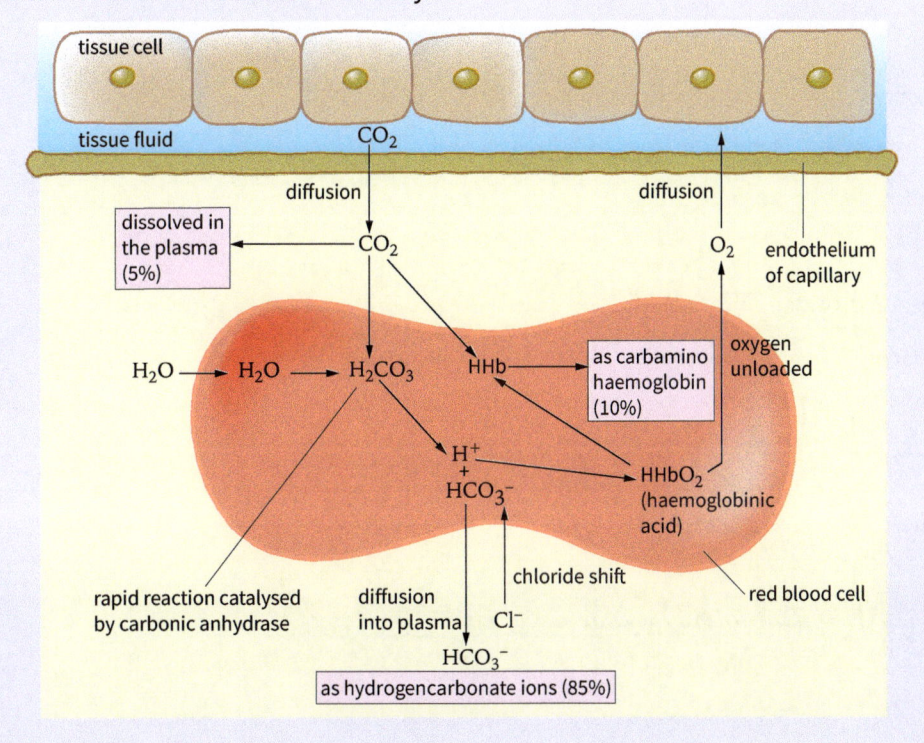

9 Knowledge

Control of heart action

The heartbeat originates in the heart muscle – it is **myogenic**.

The wave of electrical activity is initiated by the **sino-atrial node (SAN)**, which acts as a pacemaker. Located in the wall of the right atrium, it generates a wave of excitation (nerve impulses) that causes the muscle in the atrial wall to contract.

To coordinate the contraction of the heart, the **atrio-ventricular node (AVN)** in the septum delays the impulse to let the atria contract fully before the ventricles contract.

The **Purkyne tissue** distributes the impulse through the walls of the ventricles, causing the muscles to contract.

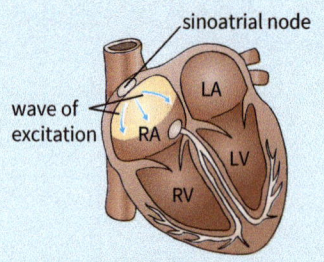

1. wave of electrical activity spreads out from the sinoatrial node
2. wave spreads across both atria, causing them to contract, and reaches the atrioventricular node 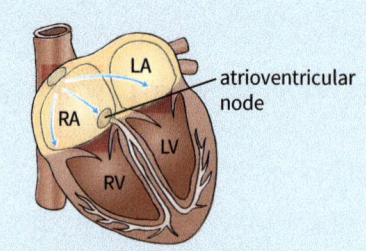 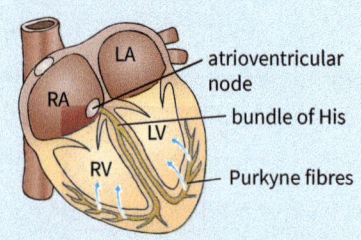
3. atrioventricular node conveys wave of electrical activity down the bundle of His in the septum between the ventricles, along the Purkyne fibres and then releases it at the apex, causing the ventricles to contract

Electrocardiograms (ECG)

An ECG is a trace of the electrical activity of the heart. A normal trace is made up of five features (PQRST).

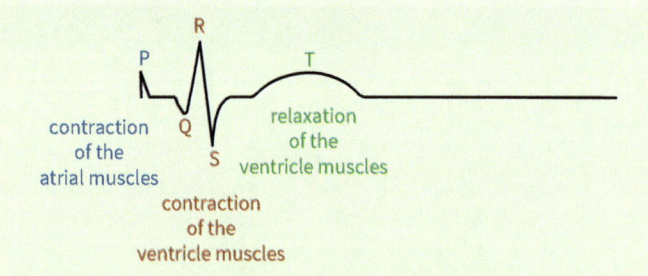

- P: contraction of the atrial muscles
- QRS: contraction of the ventricle muscles
- T: relaxation of the ventricle muscles

Abnormal heartbeats produce different ECGs.

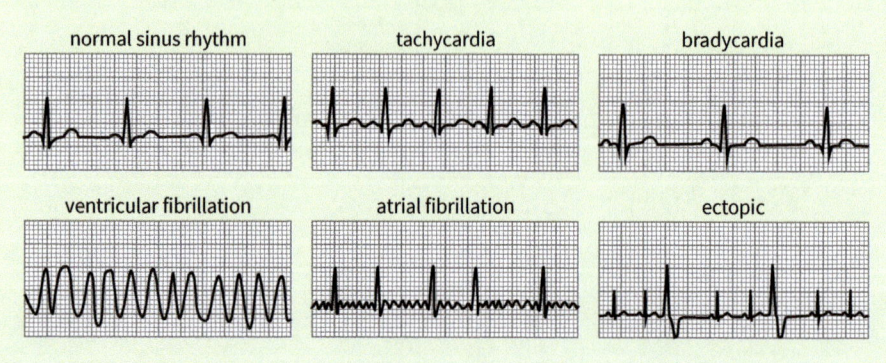

- normal sinus rhythm
- tachycardia
- bradycardia
- ventricular fibrillation
- atrial fibrillation
- ectopic

9 Transport in animals

Oxygen dissociation curve

Oxygen loading
At the alveoli, when the first oxygen molecule binds to the first haem group, the haemoglobin changes shape. This makes it easier to bind a further three oxygen molecules.

Oxygen dissociation
At the tissues, oxygen dissociates from the haemoglobin due to low partial pressure of oxygen in the tissues.

At high partial pressures of oxygen haemoglobin has a higher affinity for oxygen therefore has high saturation levels.

At low partial pressures of oxygen haemoglobin has lower affinity for oxygen there has lower saturation levels.

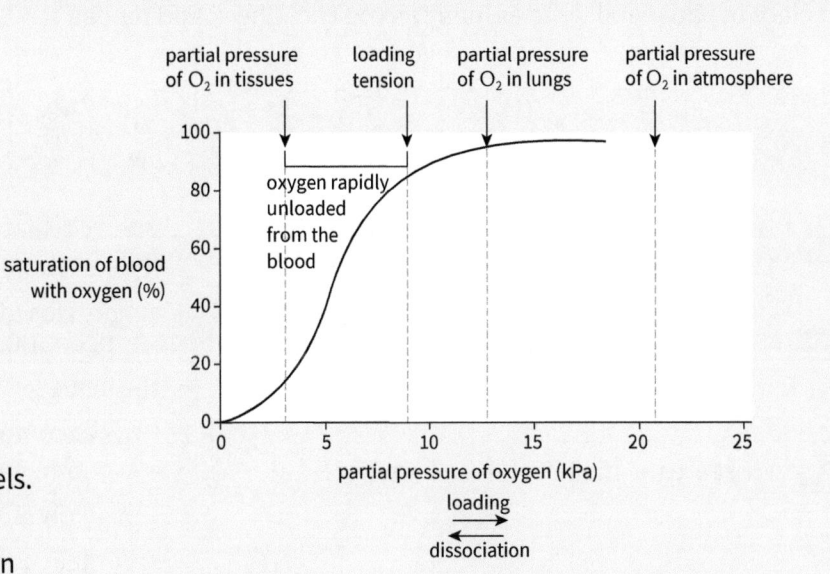

Bohr effect

Haemoglobin's **oxygen binding affinity** is inversely related to the concentration of carbon dioxide in the blood.

On the top graph, the lower part of the solid line occurs in the active tissues. The top part of the dotted line occurs at the lung capillaries.

The **dissociation** of oxyhaemoglobin is therefore higher at the tissues, where the partial pressure of carbon dioxide is higher. This is known as the Bohr effect.

A developing fetus has fetal haemoglobin, which has a higher affinity for oxygen than adult haemoglobin so that the fetus is able to receive enough oxygen from the maternal blood via the **placenta**.

The bottom graph shows that fetal haemoglobin will bond with oxygen at lower partial pressures and concentrations of oxygen compared to adult haemoglobin.

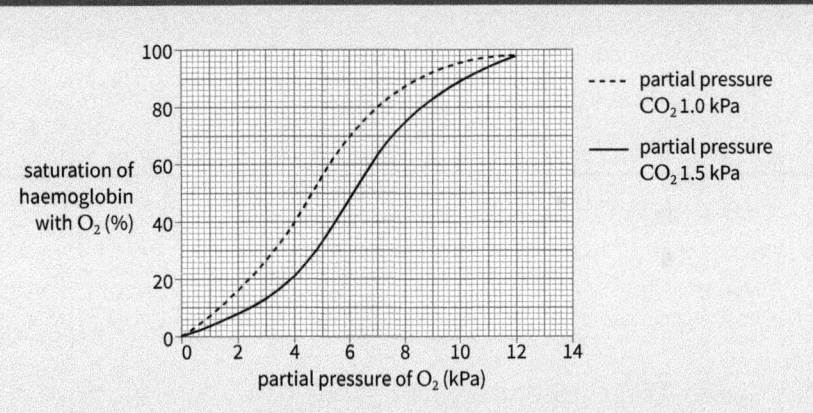

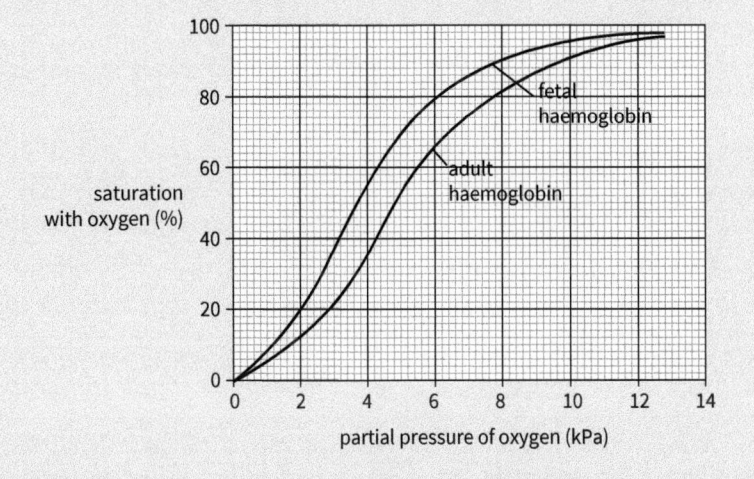

Retrieval

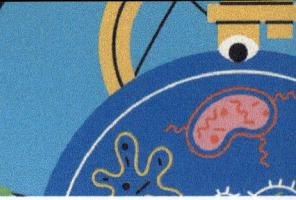

Learn the answers to the questions below, then cover the answers column with a piece of paper and write as many as you can. Check and repeat.

Questions	Answers
1. What type of circulation do insects have? Explain how it works.	open circulation, bathes all the cells in a fluid (haemolymph) where substance exchange takes place
2. Describe the circulatory system found in fish.	single, closed circulatory system: blood is pumped by the heart, through the gills, to the body, and back to the heart
3. What are the main features of arteries?	• walls contain thick layers of elastic tissue and smooth muscle tissue • high pressure
4. What are the main features of veins?	• contain elastic and muscle tissue • thinner walls and a larger lumen compared to arteries • most contain valves
5. What are the main features of capillaries?	• very small, 4–10 μm in diameter • allow only one red blood cell through at a time • blood pressure is very low • made of a single layer of epithelial cells
6. What is the difference between hydrostatic pressure and oncotic pressure in the capillaries?	hydrostatic pressure: the pressure from fluid on the walls of the capillary, usually forcing blood plasma out of the circulatory system oncotic pressure: osmotic pressure from proteins in plasma that draws water into the circulatory system
7. Explain why there are no erythrocytes or large proteins in tissue fluid.	larger components of blood such as erythrocytes and proteins are too large to squeeze through the gaps between endothelial cells in the capillary wall
8. How many chambers does the heart have? Name them.	four: left and right atria, left and right ventricles
9. How does blood pressure compare around the circulatory system?	the pulmonary system has a lower pressure than the systemic (body) system; arteries have higher pressure than capillaries and veins
10. Why does oxygen loading increase after the first haem group binds to an oxygen molecule?	the haemoglobin molecule changes shape and increase affinity for oxygen
11. What is a venule?	a very thin vein that receives blood from the capillaries
12. What is the Bohr effect?	haemoglobin's oxygen binding affinity is inversely related to the concentration of carbon dioxide in the blood

13 Describe the structure of lymph vessels.
- sac-like
- have valves
- lymph circulates via the movement of surrounding tissues

14 Name the two types of valve found in the heart.
atrioventricular and semi-lunar

15 Explain the difference between adult haemoglobin and fetal haemoglobin.
fetal haemoglobin has a higher affinity for oxygen than adult haemoglobin so that the fetus is able to receive enough oxygen at the placenta

16 Describe how the heartbeat is controlled.
- sino-atrial node (SAN) initiates wave of electrical activity (nerve impulses)
- causes muscle in atrial wall to contract
- atrio-ventricular node (AVN) in septum delays the impulse to let atria contract fully before ventricles contract
- Purkyne tissue distributes the impulse through the walls of the ventricles, causing ventricular muscles to contract

Maths skills

Practise your maths skills using the worked example and practice questions below.

Calculating cardiac output

Cardiac output is the volume of blood pumped from the left ventricle of the heart in one minute.

$$\frac{\text{cardiac}}{\text{output}} = \frac{\text{stroke}}{\text{volume}} \times \frac{\text{heart}}{\text{rate}}$$

$$CO = SV \times HR$$

Where:
- CO = cardiac output
- SV = the volume of blood pumped by the left ventricle in one heartbeat
- HR = heartbeats in one minute

Units:
- CO – cm³ per minute ($cm^3\,min^{-1}$)
- SV – cm³ per beat
- HR – beats per minute (bpm)

Worked example

Question
A patient has a heart rate of 60 bpm and a stroke volume of 75 cm³.
Calculate their cardiac output.

Answer
Remember that the equation you need is:

$$CO = SV \times HR$$

So, $CO = 75 \times 60$
     $= 4500\,cm^3\,min^{-1}$

The range for normal cardiac output is 4000–8000 $cm^3\,min^{-1}$.

Practice

1 The same patient runs on a treadmill for 1 minute and their heart rate increases to 120 bpm.
Calculate their new cardiac output.

2 An athlete has a cardiac output of 7250 $cm^3\,min^{-1}$ and a resting heart rate of 46 bpm.
Calculate their stroke volume.

3 Immediately after training, the athlete has a cardiac output of 23 000 $cm^3\,min^{-1}$.
What has their heart rate increased to?

Practice

Exam-style questions

1 A camel is a mammal that lives in the desert. It must be adapted to survive in very dry and hot conditions. An image of a camel is shown in **Figure 1.1**.

Synoptic link

2.1.5

Figure 1.1

(a) Describe the structure of the camel's heart.

....

....

....

....

....

.... [4]

(b) Using **Figure 1.1** and your own knowledge, explain the importance of both the heart and circulation to the camel.

....

....

....

....

....

.... [4]

Exam tip

Look carefully at the image provided, in this case the features of the camel, and link them to the circulatory system.

(c) (i) Explain why very dry conditions may limit osmosis into the camel's cells.

....

.... [1]

(ii) Explain how the camel is adapted to prevent osmosis being limited into the camel's cells.

....

.... [1]

9 Transport in animals

2   **Figure 2.1** shows the cardiac cycle in a healthy human from the left side of the heart.

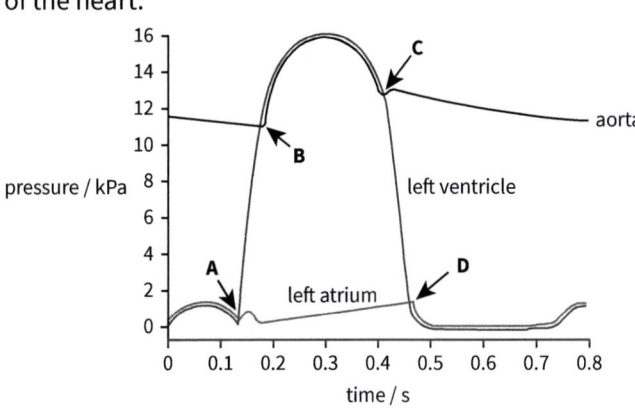

Figure 2.1

(a) Identify and explain where the atrioventricular valves and semi-lunar valves open and close on the graph.

Use the letters **A**, **B**, **C**, and **D** to refer to the specific points on the graph in **Figure 2.1**.

....

....

.... [3]

(b) Explain why atrioventricular and semilunar valves need to close.

....

.... [1]

(c) Calculate the heart rate in beats per minute from the graph in **Figure 2.1**.

> **Exam tip**
> Remember that units are important. You are asked to provide the beats per minute but this graph measures heart rate in seconds. Don't let this trip you up.

.... bpm [2]

(d) The healthy human's cardiac output is 6.2 dm³ min⁻¹.

Calculate their stroke volume including the correct unit.

.... [2]

(e) A human heart is a closed circulatory system, whereas an insect has an open circulatory system.

Suggest why insects have open circulatory systems.

....

.... [2]

3 Haemoglobin has quarternary protein structure.

(a) Describe one feature of quarternary protein structure.

.... [1]

(b) The graph in **Figure 3.1** shows the oxygen dissociation curves for both fetal and adult human haemoglobin.

Synoptic link

2.1.2

Figure 3.1

State the ratio of the oxygen saturation between fetal and adult haemoglobin at a partial pressure of oxygen of 20 mm Hg.

....

.... [1]

Exam tip

To calculate a ratio, divide the first number (fetal) by the second number (adult) to give you a value of 'x'. The ratio is then expressed as 'x : 1'.

(c) Explain the shape of the adult haemoglobin dissociation curve.

....
....
....
....
....
....
.... [6]

4 A sheep heart can be dissected in a laboratory.

(a) Before the sheep's heart is cut, water is often run through the top of the heart.

Suggest why this may be carried out.

....
.... [1]

(b) Identify two risks invoved with carrying out a dissection and explain how to manage these risks when carrying out a dissection of a sheep's heart.

....
....
....
....
.... [2]

106   **9** Transport in animals

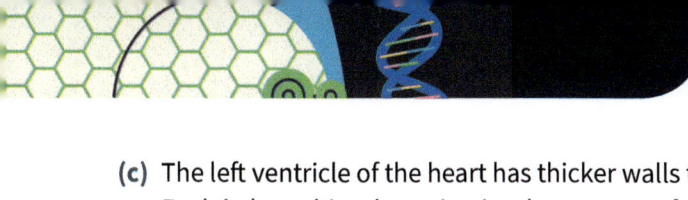

(c) The left ventricle of the heart has thicker walls than the right. Explain how this adaptation is advantageous for the circulatory system.

....
....
.... [1]

(d) A blood clot is found in the coronary artery during the dissection. Explain what the impact of this would be on the function of the heart.

....
....
.... [2]

> **Exam tip**
>
> Extra information will be provided in exam questions. Think about what is most relevant to the question – in this case, it is the blood clot.

(e) **Figure 4.1** shows data relating to cardiovascular and non-cardiovascular deaths in men and women. The investigator reviewed a sample size of 5 for each group of patients in **Figure 4.1**. The investigator interviewed the deceased patients' relatives to gain this information.

Figure 4.1

Describe the overall trend of the graph in **Figure 4.1**.

....
....
.... [2]

(f) A student made the following conclusions from the graph in **Figure 4.1**:

'As the age increases, those with cardiovascular disease have a greater chance of death.'

'More women have cardiovascular disease than men.'

Evaluate whether you can support the conclusions made by the student.

....
....
....
.... [4]

5   A man took an exercise tolerance test after complaining of chest pain during a 10 km run.

This exercise tolerance test normally involves exercising on a treadmill. However, given that the pains occurred during a run, the doctor decided to test the man's heart function using an exercise bicycle.

The man was asked to continue pedalling at a continuous rate per minute (as indicated by the digital display on the exercise bicycle) whilst the intensity (resistance) of the exercise increased.

The man produced 120 dm³ of carbon dioxide and consumed 130 dm³ of oxygen during this exercise. Resistance and heart rate are shown in **Table 5.1**.

Synoptic links

5.1.5   5.2.2

Time (min)	Resistance (arbitrary units)	Heart rate (bpm)
0	1	65
2	2	94
4	3	116
6	4	127
8	5	142
10	6	155

Table 5.1

(a) Using **Table 5.1**, calculate the percentage increase in heart rate in the first 4 minutes of exercise.

.... % [2]

(b) (i) Calculate the respiratory quotient (RQ) of the man during this exercise.

.... [2]

(ii) State what this RQ result means.

.... [1]

(c) Explain how heart rate is controlled as intensity of exercise increases.

....
....
....
....
....
.... [6]

Exam tip

This is a typical synoptic link question. Links need to be made to respiration and hormonal control of the heart.

108   9 Transport in animals

6 (a) Describe how tissue fluid is formed in humans.

....

....

....

....

....

....

....

.... [4]

(b) The data in **Table 6.1** below shows the plasma protein concentration in a person with hepatitis, which is inflammation of the liver.

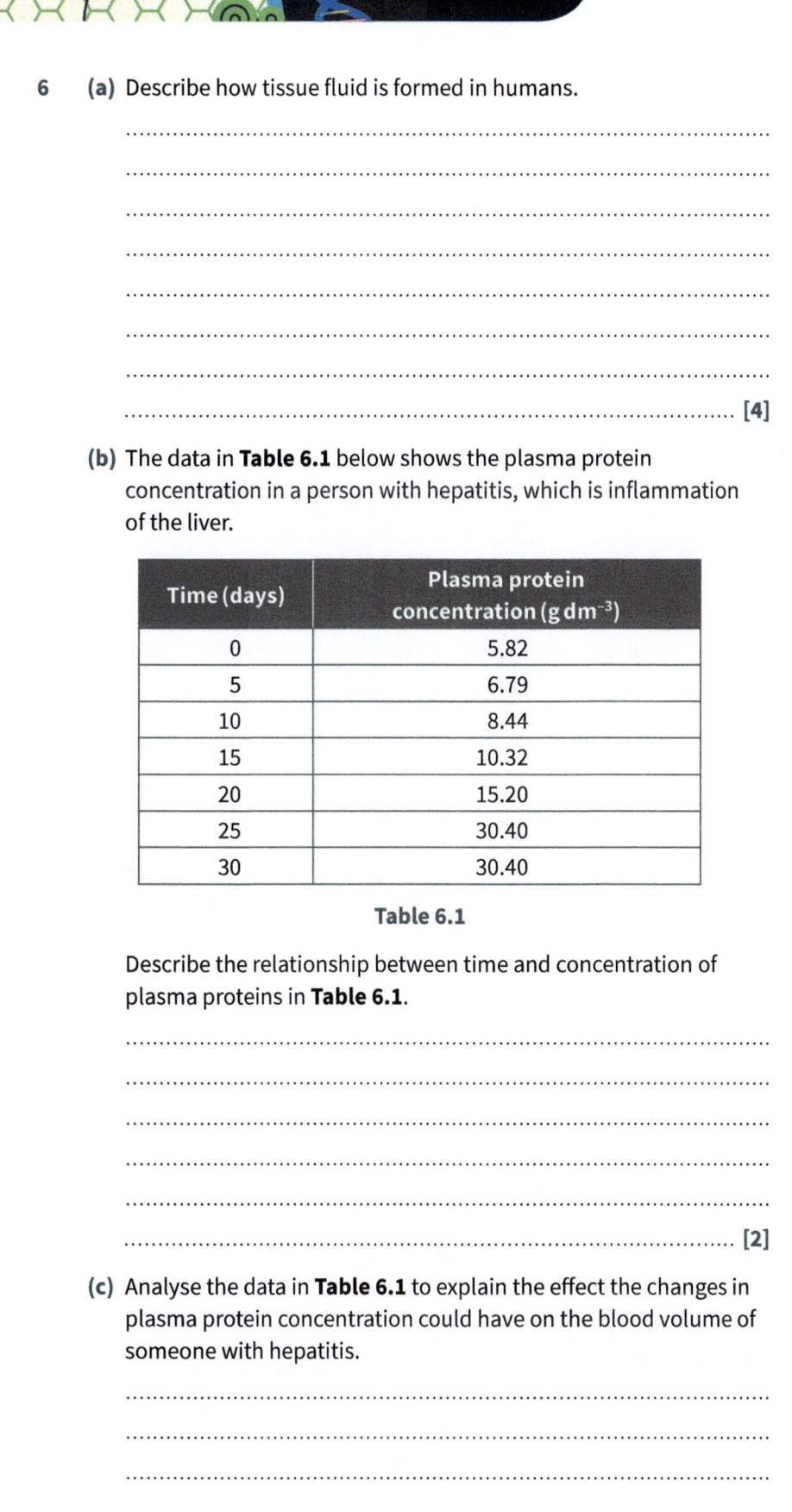

Time (days)	Plasma protein concentration (g dm^{-3})
0	5.82
5	6.79
10	8.44
15	10.32
20	15.20
25	30.40
30	30.40

Table 6.1

> **! Exam tip**
> Remember to include comparisons of the data within the description, which could also include a calculation (if appropriate).

Describe the relationship between time and concentration of plasma proteins in **Table 6.1**.

....

....

....

....

....

.... [2]

(c) Analyse the data in **Table 6.1** to explain the effect the changes in plasma protein concentration could have on the blood volume of someone with hepatitis.

....

....

....

....

....

.... [2]

Knowledge

10 Transport in plants

Transport in plants

Unicellular plants (phytoplankton) have a large **surface area to volume ratio** and can rely on diffusion for transport of nutrients into them and removal of waste out of them. As multicellular plants become larger, their surface area to volume ratio becomes smaller. **Transport systems** are essential to supply nutrients to, and remove waste from, individual cells, when plants become larger and more complex.

The **supply of nutrients** from the soil relies upon the **flow of water** through a **vascular system**, as does the movement of the products of photosynthesis.

Transport vessels

Plants transport water, sugars, and mineral ions using two types of vessel: xylem and phloem.

Xylem vessels transport water in the roots, stem, and leaves of the plant. This happens in **one** direction only, from roots to the top of the plant.

Phloem transports organic molecules, such as sucrose from photosynthesis. This can happen in **all** directions.

Xylem and phloem are arranged in **vascular bundles**. Roots have a single vascular bundle, which branches into a separate arrangement of tubes up the stem, further branching into veins of xylem and phloem in the leaves. The structural and supporting tissue is called the cortex.

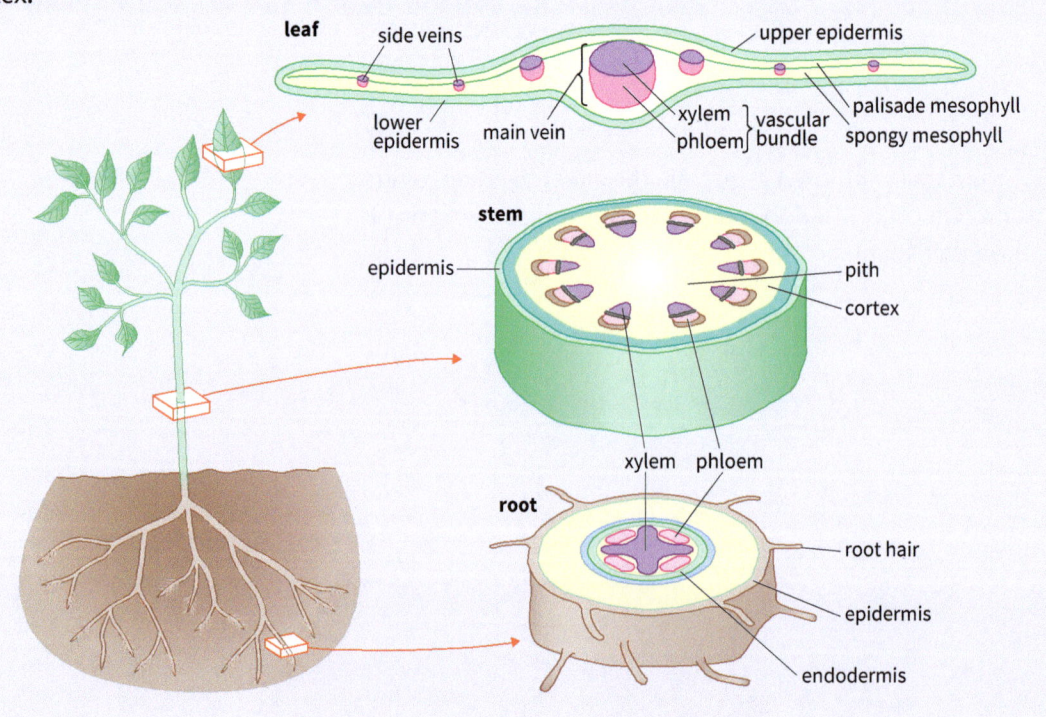

110 10 Transport in plants

Structure and function of phloem

Phloem transports organic molecules (assimilates) both up and down the plant. This is an **active** process, requiring energy in the form of ATP to move these substances.

Phloem is made up of living cells called **sieve tube elements**, which have perforated cell walls, called sieve plates, between them and **companion cells** beside them. Companion cells regulate the movement of solutes and provide ATP for active transport. Strands of cytoplasm called **plasmodesmata** connect the sieve tube element and companion cell.

Translocation

Plants transport sucrose and other substances from **sources** (e.g., leaf cells) to **sinks** (e.g., roots, meristem).

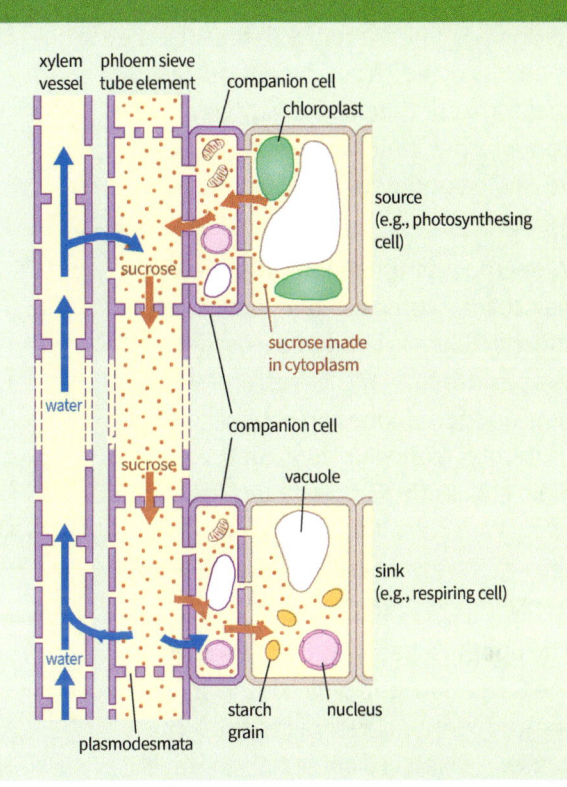

Loading and unloading of sucrose in the phloem

Loading

- At a **source** – usually a photosynthesising leaf – sucrose is loaded into the phloem.
- The companion cells use proton pumps to pump out hydrogen ions, using ATP, creating a higher concentration of hydrogen ions outside the companion cell.
- A co-transporter protein in the companion cell membrane then transports these hydrogen ions back into the cell in conjunction with sucrose molecules.
- Sucrose then diffuses from the companion cell into the sieve tube elements via plasmodesmata.
- Water moves via osmosis from the companion cell to the sieve tube elements, due to the water potential gradient set up by the movement of sucrose into the sieve tube elements previously.

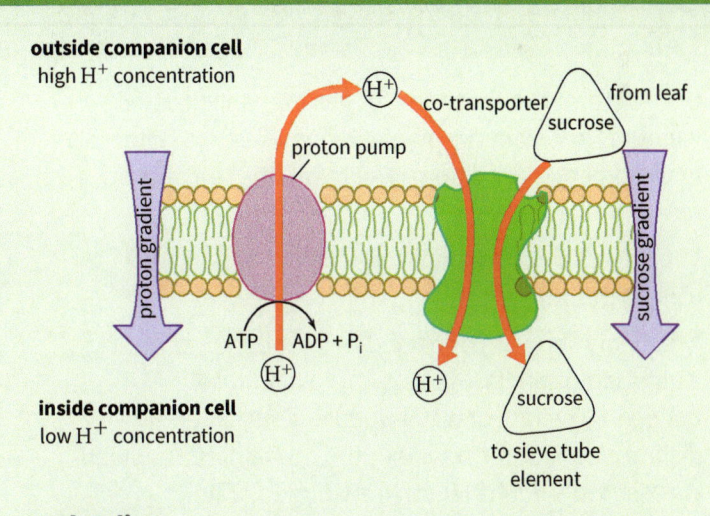

Unloading

- At a **sink** – for example, a root – the sucrose moves out of the sieve tube elements by diffusion.
- The concentration gradient is maintained by converting sucrose into glucose and fructose.
- This loading and unloading causes **mass flow** through the phloem via hydrostatic pressure and a pressure gradient.

Structure and function of xylem

Xylem vessels transport water and dissolved minerals to the tissues that need them. It is made from **dead lignified** cells that form continuous tubes. Xylem also contains pits which connect one xylem vessel to another to allow lateral water movement.

Water moves from the soil into the root hair cells by **osmosis**, then moves through the root to the xylem vessel. Water **evaporates** from the leaves, and surface tension causes cohesion between water molecules (**cohesion-tension theory**) which pulls other water molecules up the stem. Water also **adheres** to the side of the xylem vessels, creating a continuous transpiration stream.

The apoplast pathway is stopped by the Casparian strip which is found in the endodermal layer of the root. This causes all water to enter cells to travel further through the plant.

There are three pathways taken by water:
- **Apoplast:** water travels between cells
- **Symplast:** water enters cells
- **Vacuolar:** water passes through cell vacuoles

Investigating transpiration

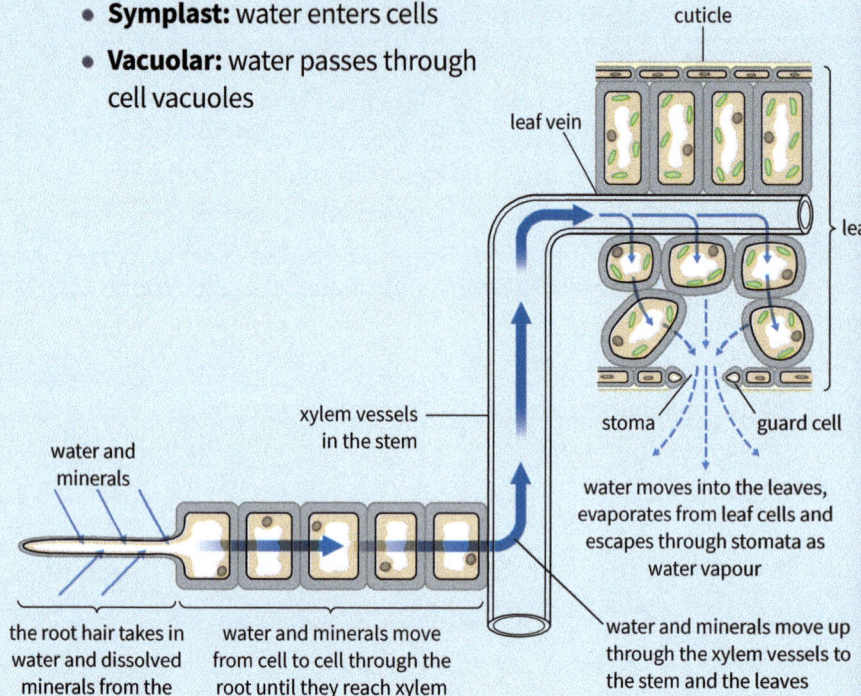

Due to stomata being open for gas exchange, water vapour is lost from the plant via transpiration. Different environmental conditions, like humidity, can affect the rate of transpiration.

The effects of these conditions can be investigated using a **potometer**.

A cut leafy shoot is connected to a rubber tube, and a graduated capillary tube, with a water reservoir in between. The rate of water uptake is measured by the distance the bubble travels in the capillary tube, which we assume is equivalent to transpiration rate.

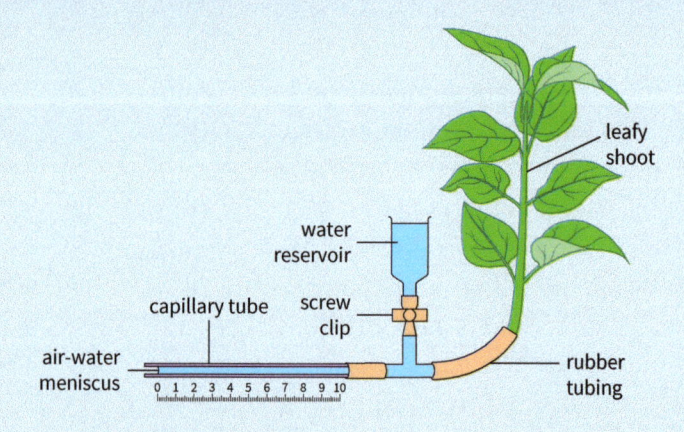

Adaptations of plants living in extremes

Xerophytes	Hydrophytes
grow in dry habitats (e.g., cacti, marram grass)	grow in or on water (e.g., water lilies)
thicker cuticle	little or no waxy cuticle
reduced leaf surface area (e.g., needles)	large, flat leaves
few, sunken stomata	minimal root system
rolled leaves (e.g., marram grass)	air pockets to aid flotation and flexible stems

Maths skills

Practise your maths skills using the worked example and practice questions below.

Calculating transpiration rates

The rate of water loss from leaves can be measured using a potometer.

A cut leafy shoot is attached to rubber tubing, which is in turn attached to a capillary tube. The system is filled with water apart from one air bubble.

The rate of transpiration is measured by the distance the air bubble travels over a specified length of time.

The conditions tested can be:
- light intensity
- wind
- humidity
- temperature

Worked example

Question

At high light intensity, the following data were collected:

Initial position of bubble: 0.5 cm
Final position of bubble: 6.0 cm
Time taken: 5 min

Calculate the transpiration rate.

Answer

So the equation you need to use is:

$$\text{transpiration rate (mm/s)} = \frac{\text{final position (mm)} - \text{initial position (mm)}}{\text{time (seconds)}}$$

You know the final and initial positions of the bubble, so you now need to find the difference between them:

$$60 \text{ mm} - 5 \text{ mm} = 55 \text{ mm}$$

Convert the time taken into seconds by multiplying the number of minutes by 60.

$$5 \text{ min} \times 60 = 300 \text{ s}$$

Finally, divide the distance travelled by the time taken to find the rate of transpiration:

$$\frac{55}{300} = 0.18 \text{ mm s}^{-1}$$

Practice

Calculate the transpiration rate for the following experiments, given the data collected.

1. Windy conditions for 5 minutes:
   Initial position of bubble: 0.5 cm
   Final position of bubble: 7.2 cm

2. Humid conditions for 25 minutes:
   Initial position of bubble: 0.5 cm
   Final position of bubble: 4.1 cm

3. Dark conditions for 18 minutes:
   Initial position of bubble: 0.5 cm
   Final position of bubble: 0.5 cm

4. Of the experiments outlined above, which condition had the smallest effect on the transpiration rate, compared to the base condition in the worked example?

Retrieval

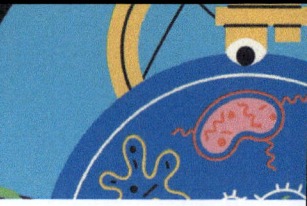

Learn the answers to the questions below, then cover the answers column with a piece of paper and write as many as you can. Check and repeat.

Questions | Answers

	Questions	Answers
1	Why can unicellular plants rely on diffusion of substances in and out of cells?	they have a large surface area to volume ratio
2	Why do larger, more complex plants need transport systems?	large, multicellular plants' surface area to volume ratios become smaller so they cannot rely on diffusion to supply nutrients to, and remove waste from, individual cells
3	What substances do plants need to move around their vascular system?	water, minerals, and sugars, such as sucrose
4	What are the two main types of vascular tubes called?	xylem and phloem
5	What are the main components of a root?	a xylem core, surrounded by phloem; this is surrounded by the endodermis, cortex, and epidermis, which contains the root hair cells
6	In a transverse section, how are vascular bundles arranged in the stems of herbaceous dicotyledonous plants?	from the outside: phloem, cambium, xylem
7	What is a potometer used for?	to measure water uptake, which is used to estimate transpiration through a plant
8	Describe the structure and function of xylem.	• dead lignified cells that form continuous tubes • transports water up the plant via the transpiration stream, as well as dissolved minerals to the tissues that need them
9	Describe the structure and function of phloem.	• living cells, called sieve tube elements • have sieve plates between them and companion cells beside them • transports organic molecules, such as sucrose from photosynthesis • this can happen in all directions
10	Describe what is meant by translocation in dicotyledonous plants.	plants transport sugars and other assimilates from sources (e.g., leaf cells) to sinks (e.g., roots, meristem) this is an active process, requiring energy to move these substances
11	Describe some adaptations of xerophytes.	• thicker cuticle • reduced leaf surface area (e.g., spines or needles) • sunken and fewer stomata • rolled leaves

10 Transport in plants

12	Explain what happens to load sucrose at a source.	• hydrogen ions are pumped out of companion cell by active transport, using ATP, creating a higher concentration of hydrogen ions outside the companion cell • sucrose is co-transported with hydrogen ions into the companion cells • sucrose diffuses into sieve tube elements through the plasmodesmata
13	Explain what happens to unload sucrose at a sink.	• sucrose moves out of the phloem by diffusion • concentration gradient is maintained by converting sucrose into glucose and fructose in the sink
14	What are xerophytes?	plants that grow in dry habitats (e.g., cacti, marram grass)
15	What are hydrophytes?	plants that live on or in water (e.g., water lilies)
16	Describe some adaptations of hydrophytes.	• minimal root system (some have aerial roots) • large, flat leaves • air pockets that aid flotation • little or no waxy cuticle • flexible stems to avoid snapping in water currents
17	Which environmental conditions increase the rate of transpiration?	increased temperature, decreased humidity, increased wind, increased light intensity
18	How are minerals transported in a leaf?	leaves have a main vein of xylem and phloem (the vascular bundle), which divides out into the leaf tissue as side veins
19	Describe the transpiration stream in dicotyledonous plants.	• water moves from the soil into the roots by osmosis from a higher to a lower water potential, moving through the root tissue to the xylem vessel • water evaporates from the leaves • this causes tension, which pulls other water molecules up the stem • water has a high surface tension, causing cohesion between water molecules (cohesion-tension theory) • water also adheres to the side of the xylem vessels • this creates a continuous transpiration stream
20	What is a potometer used for?	to measure water uptake, which is used to estimate transpiration through a plant
21	Explain how a potometer works.	• cut leafy shoot is connected underwater to a rubber tube and a graduated capillary tube, with a water reservoir in between controlled by a tap • the distance travelled by a bubble in the capillary tube is used to measure transpiration rate in different conditions

Practice

Exam-style questions

1 (a) Describe two differences between the structure of phloem and xylem vessels.

....

....

.... [3]

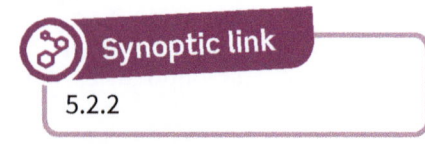

> **Synoptic link**
> 5.2.2

> **Exam tip**
> For **1 (a)**, read the question carefully. This question is asking about the structure, rather than the role, of the phloem.

The flow chart in **Figure 1.1** shows a stage of respiration in the cytoplasm of a root hair cell, where sucrose is transported to by the phloem. The sucrose is broken down into glucose.

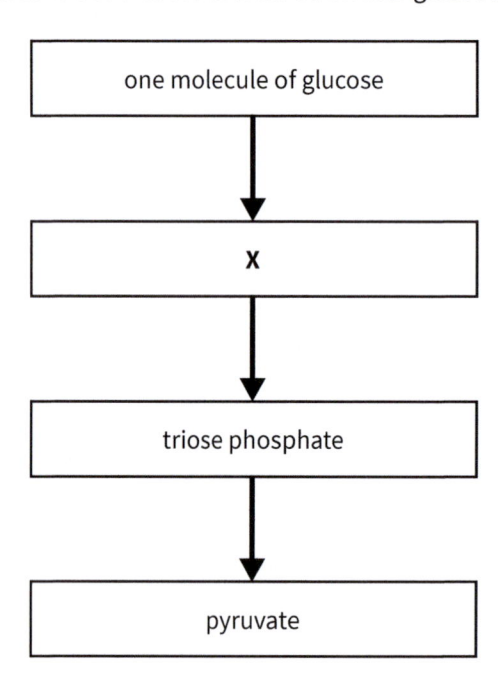

```
one molecule of glucose
         ↓
         X
         ↓
   triose phosphate
         ↓
      pyruvate
```

Figure 1.1

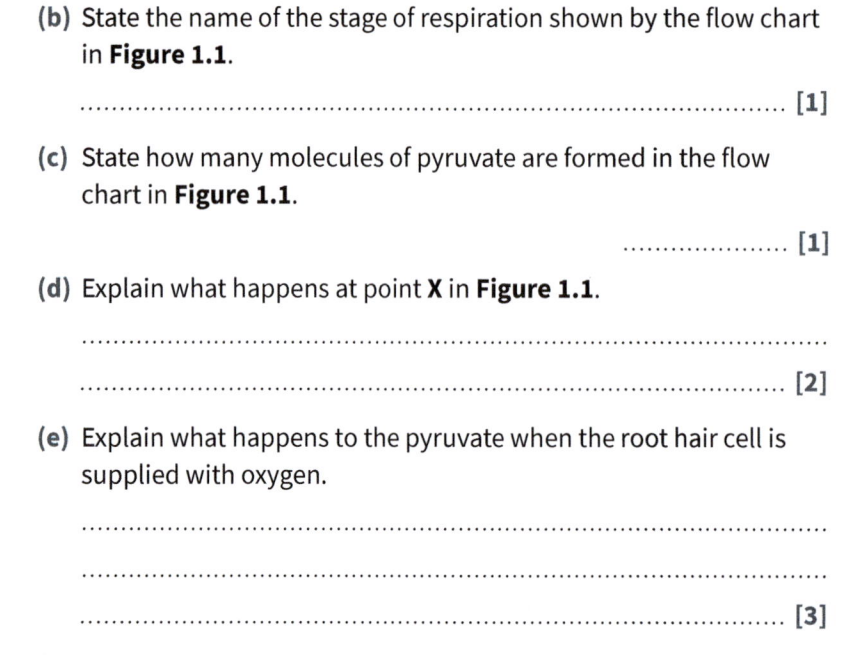

(b) State the name of the stage of respiration shown by the flow chart in **Figure 1.1**.

.... [1]

(c) State how many molecules of pyruvate are formed in the flow chart in **Figure 1.1**.

.... [1]

(d) Explain what happens at point **X** in **Figure 1.1**.

....

.... [2]

(e) Explain what happens to the pyruvate when the root hair cell is supplied with oxygen.

....

....

.... [3]

116   10 Transport in plants

2   A potometer, shown in **Figure 2.1**, is used to measure the volume of water uptake in a plant over time. A calculated rate of water uptake is used to estimate the rate of transpiration.

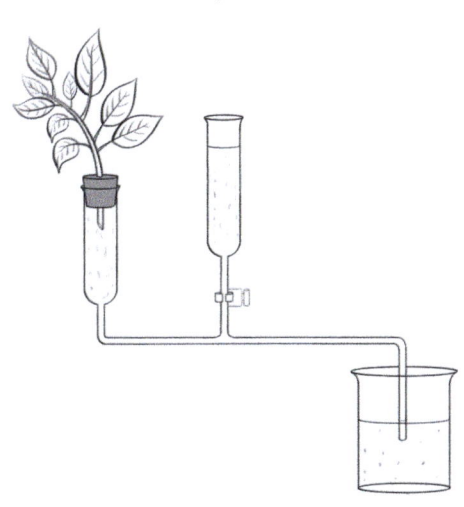

Figure 2.1

A potometer was firstly set up in a school laboratory preparation room at a temperature of 35 °C. The volume of water taken up by the plant shoot was recorded for 10 minutes.

The potometer was then moved to a school laboratory at a temperature of 18 °C.

The results of the investigation are shown in **Figure 2.2**.

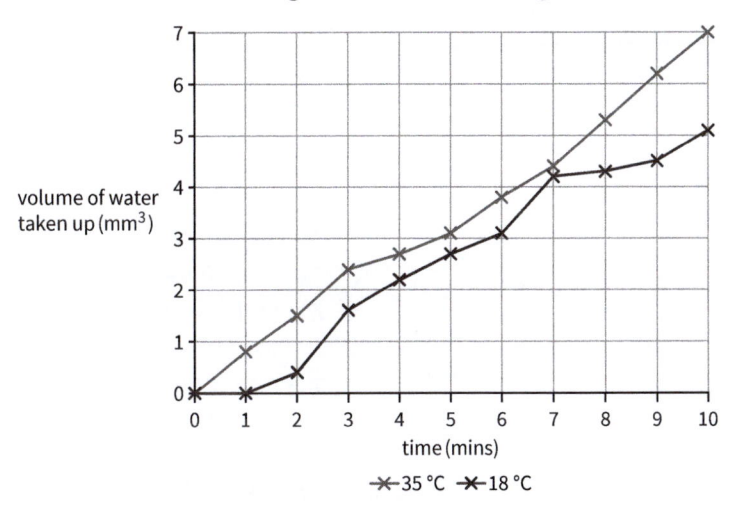

Figure 2.2

2   **(a)** Using **Figure 2.2**, calculate the mean rate of water uptake at 18 °C between 6 and 10 minutes.

> **Exam tip**
> How many minutes does the question refer to in **2(a)**?

.... [2]

(b) Explain how an increase in temperature increases the rate of transpiration in the plant shoot.

....

....

....

....

....

....

.... [6]

3   Marram grass is a xerophyte, a plant that has adapted to survive in dry regions, and is shown in **Figure 3.1**.

Synoptic link

6.3.1

Figure 3.1

(a) Explain how marram grass is adapted to prevent it losing water.

....

....

.... [2]

(b) (i) Marram grass is a pioneer species.

Explain what is meant by the term pioneer species.

....

....

.... [2]

Exam tip

Where an image has been provided in an adaptation question, refer to specific features from the image in your answer. It could also jog your memory of a key structural adaptation that links to an effective function.

(ii) Describe the stages of primary succession following the establishment of pioneer species.

....

....

....

.... [3]

(c) Suggest one way that deflected succession can be caused by humans.

....

.... [2]

4 Xylem vessels and the phloem are involved in transport in plants, as shown in the light micrograph image in **Figure 4.1**.

Figure 4.1

Synoptic link

2.1.1

(a) Using **Figure 4.1**, describe the differences between the structure of phloem and xylem.

....

....

....

....

....

....

....

.... [6]

Exam tip

Where you have been asked to describe the differences, ensure that each answer compares both tissues, for example:

'In the xylem, there is ….; whereas in the phloem there is …'

(b) Calculate the length of the vascular bundle in **Figure 4.1**.

Give your answer in standard form.

.... [2]

(c) Explain how the term magnification is different to the term resolution.

....

....

....

.... [2]

5 Light intensity is a factor that can affect the rate of photosynthesis, as shown in **Figure 5.1**.

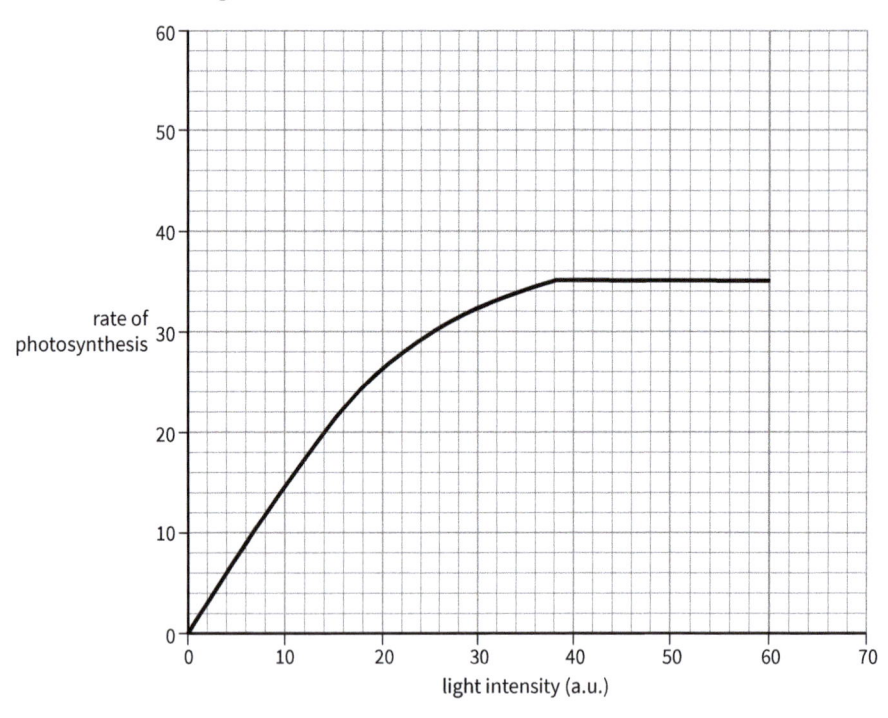

Figure 5.1

Synoptic link

5.2.1

(a) Calculate the percentage increase in the rate of photosynthesis between the light intensities of 10 and 20 arbitrary units in **Figure 5.1**.

.... % [2]

(b) Describe a method that could be used to generate the results from **Figure 5.1** for this investigation.

....
....
.... [3]

(c) This investigation includes the light-dependent reaction in photosynthesis.

Explain the steps involved in the cyclic-phosphorylation part of this process.

....
.... [2]

(d) Translocation occurs in plants between a source and a sink.

Explain how sucrose is loaded into sieve tube elements at the source.

....
....
.... [3]

Exam tip

Remember to include a reference to hydrogen ions in your answer.

6   *Pistia stratiotes,* shown in **Figure 6.1**, is a hydrophyte – a plant that has adapted to survive in wet regions.

Synoptic link
4.2.2

Figure 6.1

6   (a) Complete **Table 6.1**. [3]

Taxonomy	Name
kingdom	
genus	
species	

Table 6.1

(b) State the type of competition that occurs among members of the same species.

.... [1]

(c) Explain how *Pistia stratiotes* has adapted to the availability of water, using **Figure 6.1**.

Exam tip
Make sure to refer to the characteristics that you can see in the image provided.

....
....
....
....
....
....
....
....
.... [6]

Knowledge

11 Communicable diseases

What is a communicable disease?

A **pathogen** is an organism that causes disease.

Communicable diseases of animals and plants are caused by pathogens that can be transmitted from one organism to another.

Examples of communicable diseases:

Type of pathogen	Examples of diseases
bacterium	tuberculosis (TB; human, bovine), bacterial meningitis (human), MRSA (human), ring rot (potatoes, tomatoes)
virus	HIV/AIDS (human), influenza (animals), rubella (human), COVID-19 (animals), tobacco mosaic virus (plant)
fungus	ringworm (mammals), athlete's foot (human), black sigatoka (bananas)
protoctist	malaria (human), potato/tomato late blight

Transmission of pathogens

In order to cause disease, animal and plant pathogens must be transmitted from one organism to another, either directly or indirectly.

- **Direct** transmission:
  - person-to-person skin contact (ringworm)
  - exchange of bodily fluids (HIV/AIDS)
  - across the placenta (rubella)
  - animal bites (rabies)
  - contaminated food and drink (Salmonella)
  - sharing infected needles (HIV/AIDS, hepatitis B)

- **Indirect** transmission by:
  - a **vector*** (malaria, yellow fever)
  - droplet infection (common cold, COVID-19)
  - touching contaminated objects

*A **vector** is an organism, like a mosquito, that carries a disease-causing pathogen from one host to another.

The transmission of communicable diseases can be increased by social factors, such as poor living conditions, overcrowding, and climate.

Plant defences against pathogens

Plants have bark and a waxy cuticle to prevent entry of pathogens. They can also produce chemicals (e.g., antimicrobial enzymes, saponins, and phytoalexins, in response to pathogen attack).

Plants can also limit the spread of a pathogen by depositing **callose**. Callose, a polysaccharide, is deposited to block pores in phloem sieve plates between phloem sieve tubes to prevent pathogens spreading.

Using antibiotics to manage bacterial infection

Bacterial resistance to antibiotics has led to the development of infections such as **MRSA** (methicillin-resistant *Staphylococcus aureus*), which is now common in hospitals.

Various factors contribute to bacteria becoming resistant to antibiotics, including:
- using antibiotics to treat trivial, minor, or viral ailments
- patients not completing courses of antibiotics
- doctors prescribing antibiotics unnecessarily in response to patient demand
- use of antibiotics in intensive farming to prevent infections.

Bacteria that have developed multi-antibiotic resistance are very difficult to treat.

Possible sources of medicines

New drugs are required because:
- new pathogens are constantly emerging (e.g., SARS-CoV-2)
- many existing diseases are not yet treatable nor curable
- bacteria have become resistant to current antibiotic treatments.

Personalised medicine involves using a person's genotype to choose the best treatment. DNA sequencing and clinical information can provide individual treatment plans using medicines and lifestyle choices.

Synthetic biology involves using genetically modified bacteria or animals, and nanotechnology, to produce drugs that might be rare, expensive, or difficult to make.

Different types of immunity

Natural immunity: the body's ability to recognise, neutralise, or destroy non-self substances.

Artificial immunity: gained through deliberate exposure to antigens or antibodies.

Active immunity: immunity gained through activation of the immune system creating memory cells.

Passive immunity: immunity gained through antibodies which have been made externally.

Type of immunity	Active immunity	Passive immunity
natural immunity	• natural exposure to the antigens on pathogens, an immune response, and making of memory cells • most diseases develop only once • long-term immunity	• antibodies transferred from mother to baby via breast milk and placenta • short-term (but essential) immunity
artificial immunity	• immune response by exposure to a dead or weakened pathogen, and production of memory cells (e.g., TB, rubella). • long-term immunity	• antibodies made by another organism (e.g., rabies immunoglobulin injections) • short-term immunity as the antibodies are broken down over time

Primary non-specific defences in animals

These prevent pathogens from gaining entry to the body and include:
- the **skin** – a tough, waterproof outer layer, made up of dead keratinocytes
- **mucous membranes** – in the gut, nose, and genital areas; lined with mucus
- **chemical defences** – lysozyme in tears, hydrochloric acid in the stomach
- **blood clotting** – a mesh of protein fibres and blood cells form a scab to prevent pathogen entry through broken skin
- **inflammation** – pain, swelling, heat, and redness; damaged cells make capillaries dilate and attract white blood cells to the affected area
- **wound repair** – cells at the wound edge divide to repair damage to the skin
- **expulsion reflexes** – coughing and sneezing in response to irritation of the airways.

Phagocytes

The second line of defence is **phagocytosis**, the engulfing and destroying of pathogenic cells that have entered the body, by **phagocytes**. There are two types of phagocyte:

- **neutrophils** – multi-lobed nucleus, short-lived, found in large numbers during infections
- **macrophages** – larger than neutrophils, can display pathogen antigens on their surfaces after phagocytosis and become **antigen-presenting cells (APC)**.

1. Chemical products from the pathogen attract a phagocyte to move towards the pathogen (chemotaxis). **Opsonins** (small molecules, e.g., antibodies) bind to the pathogen, marking it for phagocytosis.
2. The phagocyte attaches to the pathogen.
3. The phagocyte surrounds and engulfs the pathogen in a vesicle called a **phagosome**.
4. **Lysosomes** move towards, and fuse with, the phagosome.
5. Lysosome enzymes digest the pathogen. Macrophages do not digest the pathogen completely and will display the pathogen's antigens on its membrane, becoming an APC.

Finally, the phagocyte secretes **cytokines**, which act as messenger molecules, attracting more phagocytes to the area.

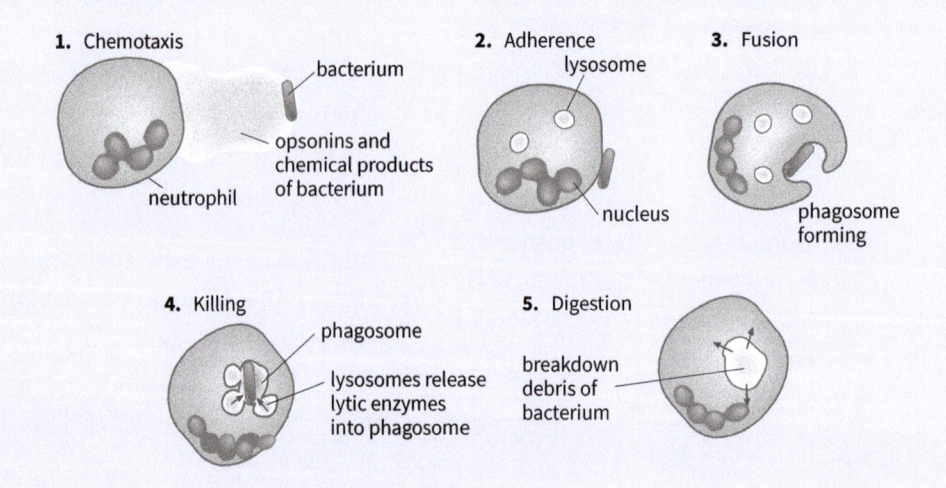

1. Chemotaxis – neutrophil, bacterium, opsonins and chemical products of bacterium
2. Adherence – lysosome, nucleus
3. Fusion – phagosome forming
4. Killing – phagosome, lysosomes release lytic enzymes into phagosome
5. Digestion – breakdown debris of bacterium

11 Communicable diseases

11

The structure and roles of B and T lymphocytes

The **specific immune response** involves white blood cells called **lymphocytes**, which are divided into two types: T and B.

Type of lymphocyte	Production location	Involved in ...	Roles in immunity	Cloned cells develop into ....
T	produced in bone marrow, mature in thymus	cell-mediated immunity	• respond to antigens inside cells • respond to own cells altered by viruses or cancer and to transplanted tissue	T helper cells T memory cells T killer cells T regulator cells
B	produced and mature in bone marrow	humoral immunity (involves antibodies)	• respond to antigens outside of cells • respond to pathogens • produce antibodies	plasma cells B memory cells

T and B lymphocytes communicate via **cell signalling** through the secretion of chemical messengers called **cytokines**.

Interleukins are a group of cytokines released by T and B lymphocytes and macrophages, to stimulate division of B and T cells.

Other cytokines include monokines and interferon.

Antibodies

An antibody is a globular protein produced by a plasma cell in response to the presence of a specific, complementary antigen.

It is composed of four polypeptide chains: two heavy chains, and two light chains. These chains are arranged in a Y shape and held together by disulphide bridges.

The tips of the antibody's Y shape form the antigen binding sites. Each tip has a variable region formed by unique amino acid sequences that produce specific tertiary structures (3D shapes). This allows them to bind to different complementary antigens.

All antibodies have the identical constant regions, the variable region is the only part of the antibody that changes.

The receptor binding site enables an antibody to attach to the cell surface membrane of a lymphocyte or to other antibodies to form antibody complexes.

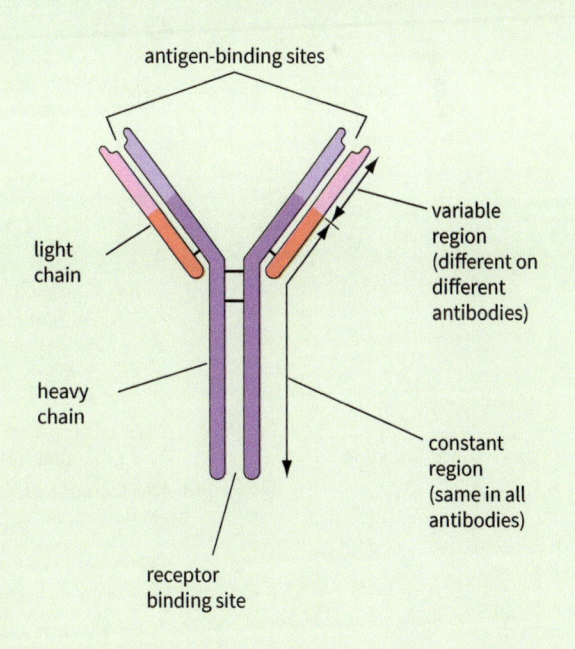

Labels: antigen-binding sites; light chain; heavy chain; receptor binding site; variable region (different on different antibodies); constant region (same in all antibodies)

Cell-mediated immunity

Cell-mediated immunity involves T lymphocytes:

1. Pathogens are engulfed by a (non-specific) macrophage, which breaks down the pathogen and becomes an **antigen-presenting** cell (APC).
2. The APC presents the pathogen's partially digested antigens to T helper cells.
3. The antigens bind to complementary receptors on one type of T helper cell – **clonal selection**.
4. The T helper cell is activated and divides rapidly. This is **clonal expansion**.
5. The cloned T cells:
   - secrete interleukins to stimulate phagocytes
   - secrete interleukins to stimulate B cells to divide
   - may become T killer cells that kill infected cells by making holes in their cell surface membranes
   - may become T regulator cells that control the immune response by inhibiting cytokine production

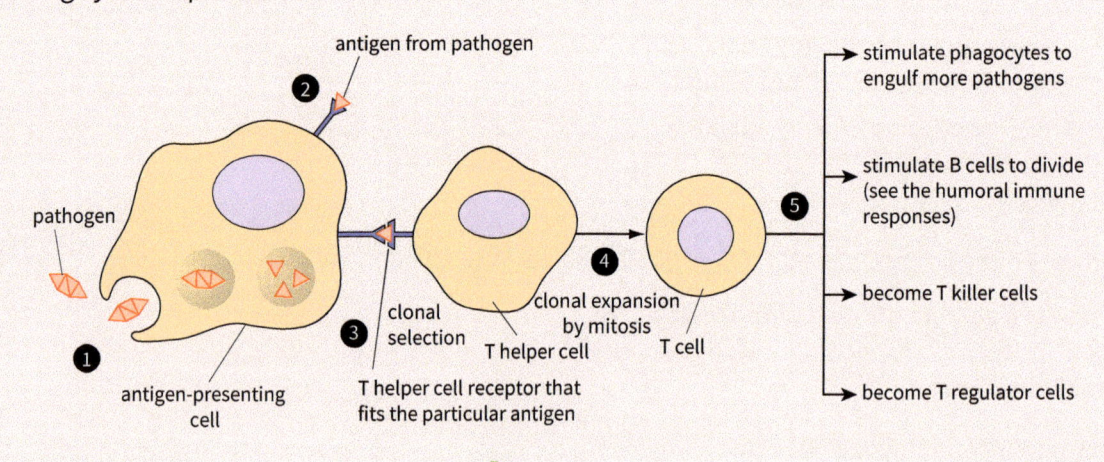

Functions of antibodies

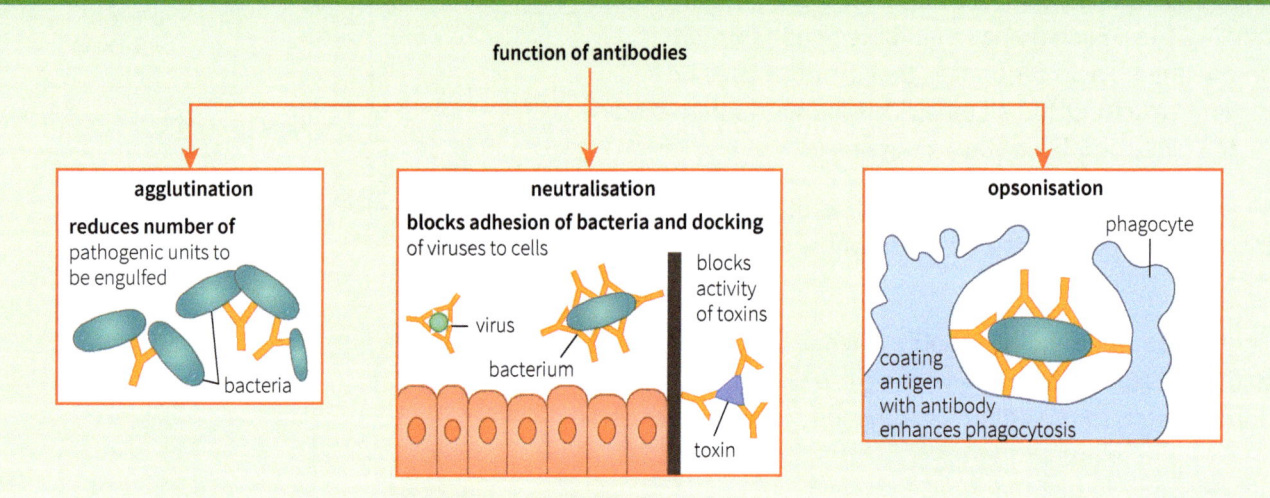

agglutination
reduces number of pathogenic units to be engulfed

neutralisation
blocks adhesion of bacteria and docking of viruses to cells
blocks activity of toxins

opsonisation
coating antigen with antibody enhances phagocytosis

126 11 Communicable diseases

Vaccinations

A **vaccination** is the introduction of a substance containing appropriate antigens into the body to stimulate artificial active immunity against a pathogen.

- **Routine vaccinations** are given to babies starting at 8 weeks of age with the 6-in-1 vaccine: diphtheria, whooping cough, hepatitis B, polio, tetanus, and haemophilus influenzae type B.
- Some pathogens cause a **pandemic**: a large-scale global outbreak. In these circumstances, vaccination programmes will target those people who are most at risk. A global vaccination programme against smallpox successfully eradicated the disease from the population in 1980.

Some pathogens mutate and change their antigens. When this happens, a new vaccine needs to be developed against the new strain of pathogen to ensure antibodies are made for the new antigen.

The humoral response – primary and secondary responses

1. Free antigens of the pathogen are taken up by phagocytes.
2. The phagocytes process and present the antigens on their cell surfaces.
3. **T helper cells** bind to the antigens, stimulate B cells to divide by mitosis, and differentiate into short-lived plasma cells and long-lived **memory cells**.
4. The plasma cells produce complementary antibodies to the antigens. This is the **primary immune response**, and the infected person will show symptoms until the pathogen is destroyed.
5. When the memory cells come into contact with the antigen again, they divide rapidly to form plasma cells and memory cells. The plasma cells rapidly produce high levels of antibodies so the pathogen is destroyed before the person feels unwell. This is the **secondary immune response**.

Autoimmune diseases

An **autoimmune disease** occurs when a person's immune system recognises their own antigens as non-self and mounts an immune response to the body's own cells. Examples of autoimmune disease include **rheumatoid arthritis**, **lupus erythematosus**, and **multiple sclerosis**.

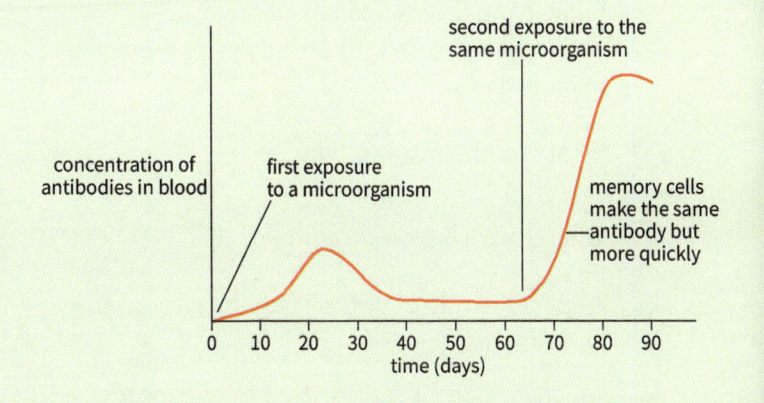

Retrieval

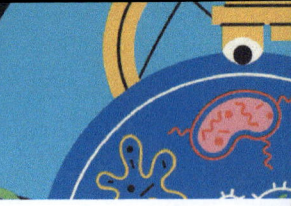

Learn the answers to the questions below, then cover the answers column with a piece of paper and write as many as you can. Check and repeat.

Questions	Answers
1. What is a pathogen?	an organism that causes a disease
2. List the four types of microorganisms that can cause disease. Give an example of each one.	• bacteria (e.g., TB, tetanus) • viruses (e.g., common cold, HIV) • fungi (e.g., athlete's foot, ringworm) • protoctista (e.g., malaria, amoebic dysentery)
3. What is a communicable disease?	a disease that can be transferred between organisms
4. Give five examples of indirect disease transmission.	infected needles, vectors, contaminated water, touching contaminated objects, droplets
5. How do plants prevent infection?	• physical barriers – bark and waxy cuticles • chemical defences such as antimicrobial enzymes
6. What is the role of callose deposition?	prevents the spread of infection throughout a plant
7. Why are new vaccines for some pathogens required?	because the pathogen mutates and its surface antigens change, so the original vaccine ceases to be effective
8. What is the process called whereby a phagocyte engulfs and destroys a pathogenic microorganism?	phagocytosis
9. What is a phagosome?	the vesicle formed when a phagocyte engulfs a pathogenic bacterium
10. What does a lysosome contain?	hydrolytic enzymes to digest/break down the pathogenic microbe
11. What is the role of plasma lymphocytes in the humoral response?	plasma cells have a main role in the primary immune response, producing antibodies
12. Which immune response is very rapid, produces high levels of antibodies, and is long lived?	secondary immune response
13. What is an autoimmune disease? Give three examples.	when a person's immune system attacks their own body, for example, rheumatoid arthritis, lupus, MS
14. What is passive immunity?	when antibodies are given to an individual via breast milk, via the placenta, or injected
15. What is MRSA?	methicillin-resistant *S. aureus* (name given to any antibiotic-resistant strain of the bacterium)
16. What is the definition of an antibody?	a protein produced by a plasma cell in response to the presence of an antigen
17. List the non-specific primary defences.	skin, mucous membranes, blood clotting, wound repair, inflammation, expulsion reflexes, chemical defences

11 Communicable diseases

Maths skills

Practise your maths skills using the worked example and practice questions below.

Standard deviation

When conducting an experiment, you are often asked to calculate the mean, median, and range of your results, but two datasets with the same mean, median, and range can have very different distributions. The distribution of results around the mean can be measured by calculating the standard deviation, and this can indicate how reliable your results are when comparing datasets.

Standard deviation (s) can be calculated by:

$$s = \sqrt{\frac{\sum(x - \bar{X})^2}{n - 1}}$$

Where:
- x = your results
- $\bar{X}$ = the mean of the results
- n = sample size

The lower your standard deviation, the closer the results are distributed around the mean, and therefore, the more reliable they are.

As the standard deviation measures the distribution of results around the mean, it can be influenced by outliers, and a strong outlier can increase the standard deviation of an otherwise reliable dataset.

Worked example

The white blood cell (CD4) counts of five patients with AIDS were taken, and the results are below:

Patient	CD4 cell count
1	530
2	368
3	472
4	231
5	334

Question
Calculate the standard deviation for these results. Give your answer to 2 decimal places.

Answer
The first thing to calculate here is the mean ($\bar{X}$):

$$\frac{(530 + 368 + 472 + 231 + 334)}{5} = 387$$

Then, subtract this mean ($\bar{X}$) from each of your results (x), and square your answer to remove negative values. Then, find the total of your squared values:

x	$x - \bar{X}$	$(x - \bar{X})^2$
530	143	20 449
368	−19	361
472	85	7225
231	−156	24 336
334	−53	2809
Total		55 180

Finally, plug this number into the equation for standard deviation, along with your sample size (n).

$$s = \sqrt{\frac{55\,180}{5 - 1}} = 117.45$$

Practice

The white cell blood counts (per μl) of 7 adult patients were measured, before and after they had received a vaccination for a strain of influenza. The results are shown below:

Patient	White blood cell count (/μl) Pre-vaccine	White blood cell count (/μl) Post-vaccine
1	4.90×10^3	2.12×10^4
2	5.80×10^3	1.95×10^4
3	6.40×10^3	1.87×10^4
4	4.20×10^3	1.85×10^4
5	6.90×10^3	2.04×10^4
6	5.60×10^3	1.89×10^4
7	9.80×10^3	1.92×10^4

1 Calculate the standard deviation for both of the datasets.
   Give your answers to 2 decimal places.

2 Compare your answers. Which dataset is more reliable?

3 Identify the outlier in the pre-vaccine sample, and explain how this might affect the standard deviation.

4 Recalculate the standard deviation of the pre-vaccine sample, excluding this outlier. Give your answer to 2 decimal places.

5 Explain how the removal of the outlier changed the reliability of the pre-vaccine sample.

Practice

Exam-style questions

1. Many different cells are involved in the non-specific and specific immune response.

   (a) Complete **Table 1.1** by naming the different immune cells that fit the description.

Immune cell	Description
	contains a lobed nucleus
	triggers secondary immune response
	contains major histocompatibility complex
	suppresses the immune response
	produces antibodies
	releases perforin
	releases histamines and cytokines
	contains a CD4 receptor

   Table 1.1 [8]

   (b) Antibodies are released as specific immunoglobulins that can target specific antigens.

   Describe their actions against pathogens.

   ....
   ....
   ....
   ....
   ....
   ....
   .... [6]

   > **Exam tip**
   >
   > You need to be familiar with the keywords to describe the roles antibodies have.

2. Malaria is a disease caused by a parasite.

   (a) The parasite enters the bloodstream to reproduce.

   (i) State the type of pathogen that causes malaria.

   .... [1]

   > **Synoptic links**
   >
   > 2.1.2.n   3.1.2.i

   (ii) Describe how the pathogen is transmitted between hosts.

   ....
   ....
   .... [2]

   (b) Sickle cell anaemia is a condition where an individual's Hb crystallises, increasing the likelihood of their red blood cells rupturing. When viewed under the microscope, these red blood cells have a half-moon, sickle shape, hence the disease is called sickle cell anaemia.

   > **Exam tip**
   >
   > For this question, you will need to draw your knowledge from previous chapters on protein structure and transport in animals.

11 Communicable diseases

(i) Describe the structure of haemoglobin.
....
....
....
.... [2]

(ii) Based on the information given, suggest one symptom these people display and explain why.
....
....
....
.... [2]

(iii) Suggest why people with sickle cell anaemia are resistant to malaria.
....
....
....
....
....
.... [3]

(c) The parasite that causes malaria reproduces inside red blood cells.

(i) Describe the action of another type of pathogen that also reproduces inside body cells leading to AIDS.
....
....
....
....
....
.... [3]

(ii) Once a T helper cell detects a cell that is infected with a pathogen, it releases interleukins to activated B cells to start the humoral immune response. Describe what happens to the B cells to destroy the pathogen.
....
....
....
....
....
....
.... [4]

3   Vaccination is a common practice used to prevent the spread of disease.

(a) Complete the following sentences by filling the gaps with the most appropriate words.

Vaccines contain .... pathogens or antigens and are injected into the bloodstream. This is an example of active, ... immunity, where the body is triggered to produce its own antibodies. A particular type of immune cell called .... cells are also produced. When the real pathogen enters the body in the future, those cells will recognise the pathogen and quickly undergo mitosis and differentiation to produce high levels of antibodies in a short amount of time. This is referred to as a .... response. However, in the case of the influenza vaccine, the vaccine may not work next year, as the viruses undergo quick mutations, changing their .... structure, meaning the immune cells made through vaccination may no longer recognise it. [5]

(b) The spread of influenza is largely stopped by flu vaccines. The vaccines are redeveloped every year due to the high mutation rate of the virus.

COVID-19 is an infectious disease caused by a virus called SARS-CoV-2. It has a spherical shape similar to the influenza virus.

(i) Suggest why flu vaccines cannot be used to limit the COVID-19 spread.

....
....
....
.... [2]

(ii) There are many types of vaccines. For the COVID-19 pandemic, mRNA vaccines are becoming the focus of research and development, where the mRNA of the pathogen is injected into the bloodstream, unlike conventional vaccines.

Suggest why mRNA vaccines may be safer than conventional vaccines for COVID-19.

....
....
....
....
....
.... [3]

(c) State one difference between active and passive immunity.

....
....
....
.... [2]

> **Exam tip**
>
> If a question asks you to simply 'state' something, there is no need to go into detail explaining what that aspect is.

11 Communicable diseases

(d) Describe what non-specific and specific mean in terms of immune defence.

State one example of each.

....
....
....
....
.... [4]

4   Different pathogens cause different diseases.

(a) Complete **Table 4.1** by stating the type of pathogen that causes each of the diseases.

Disease	Pathogen
ring rot	
black sigatoka	
potato blight	
influenza	

Synoptic link

2.1.2.m

Table 4.1   [4]

(b) When pathogens enter the body, our immune system creates antibodies as the primary response. **Figure 4.1** shows the concentration of antibodies in a person's blood following the initial infection.

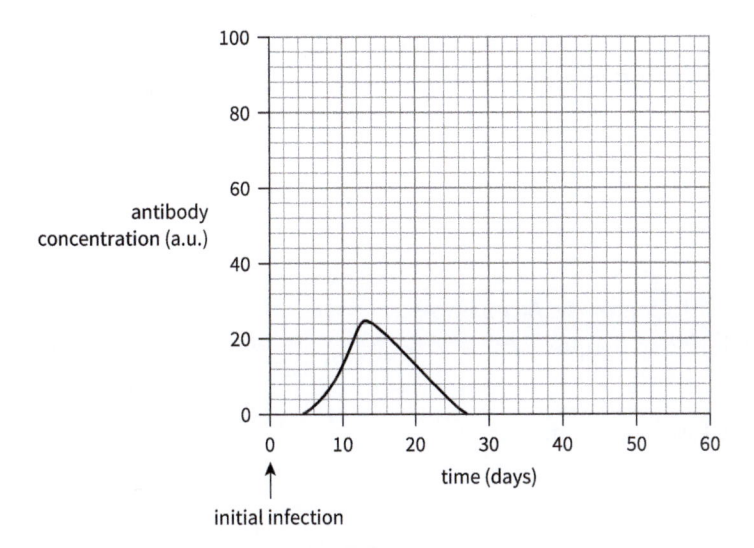

Figure 4.1

(i) Describe how the concentration of antibodies in this person's blood changes during the primary response.

....
....
....
....
.... [3]

(ii) This person was infected by the same pathogen at day 30. Draw a line on the graph to show the concentration of antibodies from day 30 onwards. [2]

(c) **Figure 4.2** shows the structure of an antibody.

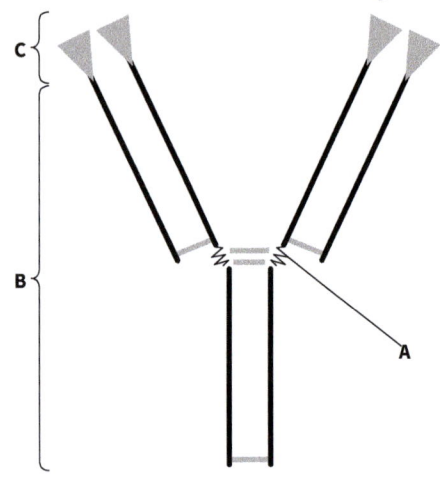

Figure 4.2

(i) State the type of bond labelled **A**.

.... [1]

(ii) State the name of region **C** and describe its function.

....
....
.... [2]

(iii) Considering the different levels of protein structures, explain how region **B** may interact with region **C**.

....
....
.... [2]

> **Exam tip**
>
> You will need to draw on your knowledge from the different levels of protein structure and the types of bond involved.

5 Autoantibodies are proteins that cause autoimmunity. An example is rheumatoid factors, which are often found in people with rheumatoid arthritis.

This is an autoimmune disease which leads to inflammation symptoms such as warm, swollen, and painful joints.

(a) Define what is meant by autoimmunity.

....
.... [1]

(b) Suggest how rheumatoid factors bring about the symptoms of rheumatoid arthritis.

....
....
....
....
....
.... [6]

> **Exam tip**
>
> To 'suggest' means to read the information given and draw conclusions based on your understanding of the topic. You will need to look for aspects within the information given that you can recognise and link to your understanding of the topic.

11 Communicable diseases

(c) Suggest a type of cell in the body that may prevent autoimmunity after an immune response to a non-self pathogen.

....

.... **[1]**

6 Influenza is the virus that causes flu. SARS-CoV-2 is a new strain of the same family of viruses, which causes a disease called COVID-19 with flu-like symptoms such as fever, coughing, or difficulty breathing. People are found to have an excessive amount of mucus in their respiratory system.

This infection can have some serious complications, such as pneumonia and acute respiratory distress syndrome (ARDS).

(a) Suggest a method of transmission of this virus.

....

.... **[1]**

(b) Suggest one way to reduce the chance of transmission and explain your suggestion.

....

....

....

.... **[2]**

(c) Based on the information given and your own knowledge, suggest which type of cell COVID-19 targets and explain how it can lead to pneumonia, which is lung inflammation.

....

....

....

....

....

.... **[3]**

(d) ARDS can be caused by an accumulation of fluids in the lungs. Symptoms include shortness of breath and fast breathing.

Explain why ARDS may cause a person to faint and collapse.

....

....

....

....

....

....

....

....

.... **[5]**

> **Synoptic links**
> 2.1.6h   3.1.1.c   3.1.1.d
> 3.1.1.e

> **Exam tip**
> You will need to use knowledge of gaseous exchange and specialised cells.

Knowledge

12 Biodiversity

Biodiversity

Biodiversity refers to the variety of living organisms within a particular area. It includes all the plants, animals, fungi, bacteria, and other microorganisms, as well as the genes they contain, and the ecosystems they inhabit.

Biodiversity is important in the study of habitats as an indicator of their health.

Maintaining biodiversity is important for the economy, aesthetics, and ecology, and action to preserve it must be taken at local, national, and global levels.

Biodiversity and variation

Biodiversity may be considered at different levels:
- Habitat biodiversity (e.g., sand dunes, woodland, meadows, streams)
- Species biodiversity (species richness and species evenness)
- Genetic biodiversity (e.g., different breeds or varieties within a species)

Why should biodiversity be maintained?

There are many reasons for maintaining biodiversity:
- **Ecological** – including protecting keystone species (interdependence of organisms) and maintaining genetic resources (e.g., crop wild species).
- **Economic** (financial) – including reducing soil depletion (continuous monoculture) so crop yields remain high.
- **Aesthetic** – including protecting beautiful landscapes, mental health, and emotional wellbeing.

136 12 Biodiversity

12

Species evenness and species richness

Species richness
- A measure of the number of different species in a habitat – the more species in a habitat the richer it is.
- Estimate using a qualitative study (i.e., observe and record the different species found in the habitat).

Species evenness
- A measure of the number of individuals of each species in a habitat.
- Requires a quantitative study:
  - plants – count individuals of each species or percentage cover
  - animals – can be counted directly, or a population estimated using a mark-recapture technique.

Calculating biodiversity

Simpson's Index of Diversity (D) can be used to calculate the biodiversity of a habitat, using both species richness and species evenness. It is always between 0 and 1.

Simpson's index of diversity:

$$D = 1 - \Sigma \left(\frac{n}{N}\right)^2$$

n = number of individuals of each species (or percentage cover for plants)
N = the total number of all individuals of all species (or percentage cover)

A Simpson's index value close to 1 shows a diverse habitat, rich in species number and population size. These habitats tend to be resilient to change (e.g., disease, famine, or drought).

A low value of Simpson's index shows a habitat dominated by one or a few species. A small change could be catastrophic for the habitat.

Calculating genetic diversity

Genetic diversity is an important indicator of population health. Monomorphic genes only have one form. However, most genes exist in several forms, alleles, which are also known as **polymorphisms**. The higher the number of polymorphisms in a population, the greater the genetic diversity.

The genetic diversity of a population can be calculated by:

$$\text{proportion of polymorphic gene loci} = \frac{\text{number of polymorphic gene loci}}{\text{total number of gene loci}}$$

Low genetic diversity can occur through inbreeding, so zoos, conservation programmes, and pedigree breeders must test regularly for polymorphisms.

Sampling

Sampling is a method of measuring the biodiversity of a habitat.

Sampling in the field can be:

- **random:**
  - where samples are measured at random sampling sites in a habitat
  - a random number generator could be used to select sites to prevent bias.
- **non-random:**
  - **stratified** – where samples are taken in proportion to the size of each population, which must be identified beforehand
  - **systematic** – where samples are taken at regular intervals (e.g., transects)
  - **opportunistic** – samples are selected deliberately.

Sampling techniques

The techniques used to sample a habitat will depend on the samples being collected and include:

- sweeping nets – to collect invertebrates in low-growing vegetation
- pitfall traps – to collect small invertebrates that are found on the soil surface or leaf litter
- pooters – to collect insects found in crevices or in sweep nets
- Tullgren funnel – to collect small invertebrates from soil and leaf litter
- kick sampling – to dislodge freshwater invertebrates on stream beds which are then collected in a pond net.

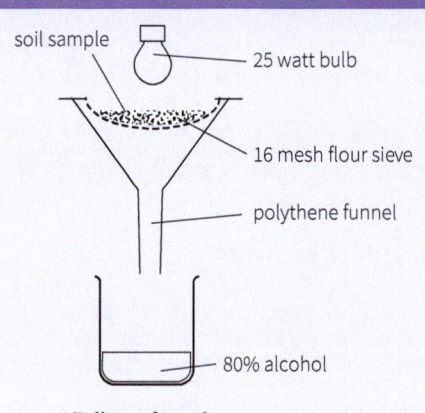

Tullgren funnel

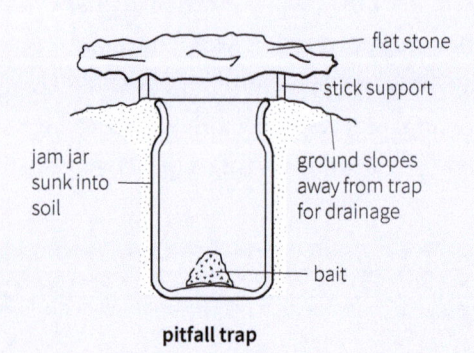

pitfall trap

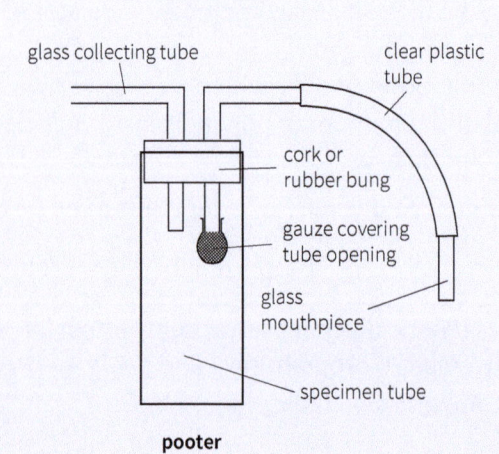

pooter

138   12 Biodiversity

12

Factors affecting biodiversity

Many factors affect biodiversity, usually by reducing it. These factors include:

- human population growth
- agriculture, including the growing of monocultures
- habitat destruction, such as deforestation for plantations
- climate change
- pollution, including plastic waste

In situ and *ex situ* methods of maintaining biodiversity

Conservation is the active management of an ecosystem to maintain biodiversity. In order to protect and maintain biodiversity, two forms of conservation exist:

In situ conservation
- Conservation in the natural habitat.
- Examples include marine conservation zones, national parks, and wildlife reserves.

Ex situ conservation
- Conservation in areas other than the natural habitat.
- Examples include seed banks, botanic gardens, and zoos' captive breeding programmes.

The Millennium seedbank stores seeds for thousands of plant species, so species can be saved from extinction

Legislation to protect biodiversity

The endangering of wildlife and loss of habitats is a global concern. At local, national, and international levels, conservation agreements exist to protect species and habitats.

Historic and current agreements include:

- The **Convention on International Trade in Endangered Species (CITES)** of wild flora and fauna – first agreed in 1973 to control the **trade** in wild species to protect their survival.
- The **Rio Convention on Biological Diversity (CBD)**, signed by 150 world leaders in 1992 to promote sustainable development.
- The **International Union of the Conservation of Nature Red List of Threatened Species** (also known as the **IUCN Red List**) was founded in 1964. The extinction risk of species is estimated through evaluating a list of specific criteria, from green (least concern) to black (extinct in the wild or extinct).

It is used all over the world to improve the conservation status of endangered species, and is considered to be the most comprehensive guide on global biodiversity.

Retrieval

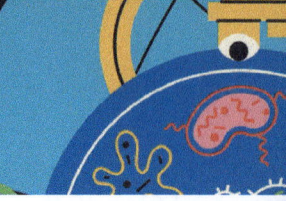

Learn the answers to the questions below, then cover the answers column with a piece of paper and write as many as you can. Check and repeat.

Questions	Answers
1. What is biodiversity?	the variety of living organisms within a particular area
2. List the three levels at which biodiversity can be considered.	habitat, species, genetic
3. List three examples of different habitats.	any three from: sand dunes, woodland, meadows, streams, oceans, rainforest,
4. List the two ways in which species diversity in a habitat is measured.	species richness and species evenness
5. What does genetic biodiversity mean?	the number of different alleles/polymorphisms per gene locus
6. What does species richness mean?	the number of different species in a habitat
7. What does species evenness mean?	the number of individuals of each species in a habitat
8. Why is calculating Simpson's index of diversity useful when studying a habitat?	it is based on both species richness and species evenness
9. What does a high index value tell you about a habitat?	the habitat is diverse and should be resilient to change (e.g., a new disease or new competition)
10. What is a pooter?	a device used to suck insects out of crevices
11. What is systematic sampling?	sampling carried out at regular intervals
12. What is stratified sampling?	when the sampling is proportional to the size of each population, which is determined beforehand
13. How would you calculate the genetic diversity within an isolated population?	divide number of polymorphic gene loci by the total number of gene loci
14. List three factors that affect biodiversity.	climate change, human activity/human population growth, agriculture
15. Give three reasons why biodiversity and habitats should be protected and maintained.	economic, aesthetic, ecological
16. Give five examples of *in situ* conservation projects.	any national park, marine reserve, protected woodland, site of special scientific interest, nature reserve
17. Give three examples of *ex situ* conservation projects.	Millennium (or other) seed bank, any zoo with a captive breeding programme, botanic garden
18. What does CITES stand for, and why was it set up?	the Convention on International Trade in Endangered Species, to control the trade of endangered wildlife
19. What does CBD stand for, and why was it set up?	Rio Convention on Biological Diversity, to promote sustainable development

12 Biodiversity

Maths skills

Practise your maths skills using the worked example and practice questions below.

Simpson's diversity index

Diversity can be measured in a number of ways, and they can tell you different things about the habitat you're studying:

Species richness: this is a measure of the number of species in a habitat.

Species evenness: this is a measure of the relative abundance of individuals from each species in a habitat.

A farmer's field and a meadow could both have the same species richness, but if the farmer's field is dominated by wheat, it has a lower species evenness and therefore lower diversity.

A good way of comparing diversity in two habitats is to calculate the Simpson's diversity index using the following equation:

$$D = 1 - \Sigma\left(\frac{n}{N}\right)^2$$

Where:

n = the total number of individuals from one species

N = the total number of individuals from all species

This equation takes both species richness and species evenness into account when calculating the diversity.

The higher the value, the higher the diversity in the habitat.

Worked example

Question

The table shows population data for two habitats, **X** and **Y**.

Species	Number of individuals	
	Habitat X	Habitat Y
wheat	10	200
field mouse	55	8
bee	105	40
beetle	90	12
total	260	260

Calculate the diversity index for habitat **X**. Give your answer to 3 significant figures.

Answer

You need to use the equation:

$$D = 1 - \Sigma\left(\frac{n}{N}\right)^2$$

You know that the total number of all individuals in the habitat is 260, so now you need to work out $\left(\frac{n}{N}\right)^2$, which is calculated per species, and shown in the table below:

Species	Number of individuals (n)	$\left(\frac{n}{N}\right)^2$
wheat	10	$(10 \div 260)^2 = 0.00148$
field mouse	55	$(55 \div 260)^2 = 0.0447$
bee	105	$(105 \div 260)^2 = 0.163$
beetle	90	$(90 \div 260)^2 = 0.119$
Total $\left(\Sigma\left(\frac{n}{N}\right)^2\right)$		0.342

Therefore,

$$D = 1 - \Sigma\left(\frac{n}{N}\right)^2$$
$$= 1 - 0.342$$
$$= 0.658$$

Practice

1. Calculate the diversity index for habitat **Y**. Give your answer to 3 significant figures.

2. Which habitat has the highest diversity?

3. Which habitat is most likely to be a farmer's field, and which is most likely to be a meadow?

   Explain your answer.

Practice

Exam-style questions

1. Kick sampling is a method that can be used to sample invertebrate populations that live on the bed of a stream.

    In kick sampling, a net is held underwater and the surrounding substrate is disturbed by kicking.

    (a) Describe how you would carry out a sampling investigation using this method.

    ....
    ....
    .... [3]

    Synoptic links
    4.1.1(a) 6.3.2(a) 6.3.2(b)

    (b) Describe one safety risk from this investigation and explain how you would manage it.

    ....
    .... [2]

    (c) The results from a kick sampling investigation are shown in **Tables 1.1** and **1.2**.

Factor	Area A	Area B
pH	3.2	6.8
temperature (°C)	4.0	11.0
number of parasitic worms	23	0

    Table 1.1

Invertebrate name	Numbers in Area A	Numbers in Area B
stoneflies	3	6
true bugs	8	15
beetles	14	20
dragonfly nymphs	2	9

    Table 1.2

    Use the data in **Tables 1.1** and **1.2** to identify, and suggest explanations for, the ideal conditions for dragonfly nymphs to survive in a stream.

    ....
    ....
    .... [3]

    > **Exam tip**
    > Remember to refer to the data provided in the tables and compare the two areas (**A** and **B**) as this is what the question specifically asks you to do.

    (d) In Area **B**, the beetles were collected over a period of 5 minutes. Calculate the rate of collection.

    ....
    .... [2]

12 Biodiversity

2 The populations of African elephants have declined constantly for the last 200 years, as shown in **Figure 2.1**.

African elephants were listed in CITES (Convention of International Trade in Endangered Species of Wild Fauna and Flora) in 1989.

Synoptic links
6.3.2(a)   6.3.2(b)

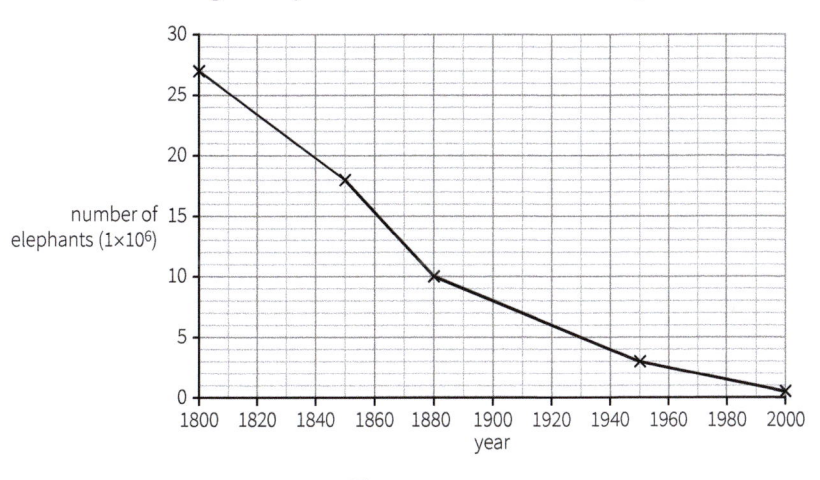

Figure 2.1

(a) Explain what is meant by the term population.
.... [1]

(b) Explain the purpose of CITES and the role it plays in the conservation of African elephants.
....
.... [2]

(c) Suggest why the population of African elephants continues to decline.
....
.... [2]

(d) Use the data in **Figure 2.1** to calculate the percentage decrease in the number of African elephants between 1800 and 1900.

.... % [2]

3 An investigation was carried out to determine the numbers of different species of butterflies in two areas (**A** and **B**).

The results are shown in **Table 3.1**.

Species of butterfly	Number of individuals	
	Area A	Area B
small tortoiseshell	3	42
red admiral	4	5
speckled wood	74	17
common blue	21	19
marbled white	6	25

Table 3.1

(a) Calculate the percentage increase in the number of marbled white butterflies from area **A** to area **B**.

........................% **[2]**

(b) Calculate the Simpson's Index of diversity (*D*) for area **B** using the following formula:

$$D = 1 - \sum \left(\frac{n}{N}\right)^2$$

.... **[3]**

(c) Area **A** has a *D* value of 0.49.

Use this value and the data provided to compare the biodiversity of area **A** and area **B**.

....

....

....

....

....

.... **[6]**

> **Exam tip**
>
> Use all of the data and the index of diversity value you have been given for area **A** to help you answer this question and to gain full marks.

4 Farming can have impacts on biodiversity, as shown in **Figure 4.1**.

number of individuals

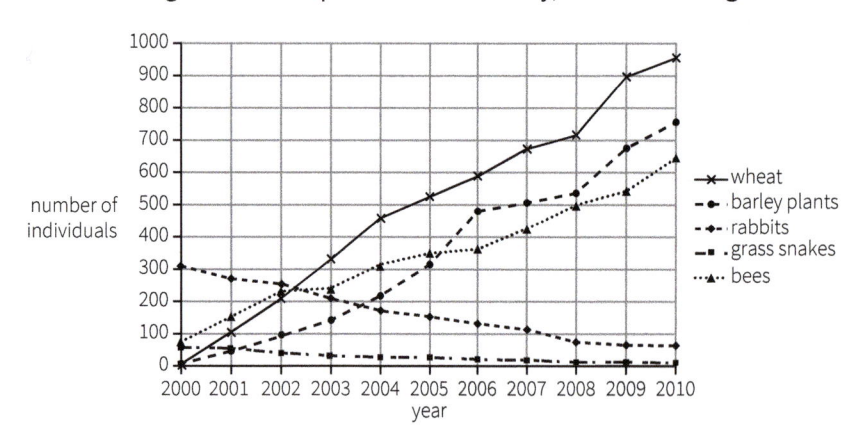

— wheat
— barley plants
— rabbits
— grass snakes
— bees

year

Figure 4.1

(a) Explain what is meant by the term species richness. **[1]**

(b) Suggest how farming could have a negative effect on biodiversity. **[2]**

(c) Suggest the measures that could be put in place to counteract these negative effects. **[2]**

(d) Explain how human population growth and climate change could further negatively effect the biodiversity of crops. **[6]**

> **Exam tip**
>
> Try to memorise as many definitions related to ecology as you can, you could be asked to recall the definitions of any of them.

144 12 Biodiversity

5   **Table 5.1** shows how Nilgiri Pipit bird (*Anthus nilghiriensis*) is classified by scientists.

(a) Complete **Table 5.1** by filling in the blank spaces.   [2]

Taxon	Specific name of taxon
Domain	Eukaryota
	Animalia
	Chordata
	Aves
	Passeriformes
	Motacillidae
Species	

Table 5.1

> **Synoptic link**
> 4.2.2

Scientists investigated genetic diversity in different bird species, as shown in **Table 5.2**.

Bird species	Total number of genes examined	Number of genes showing genetic diversity
African broadbill	467	133
collared crescentchest	328	123
sharpbill	844	596
whitehead	555	84
superb lyrebird	231	200

Table 5.2

(b) Explain what is meant by the term genetic diversity.   [2]

(c) A scientist claimed that sharpbills display the highest genetic diversity.

Evaluate this claim, and explain your reasoning.   [3]

> **Exam tip**
> Remember to calculate the proportions for sharpbills and other birds that seem high – this will help you determine your answer.

6   **Table 6.1** shows part of the primary structure of the protein responsible for eye colour in four species.

Species	Amino acid sequence					
1	arg	ser	val	tyr	glu	glu
2	arg	val	tyr	tyr	arg	glu
3	arg	val	val	tyr	glu	glu
4	tyr	ser	val	arg	glu	glu

Table 6.1

> **Synoptic links**
> 6.1.1   6.1.3

(a) Outline the different methods which are used to compare genetic diversity in isolated populations of different species.   [3]

(b) State what causes the base sequences of genes to change.   [1]

(c) Explain which species (**2**, **3** or **4**) is most closely related to species **1**, using the information provided in **Table 6.1**.   [2]

(d) Explain how a gene is inserted into a plasmid vector.   [3]

> **Exam tip**
> For part **(c)**, look carefully at each row in the table and try to identify differences in **2**, **3**, and **4** compared to **1**.

Knowledge

13 Classification and evolution

Taxonomy

All organisms share a **common ancestor**, from which they diversified into the forms we have today through variation and evolution. Because of this fact, techniques of **classification** can be used to make a **taxonomy** of life on Earth. Smaller groups are placed within larger groups, with no overlap between them. Each group is called a taxon (plural taxa).

The **hierarchy** now used, from the largest taxon to the smallest, is:

domain, kingdom, phylum, class, order, family, genus, species.

Trees of life used to be solely based on physical similarities between organisms, but now we can use many other lines of evidence, such as genetics, biochemistry, and the fossil record to construct **phylogenetic trees** to illustrate relationships.

Classification

Living organisms can be classified into groups based on their shared characteristics. Until recently, classification divided life into five **kingdoms:** Prokaryotae, Protoctista, Fungi, Plantae, Animalia.

Based on recent evidence, the new taxon **domain** comes above kingdom. There are three domains: Bacteria, Archaea, and Eukarya.

Each species is universally identified by a **binomial** consisting of the name of its **genus** and **species** (e.g., *Homo sapiens*).

Remember: the genus name must always start with a capital letter, but the species name is always be lowercase. You could lose marks for this in an exam.

Taxonomic rank	Lion	Human	Whale shark
Kingdom	Animalia	Animalia	Animalia
Phylum	Chordata	Chordata	Chordata
Class	Mammalia	Mammalia	Chondrichthyes
Order	Carnivora	Primate	Orectolobiformes
Family	Felidae	Hominidae	Rhincodontidae
Genus	*Panthera*	*Homo*	*Rhincodon*
Species	*leo*	*sapiens*	*typus*

Details of the three domains

Each of the domains contains unique ribosomal RNA (rRNA).

Bacteria (prokaryotes)	Archaea (prokaryotes)	Eukarya (eukaryotes)
They differ from Archaea as they have slightly different membranes. Hugely diverse and impossible to decide upon the number of species of bacteria as they can share genetic information through horizontal gene transfer. For example, cyanobacteria.	These often inhabit extreme environments because they have adaptations in their cell membranes to withstand high temperature, pH, and salt concentrations. They are very small in size, similar to bacteria or mitochondria.	These have membrane-bound organelles and are divided into four kingdoms: Protoctista, Fungi, Plantae, Animalia.

13

Features and evidence used in classification

A **biological species** is: a group of similar organisms that can breed together to produce fertile offspring.

For asexual organisms (e.g., bacteria and some plants), we use the **phylogenetic species definition**: the smallest group of organisms that are descended from a single common ancestor.

Classification can be achieved through comparing observable features.

Fossil record
Fossilisation occurs in particular conditions, where hard tissues (such as bones and teeth) are replaced with minerals in sedimentary rock. The fossil record is a useful tool to see how organisms evolved over time, and when different species started to appear (e.g., horses and humans). However, the fossil record is incomplete, so there are some gaps in what we know of past diversity.

DNA evidence
Comparing DNA can help determine how closely related different species are. The fewer genetic similarities, the more distantly related the species are.

Molecular evidence
Like DNA, other molecules can be compared for similarities (e.g., RNA and DNA polymerase are vital enzymes that have evolved slowly over time, but have been present since the earliest organisms).

Natural selection

In a population, not all organisms survive to be able to reproduce. Individuals die or fail to reproduce due to predation, disease, or competition for resources: food, water, space, mates, and environmental change.

There is **genetic variation** in a population.

Organisms with characteristics that allow them to survive will have a selective advantage when there is a new **selection pressure**, and are more likely to reproduce (higher **reproductive success**). This is **natural selection**.

Favourable alleles are passed onto the next generation. Those allele frequencies increase in the gene pool over many generations.

Evolution is the change of allele frequency within a population over time as a result of these processes.

Evidence for the theory of evolution by natural selection

Contribution of Darwin and Wallace
Although Charles Darwin is credited with the theory of evolution by natural selection from his fieldwork on the Galapogos islands, Alfred Russel Wallace reached a similar conclusion at the same time from his fieldwork in Malaysia. They later worked together, leading Darwin to publish *On the Origin of Species*.

Different types of variation

Intraspecific and interspecific variation
Intraspecific variation: variation between individuals within the same species.
Interspecific variation: variation between individuals in different species.

Continuous and discontinuous variation
Continuous variation: No distinct groups, quantitative differences in phenotype (e.g., mass, height).
Discontinuous variation: Distinct groups, qualitative differences in phenotypes (e.g., blood groups, eye colour).

Convergent evolution

Organisms from different taxonomic groups can have similar anatomical features. This is because they have adapted through natural selection to occupy similar niches.

For example, even though marsupials and placental mammals diverged over 100 million years ago, the **marsupial mole** and **placental mole** have evolved to converge and share these anatomical features.

This phenomenon can be seen in many marsupials and their placental counterparts.

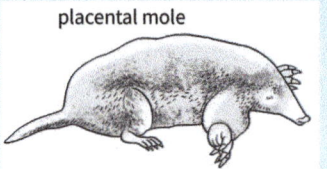

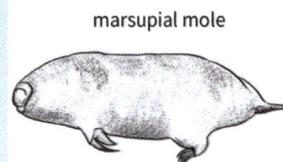

placental mole

marsupial mole

Causes of variation

Environmental
The conditions in which an organism develops can cause variation. For example, intensity of light and the supply of water and nutrients will cause variation in the phenotype of plants.

Genetic
1 **Mutation** – a random, spontaneous change in the base sequence of DNA
2 **Meiosis** – two main events that can cause variation:
   - **independent assortment** of homologous chromosomes
   - **crossing over** that happens between the non-sister chromatids of homologous chromosomes.
3 **Random fertilisation of gametes** – sperm and egg (or equivalent) meet by chance, contributing to novel combinations of alleles.

Investigating variation in a species

Quantitative investigations of variation within a species involve:
- collecting data from random samples from a single population
- calculating a mean value and the standard deviation of that mean
- interpreting mean values and their standard deviations.

Random samples must be collected to reduce the risk of sampling bias. Sampling bias can also be reduced by having a large sample size.

The standard deviation gives an indication of the range of values about the mean. A large standard deviation means there is a lot of variation between the values.

The calculation for standard deviation is:

$$s = \sqrt{\frac{\sum(x - \bar{X})^2}{n - 1}}$$

x = measured value
$\bar{X}$ = mean of all values recorded
n = number of values recorded

13 Classification and evolution

Adaptations

Adaptations are inherited features that allow an organism to survive in its niche. Adaptations can be anatomical, physiological, or behavioural.

1 **Anatomical** (related to bodily structure)
   - in high-predator environments, water fleas tend to have thicker exoskeletons than those in low-predator environments
   - some bacteria have flagella to help them move independently

2 **Physiological** (related to bodily function)
   - animal species, such as yaks, that live in high altitudes have more red blood cells that support living in low-oxygen conditions than those at low altitudes
   - plants produce bitter-tasting chemicals when being eaten and have stomata that close to prevent water loss
   - yeast change biochemical pathways in response to environmental sugar levels

3 **Behavioural** (related to behaviour)
   - fish that shoal decrease their individual chance of being eaten by a predator
   - some bacteria will move towards food sources

New species – speciation

Under certain conditions, a new species can arise from a population of an existing species.
If two populations are reproductively separated, their gene pools become different.
If these differences make it impossible for the two populations to breed and produce fertile offspring, they become two species.

Spearman's rank correlation coefficient (r_s)

This tells us the strength and direction of a correlation between two variables.
Correlation will always fall between +1.0 and –1.0.

- If r_s is a **negative** number, it shows that there is a negative relationship between the two variables.
- If r_s is a **positive** number, it shows that there is a positive relationship between the two variables.
- If r_s = 0, there is **no relationship** between the variables.

The closer r_s is to +1.0 or –1.0, the **stronger the correlation** and therefore the better it is to use for predictions.

$$r_s = 1 - \frac{6\sum d^2}{n(n^2 - 1)}$$

n = number in sample
$\sum$ = sum of
d = difference between the two variables X and Y

Retrieval

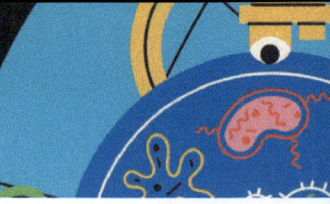

Learn the answers to the questions below, then cover the answers column with a piece of paper and write as many as you can. Check and repeat.

	Questions	Answers
1	What is taxonomy?	the science of naming, defining, and classifying groups of organisms based on their shared characteristics
2	What are the names of the five kingdoms?	Prokaryotae, Protoctista, Fungi, Plantae, Animalia
3	List the classification ranks from kingdom to species.	kingdom, phylum, class, order, family, genus, species
4	Compare the domains Bacteria and Archaea.	both prokaryotes; different properties of membranes; Archaea are usually extremophiles
5	What is the definition of a species?	a group of similar organisms that can breed together to produce fertile offspring
6	What is the phylogenetic definition of a species?	a group of individual organisms that are very similar in appearance, anatomy, physiology, biochemistry, genetics
7	Which two scientists came up with the theory of evolution through natural selection?	Charles Darwin and Alfred Russel Wallace
8	Give two examples of mammals that have a comprehensive fossil record showing their evolution.	horses and humans
9	What are the limitations of using the fossil record as evidence for evolution?	incomplete, only bones (hard parts) are fossilised
10	What are the three causes of genetic variation?	1 mutation 2 meiosis (independent assortment and crossing over) 3 random fertilisation of gametes
11	What is the difference between intraspecific competition and interspecific variation?	intraspecific variation is the variation between individuals within the same species; interspecific variation is the variation between individuals in different species
12	Define selection pressure.	a condition in the environment that gives organisms with particular alleles an advantage that allows them to survive and are thus more likely to reproduce
13	What is continuous variation? Give an example.	no distinct groups; quantitative differences in phenotype (e.g., mass, height)
14	What type of adaptation is a bird's beak to eating hard seeds?	anatomical
15	What type of adaptation is herding in zebra?	behavioural

Maths skills

Practise your maths skills using the worked example and practice questions below.

Calculating the area of a circle

The ability of an antibiotic to inhibit bacterial growth can be demonstrated using antibiotic-impregnated paper discs placed on the surface of agar that has been spread with bacteria.

After incubation, zones of inhibition around the discs (where the bacteria have not grown) can be measured, and the area of the zone of inhibition can be calculated.

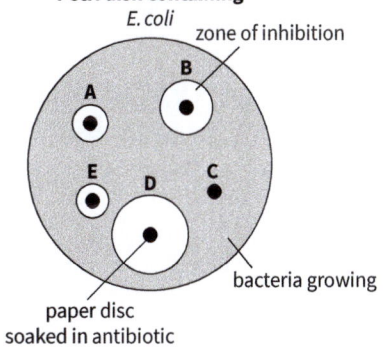

The antibiotic with the largest zone of inhibition is usually considered to be the most effective.

Worked example

Question
A zone of inhibition has a diameter of 0.7 cm. Calculate the area of the zone of inhibition.

Answer
To calculate the area of a circle, you use the equation:

$$\text{area} = \pi r^2$$

r is the radius of a circle, which the distance from the centre of a circle to the edge. Therefore, you need to halve the diameter to find r:

$$0.7 \div 2 = 0.35$$

Then you can use the π on your calculator to find the area of the circle:

$$\begin{aligned}\text{area} &= \pi r^2 \\ &= 3.14... \times (0.35)^2 \\ &= 3.14... \times 0.1225 \\ &= 0.4 \text{ cm}^2\end{aligned}$$

Practice

1 Calculate the areas for the zones of inhibition in the table below:

Antibiotic	Diameter of zone of inhibition (cm)	Area of zone of inhibition (cm²)
A	0.2	
B	2.4	
C	1.7	
D	0.3	
E	0.9	
control	0.0	

2 Which antibiotic produced the largest zone of inhibition?

3 Why might your answer to **2** not be the most effective antibiotic as a treatment for an infection by the bacterium?

4 Why do you use a control in this investigation? What would you use as a control?

Practice

Exam-style questions

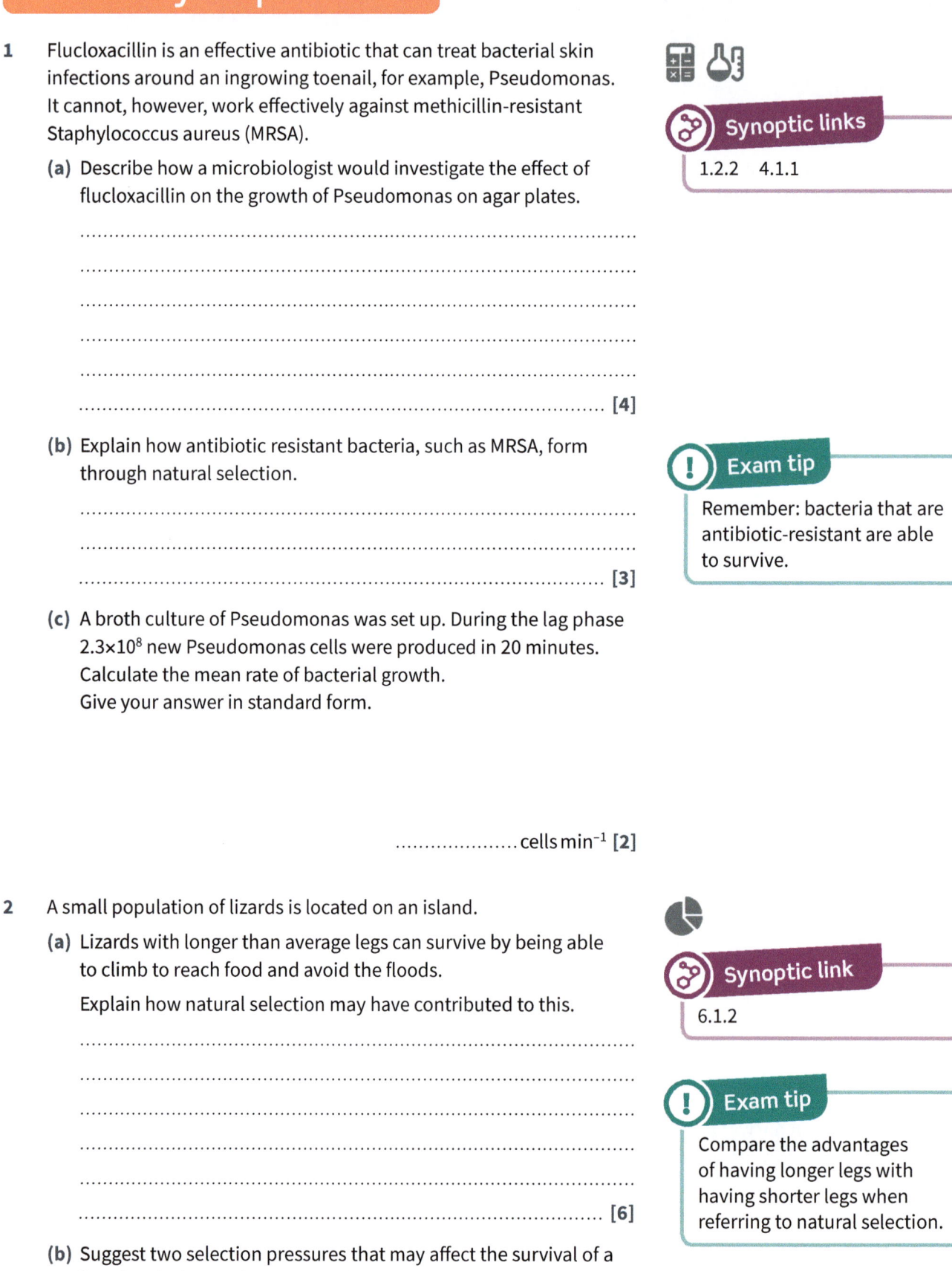

1 Flucloxacillin is an effective antibiotic that can treat bacterial skin infections around an ingrowing toenail, for example, Pseudomonas. It cannot, however, work effectively against methicillin-resistant Staphylococcus aureus (MRSA).

(a) Describe how a microbiologist would investigate the effect of flucloxacillin on the growth of Pseudomonas on agar plates.

....
....
....
....
....
.... **[4]**

Synoptic links

1.2.2   4.1.1

(b) Explain how antibiotic resistant bacteria, such as MRSA, form through natural selection.

....
....
.... **[3]**

Exam tip

Remember: bacteria that are antibiotic-resistant are able to survive.

(c) A broth culture of Pseudomonas was set up. During the lag phase 2.3×10^8 new Pseudomonas cells were produced in 20 minutes. Calculate the mean rate of bacterial growth.
Give your answer in standard form.

.... cells min^{-1} **[2]**

2 A small population of lizards is located on an island.

(a) Lizards with longer than average legs can survive by being able to climb to reach food and avoid the floods.
Explain how natural selection may have contributed to this.

....
....
....
....
....
.... **[6]**

Synoptic link

6.1.2

Exam tip

Compare the advantages of having longer legs with having shorter legs when referring to natural selection.

(b) Suggest two selection pressures that may affect the survival of a lizard with shorter than average legs.

....
.... **[2]**

13 Classification and evolution

(c) Suggest why genetic drift could be a significant problem with this population of lizards.

....
....
....
.... [2]

3   There are different intensities of the colour green in beetles that live in woodlands. Those that are darker green are more likely to survive than those that are lighter green.

The darker green beetle has the genotype **AA** and the lighter green beetle has the genotype **aa**.

(a) State which type of selection affects these beetles.
    Explain your answer. [3]

(b) An allele **A** has a frequency of 0.3. Use the Hardy-Weinberg equations below to calculate the frequency of genotypes of individuals in the whole population.

$$p^2 + 2pq + q^2 = 1 \qquad p + q = 1$$ [3]

(c) State the assumptions that must be met for the Hardy-Weinberg equation to work correctly. [3]

Synoptic link
6.1.2

Exam tip
Have a think about the type of selection that can benefit one extreme phenotype compared to another.

4   Table 4.1 shows the characteristics of the three domains.

Characteristic	Bacteria	Archaea	Eukarya
nuclear membrane	absent	absent	present
cell wall	present (peptidoglycan)	present (pseudopeptidoglycan)	present in Plantae but not in Animalia
protein synthesis initiation	formylmethionine	methionine	methionine
rRNA loop	present	absent	absent
size of ribosomes	70S	70S	80S
sensitive to antibiotics	yes	no	no
reproduction	asexual	asexual	asexual and sexual

Table 4.1

Synoptic links
2.1.2   2.1.3   HSW 5c

(a) Scientists generally agree with the three-domain model. Describe the process that led to the majority of scientists coming to such an agreement. [2]

(b) Analyse the information in **Table 4.1** to explain the evidence supporting the three-domain model of classification. [3]

(c) Methionine is the first amino acid involved in protein synthesis in Eukarya.

Describe how translation occurs to form the primary structure of a protein starting with methionine. [4]

5 *Patella rustica* (sea snails) live on rocks.

At low tide, these sea snails are at risk of dying from desiccation (dryness) so to avoid this, they clamp against the rocks.

An ecologist decided to investigate the relationship between the size of sea snails and their location on the shore.

Synoptic link

4.2.1

A 50 m transect was used, which started at the lowest water mark and extended up the shore. A 1 m² quadrat was placed at 5 m intervals along this transect and the diameters of a sample of 10 sea snails were measured.

The data are shown in **Table 5.1**.

Distance from the lowest water mark (m)	Rank of distance	Mean diameter of sea snails (mm)	Rank of mean diameters	Difference in the two ranks (d)	d^2
0	10	19.6	2	8	64
5	9	19.4			
10	8	20.2	1	7	49
15	7	16.2	7	0	0
20	6	16.8	6	0	0
25	5	17.1	5	0	0
30	4	17.2			
35	3	15.8	8	−5	25
40	2	10.4			
45	1	8.4	10	−9	81

Table 5.1

(a) State the genus of the sea snails. [1]

(b) Complete the missing data in **Table 5.1**. [3]

(c) (i) Calculate the Spearman's rank correlation coefficient for the mean diameter of sea snails and their distance from the lowest water mark, using the following equation:

$$r_s = 1 - \frac{6(\sum d^2)}{n(n^2 - 1)}$$
[3]

(c) (ii) Using your answer to **5 (c) (i)**, state and describe the correlation between the mean diameter of sea snails and their distance from the lowest water mark. [2]

(d) Another ecologist checks the data and states that there may be anomalous results.

Suggest what practical measures the ecologist could implement to reduce the likelihood of anomalous results in this investigation. [2]

6 Benzimidazole is a fungicide used to treat apple scab, which is caused by a fungus and leads to the deformation of the fruit, as shown in **Figure 6.1**.

Synoptic link
6.1.3

Figure 6.1

Table 6.2 shows the impact of using Benzimidazole fungicides on treating apple scab in an orchard where there is a significant issue.

Years after application	Incidence of apple scab (%)
0	70
2	55
4	12
6	6
7	23
8	49
9	62
10	78

Table 6.2

(a) Describe the features of the microbe that would lead to the apple scab pathogen being classified as a fungus. [2]

(b) Explain the data trends in **Table 6.2**, referring to the process of natural selection within your answer. [6]

(c) Genetic engineering using the HcrVf2 gene can create apple trees resistant to apple scab. PCR is used to produce many copies of the HcrVf2 gene.

Describe the process of PCR. [4]

Knowledge

14 Communication and homeostasis

Responding to change

Homeostasis is the maintenance of a steady internal state regardless of external changes. **Multicellular organisms** (e.g., plants and animals) use **chemical** and **electrical systems** to monitor and respond to any deviation from the body's steady state.

These changes can be brought about by:
- changes in the internal environment
- changes in the external environment.

Organisms have **communication systems** so that any response to a change is coordinated, including the activities of different organs.

Cell signalling

In order to produce a coordinated response, cells communicate with each other using **cell signalling**. This includes signalling between both adjacent cells and distant cells. A good communication system must be able to:
- cover the whole body
- enable cell to cell communication
- be specific and rapid
- give short term or long term responses.

There are two communication systems that work by cell signalling: the neuronal system and the hormonal system.

Comparing neuronal and hormonal cell signalling

System	neuronal system	hormonal system
Communication mechanism	nerve impulses	hormones
Nature of communication	electrical	chemical
Transmitted via	neurones	bloodstream
Speed of transmission	very rapid	slow
Response destination	specific muscles or glands in body	all over body but only cells in target tissues or organs respond
Effect caused by the response	localised	widespread
Speed of response	rapid	slow
Duration of the communication	short lived	can be long term
Duration of the effect	short term and temporary	short term and temporary or long term and permanent

14 Communication and homeostasis

14

Receptors and effectors in the nervous system

In order for an organism to respond to a stimulus and make changes in response to the stimulus, it must have specialised cells, **receptors**, to detect the stimulus and **effectors**, usually a **gland** or a **muscle**, to respond to it.

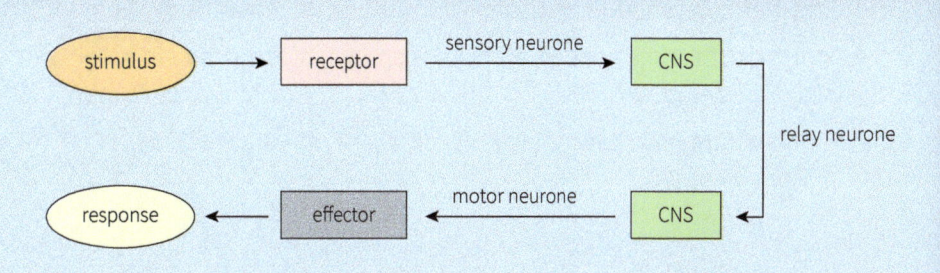

stimulus → receptor → sensory neurone → CNS → relay neurone → CNS → motor neurone → effector → response

Negative and positive feedback

Many conditions in the body are controlled by **feedback** systems.

Most feedback systems are **negative feedback** loops where a change from the set level will cause the body or cell to correct that change to bring it back to the normal value.

For example, blood glucose concentration and body temperature.

In a **positive feedback** system, the feedback causes the change to increase still further from the set level.

For example, the production of breast milk, contractions of uterine muscles during labour, and the generation of an action potential.

However, positive feedback mechanisms can be damaging to the body.

For example, when body core temperature becomes too low, positive feedback mechanisms cause the temperature to drop even lower (hypothermia).

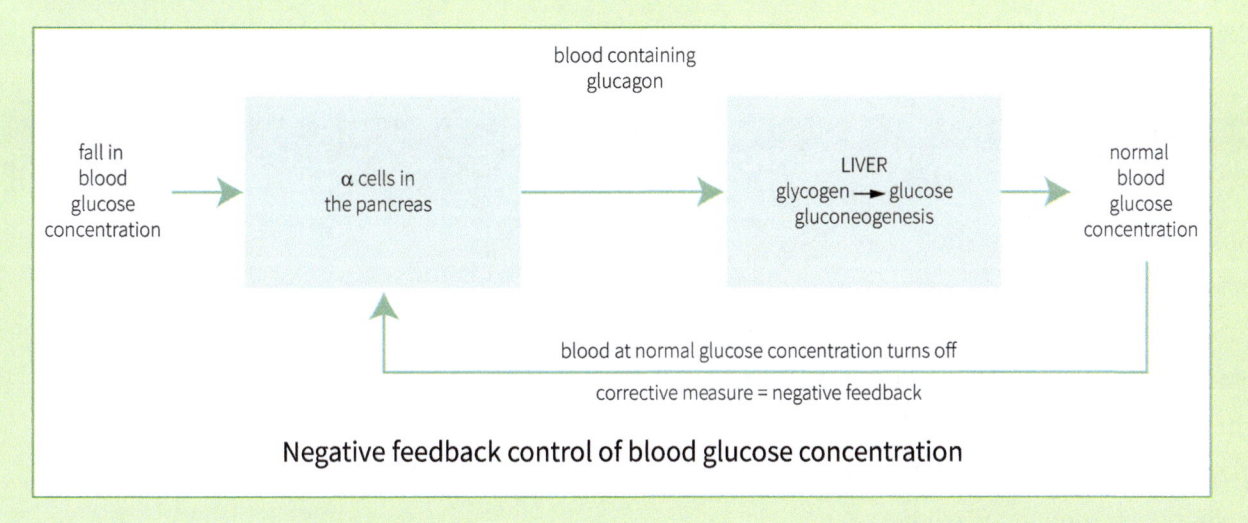

fall in blood glucose concentration → α cells in the pancreas → blood containing glucagon → LIVER glycogen → glucose gluconeogenesis → normal blood glucose concentration

blood at normal glucose concentration turns off
corrective measure = negative feedback

Negative feedback control of blood glucose concentration

Temperature control in endotherms and ectotherms

Organisms have to maintain a suitable body temperature so their enzymes can function at a specific, optimum temperature.

An organism can have two types of response to maintain an ideal body temperature.

- **Physiological** responses: automatic changes in the body. For example:
  - sweating
  - panting
  - shivering
- **Behavioural** responses: usually involve the whole organism. For example:
  - moving into the sun
  - moving into the shade

Temperature control in ectotherms

Ectotherms have a body temperature that tends to fluctuate with the external environment and they rely on external sources to keep warm or cool.

They use both physiological responses and behavioural responses to maintain a suitable body temperature.

Behavioural	Physiological
basking in the sun or moving into the shade	alter body shape to increase or decrease surface area
change body orientation to the sun	change breathing rate

Behavioural responses to change temperature

Examples of behaviour if too hot:
- move into shade
- spread limbs out
- remain inactive
- hide in burrow
- orientate body to reduce surface exposed to sun.

Examples of behaviour if too cold:
- move into sunlight and maximise surface area exposed to sun
- curl up to reduce surface area
- move about

14

Temperature control in endotherms

Endotherms (such as mammals and birds) maintain a core body temperature within very strict limits, largely independent of the external environment, through both **physiological** and **behavioural** responses.

Physiological responses

Endotherms have two types of receptors to detect changes in temperature:

a) Internal temperature is monitored and controlled by the **hypothalamus** in the brain through a negative feedback mechanism.

b) External temperature is detected by **peripheral temperature receptors** in the skin.

The hypothalamus sends nerve impulses to effectors in the skin and muscles to bring about responses to lower or raise body temperature.

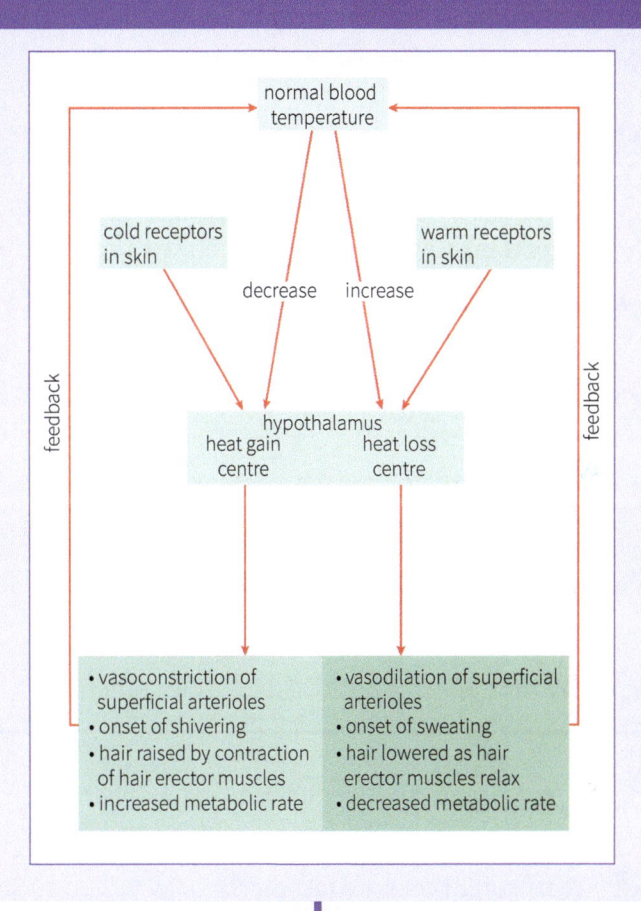

```
                    normal blood
                     temperature
        ┌─────────────────┴─────────────────┐
   cold receptors                      warm receptors
      in skin          decrease  increase    in skin
        │                                       │
        └──────────────┐         ┌──────────────┘
  feedback         hypothalamus                feedback
                  heat gain   heat loss
                   centre      centre
                      │           │
                      ▼           ▼
        • vasoconstrictionof      • vasodilation of superficial
          superficial arterioles    arterioles
        • onset of shivering      • onset of sweating
        • hair raised by contraction  • hair lowered as hair
          of hair erector muscles   erector muscles relax
        • increased metabolic rate  • decreased metabolic rate
```

Physiological changes to reduce body temperature

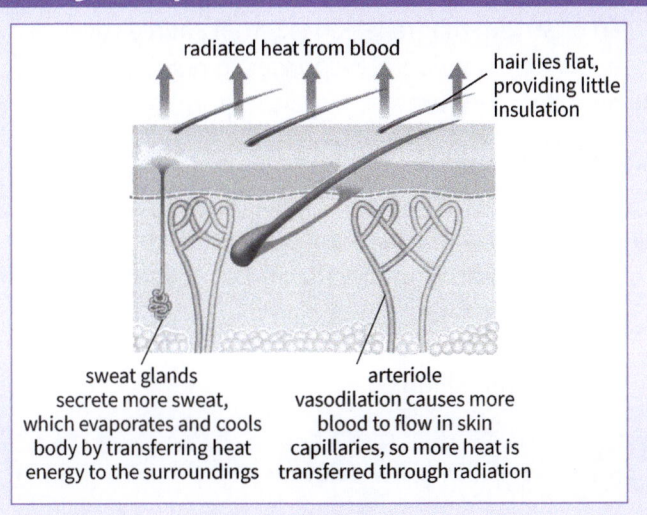

radiated heat from blood

hair lies flat, providing little insulation

sweat glands secrete more sweat, which evaporates and cools body by transferring heat energy to the surroundings

arteriole vasodilation causes more blood to flow in skin capillaries, so more heat is transferred through radiation

Physiological changes to increase body temperature

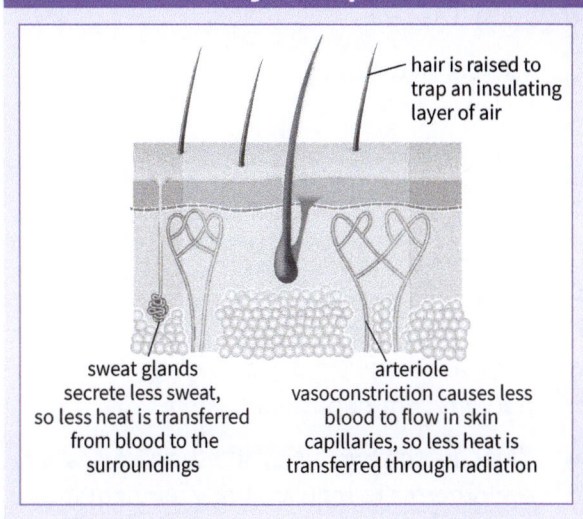

hair is raised to trap an insulating layer of air

sweat glands secrete less sweat, so less heat is transferred from blood to the surroundings

arteriole vasoconstriction causes less blood to flow in skin capillaries, so less heat is transferred through radiation

Retrieval

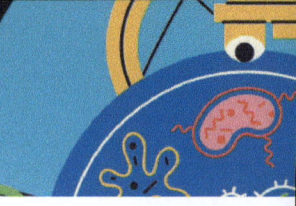

Learn the answers to the questions below, then cover the answers column with a piece of paper and write as many as you can. Check and repeat.

Questions	Answers
1. What is homeostasis?	the maintenance of a relatively stable internal environment
2. Why do organisms need communication systems?	so they can coordinate their responses to changes in their internal and external environments
3. Why does a communication system need receptors?	to detect changes in the internal and external environment
4. What are the two types of cell signalling?	hormones (chemical) and nervous (electrical) impulses
5. What is a negative feedback loop?	a change from the normal will cause the body to correct that change to bring it back to the set value
6. Give two examples of negative feedback systems.	control of blood glucose concentrations and body temperature
7. What is a positive feedback system?	where the change causes a greater move away from the set value
8. Give examples of positive feedback systems.	breast milk production, contraction of uterine muscles during labour, generation of an action potential, hypothermia
9. When can positive feedback be dangerous?	when someone is suffering from hypothermia
10. What sort of cells are receptors?	specialised cells that convert detected stimuli into nerve impulses
11. What is an endotherm?	an organism that is able to control its body temperature within strict limits independently of the external temperature
12. What is an ectotherm?	an organism that relies on external sources of heat and behavioural responses to regulate body temperature
13. Give behavioural responses of how ectotherms regulate body temperature.	move into or out of sunlight, decrease or increase exposure to sun (e.g., basking, alter breathing rate)
14. What are the properties of a good communication system?	cover the whole body, enable cell to cell communication, be specific and rapid and give short term or long term responses
15. What are the two types of effectors in the nervous communication system?	muscles and glands
16. What are the two types of response used by endotherms to regulate body temperature?	physiological and behavioural

14 Communication and homeostasis

14

Maths skills

Practise your maths skills using the worked example and practice questions below.

Calculating energy efficiency in food chains

A food chain shows the flow of energy through an ecosystem. It is important to understand how efficiently this energy is passed between trophic (feeding) levels in a food chain.

$$\frac{\text{energy transferred}}{} = \frac{\text{energy available after transfer}}{\text{energy available before transfer}} \times 100$$

Energy in food chains can be wasted through energy being needed to consume or digest the food item, some of the food item being inedible (such as bones), movement, respiration, and excretion.

The longer the food chain is, the more energy is wasted between the producer and the final consumer.

The closer the amount of energy available after the transfer is to the amount of energy available before the transfer, the more efficient the energy transfer is.

Worked example

Question
The diagram shows energy transfers along a food chain.

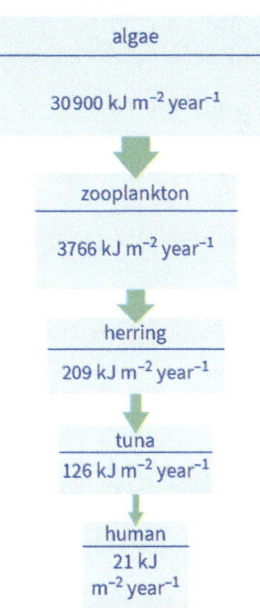

algae
30 900 kJ m^{-2} year^{-1}
↓
zooplankton
3766 kJ m^{-2} year^{-1}
↓
herring
209 kJ m^{-2} year^{-1}
↓
tuna
126 kJ m^{-2} year^{-1}
↓
human
21 kJ m^{-2} year^{-1}

Calculate the percentage efficiency of the energy transfer from algae to zooplankton.

Answer
From the diagram, you can see that:

Algae = 30 900 kJ m^{-2} year^{-1}

Zooplankton = 3766 kJ m^{-2} year^{-1}

$$\text{Efficiency} = \frac{30\,900}{3766}$$

$$= 0.122$$

Now, you can convert that value into a percentage

$0.122 \times 100 = 12.2\%$

Practice

1. Energy stored is measured over a certain area for a specific time period. Suggest a suitable unit for energy stored.

2. Calculate the energy transferred expressed as percentage efficiency between:
   a. ooplankton and herring
   b. herring and tuna
   c. tuna and humans

3. Herrings can also be eaten by humans. Humans gain 100 kJ m^{-2} year^{-1} of energy from herrings. How does this improve the percentage of energy transferred?

4. Some marine algae, including seaweed, are high in micronutrients and are edible. Should humans eat edible algae rather than fish?

Practice

Exam-style questions

1. Endotherms can use physiological responses to control body temperature.

   (a) (i) Complete **Table 1.1** by placing ticks (✓) in the relevant boxes to show whether each physiological response would have a cooling effect or a warming effect in an endotherm.

Physiological response	Warming effect	Cooling effect
hairs lying flat on skin		
shivering		
reduced metabolic rate in the liver		
increase in sweating		

   Table 1.1

   [4]

   (ii) Explain the effect that vasodilation near the skin surface has on an endotherm's body temperature.

   ....
   ....
   ....
   ....
   ....
   .... [3]

   (b) The homeostatic control of body temperature in endotherms requires a controller, receptors, and effectors.

   (i) State the locations of the sensory receptors that detect changes in body temperature in endotherms.

   ....
   ....
   ....
   .... [2]

   (ii) Name **three** effectors in an endotherm that can regulate body temperature.

   1 ....
   2 ....
   3 .... [3]

> **Exam tip**
>
> When a tick table contains two converse ideas or processes, such as 'warming' and 'cooling' in this table, you should place only one tick in each row.

14 Communication and homeostasis

(iii) The hypothalamus is sometimes described as a homeostatic controller.

Describe the role of the hypothalamus in the regulation of body temperature.

....

....

....

....

....

.... [4]

(c) Both endotherms and ectotherms can use behavioural responses to regulate body temperature.

Complete the passage below, using the most appropriate words or terms, to outline the use of behavioural responses in body temperature regulation.

Many animals bask in sunlight to absorb heat energy when they are too cold. An animal may orient its body to increase the .... exposed to the sunlight. Animals can maintain body temperature by increasing their activity. This increases the rate of .... in muscle cells, which releases heat. Some animals, especially ectotherms, press their bodies against warm ground to gain heat energy through .... **[3]**

2 Animals and plants, as multicellular organisms, need internal communication systems.

(a) State one reason why multicellular organisms need internal communication systems.

....

.... [1]

(b) A student stated that the communication systems in plants and animals are very different.

Evaluate the student's statement.

....

....

....

....

....

....

....

.... [5]

> **Synoptic links**
> 3.1.2a   5.1.2d   5.1.3
> 5.1.4   5.1.5b   5.1.5k

> **Exam tip**
> A question such as this one covers several topics; you have the potential to give an answer that overruns the allotted space. Try to stick to the key comparisons (and, in this case, avoid details of action potentials or the action of particular hormones) and ensure you have a balance of 'agree' and 'disagree' points.

(c) Homeostasis relies on communication systems, which include specific receptors and effectors.

Complete **Table 2.1** to name the receptors and effectors that are involved in each example of homeostasis.

Example of homeostasis	Receptor	Effector
control of water potential		
control of heart rate		
body temperature regulation		

Table 2.1

[6]

3. Homeostasis is controlled by negative feedback mechanisms.

(a) Outline how negative feedback regulates blood glucose concentration.

....

[6]

Synoptic links

5.1.2d 5.1.3c 5.1.4d

Exam tip

When a level of response question asks you to 'outline', concentrate on the key ideas and terms. In this case, avoid writing everything you know about the biochemistry that controls insulin secretion; this alone would use up most of the allotted answer space.

(b) Explain why water potential in the blood is maintained within a narrow range rather than being maintained at a constant value.

....

[3]

14 Communication and homeostasis

(c) Negative feedback is essential for homeostasis. However, positive feedback also occurs in some biological processes.

Explain why the generation of an action potential is an example of positive feedback.

....
....
....
....
....
.... [3]

4 (a) Paracrine signalling is a type of cell signalling. **Figure 4.1** shows a diagrammatic representation of paracrine signalling.

signalling molecules diffuse through extracellular fluid   nearby cell

Figure 4.1

Compare paracrine cell signalling with endocrine cell signalling.

....
....
....
.... [2]

> **Synoptic links**
> 4.1.1   5.1.4a

> **Exam tip**
> You should describe similarities and/or differences when you are asked to 'compare'. For some questions, you may identify only similarities or only differences. In this question, however, both similarities and differences are present.

(b) Outline the role of cell signalling in the immune system.

....
....
....
....
....
....
....
....
....
....
.... [6]

5   A mammal called the naked mole rat regulates its body temperature using the following physiological and behavioural responses:
    - At low environmental temperatures, the core body temperature of naked mole rats remains close to that of the environment.
    - At high environmental temperatures, the core temperature of naked mole rats is stable.
    - They often lie together in large groups when environmental temperature decreases.
    - They tend to move to cooler parts of their tunnel system when environmental temperature increases.
    - They possess specialised tissue called brown adipose tissue, which can release metabolic heat.

    (a) (i) State two ways in which the temperature regulation of naked mole rats is similar to that of typical endotherms.

    ....
    ....
    ....
    .... [2]

    (ii) State three ways in which the temperature regulation of naked mole rats is similar to that of typical ectotherms.

    ....
    ....
    ....
    ....
    ....
    ....
    ....
    .... [3]

    > **Exam tip**
    >
    > When a question requires a specific number of responses, as is the case here, you may think of more potential answers than are needed. Think carefully and write down only the answers in which you have the most confidence.

6   Students planned an experiment to investigate the effect of cold and hot environmental temperatures on body temperature. An outline of their plan is shown below.
    - Divide the class into two groups.
    - Take the core and peripheral body temperatures of everyone in both groups.
    - Group 1 spends time in a room set to 35 °C.
    - Group 2 spends time in a room set to 10 °C.
    - Core body temperature and peripheral body temperature are then measured again.

166   14 Communication and homeostasis

(a) Suggest additional details that should be included in the students' plan to increase the accuracy of their results.

....
....
....
....
....
....
.... [3]

> **! Exam tip**
>
> Accuracy is a measure of how close experimental results are to the true values. When asked how the accuracy of experimental results can be improved, think about what could be changed in the planning or implementation to reduce the effect of random or systematic errors.

(b) The students' core body temperature results are shown in **Table 6.1**.

Group	Number in group	Mean core temperature (°C)	Standard deviation (σ)
1 (35 °C)	13	37.0	0.12
2 (10 °C)	14	36.9	0.22

Table 6.1

(i) Calculate a value of the Student's *t*-test for these data.

Use the formula:

$$t = \frac{(\bar{x}_1 - \bar{x}_2)}{\sqrt{\frac{\sigma_1^2}{N_1} + \frac{\sigma_2^2}{N_2}}}$$

.... [4]

(ii) In this experiment, the critical value of *t* at a 0.05 probability is 2.06.

What can you conclude from the result of the *t* value you calculated in **(b)(i)**.

....
....
....
.... [2]

Knowledge

15 Excretion

Excretion

Excretion is the removal of **toxic metabolic waste** from the body. The waste products are by-products or unwanted substances from normal cellular processes. The **kidneys**, **liver**, and **lungs** are involved in the removal of toxic products of metabolism and so contribute to homeostasis.

Substances that need to be excreted from the body include:

Substance	Produced by	Removed by	Need for excretion
nitrogenous waste (urea)	deamination of amino acids in liver	kidneys	urea is toxic
carbon dioxide	cells as a waste product of aerobic respiration	lungs	excess carbon dioxide in the blood is toxic and can reduce oxygen transport and reduce blood pH

The liver

The liver is made up of cells called **hepatocytes**, which carry out many metabolic reactions, including:

- storage of **glycogen**
- **detoxification** of substances such as ethanol and hydrogen peroxide
- **deamination** (the breakdown of excess amino acids) – the liver converts amino acids into keto acids, which can be respired, and ammonia, which is very soluble and very toxic, and cannot be stored in the body. Ammonia is quickly reacted with carbon dioxide to produce urea via the **ornithine cycle**.

Structure of the liver

The liver receives blood from two blood vessels: the **hepatic artery** (carrying oxygenated blood) and the **hepatic portal vein** (carrying deoxygenated blood rich in products of digestion from the intestines). Blood leaves the liver via the **hepatic vein**.

The bile duct also leaves the liver, carrying bile from the gall bladder to the duodenum where it emulsifies fats.

The liver is divided into lobes, which are divided again into lobules.

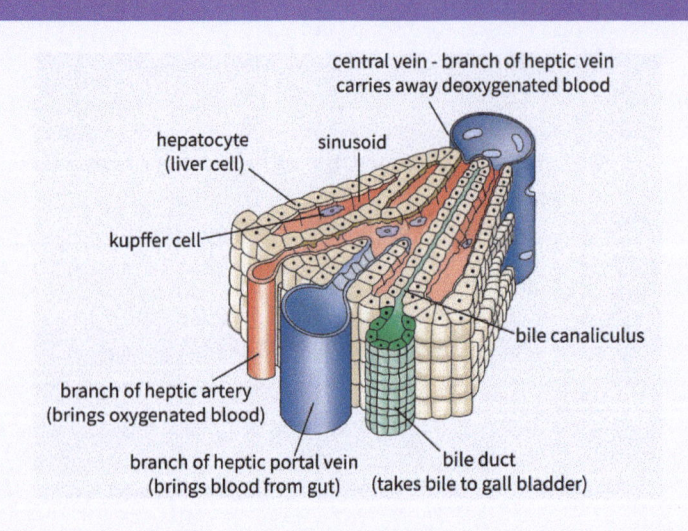

- central vein - branch of heptic vein carries away deoxygenated blood
- hepatocyte (liver cell)
- sinusoid
- kupffer cell
- branch of heptic artery (brings oxygenated blood)
- branch of heptic portal vein (brings blood from gut)
- bile canaliculus
- bile duct (takes bile to gall bladder)

15

The kidney

Kidneys have important roles in homeostasis and excretion:

- **Removing urea**, a waste product from the liver
- **Controlling the water potential** of blood plasma by removing excess water from the body.

A kidney has three main regions – the outer cortex, central medulla, and inner pelvis. It is supplied with blood by the renal artery, and the renal vein removes blood from the organ. The functional unit is the **nephron**.

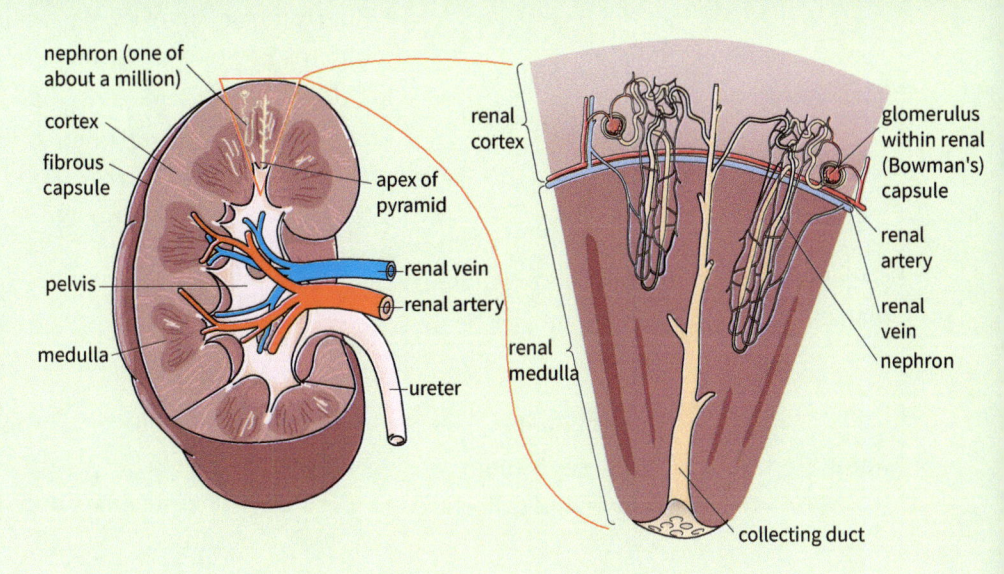

Structure of a nephron

A kidney contains a million tiny tubules called nephrons. A nephron has the following structures:

- A knot of capillaries called the **glomerulus** sits in a cup-shaped **Bowman's capsule**. The glomerulus is supplied with blood by the afferent (inward) arteriole and is drained by the efferent (outgoing) arteriole. The afferent arteriole is wider than the efferent arteriole, which creates pressure in the glomerulus, and allows **ultrafiltration** to take place between the glomerulus and Bowman's capsule.

- The Bowman's capsule drains into the **proximal convoluted tubule (PCT)**, the site of **selective reabsorption**.
- The PCT leads into the **loop of Henle** where more water is reabsorbed into the surrounding tissues.
- The **distal convoluted tubule (DCT)** connects the loop of Henle to the collecting ducts. Final water reabsorption happens in the DCT and the collecting ducts, under the influence of antidiuretic hormone (ADH), produce **urine**.

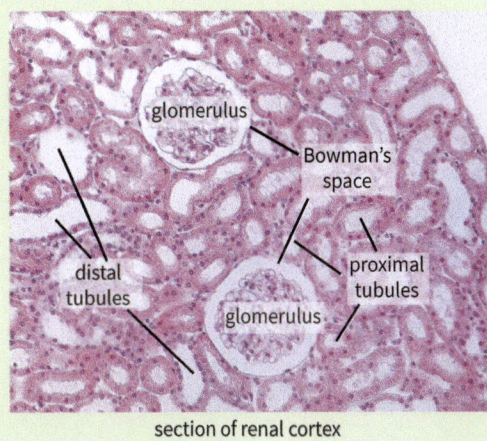

For answers and more practice questions visit www.oxfordrevise.com/scienceanswers

Even more practice and interactive revision quizzes are available on kerboodle

15 Knowledge 169

Production of urine

Stage	Takes place in	Brief outline of process
ultrafiltration	glomerulus and Bowman's capsule	• fluid is forced out of capillary blood under hydrostatic pressure into the Bowman's capsule • glucose, amino acids, urea, and inorganic ions move with it • large proteins and red blood cells cannot cross into Bowman's capsule and remain in the blood
selective reabsorption	proximal convoluted tubule	substances reabsorbed into blood: • 100% glucose • 100% amino acids • water • some inorganic ions
water reabsorption	loop of Henle distal convoluted tubule and collecting ducts	• water reabsorbed due to very negative water potential in the medulla tissue fluid • ADH changes permeability of cell membranes so more / less water is reabsorbed

The effects of kidney failure and its potential treatments

Kidney failure can be caused by a number of factors, including diabetes, infection, and hypertension (high blood pressure).

Kidney failure leads to an inability to remove toxic waste and excess water from the body, or regulate the level of water and salts, eventually resulting in death.

Glomerular filtration rate (GFR) is reduced by any type of kidney failure and is used as a measure of how serious the kidney failure is.

Kidney failure can be treated with:

- **Dialysis:**
  a) **Haemodialysis:** blood from a vein is passed through a machine that contains artificial dialysis membranes to mimic filtration in the kidney. Heparin is added to the blood to stop it clotting. Haemodialysis uses counter current flow.
  b) **Peritoneal dialysis:** fluid is placed between the patient's abdominal wall and organs, and the body's own abdominal membrane (the peritoneum) filters the blood. Waste materials move into the fluid which is then drained.

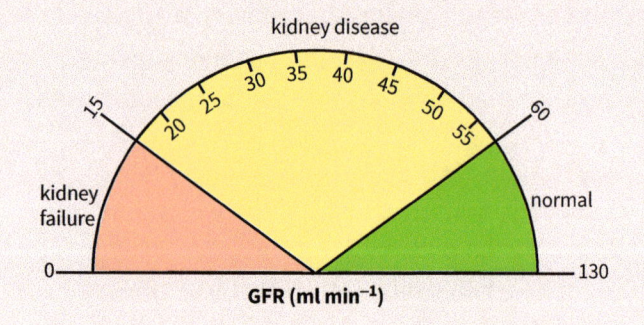

In both types of dialysis, the dialysis fluid contains glucose and mineral ions at normal blood concentrations but no urea. Urea and excess mineral ions move into the dialysis fluid by diffusion, and so are removed from the body.

- **Transplants:** a kidney from a living donor or a deceased person is surgically attached to the patient's bloodstream and bladder. Although a transplant patient will have to take immunosuppressant drugs for the remainder of their life, organ transplantation is the best life-extending procedure to treat kidney failure.

15 Excretion

Using urine for medical diagnosis

Urine is commonly used in diagnostic tests for:
- glucose concentration as an indication of diabetes mellitus
- the hormone human chorionic gonadotropin (hCG), detected during pregnancy by monoclonal antibodies on a pregnancy test
- the presence of anabolic steroids and other drugs – gas chromatography is used to test urine samples alongside known standards of drugs, so any drugs found in the urine can be identified and quantified.

Osmoregulation

Osmoregulation is the control of water potential. The water potential of plasma must be controlled to prevent osmotic problems with cells.

Osmoregulation is controlled by:
- **antidiuretic hormone (ADH)** – a hormone made by the hypothalamus and secreted by the posterior pituitary gland; acts on target cells in the collecting ducts in the kidney to increase water reabsorption into the blood
- the **hypothalamus** – a part of the brain that contains **osmoreceptors**; produces **ADH**
- the **posterior pituitary gland** – secretes **ADH**

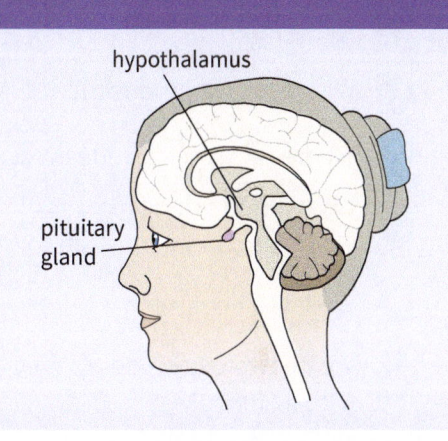

Reabsorption of water by the collecting ducts

Fluid moving into the **collecting ducts** still has a high water potential. The permeability of cell membranes in these structures is controlled by the hormone **ADH**, which conserves water in the body.

ADH makes the membranes of the collecting ducts more permeable to water, and so more water is reabsorbed into the bloodstream. ADH also causes more aquaporin proteins to be inserted into the collecting ducts of the plasma membrane.

The urine formed in the collecting ducts will be more concentrated and a smaller volume.

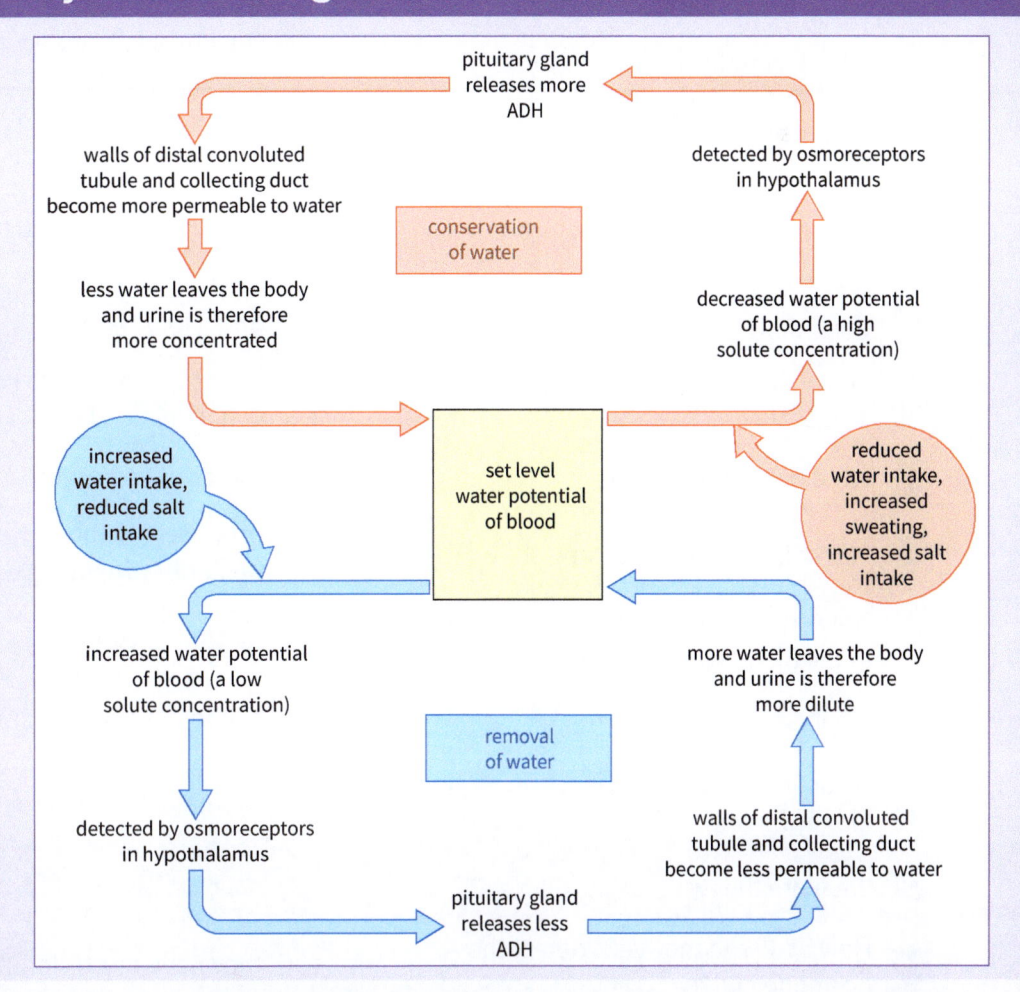

Retrieval

Learn the answers to the questions below, then cover the answers column with a piece of paper and write as many as you can. Check and repeat.

	Questions	Answers
1	What is excretion?	the removal of toxic metabolic waste products from the body
2	Give two waste products that need to be excreted.	urea and carbon dioxide
3	Where is urea produced?	in the liver / hepatocytes
4	Where is carbon dioxide produced?	cellular aerobic respiration
5	What are the three regions of the kidney and where are they in relation to each other?	outer cortex, middle medulla, inner pelvis
6	What is a nephron?	functional unit of the kidney
7	Which two blood vessels are associated with a kidney?	renal artery supplying blood, renal vein
8	List the structures of a nephron in order, starting with the glomerulus.	glomerulus, Bowman's capsule, proximal convoluted tubule, loop of Henle, distal convoluted tubule, collecting duct
9	What is ultrafiltration?	the filtering of blood into the Bowman's capsule under pressure
10	Why are large proteins and red blood cells not filtered out of the blood?	the proteins are too large (greater than 69 000 relative molecular mass)
11	Where does selective reabsorption take place?	proximal convoluted tubule
12	Which substances are reabsorbed back into the blood?	100% glucose and amino acids, some inorganic ions, and a lot of water
13	Where in the nephron does water reabsorption also occur?	loop of Henle, distal convoluted tubule, collecting ducts
14	What does ADH stand for?	antidiuretic hormone
15	Where is ADH produced and stored?	produced by the hypothalamus; stored in the posterior pituitary gland
16	How does the hypothalamus detect a change in the blood water potential?	by osmoreceptors
17	What is the role of ADH?	to conserve body water
18	What are the two main ways of treating kidney failure?	dialysis and organ transplant
19	What are the two types of dialysis?	haemodialysis and peritoneal dialysis
20	How do pregnancy tests detect the hormone hCG?	they have monoclonal antibodies specific to hCG

15 Excretion

15

Practical skills

Practise your practical skills using the worked example and practice questions below.

Developing drawing skills

An important skill is making biological drawings from dissected tissue or microscope preparations. If the rules are followed, the skill is straightforward.

Equipment for drawing: a sharp HB pencil, a pencil sharpener, an eraser, a ruler, and plain paper.

Do:
- draw what you see
- draw neat, fine, continuous lines
- draw large
- rub out mistakes
- give your drawing a title and scale
- draw label lines in pencil using a ruler – no arrows
- observe the object very carefully

Do not:
- use colour or shading of any sort
- produce a very small drawing

Worked example

Question
Draw a transverse section of a kidney. Label all the major features.

Answer
Using the dos and don'ts in the box on the left, here is the image the student produced.

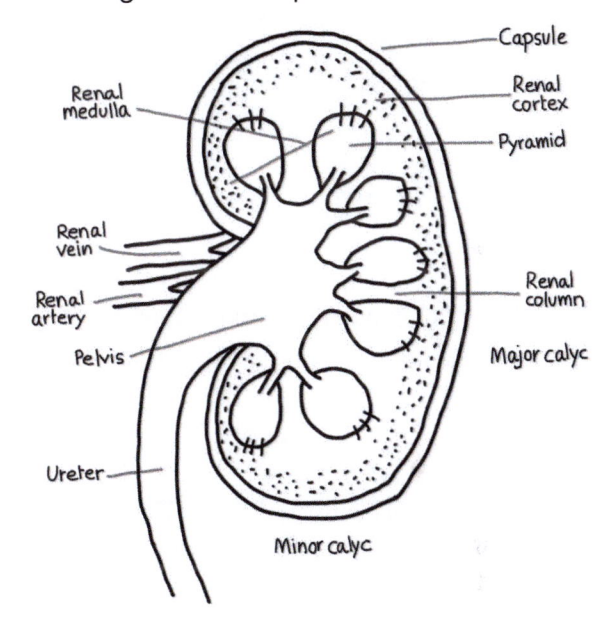

Practice

Examine the drawing in the worked example.

1 Identify what mistakes been made, and give a list of things that the student could have done differently.

2 Redraw the image correcting the mistakes.

Practice

Exam-style questions

1 A kidney can be dissected to observe its gross structure and histology.

   (a) State one safety precaution that should be taken when dissecting a kidney.

   ....

   .... [1]

   Synoptic link

   2.1.1e

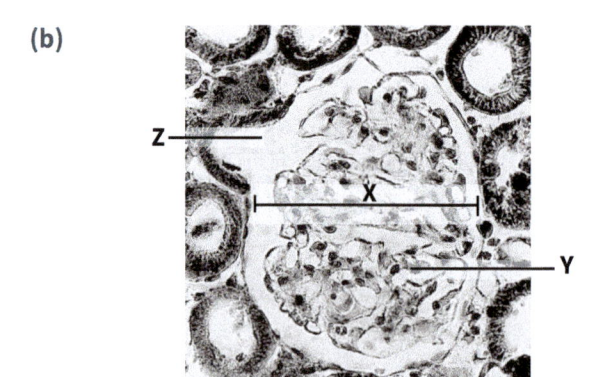

   (b)

   Figure 1.1

   A photomicrograph of a kidney nephron is shown in **Figure 1.1**.

   (i) Name the structures labelled **Y** and **Z** in the photomicrograph.

   Y ....

   Z .... [2]

   (ii) The actual length of the line labelled **X** in the photomicrograph of the kidney nephron is 120 µm.

   Calculate the microscope magnification that was used to produce this photomicrograph.

   Exam tip

   You may be asked to identify parts of a kidney nephron from photomicrographs, such as this one, which is harder than identification from diagrams. Try to study as many photomicrographs as possible before your exams.

   .... [2]

   (c) A photograph of a dissected kidney is shown in **Figure 1.2**.

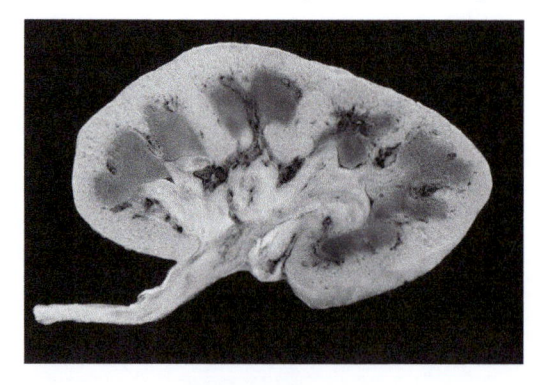

   Figure 1.2

174 15 Excretion

Sketch a simple line drawing of the kidney.

On your drawing, label the ureter, medulla, cortex, and pelvis.

[3]

2   Animals and plants excrete metabolic waste products.

(a) **Table 2.1** describes some processes that occur in animals and plants.

Write **YES** or **NO** in each box in **Table 2.1** to indicate if each statement is an example of excretion.

Process	Is this excretion?
the elimination of undigested food from an animal's body	
an animal exhaling carbon dioxide	
excess heavy metals are transferred to cells in the leaves, which are lost from a plant by abscission	
flowering plants release molecules that attract pollinators	
stercobilin is formed from the breakdown of haemoglobin and passes through the digestive system	
reed species release acid through their roots to destroy competing species	

Table 2.1   [4]

(b) One of the organs of excretion in mammals is the kidney.

(i) Describe how the glomerulus and the Bowman's capsule enable ultrafiltration to occur in a kidney nephron.

....

....

....

....

....

.... [4]

(ii) Describe the roles of the proximal convoluted tubule (PCT) and the distal convoluted tubule (DCT) in the kidney.

....
....
....
....
....
....
....
....
....
....
.... [6]

> **Exam tip**
>
> You may be able to describe transmembrane transport in the proximal convoluted tubule (PCT) in a lot of detail. However, for this level of response question, an in-depth description of transmembrane transport mechanisms may distract from more general points that you can make about the roles of these nephron regions.

3 The liver is an organ with many roles, including glycogen storage and detoxification.

(a) **Figure 3.1** shows a transmission electron micrograph of liver cells.

> **Synoptic links**
>
> 2.1.1b   2.1.1c   2.1.1g

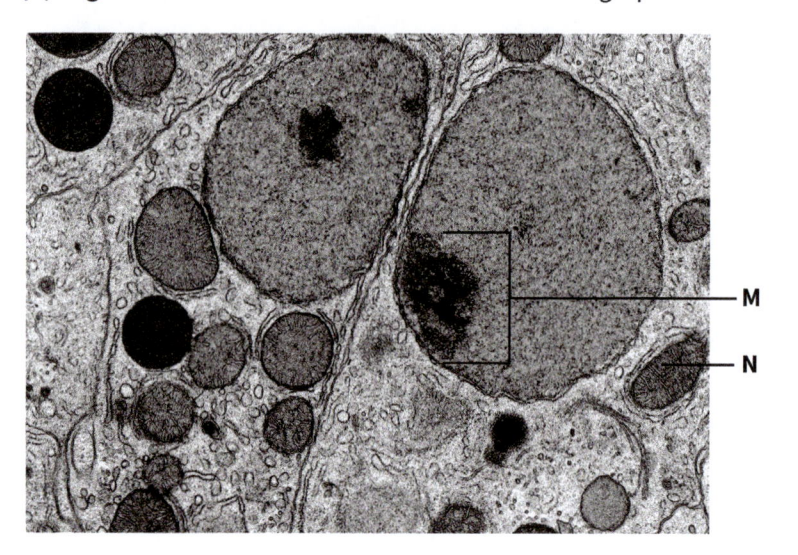

Figure 3.1

(i) Name the structures labelled **M** and **N** in **Figure 3.1**.

M ....

N .... [2]

(ii) Liver tissue can be examined using a light microscope instead of an electron microscope.

Outline how a section of liver tissue can be prepared for examination under a light microscope.

....
....
....
....
.... [3]

15 Excretion

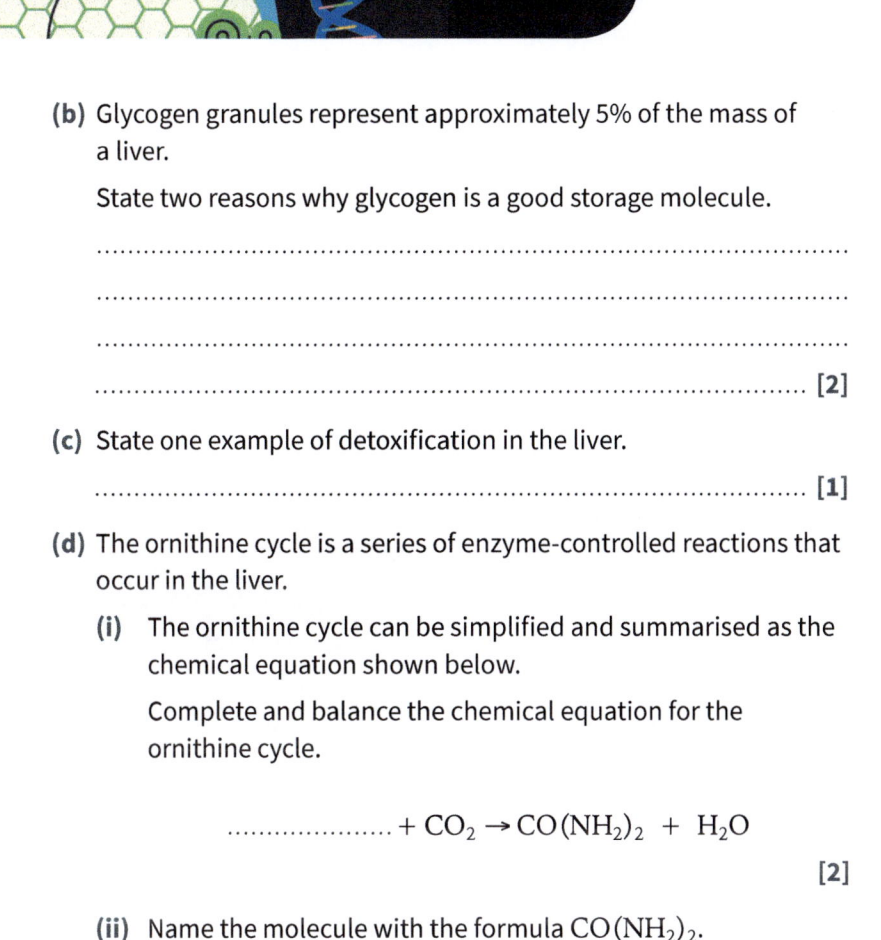

(b) Glycogen granules represent approximately 5% of the mass of a liver.

State two reasons why glycogen is a good storage molecule.

....
....
....
.... [2]

(c) State one example of detoxification in the liver.

.... [1]

(d) The ornithine cycle is a series of enzyme-controlled reactions that occur in the liver.

  (i) The ornithine cycle can be simplified and summarised as the chemical equation shown below.

  Complete and balance the chemical equation for the ornithine cycle.

  $$\text{.....................} + CO_2 \rightarrow CO(NH_2)_2 + H_2O$$

  [2]

  > **Exam tip**
  > You need to know the ornithine cycle in outline only.

  (ii) Name the molecule with the formula $CO(NH_2)_2$.

  .... [1]

4 Antidiuretic hormone (ADH) affects the volume of water reabsorbed from the collecting duct of a nephron.

(a) Place the events, **A** to **F**, in the correct order in the boxes below to outline the release and action of ADH.

  A to make ADH, neurosecretory cells in the hypothalamus are stimulated

  B ADH binds to receptors on cells in the collecting duct

  C the concentration of cAMP increases within collecting duct cells

  D osmoreceptors in the hypothalamus detect low water potential of blood

  E ADH is released from the posterior pituitary gland

  F aquaporins are inserted into the cell surface membrane

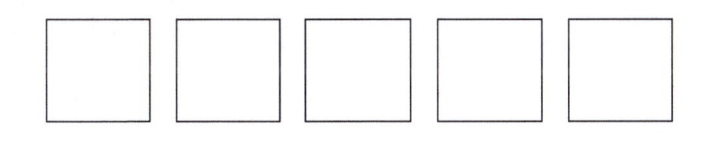

  ☐ ☐ ☐ ☐ ☐ [3]

> **Exam tip**
> When you are asked to place events in order, you can look for clues in the wording of the events (e.g., two events that mention the same cell, tissue, or molecule may be next to each other in the sequence).

(b) Describe the roles of different regions of a nephron in water reabsorption into the blood.

....
....
....
....
....
.... [6]

5   Urine samples can be analysed to detect specific molecules and to diagnose diseases.

(a) The colour of a urine sample can indicate the presence of particular substances.

Explain why urine that is red in colour may indicate kidney damage.

....
.... [2]

Synoptic link

2.1.2q

(b) The detection of glucose in urine may indicate that a person has diabetes.

(i) Explain why glucose is not normally present in urine.

....
.... [1]

(ii) Suggest a test that could be used to detect glucose in urine.

....
.... [1]

(c) Monoclonal antibodies are used in pregnancy testing.

Describe how monoclonal antibodies are used to detect pregnancy.

....
....
.... [3]

(d) Diuretics are drugs that reduce the reabsorption of water into the circulatory system from the kidney.

Diuretics can change the concentration of glucose and various ions in the blood.

Diuretics vary in their effects.

Plan a valid experimental method to compare the effects of two different diuretics on kidney function.

....
....
....
....
.... [5]

Exam tip

An experiment is valid if it measures what it is supposed to be measuring. Therefore, a valid experiment needs to control factors that are not being measured, and it requires suitable equipment and a procedure that will take appropriate measurements.

15 Excretion

6 Kidney failure can be treated using transplants or dialysis.

(a) State one advantage and one disadvantage of using kidney transplants to treat kidney failure compared to using dialysis to treat kidney failure.

Advantage: ....

....

Disadvantage: ....

.... [2]

(b) Scientists compared heart function in patients being treated with haemodialysis and patients being treated with peritoneal dialysis.

The data collected by the scientists are shown in **Table 6.1**.

Observation of heart function	Percentage of haemodialysis patients (%)	Percentage of peritoneal dialysis patients (%)
above average pressure on left atrioventricular valve	11.9	38.1
pericardial effusion (excess fluid between the heart and the pericardium, which is the tissue that protects the heart)	11.9	47.6

Table 6.1

(i) Suggest what additional information is required to assess the relative health risk to patients undergoing the two forms of dialysis.

....
....
....
....
....
.... [3]

(ii) The scientists analysed the measurements of atrioventricular valve pressure for the two groups of patients. They calculated mean values for both groups.

Suggest a statistical test that the scientists could use to compare the atrioventricular valve pressure of the two groups of patients.

.... [1]

> **Exam tip**
>
> When you are asked to decide which statistical test should be used, consider the purpose of the data. Are two groups being compared? Is the correlation between two variables being analysed? Is the difference between observed and expected data being assessed?

Knowledge

16 Neuronal communication

Structure and function of neurones

Neurones are specialised cells that conduct nerve impulses.

Sensory neurone: transmits action potentials from sensory receptors to other neurones.

Relay neurone: transmits action potentials from sensory neurones to motor neurones.

Motor neurone: transmits action potentials from the Central Nervous System to muscles or glands. However, remember that reflexes bypass the Central Nervous System.

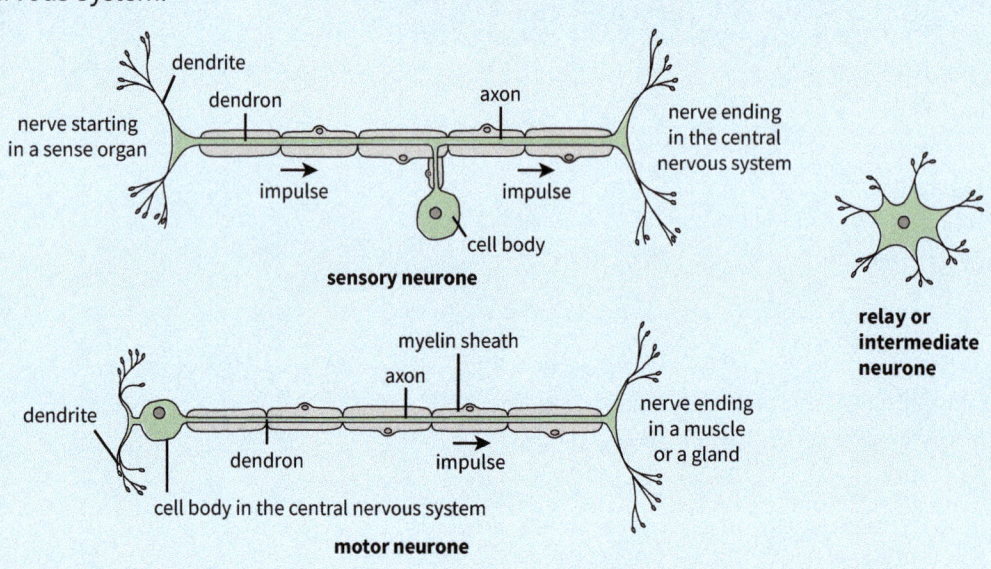

Myelination

Neurones can be myelinated (have a myelin sheath) or non-myelinated (no myelin sheath). Myelin acts as an electrical insulator, speeding up the conduction of action potentials along an axon.

Myelinated	Non-myelinated
occurs along the long axons within the nervous system (white matter)	occurs in neuronal body cells and dendrites (grey matter)
action potential jumps along axon at nodes of Ranvier by saltatory conduction	action potential occurs throughout the whole length of the axon
faster transmission	slower transmission
wider axon	narrower axon

180   16 Neuronal communication

Receptors

Receptors are specialised cells in sense organs that detect changes in the internal and external environments of an organism.

Receptors only respond to a specific stimulus and stimulation of a receptor leads to the establishment of a receptor potential.

Receptors act as **transducers**, converting a stimulus into an electrical impulse.

A **Pacinian corpuscle** is an example of a receptor. These:

- respond to the stimulus of change in pressure
- are found deep in the skin and joints
- have a **single neurone**, the ending of which is surrounded by **layers of tissue** separated by a **gel** (it resembles an onion)
- have a plasma membrane with special sodium ion channels called **stretch-mediated sodium ion channels**.

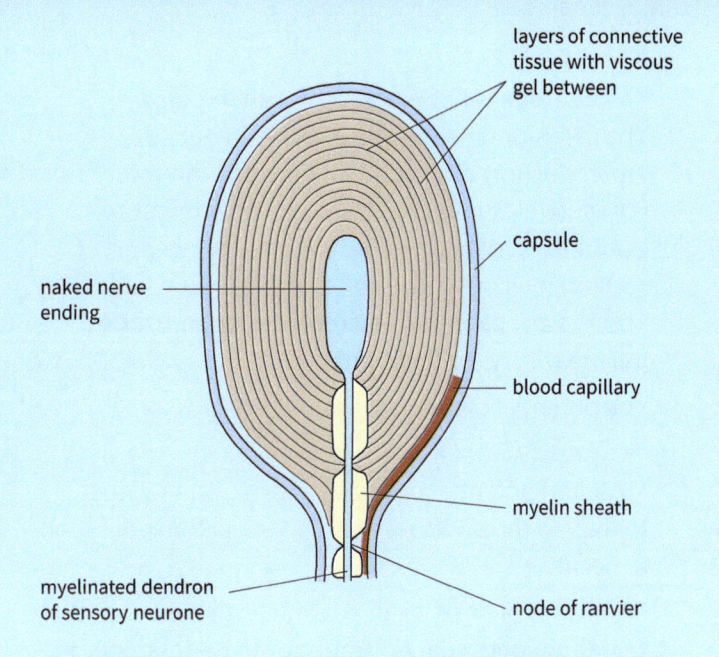

Advantages of synapses

The advantages of synapses are:

- They transmit action potentials in one direction.
- They transmit to a precise location.
- They become fatigued, protecting the system from overstimulation.

Integration synapses are important in interpretation and coordination of responses to stimuli from one or more sources.

Excitatory inputs cause depolarisation and action potentials.

Inhibitory inputs cause the neurotransmitters to bind with the postsynaptic neurone, allowing negative chloride ions to enter it. This hyperpolarises the postsynaptic neurone, making depolarisation less likely.

Summation is the additive effect caused by more than one stimulus. The strength of response is related to the amount of neurotransmitter that is produced, so several subthreshold responses can lead to a response in the postsynaptic neurone.

- **Spatial summation** occurs when impulses from different presynaptic neurones reach the threshold to cause an action potential.
- **Temporal summation** occurs when several impulses arrive in quick succession from a single presynaptic neurone, causing an action potential.

Neuronal communication

When a **sensory receptor** is stimulated, it generates an **action potential** in a **neurone**. **Synapses** enable stimuli to be transmitted between neurones.

Nerve impulses in mammals

Nerve impulses are **generated** and **transmitted** along a neurone.

1 **Resting state**

   The neurone is not transmitting an impulse. The cell is polarised – the inside and outside are oppositely charged. The inside of the cell is negatively charged. This **electrochemical gradient** is maintained by the active transport of sodium ions out of the cell and potassium ions into the cell caused by **differential membrane permeability** for these ions.

   The potential difference is about −70 mV.

Nerve impulse (an action potential)

2 An action potential takes about 3 ms. Stimuli need to reach a threshold potential for an action potential to occur.

3 Regardless of its strength, a stimulus that exceeds the **threshold potential** (−50 mV) causes **depolarisation** of the neurone and stimulation of an action potentional (the **all-or-nothing response**).

4 **Depolarisation** occurs when the distribution of the charge reverses as more sodium ions flow into the axon. Over 1 ms, **sodium ion** movement rapidly increases across the membrane of the axon, as the membrane permeability changes.

5 The action potential is reached as more sodium ions flow across the membrane. This flow continues until all voltage gated sodium ion channels are open, an example of **positive feedback**.

6 **Repolarisation** occurs as the membrane permeability for sodium ions decreases, so they stop flowing into the axon.

7 The membrane permeability for potassium ions increases, so they flow out of the axon, returning the potential difference to −70 mV.

8 The **refractory period** follows, where there is no membrane permeability to sodium and potassium ions and the neurone is unresponsive. This allows discrete impulses (they don't merge) and limits the frequency of impulse transmission (there is a time delay). The neurone returns to its resting potential.

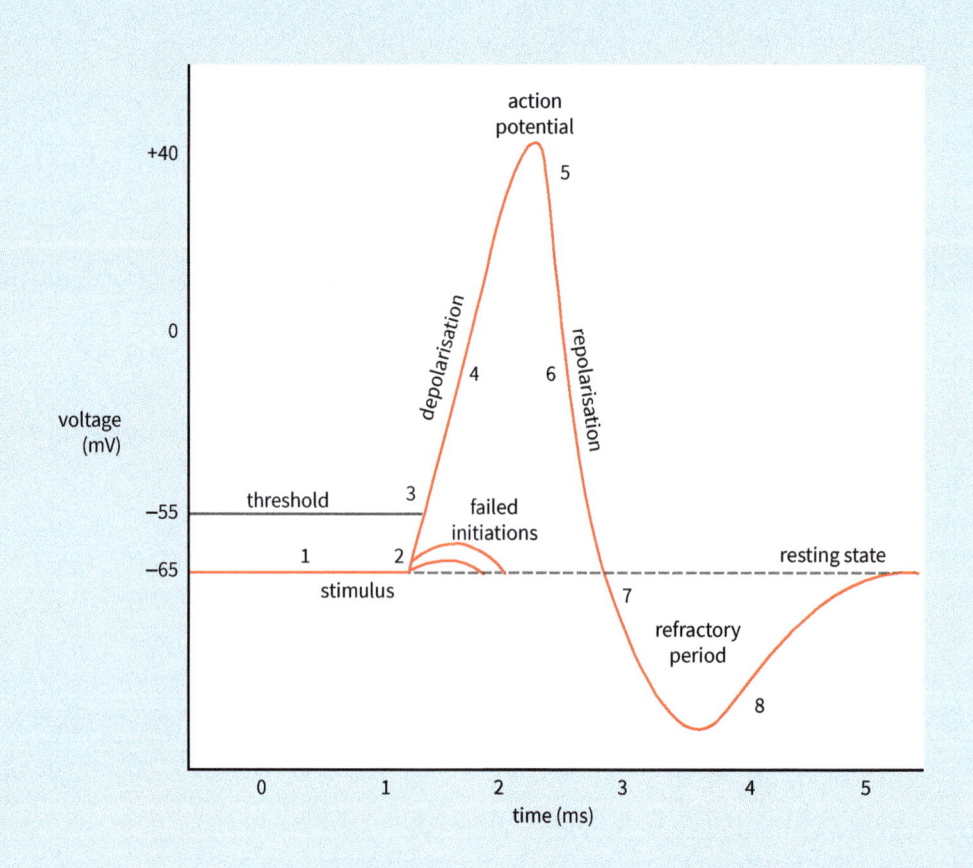

16 Neuronal communication

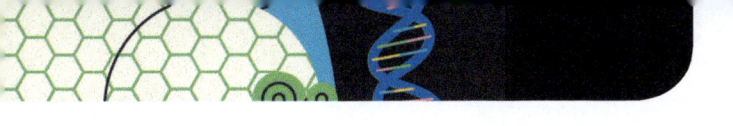

Structure and function of a synapse

A synapse is made up of:
- two neurones (presynaptic and postsynaptic)
- the gap between them (synaptic cleft).

Function
There is a chemical sequence of events that pass on an impulse between neurones.

1. The action potential arrives at the **presynaptic neurone**.
2. This action potential causes **neurotransmitter molecules** to be released into the cleft.
3. Neurotransmitter molecules bond temporarily with receptors on the **postsynaptic neurone** membrane.
4. The molecules cause **depolarisation** – if this is above the **threshold**, an action potential will be generated.
5. The release of neurotransmitter from the presynaptic membrane and deactivation of it on the postsynaptic membrane explains why neural transmission is **unidirectional**.

Cholinergic synapses

Presynaptic neurones have vesicles that contain a neurotransmitter. There are many types of neurotransmitter.

Acetylcholine (ACh) is found throughout the nervous system. Synapses using ACh are called cholinergic synapses.

1. An **action potential** arrives at the end of the presynaptic axon (the **synaptic knob**). This causes an influx of **calcium ions**, which cause vesicles to release ACh into the cleft by exocytosis.
2. ACh **diffuses** across the cleft and binds to receptors on the postsynaptic membrane, delaying the impulse by about 0.5 ms.
   Remember: Only ACh is released by exocytosis, not the vesicles containing ACh.
3. An **influx of sodium ions** occurs as ion channels open, depolarising the cell. If the **threshold potential** is reached, an action potential will be generated.
4. An enzyme (acetylcholinesterase) on the postsynaptic membrane **hydrolyses** ACh. The breakdown product choline is **reabsorbed** into the synaptic knob and recycled into ACh.

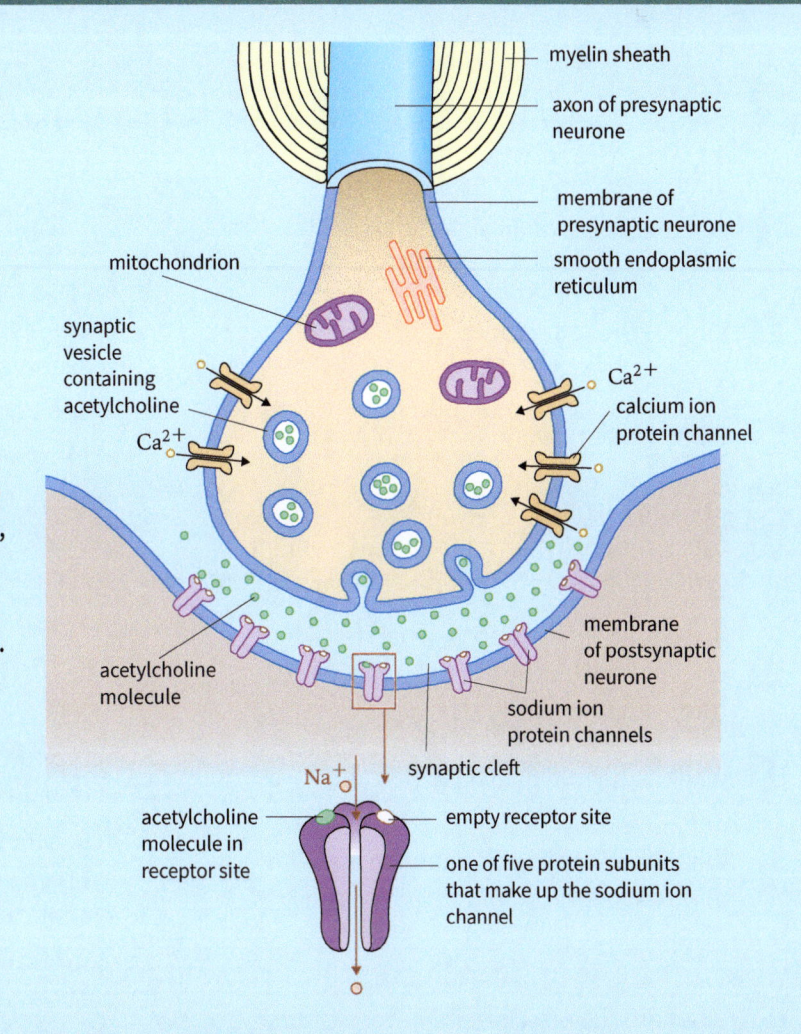

Retrieval

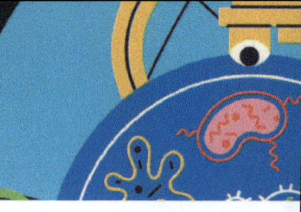

Learn the answers to the questions below, then cover the answers column with a piece of paper and write as many as you can. Check and repeat.

Questions | Answers

#	Question	Answer
1	What do receptor cells do?	detect changes in the internal and external environments of an organism
2	What is the function of a Pacinian corpuscle?	responds to pressure and vibration
3	What is a neurone?	a specialised cell that conducts nerve impulses
4	Describe the role of a sensory neurone.	transmits impulses from sensory receptors to other neurones
5	Describe the role of a relay neurone.	transmits impulses from sensory neurones to motor neurones
6	Describe the role of a motor neurone.	transmits impulses from the Central Nervous System to muscles or glands
7	What are the advantages of chemical synapses?	• transmit impulses in one direction • transmit to a precise location • become fatigued, protecting the system from overstimulation
8	List the stages of an action potential.	resting potential, threshold potential, depolarisation, repolarisation, refractory period
9	What is the refractory period?	follows the action potential, when sodium ion channels are inactive and neurone is unresponsive, preventing further impulses
10	What are the components of a synapse?	• two neurones (presynaptic and postsynaptic) • the gap between them (synaptic cleft)
11	In a cholinergic synapse, what happens to acetylcholine when it is released from the synaptic knob and what is the impact of this?	diffuses across the cleft and binds to receptors on the postsynaptic membrane, delaying the impulse by about 0.5 ms
12	In a cholinergic synapse, what determines whether the impulse is triggered in the postsynaptic neurone?	it has to reach the threshold potential
13	What is the role of myelin?	acts as an electrical insulator, speeding up the conduction of action potentials along an axon
14	What happens to acetylcholine after it binds to postsynaptic membrane receptors?	acetylcholinesterase on postsynaptic membrane hydrolyses ACh; choline is reabsorbed into the synaptic knob and recycled
15	What are the effects of inhibitory inputs?	neurotransmitters bind with receptors on the postsynaptic neurones, allowing Cl^- ions to enter the cell, and hyperpolarising the postsynaptic neurone, making depolarisation less likely

16 Neuronal communication

16 Maths skills

Practise your maths skills using the worked example and practice questions below.

Converting units

In science, using the correct units is vital for communicating information effectively. Although it seems like a simple enough procedure, this is one of the biggest areas that students lose marks in an exam, and so practising unit conversion can save you a lot of marks.

When converting units, the key thing is to ensure that the units are realistic for the context. You wouldn't measure cell size in centimetres, so you'd need to convert your answer to something more appropriate (such as micrometres).

Whatever units you use, remember that when converting to smaller units, you need to multiply by the number of smaller units needed to make the larger (e.g., there are 10 mm in 1 cm so multiply your number by 10 to convert cm into mm). When converting to larger units, you must divide by that number instead (e.g you need divide your number by 10 to convert mm into cm).

Worked example

Question

A student views a cell down a microscope that is 25 μm in length, and measures the image size to be 10 mm in length.

What is the magnification of the microscope?

Answer

When answering questions like this, your units must be consistent. Do not make the mistake of trying to mix units that are recording the same type of measurement (such as image size and actual size).

First, convert the units into μm. It doesn't matter which units you convert, just choose something that you are comfortable working with.

There are 1000 μm in 1 mm, so:

$$10 \text{ mm} \times 1000 = 10\,000 \text{ μm}$$

Then, you can substitute the numbers you know into the equation to calculate magnification.

$$\text{magnification} = \frac{\text{image size}}{\text{actual size}}$$

$$= \frac{10\,000}{25} = 400$$

Therefore, the magnification of the microscope was ×400.

Practice

1 Try the worked example again, but this time convert the units into mm instead.

2 Convert the following measurements into mm.
   a 40 cm
   b 2.5 m
   c 0.6 μm
   d 100 nm

3 Calculate which measurement is greater: 33.5 km or 3350 m.

4 Calculate which measurement is smaller: 2 μl or 0.002 cl.

5 Calculate which measurement is greater: 2.5 m³ or 25 000 mm³.

Practice

Exam-style questions

1. Sensory receptors detect stimuli and cause nervous transmission in organisms.

   (a) Cone cells in the retina of the eye detect light and this causes nerve impulses to be transmitted to the brain.

   Explain why a cone cell is an example of a transducer.

   ....

   .... [1]

   > **Exam tip**
   > You should understand the principles of sensory receptors and how they produce action potentials in sensory neurones.

   (b) A Pacinian corpuscle is a mechanoreceptor. This is a receptor found on the skin and other organs. It detects touch. A Pacinian corpuscle is shown in **Figure 1.1**.

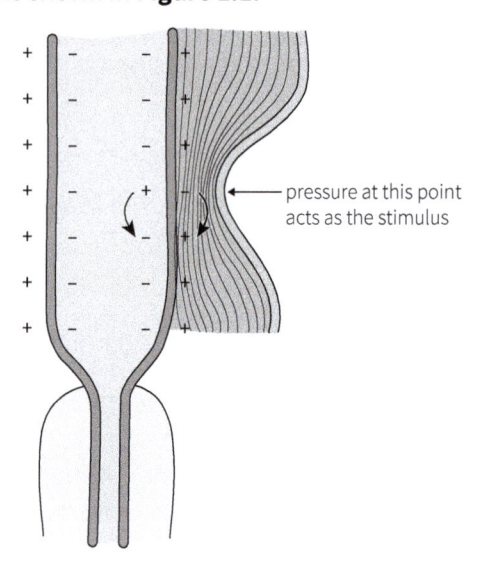

   Figure 1.1

   Explain how a Pacinian corpuscle converts the stimulus of mechanical pressure to an action potential.

   ....
   ....
   ....
   .... [3]

   (c) Olfactory receptors in the nose detect different chemical molecules and convert these stimuli to action potentials.

   (i) Suggest how olfactory receptors convert chemical stimuli to action potentials.

   ....
   ....
   .... [2]

   (ii) Suggest how different chemicals can be distinguished by olfactory receptors.

   ....
   .... [2]

16 Neuronal communication

(d) One type of pain receptor detects H⁺ ions from acids. H⁺ ions cause Na⁺ ion channels in the pain receptor membrane to open. Suggest how this type of pain receptor causes a person to feel pain.

....
....
....
....
....
.... [3]

2 (a) **Figure 2.1** shows a motor neurone.

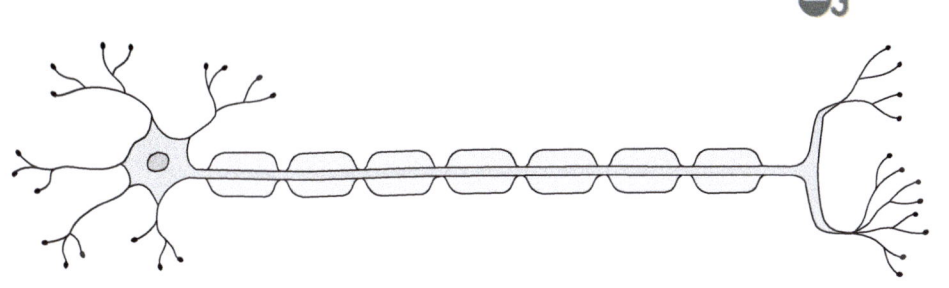

Figure 2.1

Describe two features of a motor neurone that are different from those found in sensory neurones.

....
....
....
.... [2]

> **Exam tip**
> A neurone's nucleus and rough ER are located in the cell body.

(b) The speed of nerve impulses is affected by temperature, axon diameter, and whether a neurone is myelinated or not.

Scientists measured the conduction speed in unmyelinated and myelinated neurones that had a range of axon diameters. Their results are shown in **Table 2.1**.

| Unmyelinated neurones || Myelinated neurones ||
Diameter of axon (μm)	Conduction speed (m s⁻¹)	Diameter of axon (μm)	Conduction speed (m s⁻¹)
100	8	2	19
200	10	4	37
300	14	6	53
400	17	8	70
500	20	10	85

Table 2.1

(i) State three conclusions you can draw from the data in **Table 2.1** about factors affecting a neurone's conduction speed.

....

....

....

....

.... [3]

(ii) Plot a graph to show the results for myelinated neurones.

> **Exam tip**
>
> When plotting graphs, ensure you select an appropriate scale (i.e., using up as much of the available area as possible).

[3]

(iii) Explain the effect of myelination on the speed of transmission of an action potential.

....

.... [2]

(iv) Explain why an increase in temperature up to 40 °C increases the speed of transmission of an action potential in neurones.

....

.... [1]

3 Resting potential values and action potential values vary between different types of neurone.

(a) (i) Describe how the resting potential of a neurone is established.

> **Exam tip**
>
> Remember that two forms of potassium ion channel are present in the cell membranes of neurones – voltage-gated channels, which open during an action potential, and other potassium ion channels that are always open, which help to establish resting potential.

....

....

....

.... [3]

(ii) Suggest how different resting potential values could be established in different types of neurone.

....

.... [1]

16 Neuronal communication

(b) The graphs in **Figure 3.1** show action potentials in two different types of neurone.

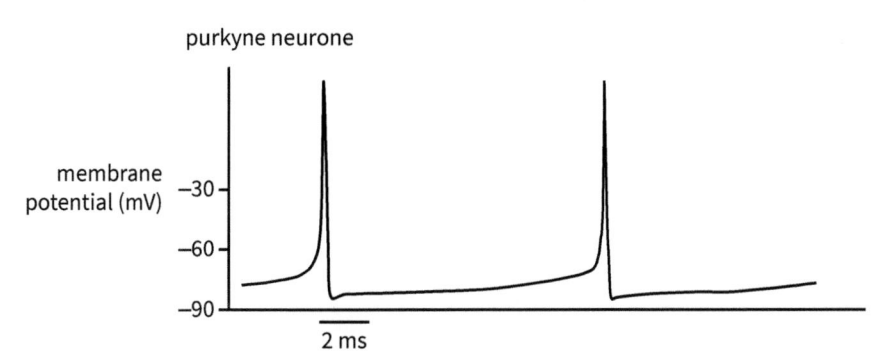

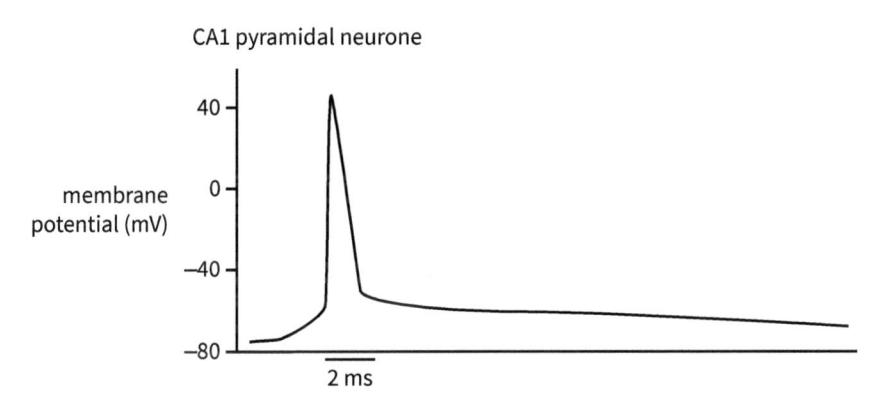

purkyne neurone

CA1 pyramidal neurone

Figure 3.1

Describe the differences between the two action potentials.

....
....
....
....
....
.... [3]

(c) The all-or-nothing principle determines when a nerve impulse is generated.

Explain the all-or-nothing principle.

....
....
....
.... [2]

4   A synapse is a junction between two neurones.

(a) Describe the roles of synapses in the nervous system.

....
....
....
.... [3]

(b) **Table 4.1** lists events in the transmission across a cholinergic synapse.

Order	Event
	voltage-gated Ca²⁺ ion channels open
	acetylcholine released by exocytosis
	sodium ion channels open on the post synaptic membrane
	acetylcholine diffuses across the synaptic cleft
	vesicles fuse with the presynaptic membrane
	acetylcholine binds to receptors on the post synaptic membrane

Table 4.1

> **Exam tip**
>
> The gap between a presynaptic and postsynaptic neurone is called the 'synaptic cleft'.

Place a number (**1–6**) in each box in **Table 4.1** to indicate the correct order of the events. [3]

(c) Describe what happens to a molecule of acetylcholine after it has bound to a receptor on a postsynaptic membrane.

....
....
....
.... [3]

5 Many chemicals, including recreational drugs, medicines, and toxins, can affect the nervous system.

(a) Tetrodotoxin is a toxin produced by pufferfish and triggerfish.

Tetrodotoxin inhibits Na⁺ ion channels.

Suggest and explain the effect of tetrodotoxin on the nervous system.

....
....
.... [2]

(b) Methamphetamine is a drug that enters vesicles containing the neurotransmitter dopamine, causing the vesicles to fuse with presynaptic membranes.

Suggest and explain the effect of methamphetamine on the nervous system.

....
....
.... [2]

(c) Cocaine is a drug that blocks the transport of dopamine back into presynaptic neurones from synaptic clefts.

Suggest and explain the effect of cocaine on the nervous system.

....
....
.... [2]

16 Neuronal communication

(d) Curare is a poisonous substance found in various South American plants.

A molecule in curare, d-tubocurarine, blocks acetylcholine receptors on postsynaptic membranes.

Suggest and explain the effect of curare on the nervous system.

....
....
....
.... [2]

> **Exam tip**
> Bear in mind that neurotransmitters can be excitatory or inhibitory.

6 Homeostasis is the regulation of conditions in the human body.

Outline the role of sensory receptors and the nervous system in homeostasis.

....
....
....
....
....
....
....
....
....
....
....
.... [6]

> **Synoptic links**
> 3.1.2g 5.1.1c 5.1.1d
> 5.1.2d 5.1.5h

7 The human body depends on communication systems to respond to any environmental changes.

Describe the differences and similarities between neuronal and hormonal communication in organisms.

....
....
....
....
....
....
....
....
....
....
.... [6]

> **Exam tip**
> When asked in a level of response question to describe similarities and differences, try to ensure that your answer is balanced. In this case, including at least two or three similarities and two or three differences should secure level 3.

For answers and more practice questions visit www.oxfordrevise.com/scienceanswers

Even more practice and interactive revision quizzes are available on kerboodle

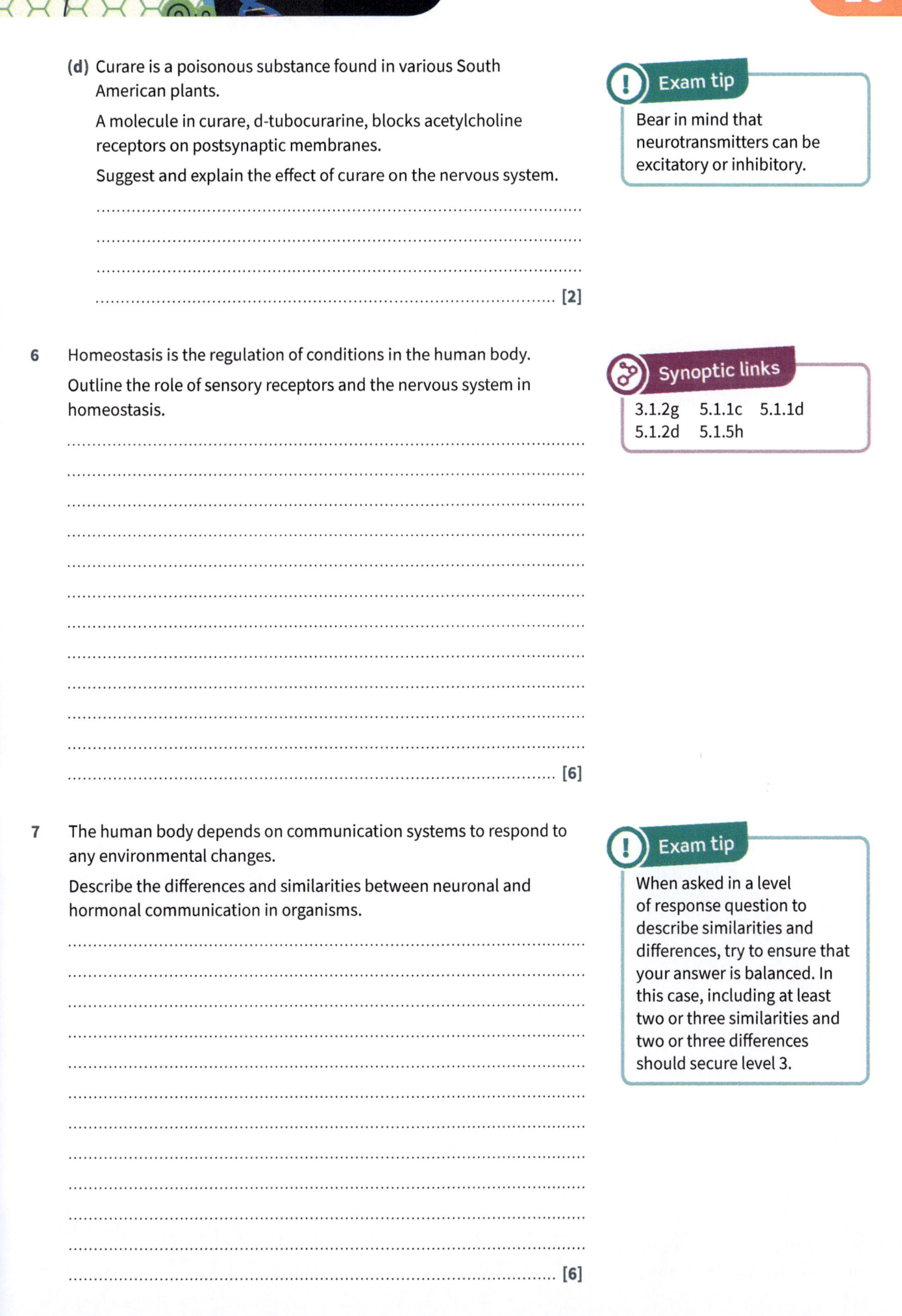

16 Practice

Knowledge

17 Hormones

The endocrine system

The **endocrine system** is a communication and control system in the body. The endocrine system is made up of **endocrine glands** that synthesise and secrete hormones directly into blood vessels flowing through the glands.

Hormones are chemical messengers that are **secreted** into the **blood**, transported in the bloodstream, and **detected** by **target cells** and **tissues**.

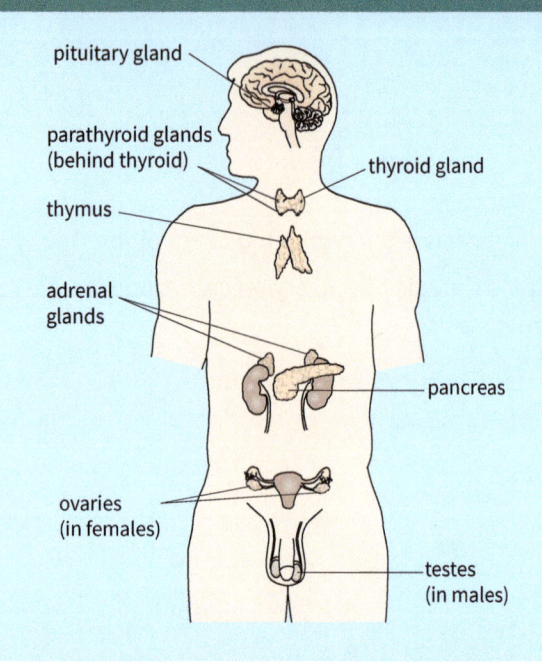

The adrenal glands

The adrenal glands are endocrine glands. They are located just above the kidneys.

An adrenal gland has a central medulla surrounded by a cortex.

The **medulla** produces and secretes adrenaline in response to stress, pain and shock. Adrenaline prepares the body for the 'fight or flight' response with numerous physiological changes including:

- increased heart rate
- pupil dilation
- increased blood glucose concentration and metabolic rate
- increased sweat production
- increased rate and depth of breathing.

The **cortex** produces steroid hormones from cholesterol. For example:

- mineralocorticoids – help control potassium and sodium ion concentration in blood
- glucocorticoids – help control metabolism of proteins and carbohydrates in the liver

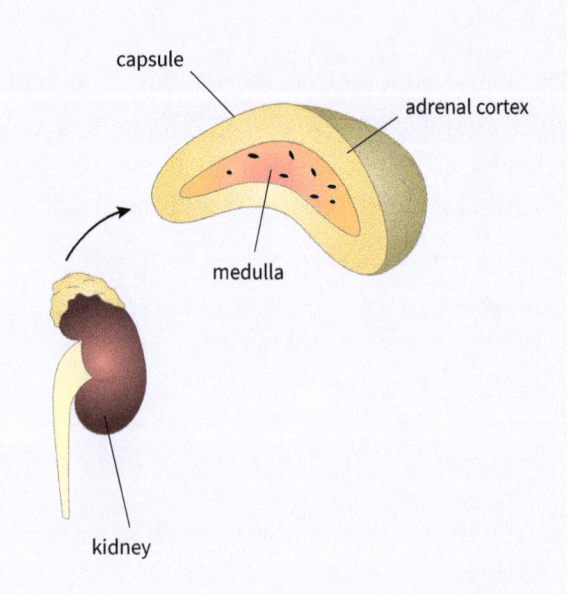

The pancreas

The **pancreas** is another example of an endocrine organ. It is a small organ found just below the stomach. The hormone-secreting cells are arranged in the islets of Langerhans. These produce insulin and glucagon, hormones that control blood glucose concentration.

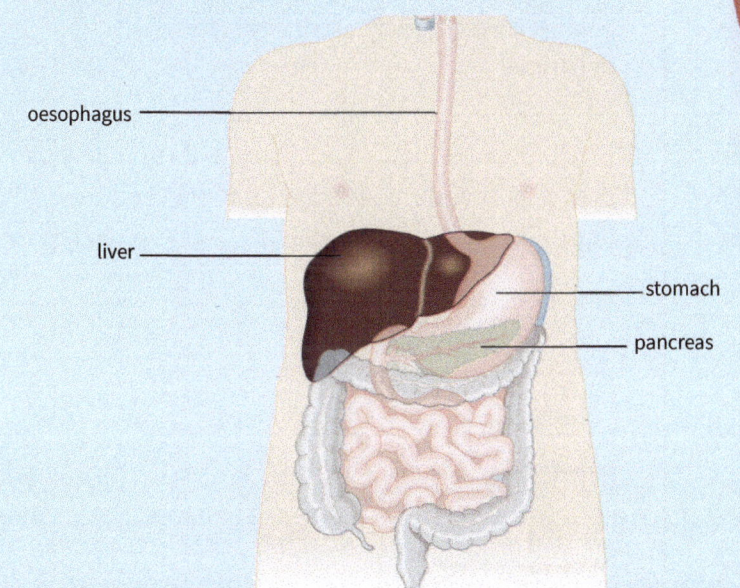

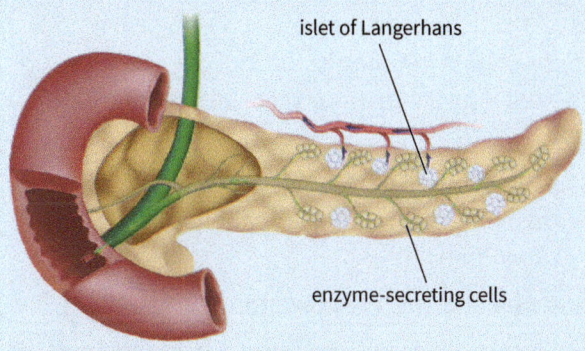

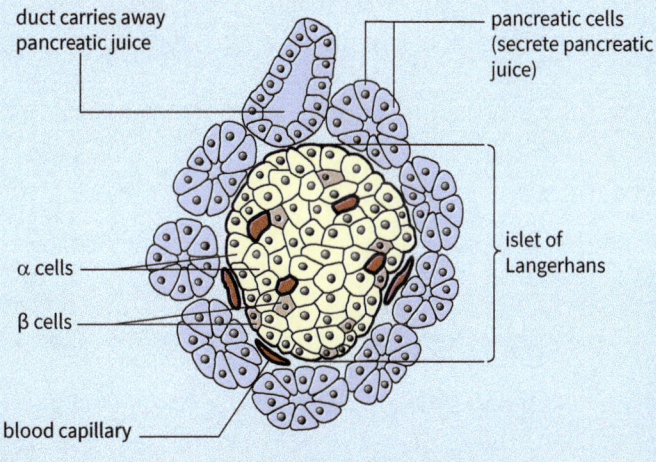

Potential treatments for diabetes mellitus

Diabetics used to be treated with insulin from the pancreas tissue of animals (e.g., pigs). However, insulin is now produced by **genetically modified bacteria** and this has many benefits including:

- less chance of a diabetic developing tolerance (so it's no longer effective) and lower risk of infection
- cheaper to manufacture
- fewer ethical objections
- exact copy of human insulin, so more effective.

Stem cells may provide a future treatment for Type I diabetics. Scientists have found precursor cells in pancreatic tissue of adult mice. If similar cells could be found in human pancreatic tissue, they could be used to produce new beta cells.

Diabetes mellitus

Diabetes mellitus is a medical condition where a person is unable to control their blood glucose concentration. There are two types of diabetes mellitus:

Type of diabetes	Cause	Treatment
type I – insulin dependent	the pancreas stops producing insulin, usually in childhood	injections of insulin, 2–4 times a day
type II – insulin independent	glycoprotein receptors on cell membranes are lost or lose sensitivity; there may be reduction in insulin production	regulate dietary carbohydrates, especially refined sugars; may require insulin or drugs to stimulate insulin production

17 Knowledge

Control of blood glucose levels – an example of negative feedback

Many homeostatic processes in the body are controlled by negative feedback. Negative feedback occurs when a change in conditions is detected and restored back to its normal level through a series of corrective measures. For example, insulin and glucagon are both involved in regulating blood glucose concentration through negative feedback mechanisms, to keep it at its normal level of 90 mg per 100 cm³ blood.

Response to decreased blood glucose
- A **fall** in blood glucose concentration below the normal is detected by alpha cells in the islets of Langerhans.
- **Alpha** cells secrete **glucagon**.
- Glucagon acts on liver cells to increase blood glucose concentration.
- Blood glucose concentration returns to normal.

Response to increased blood glucose
- A **rise** in blood glucose concentration above the normal is detected by beta cells in the islets of Langerhans.
- **Beta** cells secrete **insulin**.
- Insulin acts on target cells, particularly muscle and liver cells, to reduce blood glucose concentration.
- Blood glucose concentration returns to normal.

Flow diagram: increasing blood glucose concentration → detected by α cells of pancreas, which produce glucagon → blood glucose concentration falls → glucagon → normal blood glucose concentration 90 mg in 100 cm⁻³ blood. Glucagon effects: conversion of glycogen to glucose; conversion of amino acids to glucose; uncontrolled quantity of glucose enters from intestines. On the other side: reducing blood glucose concentration ← detected by β cells of pancreas, which produce insulin ← blood glucose concentration rises ← insulin. Insulin effects: increased cellular respiration; conversion of glucose to glycogen; conversion of glucose to fat; absorption of glucose into cells. Negative feedback loop: blood glucose concentration rises / blood glucose concentration falls.

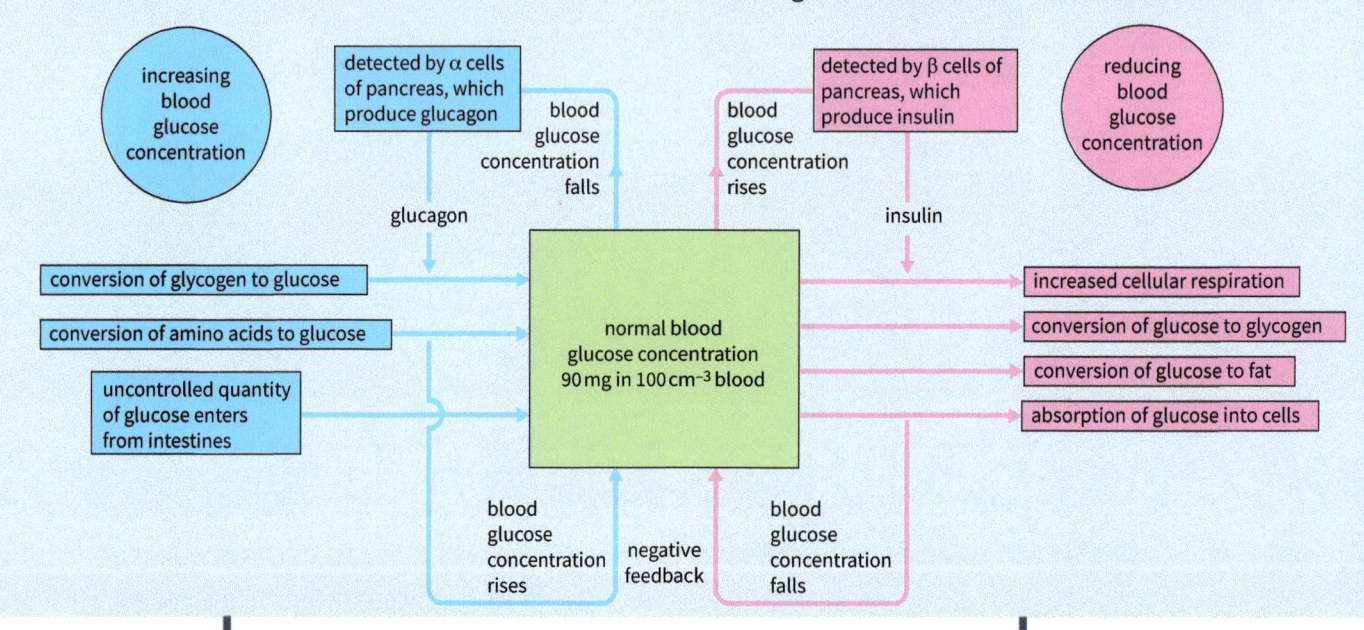

Glucagon

Glucagon works in the opposite way to insulin. Only liver cells have receptors for glucagon.

Glucagon binds to receptors on the cell surface membranes of liver cells and raises blood glucose concentration by:

1. Converting glycogen to glucose – **glycogenolysis**.
2. Converting glycerol and amino acids into glucose – **gluconeogenesis**.
3. Causing the body to use more fatty acids in respiration.

Insulin

Insulin binds to **receptors** on the cell membrane of **target cells**, particularly muscle and liver cells. It reduces blood glucose concentration by:

1. Causing more glucose channels to be inserted into the cell surface membrane, so increasing the uptake of glucose, especially by muscle cells.
2. Increasing the rate of respiration, so more glucose is used.
3. Activating **enzymes** involved in the conversion of glucose to glycogen – **glycogenesis** – in muscle and liver cells.
4. Causing excess glucose to be converted into fat.

17 Hormones

Control of insulin secretion

The secretion of insulin by beta cells has to be carefully controlled in response to changing concentrations of blood glucose.

Control of insulin levels is achieved in the following way:

1. Beta cell surface membranes contain **calcium ion channels**, which are closed,
2. There are also **potassium ion channels** in the beta cell-surface membranes, which are open. These allow potassium ions to diffuse out of the cell. The inside of the cell becomes more negative, and sets up a potential difference (p.d.) of −70 mV across the membrane.
3. Under high blood glucose concentrations, glucose molecules diffuse into the cell and are quickly respired to release ATP.
4. The increase in ATP causes the potassium ion channels to close. Potassium ions cannot move out of the cell and the p.d. across the membrane becomes less negative.
5. The change in p.d. opens the voltage-gated calcium ion channels to allow calcium ions to diffuse into the cell down their concentration gradient.
6. The calcium ions cause insulin-containing vesicles to move to, and fuse with, the cell surface membrane, releasing insulin by exocytosis.

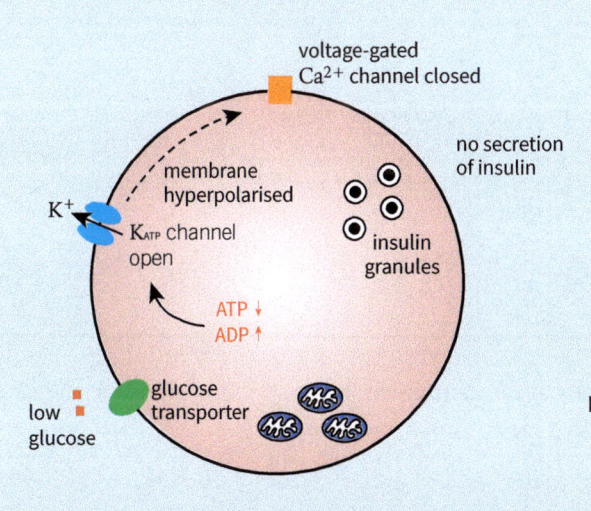

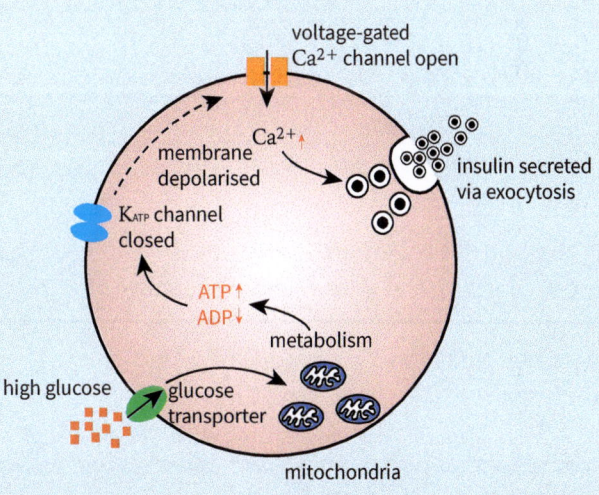

The role of the liver in controlling blood glucose concentration

The liver is the site of three important processes in the control of blood glucose levels:

1. **Glycogenesis:** the conversion of glucose to glycogen under the influence of insulin
2. **Glycogenolysis:** the conversion of glycogen to glucose under the influence of glucagon
3. **Gluconeogenesis:** the conversion of non-carbohydrates to glucose under the influence of glucagon

Liver cells (hepatocytes) are **target** cells for the hormones insulin and glucagon.

Retrieval

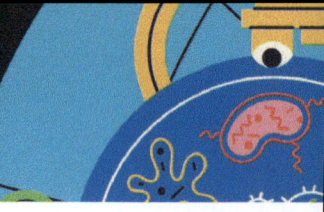

Learn the answers to the questions below, then cover the answers column with a piece of paper and write as many as you can. Check and repeat.

Questions | Answers

#	Question	Answer
1	What is the endocrine system?	the endocrine system is made up of glands that secrete hormones for communication and control
2	What are hormones?	chemical messengers
3	How are hormones transported from their organ of production to target cells?	via the bloodstream
4	Which endocrine glands sit above the kidneys?	adrenal glands
5	Describe the basic structure of an adrenal gland.	central medulla surrounded by a cortex
6	Which hormone(s) does the medulla produce, and in response to what sort of stimuli?	adrenaline, in response to stress, pain, shock, fear, or excitement
7	Which hormone(s) does the cortex produce?	mineralocorticoid and glucocorticoid
8	In the pancreas, what are the islets of Langerhans?	structures that produce the hormones insulin and glucagon
9	In the islets of Langerhans, which cells produce insulin, and which produce glucagon?	beta cells produce insulin, and alpha cells produce glucagon
10	How does glucagon raise blood glucose concentration?	activates enzymes in target cells to increase conversion of glycogen to glucose (glycogenolysis), and gluconeogenesis
11	Do potassium ions normally move into or out of a beta cell, and what does this movement cause?	K^+ move out of the cell to create a potential difference of –70 mV across the membrane
12	What triggers the potassium ion channels to close?	extra ATP produced through respiration of additional glucose
13	Why do the calcium ion channels open?	potassium ion channels close, potassium ions can no longer move out of the cell, the p.d. becomes less negative (depolarises), calcium ion channels open
14	What is the role of calcium ions in the beta cell?	they cause insulin-containing vesicles to move towards and fuse with the cell-surface membrane, releasing insulin by exocytosis
15	Which type of diabetes is insulin dependent?	type I
16	How is type II diabetes controlled?	by restricting carbohydrate intake in the diet; sometimes drugs that stimulate insulin production, occasionally insulin injections
17	Write a definition for diabetes.	a medical condition where the patient is unable to control their blood glucose concentration

17 Hormones

17

Practical skills

Practise your practical skills using the worked example and practice questions below.

Draw a calibration curve

A calibration curve can be used to determine the concentration of an unknown sample of a substance by comparing it to a set of standard samples of a known concentration.

For example, the wavelength of light that passes through urine samples with different known concentrations of glucose (absorbance) could be measured using a colorimeter. The calibration curve this produces then allows the unknown glucose concentration of a urine sample to be determined by measuring the light absorbance and finding that point on the curve.

Worked example

Question

The test for a reducing sugar (Benedict's reagent) is carried out on known concentrations of glucose.

Glucose concentration (mmol dm^{-3})	Absorbance (a.u.)
0.0	0.000
0.6	0.002
1.2	0.056
1.8	0.140
2.4	0.218
3.6	0.346
4.8	0.477
6.0	0.629

Draw a calibration curve of these results.

Answer

This is a good test of your graph drawing skills. It's extremely important that you plot your points accurately, and make your curve as smooth as possible, otherwise your readings of unknowns could be inaccurate.

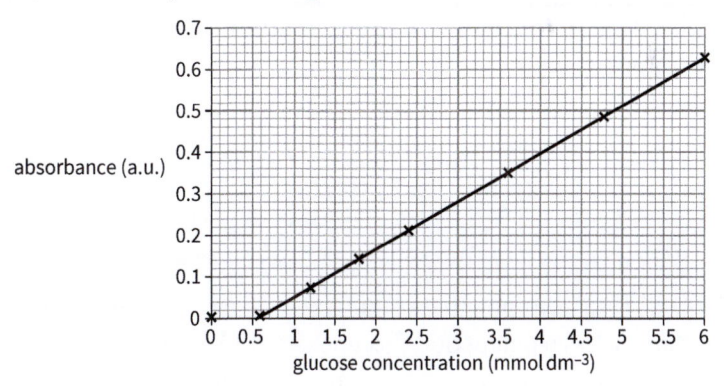

Practice

1 Three samples are tested and have the following absorbances. Determine what the glucose concentrations of the urine samples are. Give your answer to 2 significant figures.

   a 0.100   b 0.550   c 0.325

2 Three samples are known to have the following glucose concentrations. Predict what the absorbance values will be. Give your answer to 2 significant figures.

   a 1.5   b 3.0   c 5.8

3 A student uses the calibration curve to predict that the absorbance of a sample with 10 mmol dm^3 would be 1.122. State if you think this prediction is valid, and explain your answer.

For answers and more practice questions visit www.oxfordrevise.com/scienceanswers

Even more practice and interactive revision quizzes are available on kerboodle

17 Retrieval 197

Practice

Exam-style questions

1 The adrenal glands secrete different types of hormone from their medulla and cortex regions.

Synoptic links
2.1.3g 2.1.5di 5.1.5j

(a) Complete **Table 1.1** by placing ticks (✓) in the relevant boxes to show the features of the adrenal cortex and adrenal medulla.

Feature	Cortex	Medulla
secretes steroid hormones		
secretes hormones that affect carbohydrate metabolism		
secretes noradrenaline		
located on the outside of the adrenal glands		

Table 1.1 [4]

(b) Describe the cellular effects caused by adrenaline when it binds to its target cell.

....
....
....
....
....
.... [5]

(c) Explain how steroid hormones can pass through cell surface membranes.

....
....
....
.... [2]

(d) Prolactin is a hormone that stimulates milk production in mammals. It is a polypeptide composed of 198 amino acids.

(i) State the name of the organelle responsible for synthesising prolactin.

.... [1]

(ii) Suggest and explain how prolactin causes an effect in its target cells.

....
....
....
....
.... [2]

Exam tip

When you are asked to 'suggest', the question will usually require you to apply your understanding of a topic to a novel example.

17 Hormones

2   A photomicrograph of pancreatic tissue is shown in **Figure 2.1**.

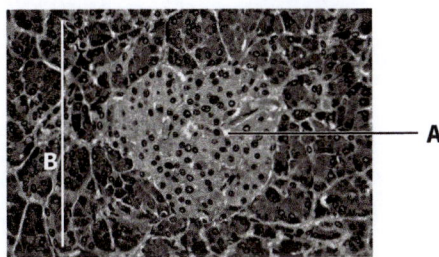

Figure 2.1

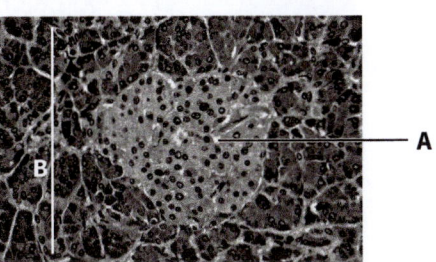

(a) Describe the structure and function of the tissue labelled **A**.

....
....
....
.... [4]

> **Synoptic link**
>
> 2.1.1e

(b) The microscope magnification used to produce **Figure 2.1** was ×500. Calculate the object length of the line labelled **B** in **Figure 2.1**.

.... [2]

> **Exam tip**
>
> You may be asked to calculate microscope magnification or the object size of biological material. In both cases, you will need to measure the size of the image provided as accurately as possible.

3   Blood glucose concentration is regulated by alpha and beta cells in the pancreas.

(a) Place the events, **A** to **H**, in the correct order in the boxes below to outline how the secretion of insulin is controlled in the beta cells of the pancreas.

   A K^+ ion channels close
   B   glucose is metabolised to produce ATP
   C Ca^{2+} ions diffuse into the beta cell
   D K^+ ion concentration increases inside the beta cell
   E   glucose enters a beta cell through a transporter protein
   F   ATP binds to K^+ ion channels
   G   voltage-gated Ca^{2+} ion channels open
   H   secretory vesicles release insulin via exocytosis

   ☐ ☐ ☐ ☐ ☐ ☐ ☐ ☐   [4]

(b) Describe the roles of the pancreas and the liver in raising blood glucose concentration.

....
....
....
....
....
.... [6]

> **Exam tip**
>
> Note that this level of response question requires only one side of the blood glucose homeostasis story: how glucose concentration is increased. Writing about the effect of insulin here would be irrelevant.

4 Type 1 and type 2 diabetes are the most common forms of diabetes mellitus.

(a) Complete **Table 4.1** to outline the features of type 1 and type 2 diabetes mellitus.

Feature	Type 1 diabetes	Type 2 diabetes
cause		
typical age at onset		
usual treatment		

Table 4.1

Synoptic link

6.1.2bi

Exam tip

The space provided in a table indicates the length of answer that is expected. In this question, you are asked to 'outline' the features, which means your answers can be single words, terms, or short sentences.

[5]

(b) Compare the genetic and environmental influence on the development of type 1 and type 2 diabetes.

....
....
.... [3]

(c) Latent Autoimmune Diabetes of Adulthood (LADA) is a form of type 1 diabetes that tends to develop in adulthood.

Suggest why LADA can be misdiagnosed as type 2 diabetes.

....
.... [1]

(d) Double diabetes occurs when someone with type 1 diabetes develops insulin resistance, which is a key feature of type 2 diabetes.

Suggest how double diabetes should be treated.

....
.... [2]

(e) Maturity-onset diabetes of the young (MODY) is a heritable condition that shows autosomal dominant inheritance.

Calculate the probability of two parents who are both heterozygous for the MODY gene having a child with MODY.

.... [1]

200 17 Hormones

5 Describe the current treatments and potential future treatments for diabetes mellitus.

....

....

....

....

....

....

....

.... [6]

> **! Exam tip**
>
> Read the wording of level of response questions carefully. There are four facets to this answer: current treatments, potential future treatments, and both types of diabetes. It would be easy to overlook type 2 diabetes when answering this question.

6 In an oral glucose tolerance test, a person is given a specific amount of glucose. Their blood glucose concentration is then monitored over several hours.

The following shows the responses of two people to an oral glucose tolerance test:

1   a person with type 2 diabetes
2   a healthy person.

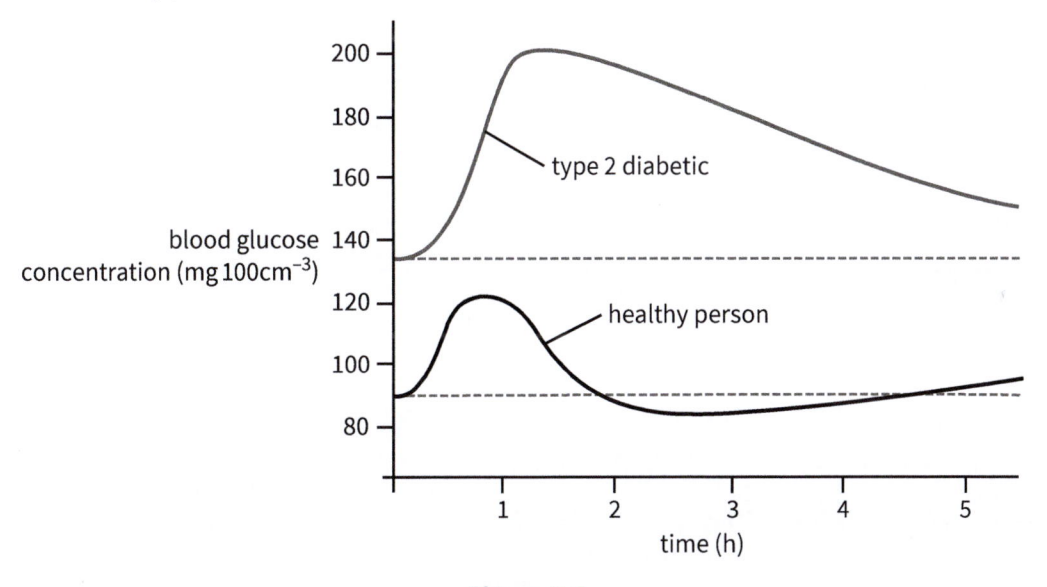

Figure 6.1

(a) (i) Describe the differences in the responses of a healthy person and a type 2 diabetic shown in **Figure 6.1**.

....

....

.... [3]

(ii) Explain the differences in the responses of a healthy person and a type 2 diabetic shown in **Figure 6.1**.

....

....

.... [3]

> **! Exam tip**
>
> Take note of whether you are being asked to 'describe' or 'explain' data from a graph. Some questions will require you to do both.

For answers and more practice questions visit www.oxfordrevise.com/scienceanswers

Even more practice and interactive revision quizzes are available on kerboodle

17 Practice   201

Knowledge

18 Plant and animal responses

Plant responses

Plants respond to abiotic factors and changing conditions in their environments through **defence mechanisms** and **tropisms**.

Plants have defence mechanisms to respond to herbivory. **Chemical defences** include production of:

- **tannins** – reduce nutritional value of plants by preventing digestion of proteins in herbivores and can be toxic
- **alkaloids** – give plants a bitter taste and can be toxic
- **pheromones** – plants being grazed release pheromones which alert some nearby plants to increase tannin production.

Some plants also respond to touch – the sensitive plant *Mimosa pudica* folds its leaflets when touched.

All plants display **tropisms**. A tropism is a growth response to a directional stimulus, and can be towards (positive tropism) or away from (negative tropism) the stimulus.

Stimuli that generate tropisms include:

- light – phototropism
- water – hydrotropism
- gravity – gravitropism / geotropism
- chemicals – chemotropism
- contact – thigmotropism (how climbers curl shoots around supports).

Plant hormones

Plant responses to abiotic stress and environmental changes are coordinated by **plant hormones**. Hormones are involved in:

Leaf fall in deciduous plants
Levels of **cytokinins** in a leaf decline, and the leaf will start to age and brown.

The level of **auxins** in the leaf also starts to decrease, which has two effects:

1 Cells in the abscission layer (between the petiole and the stem) become more sensitive to **ethene**.
2 More ethene is produced.

This increases production of cellulase, which digests cells in the abscission layer, causing the leaf to fall.

Seed germination
Water is absorbed by the seed. **Gibberellins** diffuse from the embryo to the aleurone layer, where they stimulate the production of amylase. Amylase hydrolyses the starch food store, thus releasing glucose for the embryo. Germination begins.

Stomatal closure
When flowering plants experience water stress (a lack of water), they close their stomata. This is brought about by **abscisic acid** which binds to receptors on guard cells. This causes a change in pH in the cytoplasm, and both positive and negative ions leave the guard cell. The water potential of the cell increases, causing water to leave the cell, and the cell loses turgidity. The stoma closes.

202 18 Plant and animal responses

18

Experimental evidence for the roles of plant hormones – auxins

Auxins produced in the apex (top bud of a stem) inhibit the growth from lateral buds. If the apical tip is removed, the plant grows from lateral buds. This is called **apical dominance** and was demonstrated in a series of experiments.

1. Paste containing auxins were applied to the cut shoot and the lateral buds did not grow. But this may have been due to another factor, such as another hormone being produced in response to oxygen exposure.

2. A ring of auxin transporter inhibitor applied below the apical tip allowed lateral growth. This suggested normal levels of auxins inhibit lateral growth but low levels promote lateral growth. However, this assumes a direct link between hormone concentration and plant growth – more variables may be involved.

3. A direct link was proven when researchers discovered auxin concentrations in lateral buds increase when the apical tip is removed.

Two other plant hormones, abscisic acid and cytokinins, may also have a role in apical dominance.

The effect of plant hormones on growth can be investigated using concentrations of hormones prepared using a serial dilution.

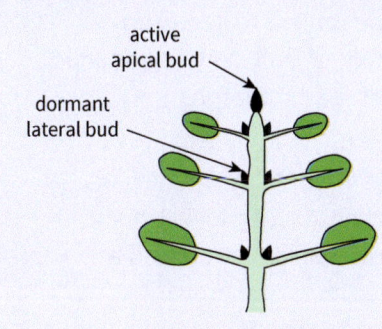

Experimental evidence for the roles of plant hormones – gibberellins

1. When gibberellins (GA_3) were applied to dwarf varieties of plants, like cabbages and peas, they all grew taller. Researchers could assume that gibberellins caused stem elongation but they needed to show that gibberellins would cause these effects using naturally occurring concentrations of gibberellins in parts of the plants where they normally occur.

2. Researchers found that tall pea plants had higher concentrations of a similar gibberellin, GA_1, than dwarf pea plants. All the plants were genetically identical apart from a single allele, *Le/le*. The allele *Le* in the tall plants was found to code for an enzyme that synthesised GA_1 from a precursor, GA_{20}. The allele *le* in the dwarf plants did not produce this enzyme.

3. GA_1 was confirmed as the hormone that causes stem elongation by grafting a homozygous *le* dwarf pea plant onto rootstock that could produce the enzyme but could not produce GA_{20}. The grafted dwarf pea plant grew to a normal height because it synthesised GA_1 using its own GA_{20} and the enzyme from the grafted rootstock.

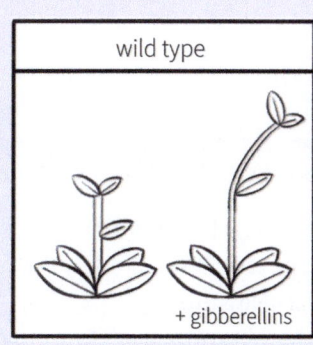

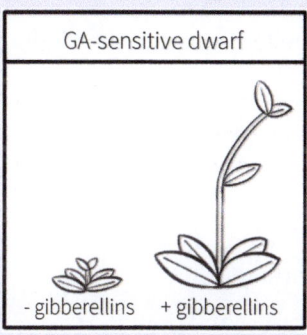

The commercial use of plant hormones

Some plant hormones have important roles commercially.

Control fruit ripening
Ethene is used to speed up ripening of fruit such as bananas, apples, and tomatoes.

Restricting ethene can also be useful to delay ripening of fruit. Low oxygen levels, high carbon dioxide levels, and a low temperature prevent ethene synthesis.

Rooting powders
Synthetic auxins are used in rooting powders because they stimulate the growth of roots from cut stems.

They are used to encourage cuttings to make roots.

Hormonal weed killers
Synthetic auxins are used as selective weed killers to kill broad-leaved weeds (dicotyledonous) in fields of narrow-leaved monocotyledons (e.g., wheat).

The auxins increase the rate of growth of the weeds. The weeds are unable to absorb enough nutrients and energy from their surrounding to keep up with the accelerated growth rate and soon die.

The human brain

The brain is found at the top end of the spinal cord. It consists of white matter on the inside and grey matter on the outside. The human brain has three distinct regions: the forebrain (the **cerebrum**), the midbrain, and the hindbrain. The brain is surrounded by three membranes called the meninges and is encased in the skull.

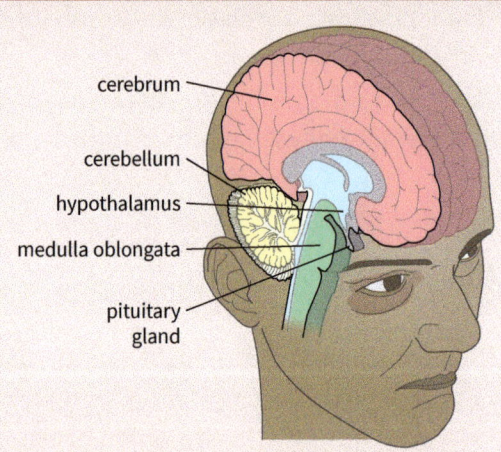

Structure	Function
cerebrum – divided into two hemispheres connected by the corpus callosum	• receives sensory information, interprets it, and sends out motor impulses to bring about a voluntary response • site of learning, reasoning, intelligence, personality, memory, conscious thought
cerebellum – part of the hindbrain	• coordinates muscle movement such as balance and fine movement
medulla oblongata – part of the hindbrain	• controls non-skeletal muscle • control centre for the autonomic nervous system • contains regulatory centres – cardiac and respiratory centres
hypothalamus – found at the base of the forebrain	• controls most of the body's homeostatic mechanisms • links the nervous and endocrine systems
pituitary gland	• regulated by the hypothalamus, stores hormones, such as ADH

18

Organisation of the mammalian nervous system

The mammalian nervous system is divided into the central nervous system (CNS) and the peripheral nervous system (PNS). The PNS is then further subdivided into the autonomic and the somatic nervous systems.

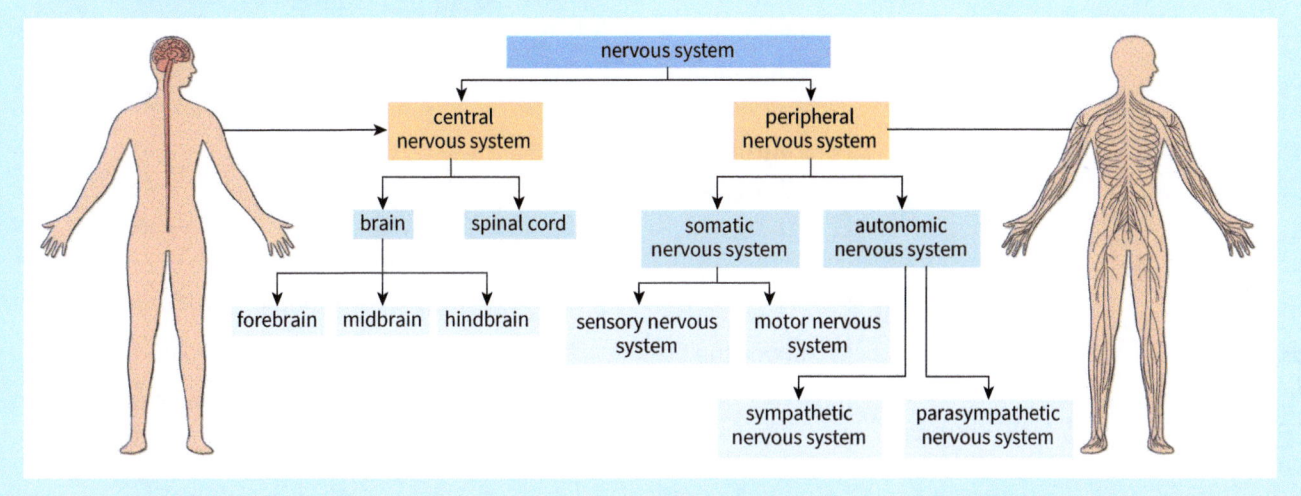

```
                        nervous system
                       /              \
              central                   peripheral
              nervous system            nervous system
              /         \              /            \
         brain       spinal cord   somatic        autonomic
                                   nervous system  nervous system
        /    |    \                /       \       /         \
  forebrain midbrain hindbrain  sensory  motor  sympathetic parasympathetic
                                nervous  nervous nervous    nervous
                                system   system  system     system
```

Endocrine response

The **'fight or flight'** response in mammals to environmental stimuli is an important survival mechanism that requires coordination of both the nervous system and the endocrine system, via the hypothalamus.

The hormone **adrenaline** is released through signalling of the sympathetic nervous system during a fight or flight response and has multiple effects on the body due to **cell signalling**.

Adrenaline acts as a **first messenger** and binds to a complementary receptor on the cell surface membrane of a target cell. The hormone-receptor complex activates **adenylyl cyclase**, which in turns converts ATP to **cyclic AMP** (cAMP). cAMP acts as a **second messenger** and activates a cascade of enzyme activity within the cell.

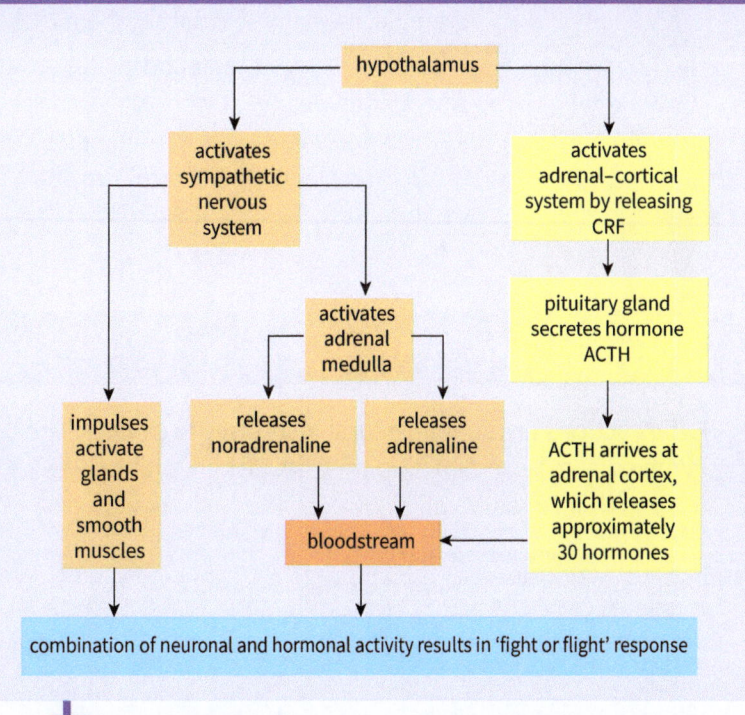

```
                        hypothalamus
                       /            \
           activates                  activates
           sympathetic                adrenal-cortical
           nervous                    system by releasing
           system                     CRF
              |                          |
              |                       pituitary gland
              |                       secretes hormone
           activates                  ACTH
           adrenal                       |
           medulla                       |
          /      \                    ACTH arrives at
   releases    releases               adrenal cortex,
   noradrenaline adrenaline           which releases
                                      approximately
   impulses      |                    30 hormones
   activate    bloodstream ←──────────┘
   glands
   and
   smooth
   muscles
```

combination of neuronal and hormonal activity results in 'fight or flight' response

Effects of hormones and nervous mechanisms on heart rate

The sinoatrial node in the wall of the right atrium of the heart is connected to the cardiovascular centre in the medulla oblongata in the brain by the autonomic nervous system. The autonomic (self governing) nervous system influences heart rate to slow it down, via the parasympathetic nervous system, or increase it via the sympathetic nervous system.

Myogenic heart muscle responds directly to adrenaline to increase the heart rate when adrenaline is present in the blood.

18 Knowledge 205

Mammalian muscle

Type of muscle	Location	Function	Structure
cardiac	• heart only	• pumps blood • myogenic (initiates own contractions) • controlled by autonomic NS	• fibres are made of many cells in rows • striated (striped) appearance • cells are divided by intercalating discs
skeletal (also called voluntary or striated muscle)	• makes up the bulk of the muscle in the body • attaches to bone by non-elastic tendons	• moves the body under voluntary control of the somatic NS	• a muscle is made up of hundreds of muscle fibres, which in turn contain myofibrils
involuntary (also called smooth muscle)	• in organ walls, for example, uterus, intestines, bladder • smooth muscles are also present in the iris and blood vessels	• under control of the autonomic NS • found in antagonistic pairs, for example, to control size of the pupil	• no fibres or striations • cells appear elongated into spindle shapes

Reflex actions

Reflex actions are simple, neural responses to danger. The brain is not involved in reflex actions, so they are fast, involuntary, often protective actions that aid survival.

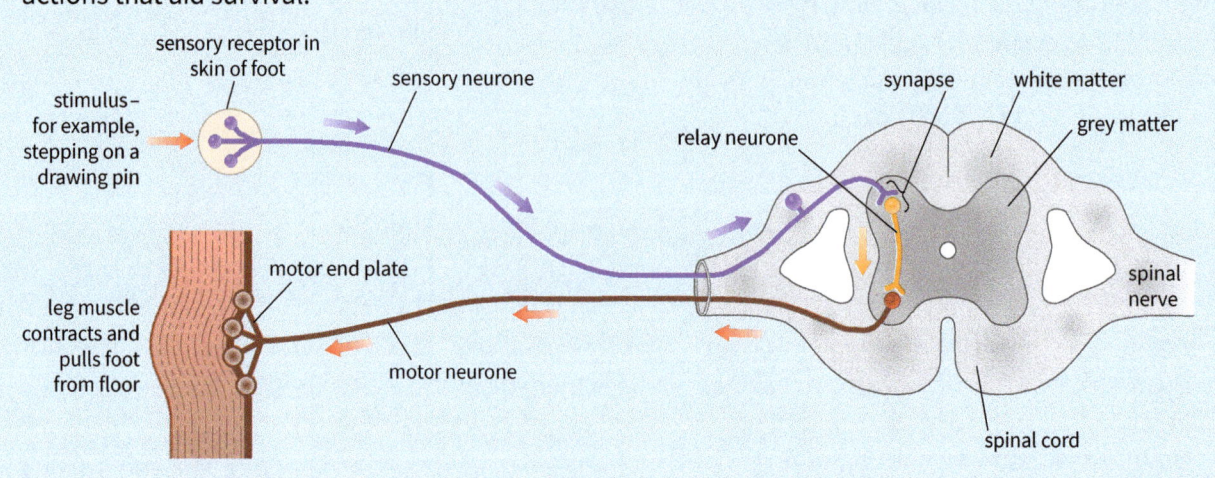

Neuromuscular junctions

A **neuromuscular junction** is the place where a motor neurone meets a muscle fibre.

There are many neuromuscular junctions along the length of muscle tissue to ensure the muscle contracts rapidly and forcefully.

When a nerve impulse arrives at the junction, acetylcholine is released into the synaptic cleft. It binds to its receptor on the postsynaptic membrane (sarcolemma) which allows sodium ions to rapidly enter the muscle fibre, causing depolarisation of the membrane and muscle contraction.

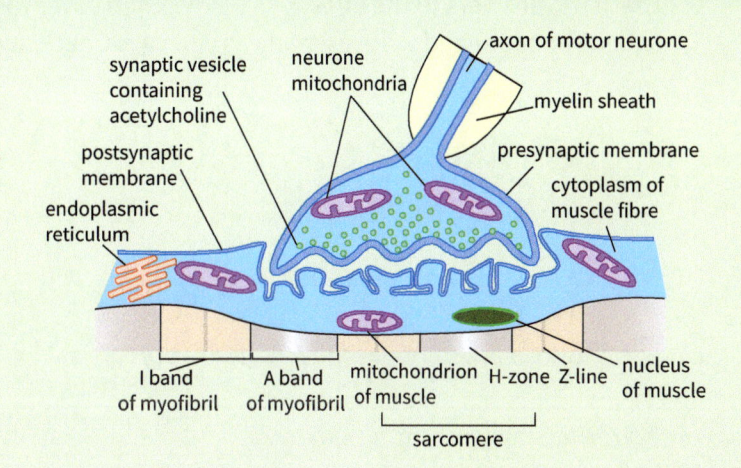

The sliding filament model

Two protein filaments are involved in muscle contraction:

- **actin** – two thin strands, which are twisted together
- **myosin** – thick filaments with heads at each end, arranged in bundles

A myosin head forms a cross bridge with actin in the presence of calcium ions, releasing inorganic phosphate from hydrolysed ATP. The head bends (releasing ADP) and pulls actin over the myosin – the '**power stroke**'. New ATP attaches to the myosin head causing it to detach from actin. As ATP is hydrolysed, the released energy re-cocks the myosin head.

A muscle fibre only contains enough ATP to allow for 1–2 seconds of contraction. Creatine phosphate maintains a supply of ATP in a muscle cell by rapidly transferring inorganic phosphate to ADP.

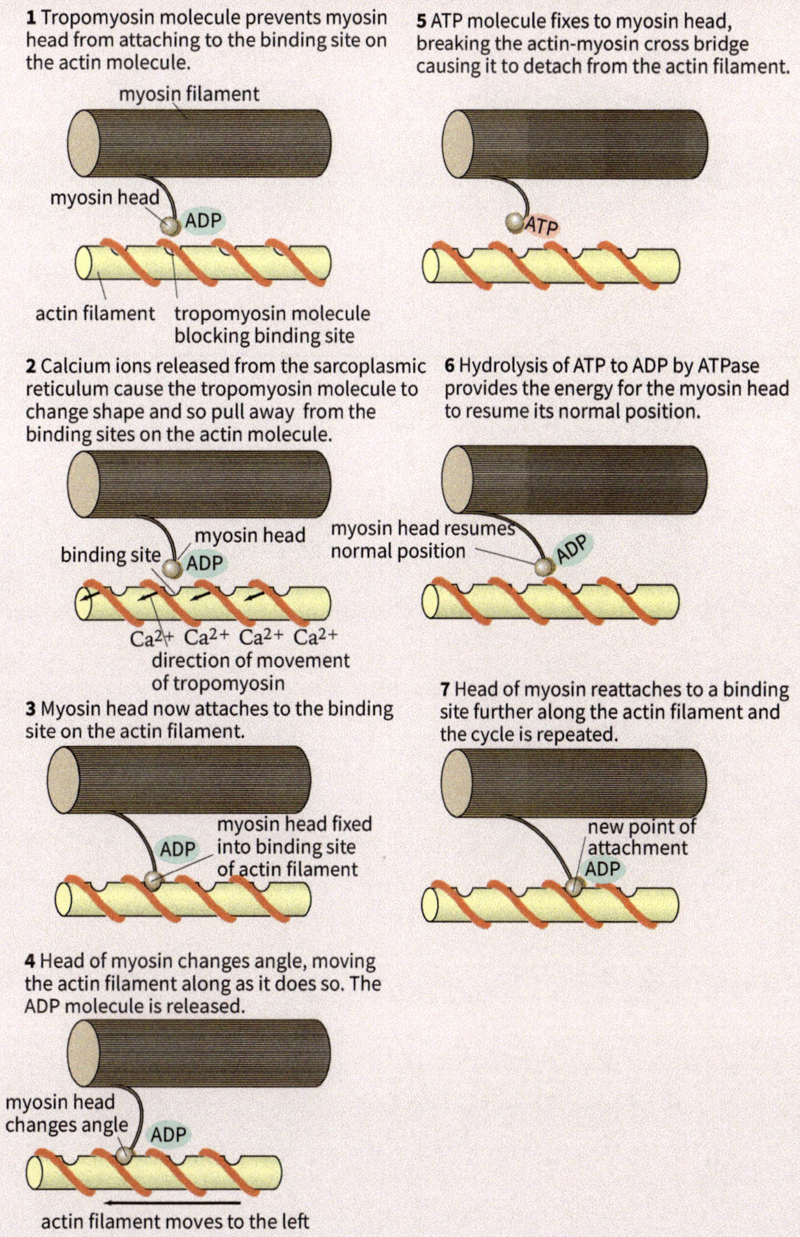

1 Tropomyosin molecule prevents myosin head from attaching to the binding site on the actin molecule.

2 Calcium ions released from the sarcoplasmic reticulum cause the tropomyosin molecule to change shape and so pull away from the binding sites on the actin molecule.

3 Myosin head now attaches to the binding site on the actin filament.

4 Head of myosin changes angle, moving the actin filament along as it does so. The ADP molecule is released.

5 ATP molecule fixes to myosin head, breaking the actin-myosin cross bridge causing it to detach from the actin filament.

6 Hydrolysis of ATP to ADP by ATPase provides the energy for the myosin head to resume its normal position.

7 Head of myosin reattaches to a binding site further along the actin filament and the cycle is repeated.

For answers and more practice questions visit www.oxfordrevise.com/scienceanswers

Even more practice and interactive revision quizzes are available on kerboodle

Retrieval

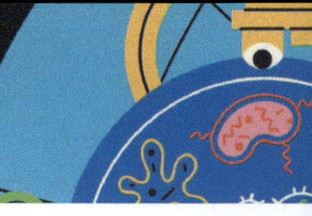

Learn the answers to the questions below, then cover the answers column with a piece of paper and write as many as you can. Check and repeat.

	Questions	Answers
1	What does herbivory stimulate in plants?	defence mechanisms
2	How do pheromones prevent herbivory?	grazed plants release them to stimulate neighbouring plants and some increase production of tannins
3	What is a tropism?	a growth response to a directional stimulus
4	List five different types of tropism.	gravitropism / geotropism, phototropism, hydrotropism, thigmotropism (response to contact), chemotropism
5	What is the difference between a negative tropism and a positive tropism to a stimulus?	positive is growth towards, negative is growth away from the stimulus
6	List the names of the three plant hormones involved in deciduous leaf fall.	ethene, cytokinins, auxins
7	How do auxins produce leaf fall?	decreasing levels of auxins cause cells in the abscission layer to become more sensitive to ethene, which increases production of cellulase
8	Which plant hormone is involved in stomatal closure?	abscisic acid
9	Under which conditions do stomata close?	water stress / lack of water
10	Which plant hormone has been shown to cause apical dominance?	auxin
11	Which hormones have been shown to cause stem elongation and seed germination?	gibberellins
12	List the three regions of the brain.	forebrain, midbrain, hindbrain
13	Where is the cerebrum and what is its role?	the forebrain; site of learning, reasoning, intelligence, personality, memory, conscious thought
14	Which part of the brain is responsible for balance and fine movement?	cerebellum
15	What are the two subdivisions of the nervous system, and what makes up these two subdivisions?	central nervous system (CNS) – brain and spinal cord peripheral nervous system (PNS) – autonomic and somatic nervous systems
16	List the pathway of a reflex action.	stimulus – receptor - sensory neurone – relay neurone – motor neurone – effector – response
17	How does stimulation of the sympathetic nerve system affect heart rate?	increases heart rate
18	What are the three types of mammalian muscle?	cardiac, skeletal, involuntary

208 18 Plant and animal responses

Maths skills

Practise your maths skills using the worked example and practice questions below.

The Student's *t*-test

The Student's *t*-test is a statistical test used to compare the means of two data sets to test a hypothesis, and tells you if the difference between the sets is significant and not due to chance.

The Student's *t*-test is calculated using the following formula:

$$t = \frac{(\bar{x}_1 - \bar{x}_2)^2}{\sqrt{\frac{\sigma_1^2}{N_1} + \frac{\sigma_2^2}{N_2}}}$$

$\bar{x}$ = mean of each data set
σ = standard deviation of each data set
N = number of elements in each data set

Worked example

Question

Five students from years 7, 9, and 13 were tested for their reaction times by measuring the distance the ruler fell before it was caught. Their results are displayed in the table below, and their null hypothesis is that age will have no effect on reaction times.

Calculate the *t* value for years 7 and 9. Give your answer to 3 significant figures.

Student number	Year 7 reaction time (cm)	Year 9 reaction time (cm)	Year 13 reaction time (cm)
1	16.2	11.1	9.4
2	17.5	7.6	10.6
3	19.9	10.9	6.7
4	12.0	7.1	8.1
5	12.3	10.5	10.1

Answer

This is a long calculation so take this step by step. All numbers are given to 3 significant figures.

Step 1: Calculate the mean values for each data set. $\bar{x}_1 = 15.6$ $\bar{x}_2 = 9.44$
Step 2: Calculate the standard deviation for each data set (see the maths skills in **Chapter 11**).
$\sigma_1 = 3.402$ $\sigma_2 = 1.93$
Step 3: Calculate *t* by putting all your calculated values into the formula.

$$t = \frac{(15.6 - 9.44)}{\sqrt{\frac{3.402^2}{5} + \frac{1.93^2}{5}}} = 3.52$$

Step 4: Compare your value of *t* against a table of values of *t*. Remember the degrees of freedom is the number of elements minus one (i.e., 5 – 1).
If your value for *t* is greater than the value given for $p = 0.05$, the difference between the means is considered significant, so you can reject the null hypothesis.

Practice

1 Calculate the *t* values for the years 9 and 13, and 7 and 13 groups.

   Give your answers to 3 significant figures.

Practice

Exam-style questions

1   The sliding filament model describes the contraction of muscles.

(a) Place the events, **A** to **H**, in the correct order in the boxes below to describe the sliding filament model of muscle contraction.

   A   myosin-binding sites on actin are uncovered
   B   troponin changes shape
   C   the power stroke
   D   ADP is released from the myosin head
   E Ca^{2+} ions bind to troponin
   F   myosin head binds to actin, forming cross bridges
   G   tropomyosin moves
   H   myosin head binds to ATP, causing it to detach from actin

   ☐ ☐ ☐ ☐ ☐ ☐ ☐ ☐   [4]

(b) Skeletal muscle and involuntary smooth muscle have different structures and functions.

(i) Complete **Table 1.1** by placing ticks (✓) in the relevant boxes to outline the characteristics of skeletal and involuntary smooth muscle.

Characteristic	Skeletal muscle	Involuntary smooth muscle
striated		
controlled only by the autonomic nervous system		
attached to tendons		
contains actin and myosin		

Table 1.1   [4]

(ii) State one location of smooth muscle in a mammalian body.

....

.... [1]

210   18 Plant and animal responses

(c) **Figure 1.1** shows a longitudinal cross section of mammalian skeletal muscle tissue.

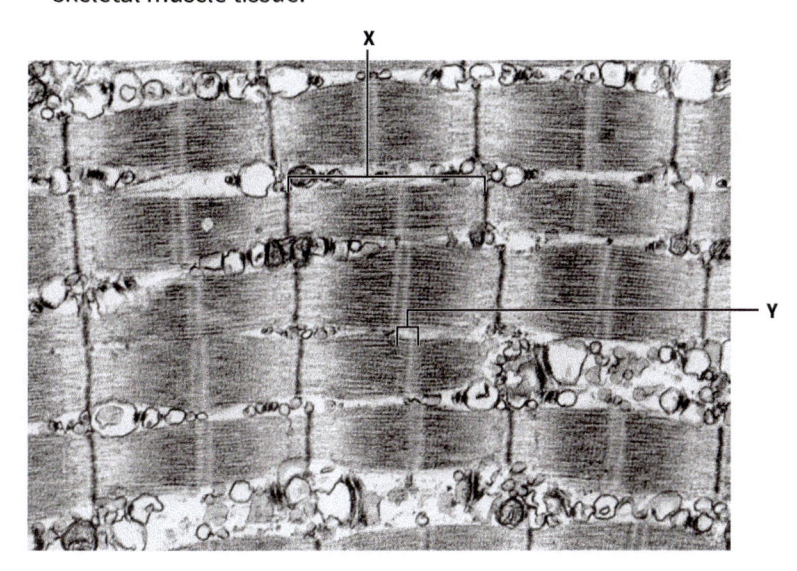

Figure 1.1

(i) State the name of the section of muscle tissue labelled **X** in the image above.

.... [1]

(ii) Explain why the section labelled **Y** in the image above changes length during muscle contraction.

....
....
....
....
....
....
....
.... [3]

> **Exam tip**
> You may be asked to examine and interpret either diagrams or micrographs of muscle tissue.

2   Hormones have a range of roles in plants.

(a) Complete **Table 2.1** to outline the roles of hormones in plants.

Role	Hormone
causing leaf loss (abcission)	
controls apical dominance	
	gibberellin

Table 2.1 [3]

> **Synoptic link**
> 2.1.2q

(b) A group of students planned an experiment to investigate the effect of the plant hormone ethene on the rate of fruit ripening.

The students based their experimental method on two pieces of knowledge:
- Bananas release ethene.
- Starch is broken down when fruits ripen.

The students followed these five steps in their experiment:

(1) Seal eight plastic bags, each with one unripe pear inside.

(2) Place a banana inside four of these bags (the test bags).

(3) Record observations of the appearance of the fruit.

(4) After three days, test the pears by staining them with iodine solution.

(5) Compare the level of iodine staining on the pears in the test bags and the pears in the control bags.

(i) Describe three improvements to the students' method.

....
....
....
....
....
.... **[3]**

(ii) Explain why the students expected the pears in the control bags to show a higher level of iodine staining.

....
....
....
....
....
.... **[2]**

> **! Exam tip**
>
> When you are asked to suggest improvements to an experimental method, you can consider several questions: are the equipment and apparatus appropriate (with a high resolution and low uncertainty)? Is the sample size large enough? Are other variables being controlled?

(c) Another group of students investigated the effect of the hormone cytokinin on the rate of ageing in plants.

The students wanted to produce a 0.005 mol dm^{-3} solution of cytokinin from a starting solution of 1 mol dm^{-3}.

Describe how the students can produce the 0.005 mol dm^{-3} solution of cytokinin.

.... **[3]**

3 Many scientists have researched the effects of plant hormones and environmental factors on flowering in plants.

(a) One scientist investigated the effect of periods of darkness and light exposure on flowering in cocklebur plants. Each plant was subjected to a fixed duration of 'nights' (periods of darkness) over several weeks and observed to see whether it produced flowers. Some plants were exposed to light during their periods of darkness.

The scientist's results are shown in **Table 3.1**.

Period of darkness during each 24h day (h)	Light exposure during the period of darkness?	Flower production?
6.5	no	no
6.5	far-red light	yes
8.5	no	yes
12.5	red light after 6 hours	no
12.5	red light after 6 hours, followed by far-red light	yes

Table 3.1

What conclusions can you draw from these results about the effect of darkness and light exposure on flowering in cocklebur plants?

....
....
....
....
....
....
.... [4]

> **Exam tip**
>
> The number of marks available in a question indicates the number of points you should include. You should be looking to include four conclusions in this particular answer.

(b) Flowering is one factor that can be controlled when growing plants for commercial purposes.

Outline the uses of named plant hormones when growing plants for commercial purposes.

....
....
....
....
....
....
....
.... [6]

4 (a) Outline the organisation of the mammalian nervous system.

....
....
....
....
....
....
....
....
....
.... [6]

Synoptic links

5.1.3b 5.1.3c

(b) **Figure 4.1** shows the structure of a human brain in longitudinal section.

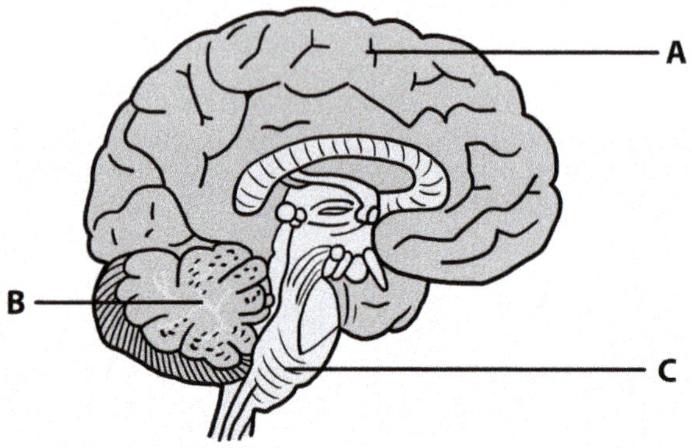

Figure 4.1

Name the parts of the brain labelled **A**, **B**, and **C**, and state their functions.

Name of **A**: ....

Function of **A**: ....

Name of **B**: ....

Function of **B**: ....

Name of **C**: ....

Function of **C**: .... [6]

(c) Motor neurones transmit nervous impulses from the brain to effectors.

Explain how the structure of a motor neurone cell is adapted to carry out its function.

....
....
....
....
.... [3]

Exam tip

To answer this question, you will need to describe a structural feature of a motor neurone and then explain how this feature is adapted to the function of the cell.

214 18 Plant and animal responses

5 Reflex responses help organisms to survive because they are fast, requiring only one or two synaptic connections.

(a) State two other general features of reflex responses that help organisms survive.

....

.... [2]

> **Exam tip**
> Here, 'general features' implies characteristics found in all reflex responses. Do not describe specific examples of reflexes.

(b) Students planned to investigate how the speed of reflex responses changes with age.

(i) Suggest two variables that the students should control in their investigation.

....

.... [2]

(ii) State the statistical test that the students should use to analyse the relationship between age and the speed of reflex responses.

.... [1]

(c) Most reflexes rely on synaptic connections between sensory neurones and relay neurones in the spinal cord.

Describe two differences between the structure of a relay neurone and the structure of a sensory neurone.

....

....

....

.... [2]

6 Adrenaline is a hormone that is secreted during the fight or flight response to an environmental stimulus.

(a) (i) State the name of the branch of the autonomic nervous system that is responsible for stimulating the release of adrenaline.

.... [1]

(ii) Vasopressin is a non-steroid hormone, like adrenaline.

Suggest the mechanism by which vasopressin produces an effect in its target cell.

....

....

....

....

....

.... [4]

> **Exam tip**
> You are not required to know about vasopressin. However, you are told that it is similar to adrenaline (i.e., it is non-steroidal and therefore will not pass through cell surface membranes). You should have learned how adrenaline affects target cells.

Knowledge

19 Photosynthesis

Photosynthesis: an overview

Photosynthesis has two groups of reactions:

- The **light-dependent reactions** where light energy is absorbed by pigments, such as chlorophyll, and a water molecule is split by photolysis.
- The **light-independent reactions** where carbon dioxide is synthesised into useful organic compounds.

Photosynthesis uses carbon dioxide and produces oxygen as a by-product.

The word equation for photosynthesis is:

carbon dioxide + water → glucose + oxygen

The symbol equation for photosynthesis is:

$6CO_2 + 6H_2O \rightarrow C_6H_{12}O_6 + 6O_2$

Respiration uses oxygen and produces carbon dioxide as a by-product.

The word equation for respiration is:

glucose + oxygen → carbon dioxide and water

The symbol equation for respiration is:

$C_6H_{12}O_6 + 6O_2 \rightarrow 6CO_2 + 6H_2O$ (+ energy)

The structure of a chloroplast

Photosynthesis occurs in the chloroplasts. The light-dependent reactions occur on the thylakoid membranes and the light-independent reactions occur in the stroma.

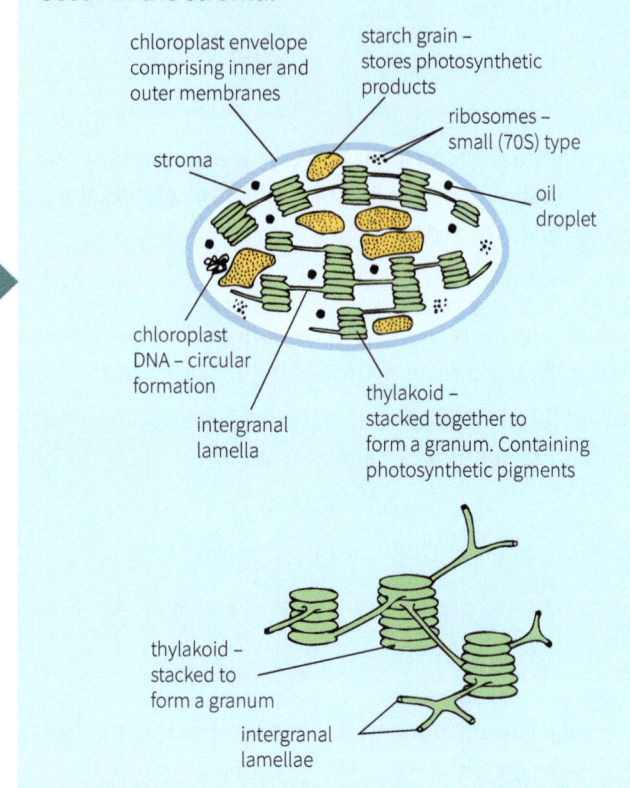

Labels:
- chloroplast envelope comprising inner and outer membranes
- starch grain – stores photosynthetic products
- ribosomes – small (70S) type
- stroma
- oil droplet
- chloroplast DNA – circular formation
- intergranal lamella
- thylakoid – stacked together to form a granum. Containing photosynthetic pigments
- thylakoid – stacked to form a granum
- intergranal lamellae

Flow chart of photosynthesis

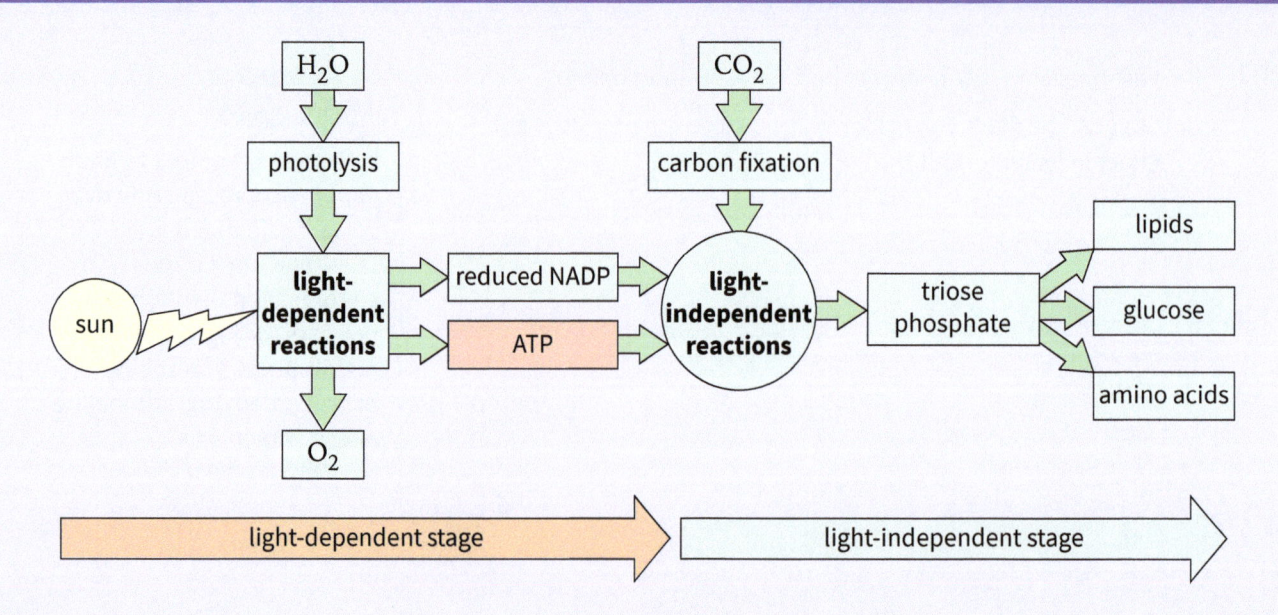

sun → light-dependent reactions

H₂O → photolysis → light-dependent reactions

light-dependent reactions → reduced NADP → light-independent reactions
light-dependent reactions → ATP → light-independent reactions
light-dependent reactions → O₂

CO₂ → carbon fixation → light-independent reactions

light-independent reactions → triose phosphate → lipids / glucose / amino acids

light-dependent stage | light-independent stage

216 19 Photosynthesis

Light-independent reactions

This is when carbon from carbon dioxide is used to synthesise organic molecules such as simple sugars. These reactions occur in the stroma of the chloroplasts.

This is done in a cycle (the Calvin cycle) that uses enzymes to synthesise intermediate organic molecules, using reduced NADP and ATP from the light-dependent reactions.

Calvin cycle

Carbon dioxide (1) reacts with **ribulose bisphosphate** (RuBP) (a simple sugar) (2).

This is catalysed by the enzyme **rubisco** and forms **two** molecules of **glycerate 3-phosphate** (GP) (3).

GP is reduced to **triose phosphate** using ATP (4) and reduced NADP (5) from the light-dependent reaction.

Some **triose phosphate** is used to regenerate RuBP (7), while the rest is used to make **useful organic compounds** within the plant (6).

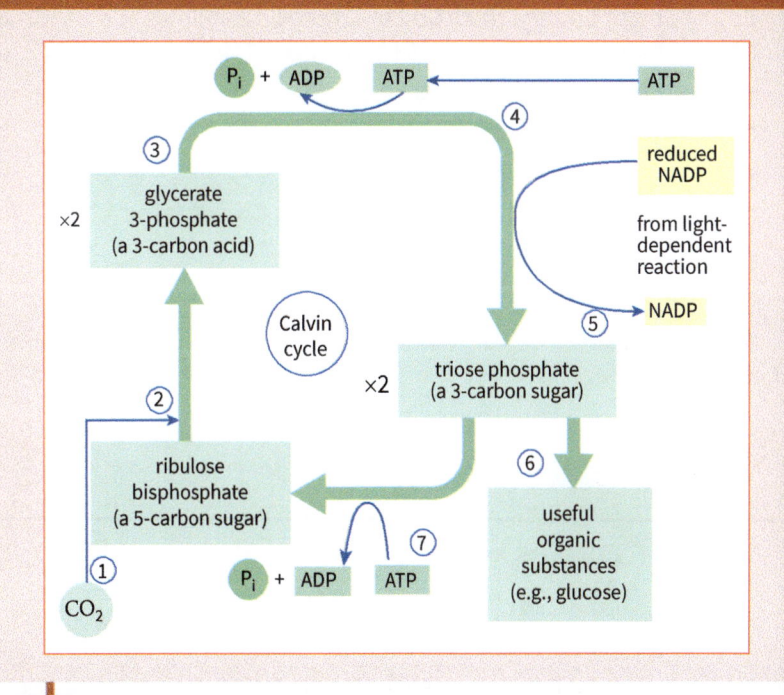

Uses of triose phosphate

Triose phosphate (TP) is a 3-carbon sugar. In the cell it is used to make important substances for the plant.

These include:

- Glucose (6-carbon sugar), used in cellular respiration.
- Cellulose, a polymer of glucose, used as a structural component of cell walls.
- Starch, a polymer of glucose, stored as granules as energy reserves.
- Disaccharides, a variety of useful sugars, such as sucrose in fruit.
- Lipids, made to store energy.
- Amino acids, to make proteins.

Light-dependent reactions

1. Light energy is absorbed by pigments in photosystem II and boosts electrons to a higher energy level.
2. The electrons are received by an electron acceptor.
3. The electrons are passed from the electron acceptor along a series of electron carriers to photosystem I. The energy lost by the electrons is captured by converting ADP to ATP. Light energy has thereby been converted to chemical energy.
4. Light energy absorbed by photosystem I boosts the electrons to an even higher energy level.
5. The electrons are received by another electron acceptor.
6. The electrons which have been removed from the chlorophyll are replaced by pulling in other electrons from a water molecule.
7. The loss of electrons from the water molecule causes it to dissociate into protons and oxygen gas.
8. The protons from the water molecule combine with the electrons from the second electron acceptor and these reduce nicotinamide adenine dinucleotide phosphate (NADP) to form reduced NADP (NADPH).
9. Some electrons from the second acceptor may pass back to the chlorophyll molecule by the electron carrier system, yielding ATP as they do so. This process is called cyclic photophosphorylation.

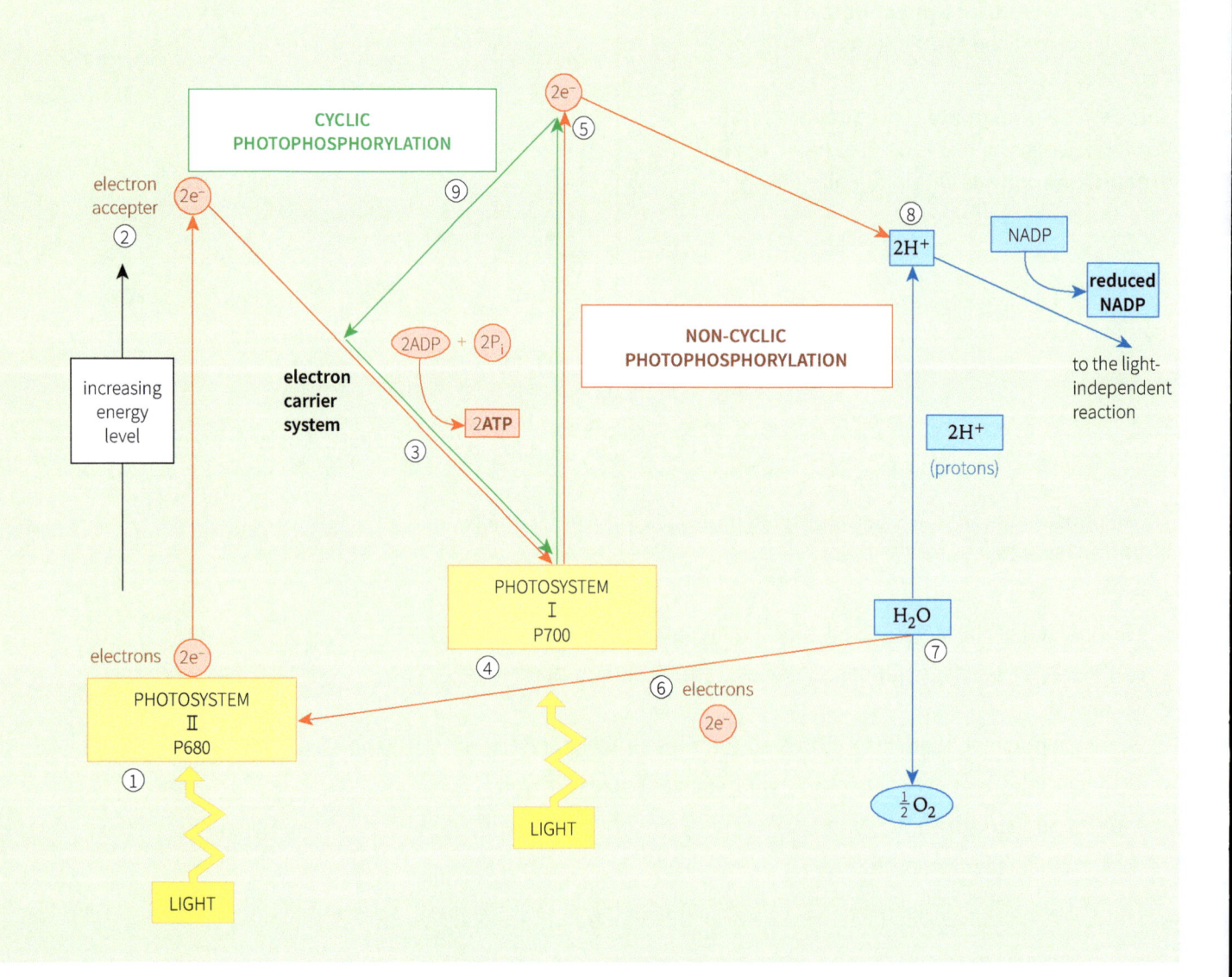

218 19 Photosynthesis

19

Factors affecting the rate of photosynthesis

Factors that affect the rate of photosynthesis are known as **limiting factors**. These factors have physiological and biochemical effects.

Saturation point refers to the point when changing a particular factor has no further effect and another limiting factor takes over.

Note that although water stress is not a limiting factor, when water is scarce the stomata close, stopping gas exchange.

Factor	Physiological	Biochemical
carbon dioxide concentration	Atmospheric concentration is 0.04% and slowly increasing. Saturation point is at 0.4% when stomata close.	At low concentrations, the reaction rate of RuBP to GP slows down. This causes levels of RuBP to increase and levels of GP and TP to decrease.
light intensity	The more intense the light, the higher the rate of photosynthesis.	Photosystems and photosynthetic pigments absorb more light and the light-dependent reactions increase. At low light intensity, the supply of ATP and reduced NADP will decrease, slowing the rate of the light-independent reactions.
temperature	As the temperature increases, so does the rate of photosynthesis.	Enzymes, such as rubisco, become inactive at low temperatures and denature at high temperatures. Proteins that make up chloroplasts and their internal membranes may be denatured.

Photosynthetic pigments

Photosynthetic pigments are **chlorophylls** and carotenoids. Along with proteins they form **light-harvesting systems** to efficiently transfer light energy in the **photosystems**.

There are two chlorophyll molecules:

- **chlorophyll a**, a yellow-green colour
- **chlorophyll b**, a blue-green colour

Each chlorophyll absorbs different wavelengths of light. These molecules are located within the **photosystems** on the thylakoid membrane in chloroplasts.

Thin layer chromatography (TLC) can be used to separate the two pigments.

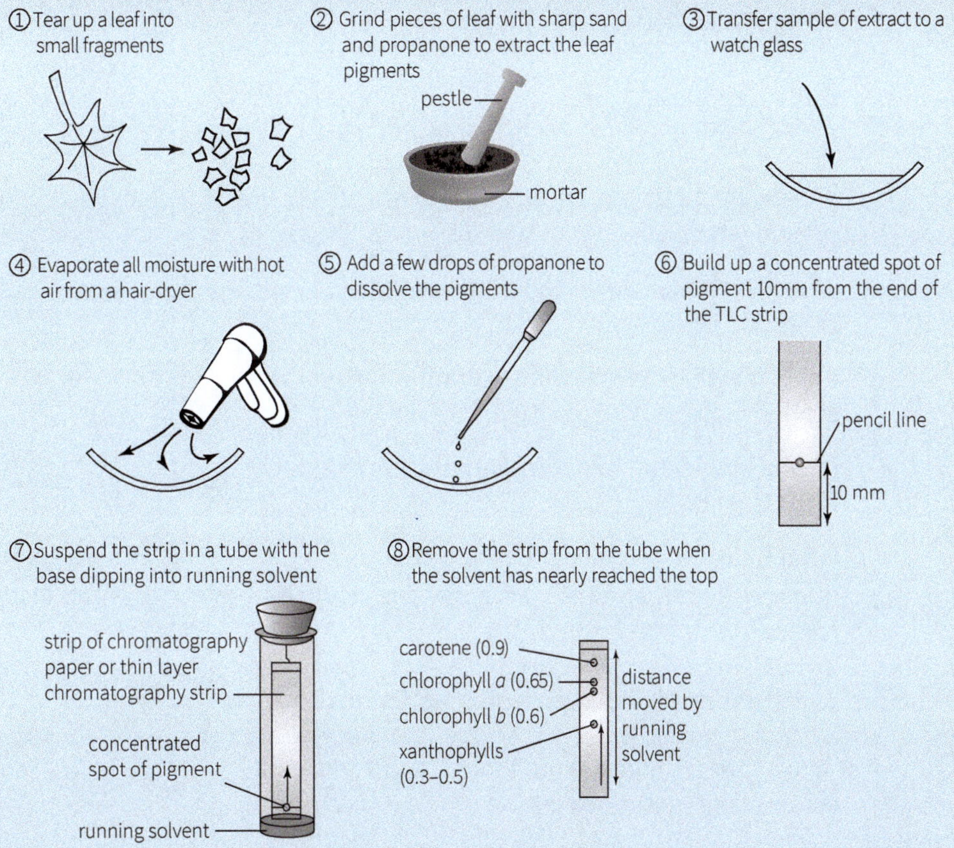

① Tear up a leaf into small fragments

② Grind pieces of leaf with sharp sand and propanone to extract the leaf pigments — pestle, mortar

③ Transfer sample of extract to a watch glass

④ Evaporate all moisture with hot air from a hair-dryer

⑤ Add a few drops of propanone to dissolve the pigments

⑥ Build up a concentrated spot of pigment 10mm from the end of the TLC strip — pencil line, 10 mm

⑦ Suspend the strip in a tube with the base dipping into running solvent — strip of chromatography paper or thin layer chromatography strip, concentrated spot of pigment, running solvent

⑧ Remove the strip from the tube when the solvent has nearly reached the top — carotene (0.9), chlorophyll a (0.65), chlorophyll b (0.6), xanthophylls (0.3–0.5), distance moved by running solvent

Retrieval

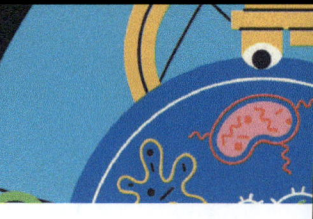

Learn the answers to the questions below, then cover the answers column with a piece of paper and write as many as you can. Check and repeat.

Questions | Answers

#	Questions	Answers
1	What are the two groups of reactions of photosynthesis called?	light-dependent reactions and light-independent reactions
2	What happens to chlorophyll when it absorbs light?	it becomes photoionised and the energy of electrons is increased, producing ATP and reduced NADP
3	Where is chlorophyll found?	on the internal membranes of chloroplasts (thylakoid membranes) in photosystems
4	How is carbon dioxide taken into the cell biochemistry?	it reacts with ribulose bisphosphate (RuBP) (a simple sugar); this is catalysed by the enzyme rubisco
5	What is the role of the Calvin cycle in photosynthesis?	to fix carbon dioxide and make it into useful organic compounds (simple sugars)
6	What are the sources of energy for the Calvin cycle?	from the light-dependent reactions, ATP and reduced NADP
7	What is the product of carbon dioxide reacting with RuBP?	two molecules of glycerate 3-phosphate (GP)
8	What is triose phosphate used for?	regeneration of RuBP and making useful organic molecules within the plant
9	What are the types of useful organic compounds produced by photosynthesis?	glucose, cellulose, starch, disaccharides, lipids, and amino acids
10	What happens to water during photosynthesis?	photolysis: during the light-dependent reactions, it is split to produce oxygen, two electrons, and two protons to reduce NADP
11	What is the balanced symbol equation for photosynthesis?	$6CO_2 + 6H_2O \rightarrow C_6H_{12}O_6 + 6O_2$
12	Where in the cell do the light-independent reactions take place?	stroma of chloroplasts
13	In the Calvin cycle, what is glycerate 3-phosphate (GP) reduced to?	triose phosphate
14	In which reactions of photosynthesis is carbon dioxide taken in?	light-independent
15	What happens to the biochemistry of photosynthesis when the concentration of carbon dioxide is reduced?	the conversion of RuBP to GP slows down; this causes levels of RuBP to increase and levels of GP and TP to decrease
16	Which limiting factors cause stomata to close?	high carbon dioxide concentration and high temperature
17	Which other useful organic compounds are synthesised from glucose?	disaccharides, cellulose, starch

19 Photosynthesis

Maths skills

Practise your maths skills using the worked example and practice questions below.

Calculating percentage of uncertainty

All measurements have some level of uncertainty. It is important that scientists are aware of sources of uncertainty and the degree of uncertainty.

When taking a reading of a single value, the uncertainty can be determined by halving the resolution of the apparatus you're using.

For example, the resolution of a thermometer is 1 °C, so the uncertainty (or maximum error) is ±0.5 °C.

When taking a measurement between two values, you have two readings that have some degree of uncertainty. Therefore, you must multiply your uncertainty for a single reading by two to get your overall uncertainty.

For example, the resolution of a digital balance is 0.1 g, so the uncertainty for one reading is ±0.05 g. However, when measuring change in mass, both the initial and final points have uncertainties, so the overall uncertainty is ±0.1 g.

Percentage error is a way of calculating the total possible error in an experiment. This can be calculated by:

$$\% \text{ error} = \frac{\text{maximum error}}{\text{measured value recorded}} \times 100$$

If you are calculating the percentage error of an experiment that uses several measurements, your percentage error is the total percentage errors of all the measurements taken.

Worked example

A student is investigating the effect of temperature on the amount of water evaporation from a piece of potato.

The student measures the initial weight of the potato piece, then measures the final weight after 2 hours to determine the change in mass at different temperatures.

The potato pieces are weighed on a digital top-pan balance with a resolution of 0.1 g.

The results are:

Initial weight: 5.2 g

Final weight: 4.6 g

Question
What is the percentage error of the change in mass?

Answers
For the change in mass, the value recorded is:

$$5.2 - 4.6 = 0.6 \text{ g}$$

As the resolution is 0.1 g, the uncertainty is 0.05 g per measurement. Because there are 2 measurements, the total uncertainty is 0.1 g.

Therefore:

$$\% \text{ error} = \frac{0.1}{0.6} \times 100$$
$$= 16.7\%$$

Practice

1. A student collected the following measurements listed below.

   Calculate the percentage error for each.

   Give your answers to 3 significant figures.

   a. A temperature change from 20 °C to 8.5 °C, measured on a digital thermometer. The maximum error for each reading is 0.1 °C.

   b. A mass of 6.29 g measured on a digital top pan balance. The maximum error for the reading is 0.01 g.

   c. A volume of acid measured at 24.5 cm^3. The maximum error for the measurement is 0.6 cm^3.

2. The percentage error for a difference in mass of 2.76 g is 7.24%. Calculate the absolute uncertainty of each measurement taken.

3. The percentage error for a temperature reading of 27 °C is 1.85%. Calculate the absolute uncertainty of the reading.

Practice

Exam-style questions

1 **Figure 1.1** shows the light-dependent stage of photosynthesis.

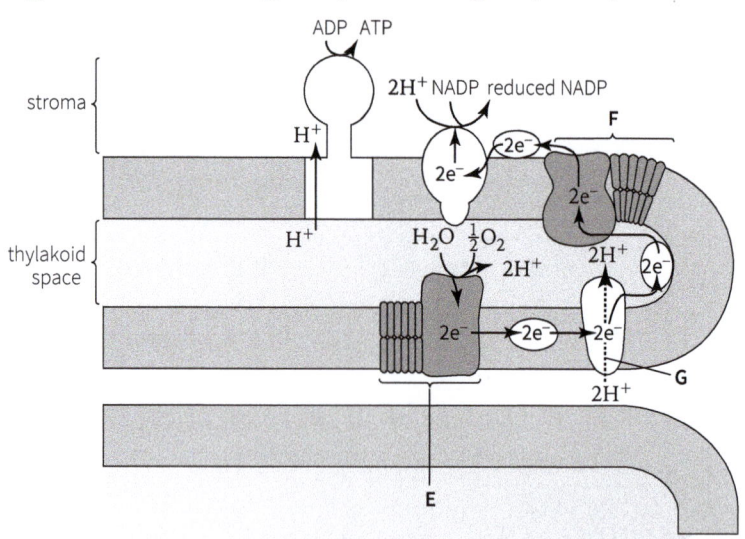

Figure 1.1

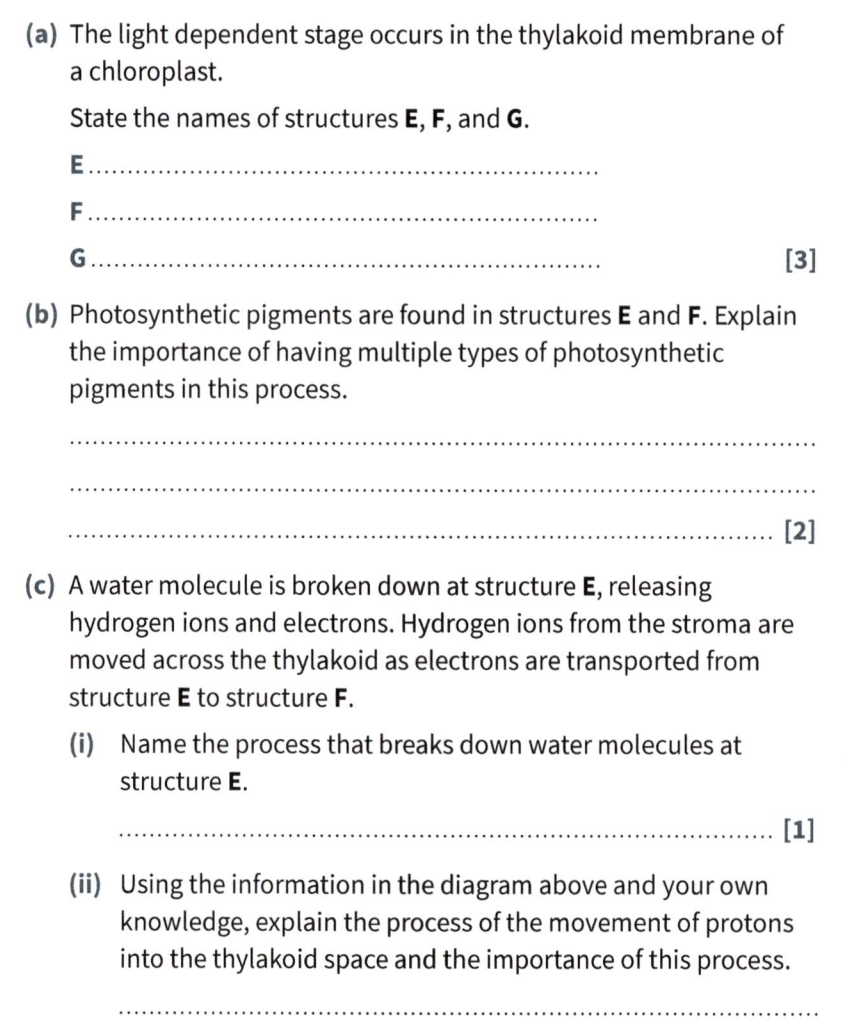

(a) The light dependent stage occurs in the thylakoid membrane of a chloroplast.

State the names of structures **E**, **F**, and **G**.

E ....

F ....

G .... [3]

(b) Photosynthetic pigments are found in structures **E** and **F**. Explain the importance of having multiple types of photosynthetic pigments in this process.

....
....
.... [2]

(c) A water molecule is broken down at structure **E**, releasing hydrogen ions and electrons. Hydrogen ions from the stroma are moved across the thylakoid as electrons are transported from structure **E** to structure **F**.

(i) Name the process that breaks down water molecules at structure **E**.

.... [1]

(ii) Using the information in the diagram above and your own knowledge, explain the process of the movement of protons into the thylakoid space and the importance of this process.

....
....
....
.... [3]

> **Exam tip**
>
> For question **1(c)(ii)**, you must make reference to the diagram provided and include your own knowledge, such as keywords and processes that may not have been clearly shown in the diagram. Using the diagram alone or your own knowledge alone will not secure you full marks.

222 19 Photosynthesis

(d) Certain ancient bacteria have bacteriochlorophylls, which allow them to carry out anoxygenic photosynthesis, as shown in **Figure 1.2**.

$$6CO_2 + 12H_2S \rightarrow C_6H_{12}O_6 + 12S + 6H_2O$$

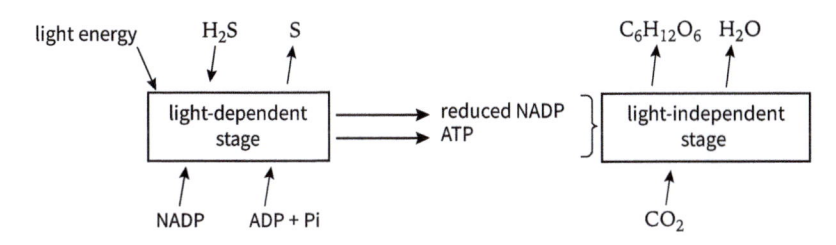

Figure 1.2

(i) Scientists have argued that these bacteria existed before multicellular plants existed.

Suggest why.

.... [1]

(ii) Using the information given and your own knowledge, describe one similarity and one difference between the light-dependent stage in present-day multicellular plants and anoxygenic photosynthesis.

....
....
....
.... [3]

2   **Figure 2.1** is an electron micrograph of the cross-section of a chloroplast.

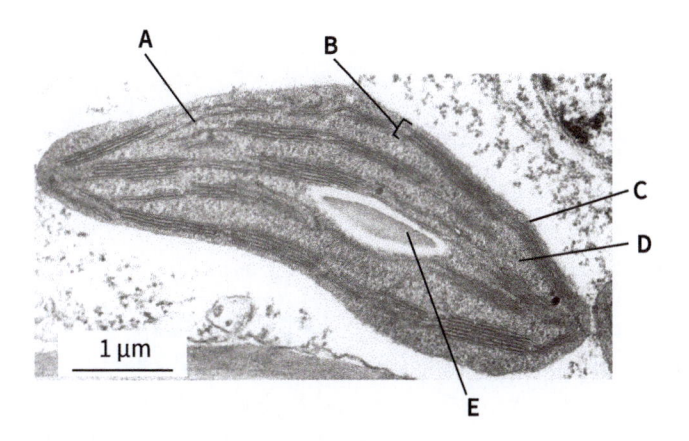

Figure 2.1

Synoptic links

2.1.1.g   2.1.1.k   5.2.2.b

(a) State the names of structures **A** to **E** in **Figure 2.1**.

A ....
B ....
C ....
D ....
E .... [5]

Exam tip

You will be expected to interpret electron micrographs and label the structures within, so make sure you do lots of practice to get used to looking at them.

(b) Using the letters **A** to **E**, from your answer to part **(a)**, complete **Table 2.1** to show the descriptions of the different structures.

Letters may be used once, more than once, or not at all.

Function	Structure
site of light-independent stage	
where chemiosmosis occurs	
highest concentration of hydrogen ions	
contains ribulose bisphosphate (RuBP)	

Table 2.1

[4]

(c) The endosymbiotic theory describes how mitochondria and chloroplasts were previously prokaryotic organisms that were engulfed and inhabited the cytoplasm of eukaryotic cells.

Describe two pieces of evidence using the structures of mitochondria and chloroplasts to support this theory.

....
....
....
.... [2]

3   The rate of photosynthesis is affected by different environmental factors. **Figure 3.1** shows how light intensity affects the rate of photosynthesis.

Synoptic links

2.1.4.f   3.1.3.c.i

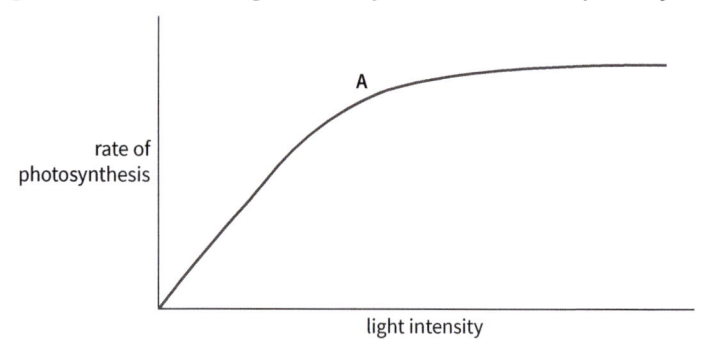

Figure 3.1

(a) Describe and explain how light intensity affects the rate of photosynthesis up to point **A**.

....
....
....
.... [2]

Exam tip

Make sure your answer includes a description of the pattern shown in the graph *and* an explanation for it. If the graph has actual numerical data, then make sure to also quote those figures where appropriate. Only giving a description or an explanation will not score you full marks.

224   19 Photosynthesis

(b) Temperature is a limiting factor of photosynthetic rate as temperature affects enzyme activity.

(i) Name two enzymes involved in photosynthesis.

1 ....

2 .... [2]

(ii) Describe an event in plants that causes carbon dioxide to become limiting.

Explain in what situations this event would occur.

....
....
....
....
....
....
.... [4]

(iii) Under hot and dry conditions, photorespiration can occur, where ribulose bisphosphate is converted into a toxic two-carbon molecule called 2-phosphoglycolate.

Using **Figure 3.2**, suggest how a high oxygen concentration may promote photorespiration and why this is not ideal for farmers.

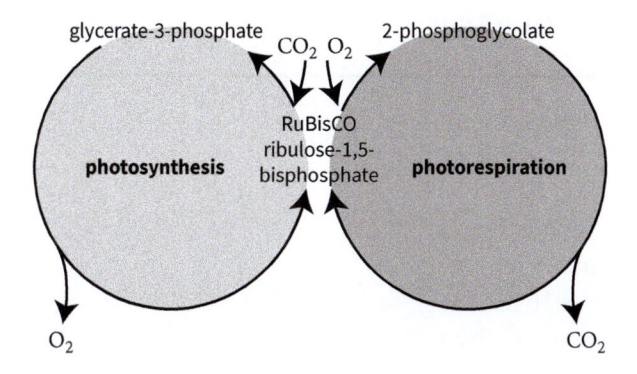

Figure 3.2

> **Exam tip**
>
> In your exams, you are going to be asked questions that haven't been covered in your class. Don't panic! Just look at the information you've been given, and you'll see that you can apply the concepts that you've learned to this unfamiliar context.

....
....
....
....
....
....
.... [4]

4   **Figure 4.1** shows part of the light-independent stage of photosynthesis.

```
           A              B
RuBP ─────────► GP ─────────► glucose ─────► starch
                     C
```

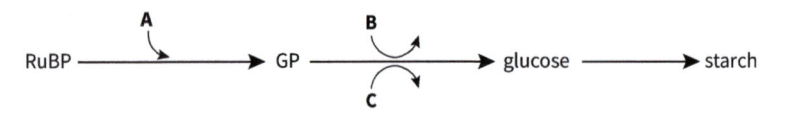

Figure 4.1

(a) Identify compounds **A**, **B**, and **C**.

A ....

B ....

C .... [3]

(b) Glycerate-3-phosphate (GP) is first converted to another compound, before forming glucose.

This stage is omitted from the diagram above.

(i) Name this compound made from GP.

.... [1]

(ii) Suggest where compounds **B** and **C** originated from.

....

....

....

.... [2]

(iii) Explain the importance of compounds **B** and **C** in the conversion of GP to the compound you named in **(b)(i)**.

....

....

....

.... [2]

(iv) With the addition of other chemicals, plants can use the products of the light-independent reactions to produce compounds essential to the growth of a plant, such as proteins.

Suggest two compounds other than glucose, starch, and proteins that can be made, and in each case state the molecules needed to achieve this.

....

....

....

....

....

....

.... [4]

> **Exam tip**
>
> Exams tend to present only part of a process or present them in a manner that may be unfamiliar to you. Make sure you learn the whole process detailing the different stages of photosynthesis so as to avoid any confusion in your exam questions.

5   Phosphorylation is the addition of an inorganic phosphate group to a compound. One example of this is when ADP is phosphorylated to make ATP.

Synoptic links
5.2.2.c   5.2.2.d   5.2.2.e
5.2.2.f   5.2.2.g

(a) There are many types of phosphorylation.

(i) Place a tick (✓) in the correct box in **Table 5.1** to illustrate the difference between the three different types of phosphorylation given.

Description	Photophosphorylation	Oxidative phosphorylation	Substrate-level phosphorylation
photosystem I is involved			
electron transport chain is involved			
occurs in the cytoplasm			
occurs in plant cells			

Table 5.1

[4]

(ii) There are two types of photophosphorylation: cyclic and non-cyclic.

Outline two differences between them.

....
....
....
....
.... [2]

(b) Photosynthesis and respiration both involve phosphorylation to make ATP at various stages.

Coenzymes are often involved at these stages to carry hydrogen atoms from one compound to another. NAD, FAD, and NADP are all examples of coenzymes.

Describe their role within a palisade mesophyll cell.

Exam tip

This is an extended response question. You will not score marks based on the number of points made, but only if your answer is well-written with accurate and relevant information. Consider carefully what content is needed and avoid including extra, irrelevant points.

....
....
....
....
....
....
....
.... [6]

6 **Figure 6.1** shows an experiment investigating the effect of light intensity on the rate of photosynthesis in an aquatic plant.

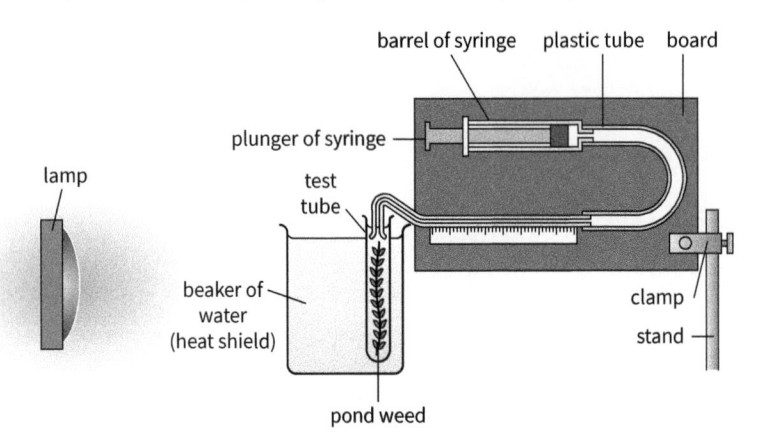

Figure 6.1

The rate of photosynthesis is calculated by measuring the oxygen produced over a set period of time. The gas is collected in the capillary tube, which produces an air bubble that extends along the capillary tube.

Its length is then measured along the scale at the end of the experiment.

The distance (*d*) between the lamp and the plant varies to change the light intensity.

Table 6.1 shows how light intensity varies with distance.

Distance from lamp to plant (cm)	Light intensity $\left(\frac{1}{d^2}\right)$
4	0.0625
8	0.0156
12	0.0069
16	0.0039
20	0.0025
24	
60	0.0003

Table 6.1

(a) Calculate the light intensity $\left(\frac{1}{d^2}\right)$ when the lamp is 24 cm away from the plant.

.... [2]

(b) The length of the air bubble is measured in mm.

State what additional information is needed to calculate the volume of gas produced.

....

.... [1]

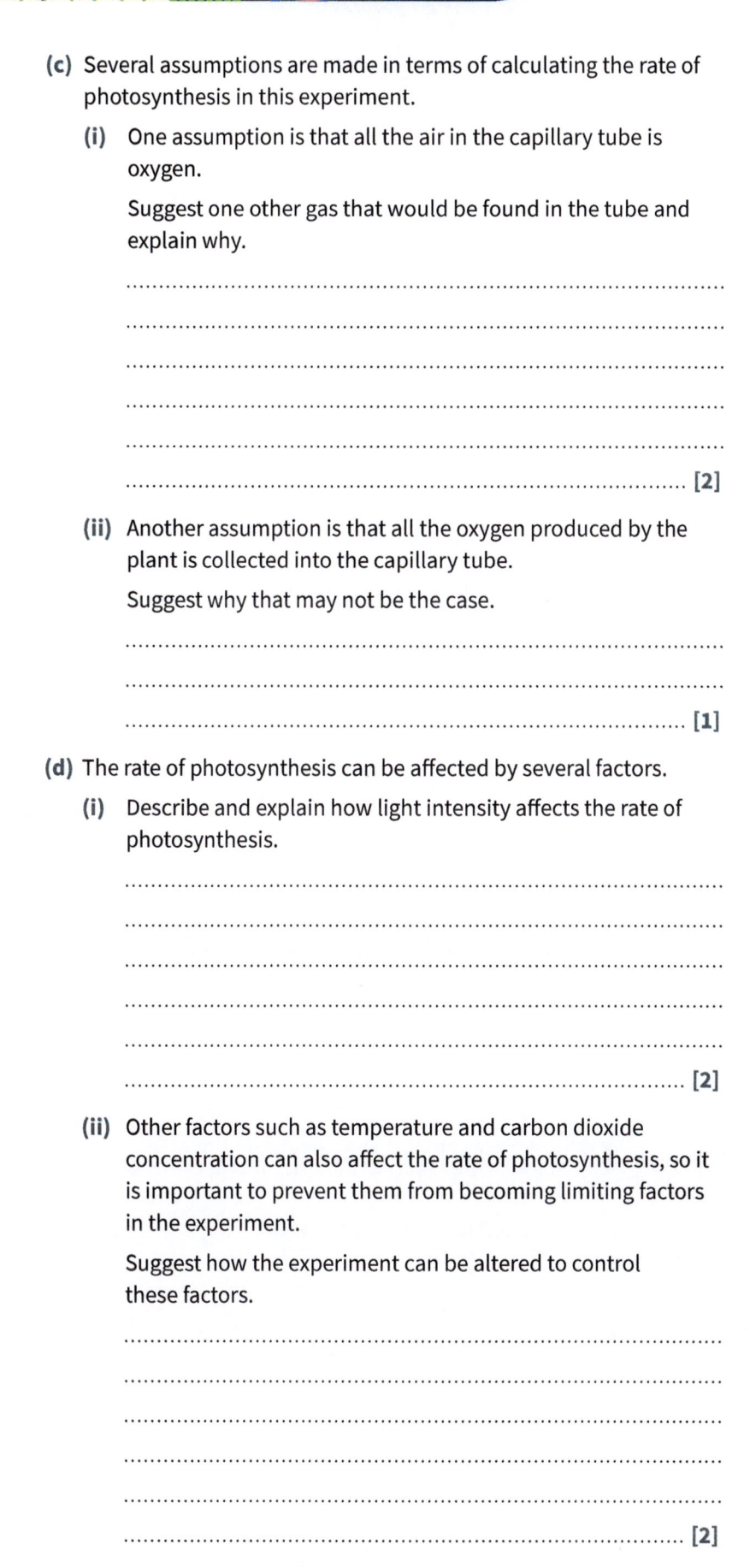

(c) Several assumptions are made in terms of calculating the rate of photosynthesis in this experiment.

(i) One assumption is that all the air in the capillary tube is oxygen.

Suggest one other gas that would be found in the tube and explain why.

....
....
....
....
....
.... [2]

(ii) Another assumption is that all the oxygen produced by the plant is collected into the capillary tube.

Suggest why that may not be the case.

....
....
.... [1]

(d) The rate of photosynthesis can be affected by several factors.

(i) Describe and explain how light intensity affects the rate of photosynthesis.

....
....
....
....
....
.... [2]

> **Exam tip**
>
> Simply stating how the rate of photosynthesis changes with increasing light intensity is not a sufficient explanation. You must include details and use comparative words to fully explain its impact on the actual process of photosynthesis.

(ii) Other factors such as temperature and carbon dioxide concentration can also affect the rate of photosynthesis, so it is important to prevent them from becoming limiting factors in the experiment.

Suggest how the experiment can be altered to control these factors.

....
....
....
....
....
.... [2]

Knowledge

20 Respiration

Respiration

Cells use ATP as their immediate energy source. Respiration transfers energy stored in complex organic molecules (e.g., glucose) to ATP by phosphorylation.

The energy stored in ATP is required for many cellular processes, for example:

- active transport for the conduction of nerve impulses and uptake of nitrates by root hair cells
- muscle contraction
- anabolic processes (synthesis of proteins and amino acids for growth and repair of tissues).

The process of respiration is common in all organisms, providing indirect evidence for evolution.

There are two types of respiration:

- Aerobic respiration – requires oxygen, produces water, carbon dioxide and many molecules of ATP.
- Anaerobic respiration – takes place in the absence of oxygen and produces a small amount of ATP. In plants and fungi, it also produces carbon dioxide and ethanol; animals produce lactate (lactic acid).

Aerobic respiration

Aerobic respiration is a four-stage process:

1. **Glycolysis** – 6-carbon glucose is split into two molecules of 3-carbon pyruvate.
2. **Link reaction** – 3-carbon pyruvate is oxidised into acetylcoenzyme A (acetyl CoA, a 2-carbon molecule) and carbon dioxide.
3. **Krebs cycle** – Acetyl CoA enters a cycle of redox reactions that produce ATP and a large number of electrons stored in reduced NAD and reduced FAD.
4. **Electron transport chain** – the electrons stored in reduced NAD from the Krebs cycle are used to generate ATP, with water as a waste product.

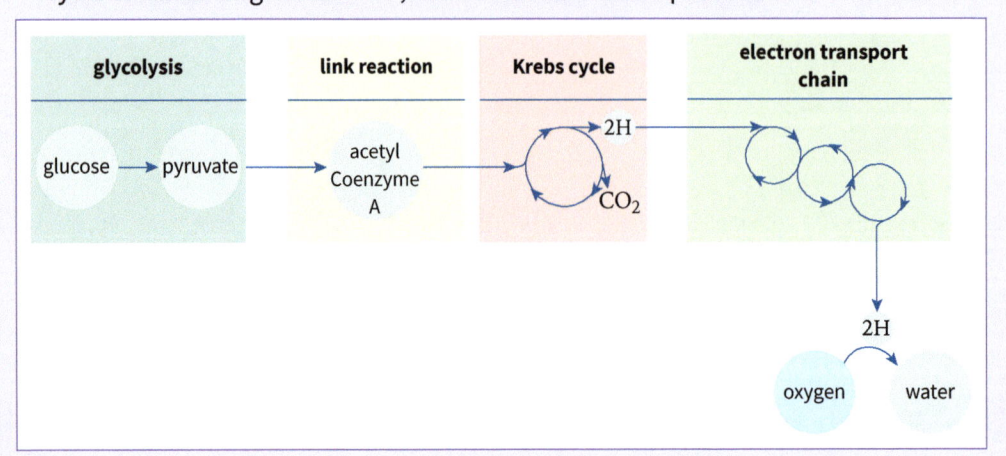

Anaerobic respiration

If oxygen is not present, anaerobic respiration occurs, which involves glycolysis. There are two main types of anaerobic respiration in eukaryotic cells:

- In some microorganisms such as yeast, pyruvate is converted to ethanol via ethanal. Ethanal accepts a hydrogen atom from reduced NAD. NAD is free to act as a coenzyme in glycolysis again.
- In animal cells, pyruvate is converted to lactate:

  pyruvate + reduced NAD → lactate + NAD

During strenuous exercise, lactate can build up in muscles, causing a drop in pH which affects enzyme activity. Lactate is transported to the liver where it is oxidised back to pyruvate. Pyruvate then enters the link reaction or is converted into glycogen. The re-oxidised NAD can be used in further glycolysis.

During anaerobic respiration one molecule of glucose generates two molecules of ATP (by glycolysis only). Anaerobic respiration ensures a small, steady amount of ATP is produced even in the absence of oxygen. Hydrogen atoms are removed from reduced NAD so the coenzyme can continue to accept hydrogen atoms from triose phosphate, thus allowing glycolysis to proceed. Without fermentation and the re-oxidising of reduced NAD, glycolysis would stop and ATP production would cease.

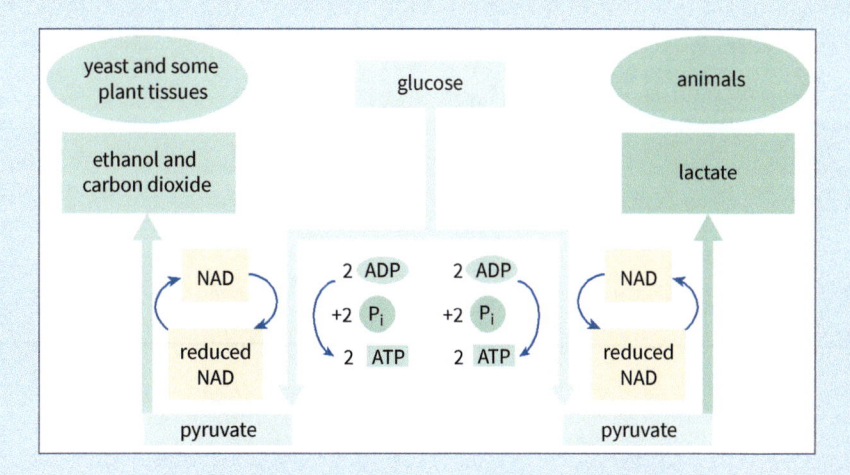

Respiratory substrates

A respiratory substrate is an organic substance that can be used during respiration.

Different respiratory substrates generate varying amounts of ATP depending on the number of hydrogen atoms a molecule of substrate has.

More hydrogen atoms mean more protons, which means more ATP.

Respiratory substrate	Mean energy value (kJ g^{-1})
carbohydrate	15.8
protein	17.0
lipid	39.4

Respiratory quotient

The respiratory quotient (RQ) is the ratio of carbon dioxide produced to oxygen consumed during respiration.

The RQ gives information about the type of substrate being respired. Carbohydrates have an RQ of 1, lipids approximately 0.7, and proteins between 0.8 and 0.9.

$$RQ = \frac{CO_2 \text{ produced}}{O_2 \text{ consumed}}$$

Glycolysis

Glycolysis is the first stage of anaerobic and aerobic respiration. It occurs in the cytoplasm.

It is an anaerobic process in three stages:

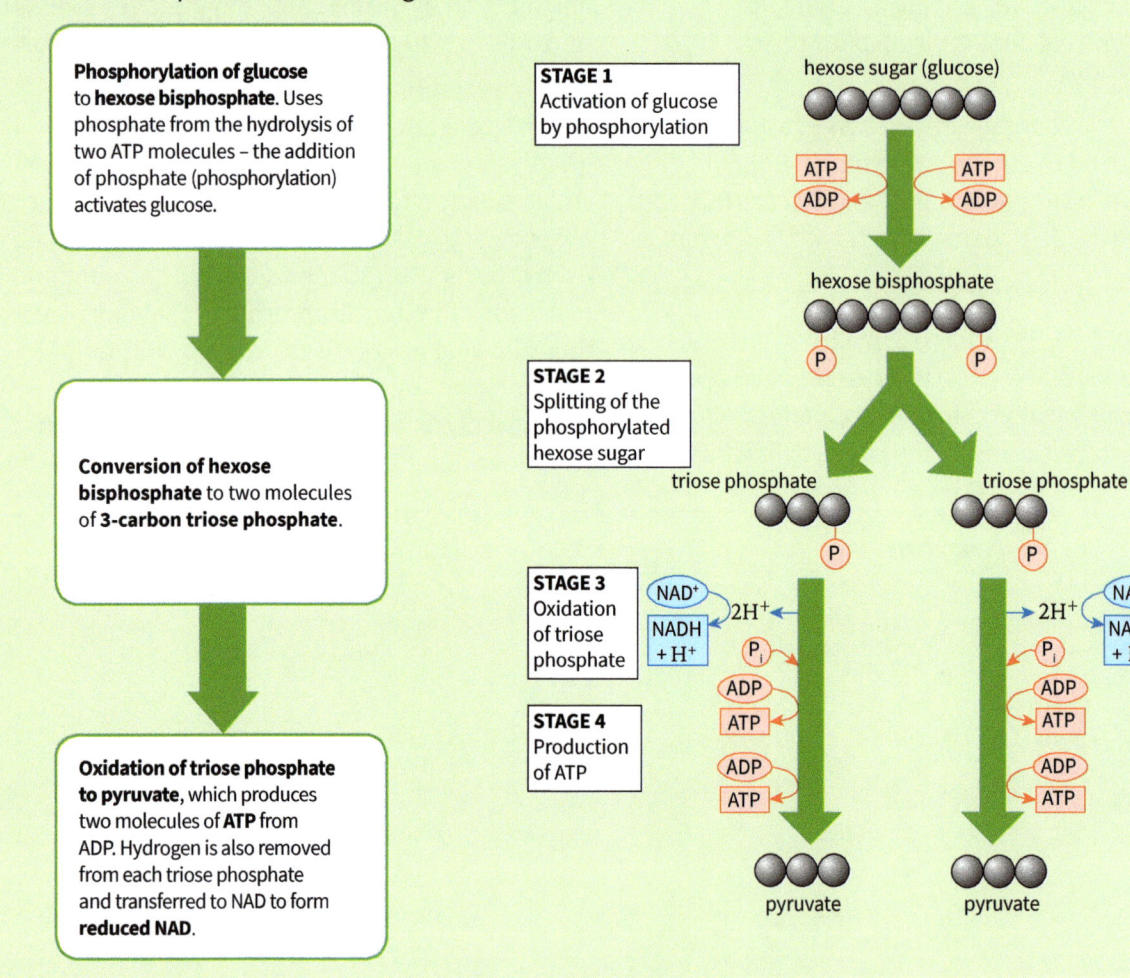

Phosphorylation of glucose to **hexose bisphosphate**. Uses phosphate from the hydrolysis of two ATP molecules – the addition of phosphate (phosphorylation) activates glucose.

Conversion of hexose bisphosphate to two molecules of **3-carbon triose phosphate**.

Oxidation of triose phosphate to pyruvate, which produces two molecules of **ATP** from ADP. Hydrogen is also removed from each triose phosphate and transferred to NAD to form **reduced NAD**.

STAGE 1 Activation of glucose by phosphorylation

hexose sugar (glucose) → hexose bisphosphate

STAGE 2 Splitting of the phosphorylated hexose sugar

→ triose phosphate + triose phosphate

STAGE 3 Oxidation of triose phosphate

STAGE 4 Production of ATP

→ pyruvate + pyruvate

Remember:
- one molecule of glucose gives rise to **two** molecules of pyruvate
- therefore, glycolysis yields **two** molecules of reduced NAD and a **net** gain of **two** ATP

Aerobic respiration – the link reaction

If oxygen is present, the link reaction joins glycolysis to the Krebs cycle. Pyruvate from glycolysis enters the mitochondrial matrix by active transport.

- Pyruvate is decarboxylated (carbon dioxide removed) to form acetate, one molecule of reduced NAD is generated, and one molecule of carbon dioxide is released.
- Acetate combines with coenzyme A (CoA) to produce acetyl coenzyme A (acetyl CoA).

    pyruvate + NAD + CoA → acetyl CoA + carbon dioxide + reduced NAD

Acetyl CoA then moves to the Krebs cycle.

20 Respiration

The Krebs cycle

This step takes place in the mitochondrial matrix, and occurs **twice** per glucose molecule.

During the Krebs cycle:

- Acetyl CoA reacts with oxaloacetate (four-carbon) to form citrate (six-carbon), which enters the Krebs cycle. CoA is regenerated.
- In a series of dehydrogenation (removal of hydrogen) and decarboxylation reactions, the Krebs cycle regenerates oxaloacetate and reduces coenzymes NAD and FAD.
- ATP is formed by substrate-level phosphorylation.
- Carbon dioxide is produced.

Other respiratory substrates also enter the Krebs cycle. Deaminated amino acids (with NH_2 removed) can enter the Krebs cycle directly. Acetates, from the breakdown of fatty acids from lipids, can enter the Krebs cycle via coenzyme A.

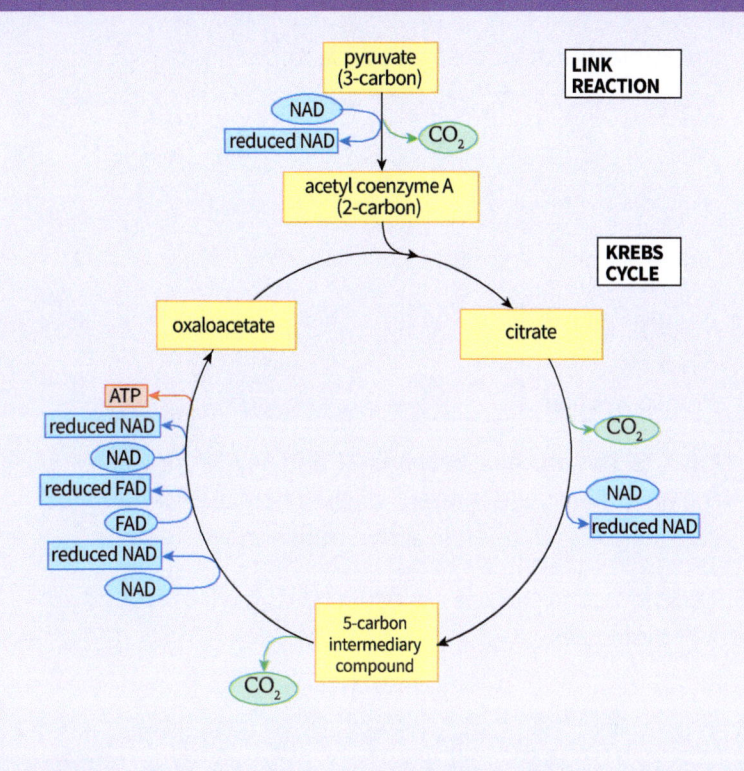

The electron transport chain (ETC)

The electron transport chain (ETC) takes place across the cristae membrane.

- The energy stored by the electrons in reduced NAD is used to generate ATP.
- ATP is synthesised by oxidative phosphorylation, which is driven by the transfer of electrons down the ETC and the movement of protons across the inner mitochondrial membrane. This is known as **chemiosmotic theory**.
- At the end of the ETC, the electrons and protons form hydrogen, which reacts with oxygen to form water. **Oxygen is therefore the final electron acceptor.**
- The enzymes required for this process, including ATP synthase, are embedded in the cristae membrane.

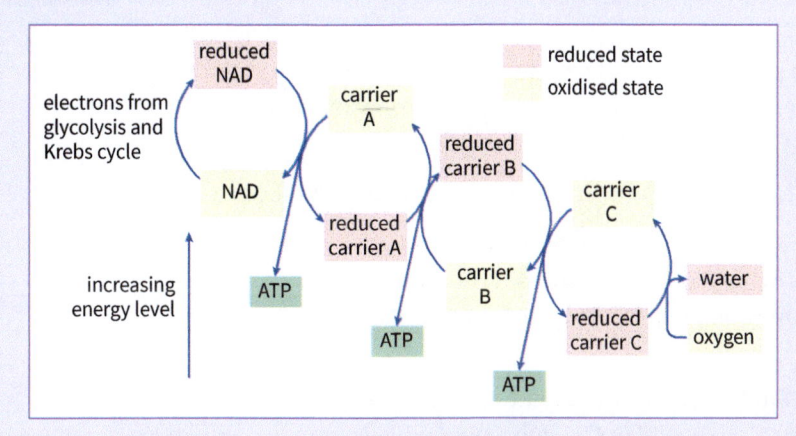

A summary of aerobic respiration

One molecule of glucose gives rise to:

Stage	ATP	Reduced NAD	Reduced FAD	Carbon dioxide
glycolysis	2 (net)	2	0	0
link reaction	0	2	0	2
Krebs cycle	2	6	2	4
electron transport chain	26–34	0	0	0

The ETC can produce between 26 and 34 ATP molecules, but the maximum yield is rarely reached because membranes can 'leak' ATP, or use it in active transport.

Therefore, one glucose molecule tends to yield around 30 ATP molecules.

Substrate-level phosphorylation vs. oxidative phosphorylation

Substrate-level phosphoryl-ation	Oxidative phosphoryl-ation
forms ATP by direct transfer of a phosphate group from a reactive intermediate chemical to ADP	forms ATP by chemiosmosis in the ETC
occurs in glycolysis and the Krebs cycle	occurs in the presence of oxygen

The chemiosmotic theory explained

Chemiosmosis is the diffusion of hydrogen ions (protons) across a partially permeable membrane, which is linked to the generation of ATP during respiration.

This process takes place in oxidative phosphorylation (aerobic respiration) and photophosphorylation (photosynthesis).

1 Reduced NAD is re-oxidised by dehydrogenase enzymes. The hydrogens are passed to an electron acceptor embedded in the inner mitochondrial membrane. The hydrogen atoms split into electrons and protons.

2 The electrons pass along a chain of electron carriers in a series of redox reactions.

3 As the electrons pass between the electron carriers, they lose energy.

This energy is used to pump (actively transport) the protons from NAD across the cristae/thylakoid membrane into the intermembrane/thylakoid space.

4 A charge gradient builds up across the inner mitochondrial/thylakoid membrane with a store of potential energy.

5 The protons diffuse down this gradient, back through the cristae/thylakoid membrane via protein channels associated with ATP synthase.

Some of the energy from the protons is used to combine ADP and inorganic phosphate to produce ATP; the remaining energy is transferred as heat.

Mitochondria

In eukaryotic cells, mitochondria are the organelles that carry out aerobic respiration. They are rod-shaped structures approximately 1 µm in diameter by 2–5 µm long.

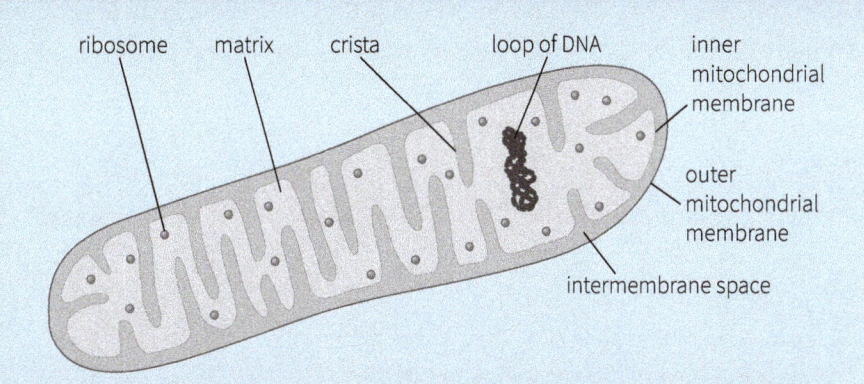

Labels on diagram: ribosome, matrix, crista, loop of DNA, inner mitochondrial membrane, outer mitochondrial membrane, intermembrane space

Component	Features
smooth outer mitochondrial membrane	• contains proteins, some of which form channels or are carriers that allow the passage of molecules, such as pyruvate
inner mitochondrial membrane	• folded into many cristae to give a large surface area • impermeable to most small ions, including hydrogen ions, embedded with many electron carriers, and ATP synthase enzymes
matrix	• gel-like • location of the link reaction and the Krebs cycle • contains mitochondrial DNA and 70S ribosomes
mitochondrial DNA	• codes for enzymes and other proteins

The importance of coenzymes in cellular respiration

During respiration, hydrogen atoms are removed from substrate molecules by dehydrogenase enzymes. However, these enzymes are not very efficient, and they require coenzymes to increase their efficacy.

Coenzymes are small, non-protein, organic molecules.

Three coenzymes are involved in respiration:

- NAD
  - a hydrogen acceptor
  - reduced during glycolysis, the link reaction and the Krebs cycle
  - reoxidised when it delivers hydrogen atoms, which are then split into electrons and hydrogen ions (protons) in the electron transport chain
- FAD
  - a hydrogen acceptor
  - reduced during the Krebs cycle
  - bound to the cristae
- Coenzyme A (CoA)
  - carries an acetyl group (from pyruvate and also from fatty acids and amino acids) from the link reaction to the Krebs cycle.

Retrieval

Learn the answers to the questions below, then cover the answers column with a piece of paper and write as many as you can. Check and repeat.

	Questions	Answers
1	What is the role of respiration?	to provide energy in the form of ATP to living cells
2	Why can glycolysis take place in both aerobic respiration and anaerobic respiration?	it does not require oxygen
3	Where does glycolysis take place in a cell?	in the cytoplasm (cytosol)
4	How many molecules of ATP are used during glycolysis?	two
5	Why is ATP required for glycolysis?	to activate glucose (make glucose more reactive)
6	In total, how many molecules of ATP are generated by glycolysis?	four
7	How many molecules of reduced NAD are produced by glycolysis?	two
8	Is carbon dioxide produced during glycolysis?	no
9	After glycolysis, what happens to pyruvate in animal cells during anaerobic respiration?	converted to lactate with the addition of hydrogen from reduced NAD
10	What happens to lactate after anaerobic respiration?	when oxygen becomes available, lactate is converted back to pyruvate or converted to glycogen in the liver
11	What is the net gain of ATP from one molecule of glucose during anaerobic respiration?	two molecules
12	After glycolysis, list the subsequent stages of aerobic respiration in the correct order.	link reaction, Krebs cycle, electron transport chain / oxidative phosphorylation
13	In addition to pyruvate, what other substances can be used to generate reduced coenzymes via the Krebs cycle?	acetates (from fatty acids produced when lipids are broken down) and deaminated amino acids
14	How many molecules of ATP, reduced NAD, reduced FAD, and carbon dioxide are produced from one molecule of pyruvate in the Krebs cycle?	1 ATP 3 reduced NAD 1 reduced FAD 2 carbon dioxide
15	What does NAD gain when it is reduced?	a pair of hydrogen atoms
16	Where does the Krebs cycle take place?	mitochondrial matrix
17	Where does the electron transport chain take place?	across the inner mitochondrial membrane/cristae

20 Respiration

20

🧪 Practical skills

Practise your practical skills using the worked example and practice questions below.

Identifying plant pigments from chromatograms

Worked example

The photosynthetic pigments found in chloroplasts can be separated and identified using paper chromatography.

A solvent is used to separate the pigments according to their solubility in that solvent. The distance a pigment travels relative to the solvent front from the origin can be used to calculate the R_f value of the pigment, which will identify the pigment.

$$R_f = \frac{\text{distance travelled by pigment}}{\text{distance travelled by solvent}}$$

Remember to start your measurements at the origin of the pigments.

The distance between the origin and the pigment is how far the pigment travelled.

The distance between the origin and the solvent front is how far the solvent travelled.

Question

The diagram shows paper chromatography of various pigments.

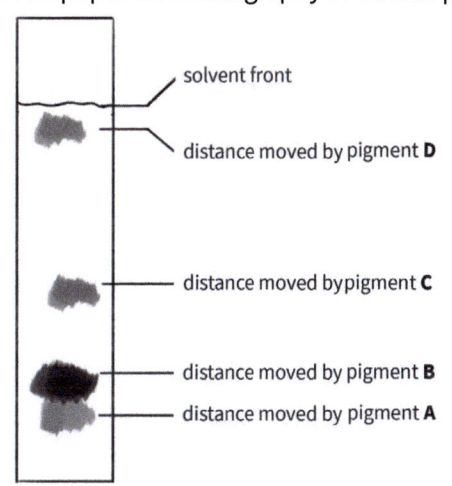

- solvent front
- distance moved by pigment **D**
- distance moved by pigment **C**
- distance moved by pigment **B**
- distance moved by pigment **A**

Calculate the R_f value for pigment **C**.

Answer

Remember to be precise when taking your measurements. You want to start all your measurements at the centre of the origin, and finish them at the centre of the pigment or solvent front.

$$R_f = \frac{\text{distance travelled by pigment}}{\text{distance travelled by solvent}}$$

$$= \frac{2.4 \text{ cm}}{3.3 \text{ cm}} = 0.73$$

Practice

1 Using the image in the worked example, calculate the R_f values for:
   a pigment **A**   b pigment **B**   c pigment **D**

2 Use the table to identify pigments **A**, **B**, **C**, and **D**.

Pigment	R_f value
chlorophyll *a*	0.59
chlorophyll *b*	0.42
xanthophylls	0.15
carotenes	0.98
phaeophytin	0.75

3 Why is there some variation between the R_f values recorded in the investigation and standard R_f values?

Practice

Exam-style questions

1 **Figure 1.1** shows a mitochondrion in an animal cell.

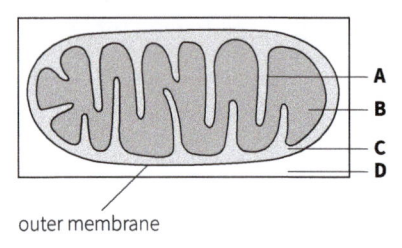

Figure 1.1

(a) For each of the following statements, identify the corresponding letter (**A–D**) in **Figure 1.1**.

The site of glycolysis ....

Where electron carriers are found ....

The site with the highest concentration of protons ....

Where acetyl coenzyme A is found .... [4]

(b) Site **D** is also the site of anaerobic respiration.

Figure 1.2 outlines the process of anaerobic respiration in some plant cells.

Figure 1.2

(i) State the names of compounds **W–Z**.

W ....

X ....

Y ....

Z .... [4]

(ii) State the enzyme involved in the conversion of pyruvate into compound **W**.

.... [1]

(iii) Describe two differences between anaerobic respiration in mammalian muscle cells and plant cells.

....
....
....
....
.... [4]

> **Exam tip**
>
> Make your answer comparative by describing both aspects. A correct description of just one side will not score full marks.

2   All living organisms carry out cellular respiration, producing ATP.

(a) Explain the importance of cellular respiration in living organisms.
    ....
    ....
    .... [2]

Synoptic links
2.1.3.c   5.2.1.d

(b) The main product of cellular respiration is ATP.

(i) Draw a labelled diagram to show the structure of an ATP molecule.

[2]

(ii) The final stage of aerobic respiration is oxidative phosphorylation, which produces most of the ATP molecules in the whole reaction.

Describe the process of oxidative phosphorylation.
....
....
....
....
....
.... [6]

(iii) Apart from oxidative phosphorylation, state two other ways that a plant cell can produce ATP.

Include the site of these reactions.
....
....
....
.... [4]

Exam tip

You will need to draw knowledge from previous chapters on other metabolic reactions carried out in plants.

3   (a) Complete **Table 3.1** by adding a tick to any true statement.

Characteristic	Mitochondrion	Cytoplasm	Chloroplast
ATP synthase is present			
electrons pass through electron carriers			
electrons are excited by light			
coenzymes are present			

Table 3.1

[4]

Synoptic links
2.1.5.d.i   5.2.1.d   5.2.1.e

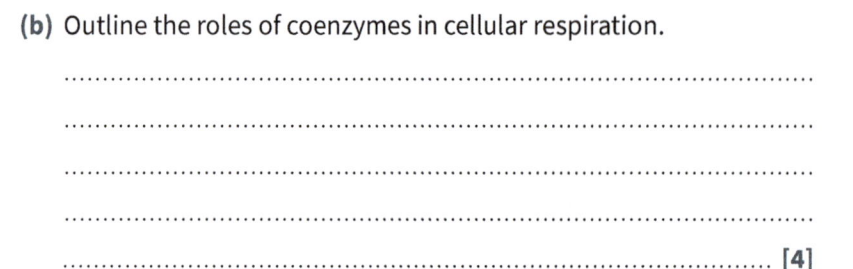

(b) Outline the roles of coenzymes in cellular respiration.

....

....

....

....

.... [4]

(c) Chemiosmosis is a mechanism where protons move across ATP synthase to produce ATP, as shown in **Figure 3.1**.

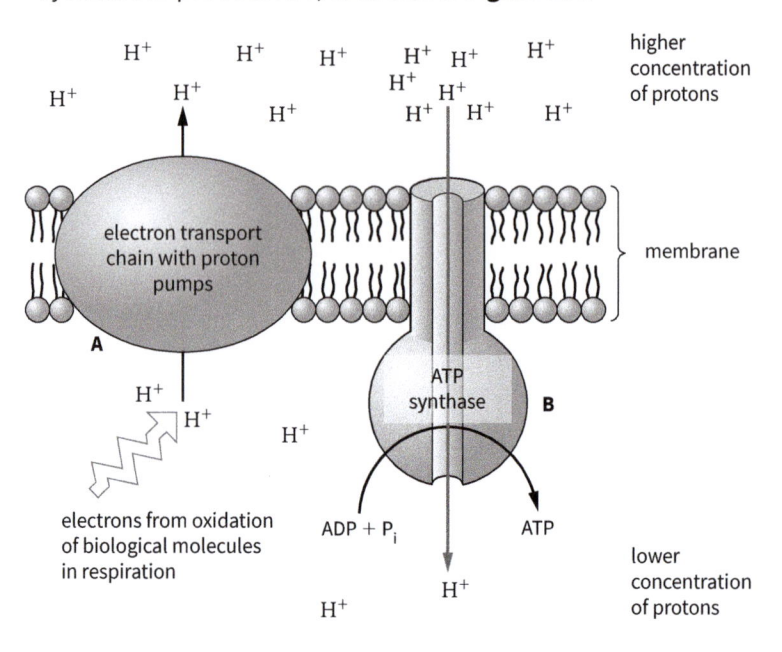

Figure 3.1

(i) State the two processes by which protons move across the membranes in **Figure 3.1**.

A ....

B .... [2]

(ii) This mechanism also occurs in chloroplasts.

Describe one difference in how this process occurs in chloroplasts compared to mitochondria.

....

....

.... [2]

!) **Exam tip**

You will need to draw on your knowledge of photosynthesis. Ensure your descriptions are comparative in order to gain full marks.

4 (a) Explain what a respiratory quotient is and outline its importance.

....

....

.... [2]

(b) The equation below shows the aerobic respiration of compound **A**, $C_{55}H_{98}O_6$, in plant cells.

$$2C_{55}H_{98}O_6 + 153O_2 \rightarrow 110CO_2 + 98H_2O$$

240 20 Respiration

(i) Calculate the respiratory quotient of compound **A**.
Give your answer to 3 significant figures.

.... [2]

> **Exam tip**
> Make sure to show your working, as you may still gain some marks for clear and correct steps even if your final answer is wrong.

(ii) Based on your calculated RQ value, determine the type of respiratory substrate of compound **A**.
Explain your choice.

....
....
.... [2]

(iii) Suggest why the calculated RQ value of compound **A** is only an estimation and not an accurate calculation.

....
.... [1]

(c) Carbohydrates, lipids, and proteins are all respiratory substrates.

(i) Describe how proteins are processed to enter cellular respiration.

....
....
....
.... [3]

(ii) Proteins are regarded as the last resort in cellular respiration. If available, carbohydrates and lipids are always used first. Suggest why this is the case.

....
....
.... [2]

5 **Figure 5.1** shows how fatty acids can be processed to enter the Krebs cycle.

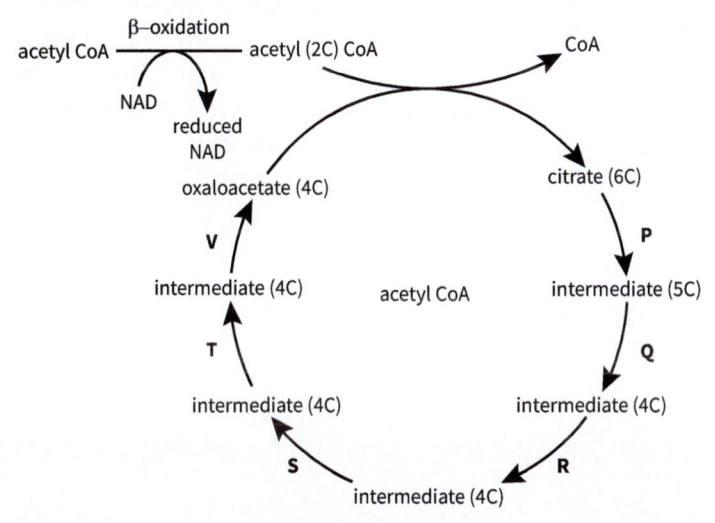

Figure 5.1

(a) Decarboxylation occurs in several stages within cellular respiration.

(i) Using the letters in **Figure 5.1**, state the stages where decarboxylation occurs in the Krebs cycle.

.... [1]

(ii) State the product of decarboxylation.

.... [1]

(iii) Name two other stages of cellular respiration in yeast where decarboxylation can occur.

....
.... [2]

(b) ATP molecules are also produced in the Krebs cycle.

(i) State the name of the reaction that produces ATP in the Krebs cycle.

.... [1]

(ii) State the number of ATP molecules made in **one** cycle, shown in **Figure 5.1**.

.... [1]

(c) Coenzymes NAD and FAD pick up hydrogen atoms from the substrates within the Krebs cycle.

(i) State the number of reduced NAD and reduced FAD molecules that are made from **one** acetyl coenzyme A.

reduced NAD: ....

reduced FAD: .... [2]

(ii) Describe what happens to these reduced coenzymes.

....
....
.... [3]

(d) Liver cells use the enzyme ethanol dehydrogenase to process ethanol. This enzyme converts ethanol into ethanal, which is a less toxic chemical. It can also work in the opposite direction in anaerobic respiration of some plants cells and yeasts.

Using your own knowledge, the information given here, and the figure above, suggest why a fatty liver is a symptom of excessive ethanol intake.

> **! Exam tip**
>
> Make sure to use both your own knowledge and draw links to the information to secure maximum marks.

....
....
....
....
....
.... [3]

20 Respiration

6 (a) Triglycerides can be broken down as a respiratory substrate.

(i) Explain why the breakdown of triglycerides is considered a hydrolysis reaction.

....
....
....
....
....
.... [2]

(b) **Figure 6.1** shows the process of oxidative phosphorylation in a normal mitochondrion.

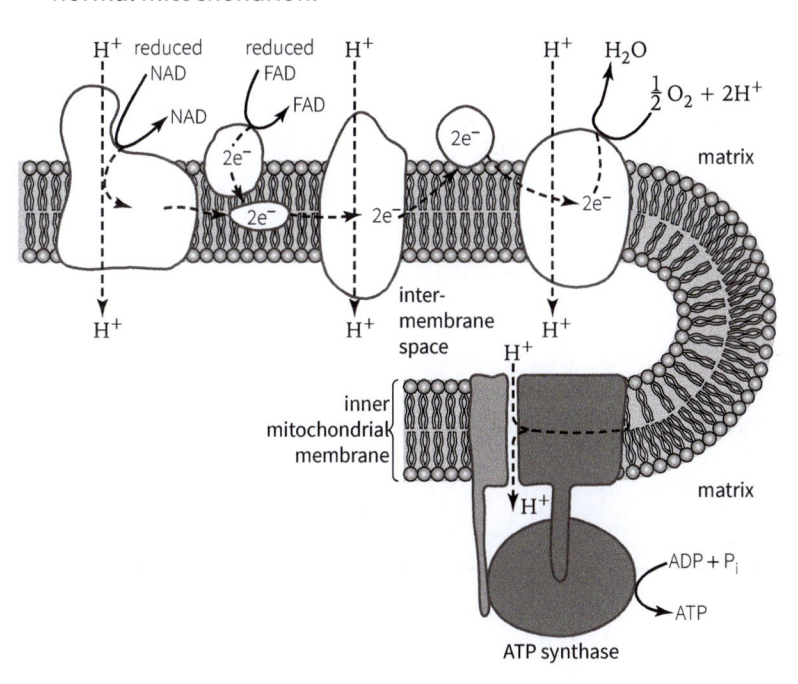

Figure 6.1

Some people are able to eat lots of food without gaining mass. These people also tend to become hungry more quickly and lose weight easily.

Their mitochondria have been found to have more hydrogen ion channels on the inner mitochondrial membrane than usual.

Using the information provided and your own knowledge, suggest why these people cannot gain mass despite eating a lot.

....
....
....
....
....
....
....
.... [6]

Synoptic links

2.1.2.h 2.1.2.i 2.1.5d.i

Exam tip

Your answer should include a description of what would happen in the mitochondrion, and an explanation of the symptoms mentioned in the question. This is also an extended response question, so remember to only include accurate and relevant information.

Knowledge

21 Cellular control

Introduction

Cellular control is the way in which cells control metabolic reactions. It determines how organisms grow, develop, and function.

Gene mutations

A **gene mutation** is a change in the amount or arrangement of DNA in a gene.

Some mutations can result in a different amino acid sequence in the encoded polypeptide through a change in only one triplet codon. The resulting protein may become non-functional, and may have a **harmful effect**, especially if the amino acid that is changed is located in the active site.

However, due to the degenerate nature of the genetic code, not all such mutations result in a change to the encoded amino acid – they have a **neutral effect**.

Some mutations may have a **beneficial effect** if they confer an advantage to the organism. This is the basis for evolution.

Types of mutation

Type of mutation	Change in base sequence	Effect on polypeptide
addition	The addition of one or more nucleotides, resulting in a frameshift to the right. An addition of three bases will not cause a frameshift but the insertion of a new amino acid.	If a frameshift occurs, the polypeptide will be disrupted, with a different amino acid sequence. The resulting protein may be non-functional.
deletion	Deletion of nucleotides, resulting in a frameshift to the left. A deletion of three bases will not cause a frameshift but an amino acid will be missing from the polypeptide.	If a frameshift occurs, the polypeptide will be disrupted, with a different amino acid sequence. The resulting protein may be non-functional.
substitution	One nucleotide is substituted for another.	Three possibilities: • Non-sense: the new sequence is a STOP codon, so the polypeptide would be truncated. • Mis-sense: the triplet codes for a different amino acid, the effect of which will depend on the substituted amino acid and where in the protein it is found. • Silent: the substituted nucleotide still codes for the same amino acid.

21

Control of gene expression at post-translational level

The hormone adrenaline is an example of gene expression control after translation by activation of enzymes through **cyclic AMP (cAMP)**:

1. Adrenaline binds to specific receptors on target cell surface membranes to form a hormone-receptor complex.
2. The hormone-receptor complex activates adenylate cyclase, inside the membrane.
3. Adenylate cyclase converts ATP into cyclic AMP (cAMP).
4. **cAMP** acts as a second messenger and activates enzymes in the cytoplasm.

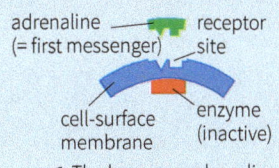

1 The hormone adrenaline approaches receptor site.

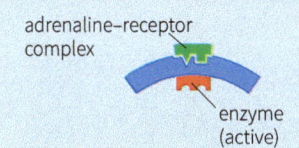

2 Adrenaline fuses to receptor site, and in doing so activates an enzyme inside the membrane.

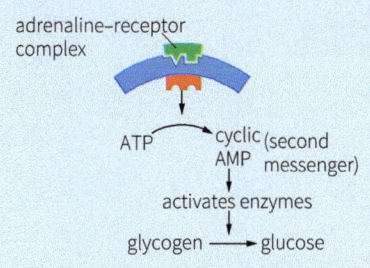

3 The activated enzyme converts ATP to cyclic AMP, which acts as a second messenger that activates other enzymes that, in turn, convert glycogen to glucose.

Homeobox genes

The development of body plans in different organisms is controlled by **homeobox genes**, which are arranged in **Hox clusters**.

Homeobox gene sequences in plants, animals, and fungi are highly conserved (i.e., there are very few differences in homeobox genes between organisms from different kingdoms).

Hox genes control body plan development in specific patterns at set stages in embryos of both invertebrates and vertebrates.

They control organ positioning and which end becomes the head and tail. They are activated and expressed in the same order from the head to the tail.

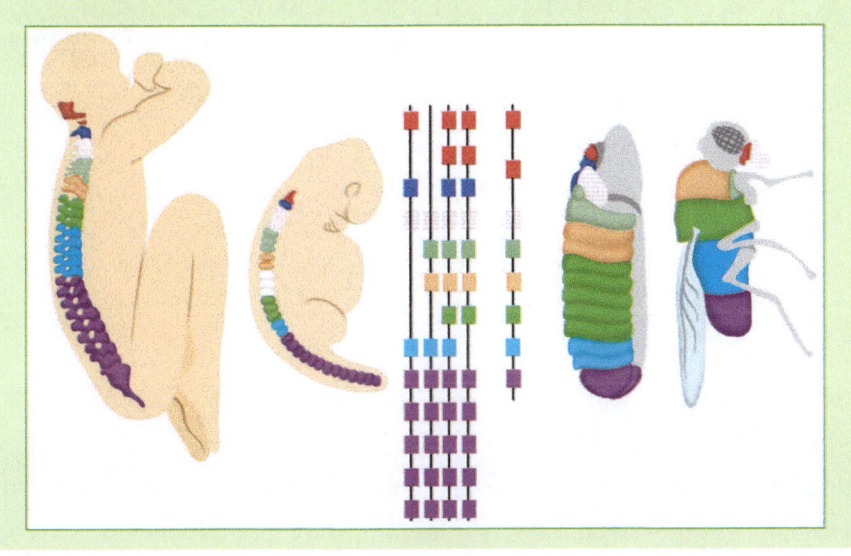

21 Knowledge

Regulation of gene expression

Gene expression is controlled at the **transcriptional, post-transcriptional**, and **post-translational** levels by different regulatory mechanisms.

Control of gene expression at transcriptional level

The **lac operon**, found in *E. coli*, is an example of gene expression control at the transcription level.

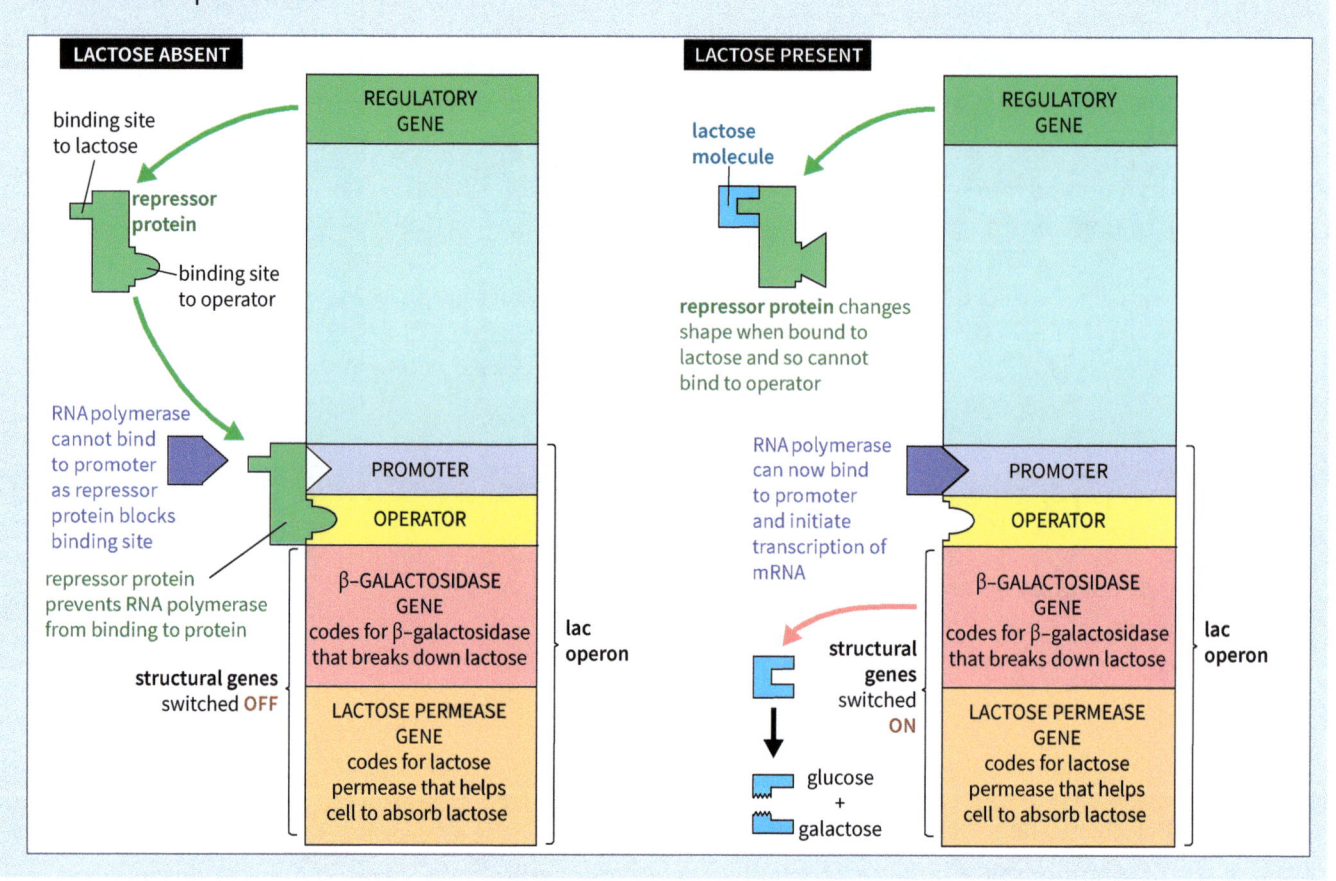

LACTOSE ABSENT

- binding site to lactose
- repressor protein
- binding site to operator
- RNA polymerase cannot bind to promoter as repressor protein blocks binding site
- repressor protein prevents RNA polymerase from binding to protein
- structural genes switched OFF

REGULATORY GENE
PROMOTER
OPERATOR
β-GALACTOSIDASE GENE — codes for β-galactosidase that breaks down lactose
LACTOSE PERMEASE GENE — codes for lactose permease that helps cell to absorb lactose
} lac operon

LACTOSE PRESENT

- lactose molecule
- repressor protein changes shape when bound to lactose and so cannot bind to operator
- RNA polymerase can now bind to promoter and initiate transcription of mRNA
- structural genes switched ON
- glucose + galactose

REGULATORY GENE
PROMOTER
OPERATOR
β-GALACTOSIDASE GENE — codes for β-galactosidase that breaks down lactose
LACTOSE PERMEASE GENE — codes for lactose permease that helps cell to absorb lactose
} lac operon

Control of gene expression at post-transcriptional level

In eukaryotic cells, transcription of a gene produces short strands of pre-mRNA which must be processed into a single strand of mature mRNA before the gene can be translated.

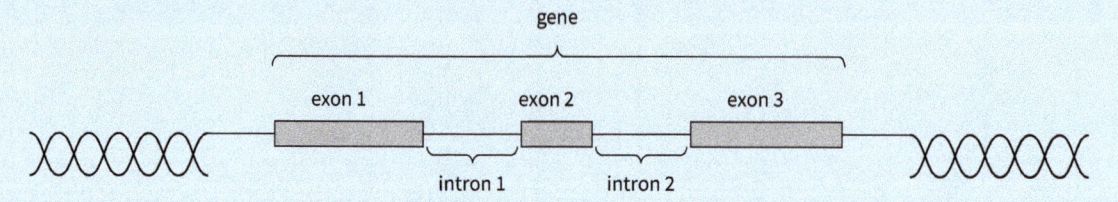

gene: exon 1 — intron 1 — exon 2 — intron 2 — exon 3

Non-coding sequences, called **introns**, are removed from pre-mRNA and the remaining coding sequences, called **exons**, are joined together.

A nucleotide cap is added to the 5' end, and a tail of adenine nucleotides is added to the 3' end.

These modifications take place in the nucleus and regulate translation of the mRNA.

21 Cellular control

21

Mitosis and apoptosis

Mitosis and **apoptosis** are important mechanisms for controlling the development of body form.

Mitosis is controlled by a balanced expression of tumour-suppressing genes (which inhibit mitosis) and proto-oncogenes (which stimulate mitosis).

Once cells have divided about 50 times, they undergo **apoptosis** – a controlled cell death ensuring surrounding cells remain undamaged.

Apoptosis in hand development

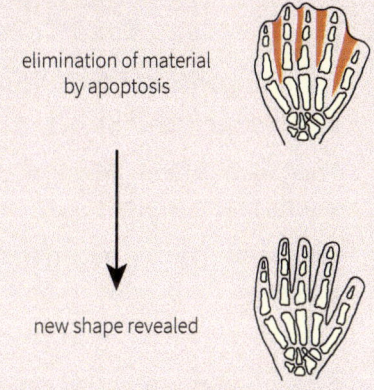

elimination of material by apoptosis

new shape revealed

Genes that regulate the cell cycle and apoptosis respond to internal and external cell stimuli, such as cytokines, hormones, growth factors, alcohol, and stress.

The effect of alcohol on prenatal mitosis and apoptosis

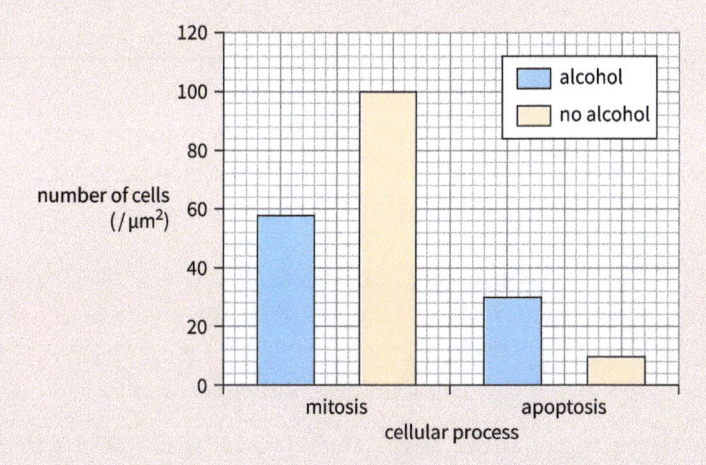

Transcription factors

In eukaryotes, transcription of genes can be stimulated or inhibited by **transcription factors**.

Each transcription factor binds to a specific region of DNA and regulates the process of transcription.

Transcription factor binding sites can be blocked by an inhibitor, preventing the transcription factor from binding to the DNA, thereby 'switching on or off' the target gene.

Retrieval

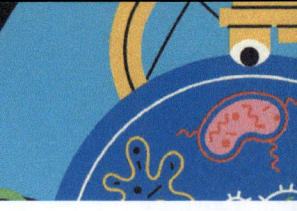

Learn the answers to the questions below, then cover the answers column with a piece of paper and write as many as you can. Check and repeat.

Questions	Answers
1. What is a gene mutation?	a change in the amount or arrangement of DNA in a gene
2. Will a mutation always result in a different amino acid being inserted in a polypeptide?	no
3. Explain your answer to **3**.	the mutation in the triplet codon may still code for the same amino acid, or is a STOP codon
4. What is a frameshift?	when an addition, deletion, or duplication mutation results in the triplet code being read from a new point
5. How can a mutation have a neutral effect?	the genetic code is degenerate so some amino acids are coded for by more than one triplet
6. What is a transcription factor?	a chemical that binds to specific regions of DNA to regulate transcription
7. Where are transcription factors usually found in the cell?	in the cytoplasm
8. What sort of mutation can have a neutral effect?	a substitution mutation
9. Why can some mutations have a beneficial effect?	if the mutation results in giving the organism a selective advantage
10. How are structural genes on the lac operon prevented from being transcribed when lactose is absent?	a repressor protein binds to the operator and partly covers the binding site of RNA polymerase on the promoter region
11. Which gene codes for the repressor protein for the lac operon?	the regulatory gene
12. How is the action of the repressor protein inhibited when lactose is present?	the repressor protein/lactose complex changes shape and cannot bind to the operator
13. What is the role of RNA polymerase when the repressor protein is bound to lactose?	RNA polymerase can bind to the promoter region and transcribe the structural genes
14. Where do post-transcription modifications of pre-mRNA take place?	in the nucleus
15. How do post-transcriptional changes control gene expression?	regulate translation
16. What is an exon?	a section of a gene coding for an amino acid sequence
17. What is an intron?	a non-coding section of a gene
18. What is pre-mRNA?	mRNA containing both exons and introns
19. What is mature mRNA?	mRNA that contains no introns, just exons

21 Cellular control

20 What is the role of cyclic AMP in post-translational control of gene expression?	activates proteins (e.g., enzymes in the cytoplasm)
21 What is the precursor of cyclic AMP?	ATP

Maths skills

Practise your maths skills using the worked example and practice questions below.

Hardy–Weinberg equilibrium

The Hardy–Weinberg principle calculates the proportions of dominant and recessive alleles in a population provided:

1. There are no mutations.
2. There is no flow of alleles into or out of the population.
3. The is no selection pressure.
4. The population size is large.
5. Mating is random.

In a population,

$$p + q = 1$$
$$p^2 + 2pq + q^2 = 1$$

Where:
- p = homozygote dominant alleles
- q = homozygote recessive alleles
- pq = heterozygotes

Worked example

Question
If one person in 10 000 displays a characteristic caused by a recessive allele, **g**, how many carriers, **Gg**, will be in the population?

Answer
You know that:

$$p + q = 1 \qquad p^2 + 2pq + q^2 = 1$$

You need to calculate the value of **Gg**, or $2pq$.

Step 1: Calculate p and q.

You know sufferers, or **gg** (q^2), have a frequency of 1 in 10 000. Therefore:

$$q^2 = \frac{1}{10\,000} = 0.0001$$

So, $q = 0.01$

As $p + q = 1$, then $p = 1 - q$

$p = 1 - 0.01 \qquad p = 0.99$

Step 2: Calculate $2pq$ (the number of carriers) by substituting in the values for p and q.

$$2pq = 2 \times p \times q$$
$$= 2 \times 0.99 \times 0.01 = 0.0198$$

So, the frequency of $2pq$ (**Gg**) = 0.0198

In a population of 10 000, the number of carriers would be:

$0.0198 \times 10\,000 = 198$ with a genotype of **Gg**.

So there would be 198 carriers with the genotype **Gg**.

Practice

1. In a population of 2000, one person suffers from cystic fibrosis.
   How many carriers are there in the population?

2. Calculate the frequency of a heterozygous genotype if the frequency, p, of the dominant allele is 0.942.

   Express your answer as a percentage of the population.

Practice

Exam-style questions

1. DNA mutations can be caused by the insertion, deletion, or substitution of one or more nucleotides.

   (a) A DNA base sequence is shown below. The DNA sequence starts at **C**.

   C T A C C C C T G A A A A T T

   Complete **Table 1.1** to state how many triplet codes in this sequence would be changed by the mutations that are described.

Mutation	Number of triplet codes that are changed
substitution of guanine	
deletion of the initial cytosine base	
insertion of cytosine after the first adenine base	
insertion of three cytosine bases before guanine	

   Table 1.1

   [4]

   Synoptic links
   2.1.2m   2.1.3g

   Exam tip

   Insertion and deletion mutations, by and large, have a more significant effect on a DNA base sequence than substitution mutations. Insertions and deletions cause frameshifts – all triplets in the base sequence after the mutation may be changed.

   (b) Basmati rice has a distinctive smell and flavour.

   These properties are the result of several genetic mutations in one gene.

   Sections of the original allele and the mutated allele, which is responsible for the distinctive smell and flavour, are shown below.

   Original allele base sequence:
   A A A C T G G T A A A A A G A T T A T G G C T T C A G C T G

   Mutated allele base sequence:
   A A A C T G G T A T A T A T T T C A G C T G

   (i) Describe the substitution mutation that occurred in the base sequence.

   ....
   ....
   ....
   ....
   ....
   .... [3]

   (ii) Describe the deletion mutation that occurred in the base sequence.

   .... [1]

250 21 Cellular control

(c) (i) Explain why a DNA mutation may change the function of the protein for which a gene codes.

....
....
....
....
.... [3]

(iii) Describe three reasons why a DNA mutation might not produce a change in the function of a protein.

....
....
....
....
.... [3]

2 Many diseases are caused by genetic mutations.

(a) Sickle-cell anaemia is caused by a substitution mutation in the gene coding for the β-globin subunit of haemoglobin.

A thymine base is replaced by adenine in the sickle-cell mutant allele.

> **Synoptic links**
> 2.1.2m   2.1.3a
> 2.1.3g   6.1.2bi

(i) Describe how the sickle-cell mutation would change the structure of mRNA that is transcribed.

....
....
....
.... [1]

(ii) The substitution mutation causes the amino acid glutamic acid to be replaced by valine in the primary structure of β-globin.

This change causes haemoglobin molecules to aggregate, which distorts the shape of red blood cells.

Suggest how the substitution of a single amino acid in the structure of haemoglobin affects its properties.

....
....
....
....
.... [2]

(b) A condition called fragile X syndrome is caused by the insertion of many CGG triplets in the *FMR1* gene.

Methylation of the CGG triplets prevents transcription of the *FMR1* gene, leading to intellectual disability.

Suggest how transcription of the *FMR1* gene is prevented.

....

....

....

....

....

.... [2]

(c) A genetic condition called cystic fibrosis is a result of a recessive allele that is caused by a deletion mutation.

  (i) Explain why deletion mutations are more likely to be harmful than substitution mutations.

  ....

  ....

  ....

  .... [2]

  (ii) State the genotypes of parents that would have a 50% probability of producing offspring with cystic fibrosis.

  .... [1]

> **Exam tip**
>
> Many exam questions focus on harmful mutations, such as those that cause genetic disorders. However, bear in mind that mutations can also be neutral (i.e., silent) or beneficial. Mutations that result in improvements to polypeptide products are the basis of evolution.

3 Gene expression in eukaryotes can be controlled at the transcriptional, post-transcriptional, and post-translational levels.

  (a) Complete **Table 3.1** to describe how gene expression is controlled at different levels.

Level	Control mechanism	Description
transcription	transcription factors	
post-transcription	mRNA processing to produce mature mRNA	
		nucleotides are deleted, added, or substituted
post-translation	protein modification	

Table 3.1 [4]

252 21 Cellular control

(b) Prokaryotes such as *E. coli* control gene expression at the transcriptional level using operons.

Describe how the transcription rate of structural genes is increased in *E. coli* when molecules of lactose are present. [5]

> **Exam tip**
> Operons enable prokaryotes to control transcription rates. Eukaryotes rely on transcription factors to do the same job.

4 Homeobox genes control the development of eukaryotic organisms.
  (a) (i) Outline the role of homeobox genes in the development of eukaryotic organisms. [3]
     (ii) Explain why homeobox genes are expressed in a specific order during development. [1]
     (iii) State the difference between the terms homeobox and Hox gene. [2]
  (b) The estimated numbers of homeobox genes in different species are shown in **Table 4.1**.

Major group	Species	Number of homeobox genes
invertebrates	nematode (*C. elegans*)	92
	fruit fly	99
	mosquito	83
vertebrates	zebrafish	289
	pufferfish	239
	mouse	242
	human	230

Table 4.1

A student suggested that the number of homeobox genes is correlated with the complexity of an organism.

Evaluate the student's suggestion. [2]

> **Exam tip**
> Remember to consider both sides of an argument when you are asked to evaluate a statement or conclusion.

> **Synoptic link**
> 4.1.1ei

5 Mitosis and apoptosis are processes that are crucial to the development of structures in the body.
  (a) Outline how mitosis and apoptosis form fingers and toes in animals. [2]
  (b) Suggest the role of the immune system in the process of apoptosis. [2]
  (c) Cells that are damaged by infection or injury can burst and release hydrolytic enzymes. This is known as necrosis.

  Describe how apoptosis is different from necrosis. [2]

> **Exam tip**
> Apoptosis and mitosis are both occurring at staggering rates, even in adult organisms. A tissue or organ that remains the same size must be experiencing similar rates of mitosis and apoptosis.

> **Synoptic link**
> 2.1.3g

6 Using examples, describe how the development of an organism is controlled using mitosis and apoptosis. [6]

7 Describe how the expression of genes can be controlled in eukaryotes before and after transcription. [6]

> **Exam tip**
> Your instinct may be to assume that introns are retained by mature mRNA. This is not the case! Introns are removed while exons remain. Think of 'e' for 'essential', or 'i' for 'interfering' introns.

21 Practice

Knowledge

22 Patterns of inheritance

Environmental and genetic variation

Phenotypic variation, the observable characteristics of an organism, is a combination of genetic and environmental factors. Examples include:

1. Plants have green leaves because their genes code for chlorophyll. However, green leaves may turn yellow, a condition called chlorosis, through a lack of magnesium ions in the soil or a viral infection.
2. Body mass is affected by genetics but is also hugely influenced by diet, especially at the extremes of high and low body mass.

Continuous and discontinuous variation

Variation is influenced by the number of genes involved.

Discontinuous variation

Qualitative differences between phenotypes that have distinctive groups (e.g., blood group).

- Different alleles at the same locus have a large effect.
- Caused by gene mutation.
- Include dominant, recessive, and co-dominant patterns of inheritance.

Continuous variation

Quantitative differences between phenotypes where there is a large range of variation within a population (e.g., height, hoof size in horses).

- Controlled by two of more genes, each of which contributes to the phenotype.
- Different alleles at each locus have little effect.
- A large number of unlinked genes may have a combined effect on the 'polygenic' characteristic.

Genetic variation through sexual reproduction

During sexual reproduction, genetic variability is increased by:

1. The formation of gametes (sex cells) during which:
   - Alleles are redistributed during crossing over (where non-sister chromatids exchange alleles) in prophase I
   - Genetic reassortment occurs during metaphase I due to random distribution and segregation of parental homologous chromosomes
   - Genetic reassortment occurs during metaphase II due to random distribution and segregation of sister chromatids
   - Random mutations occur.
2. The random fusion of gametes at fertilisation.

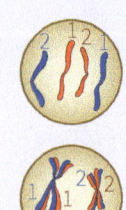

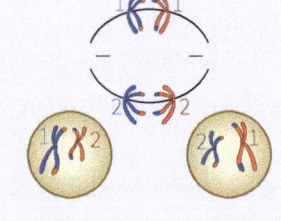

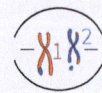

22

Factors affecting the evolution of a species

Stabilising selection
- Eliminates extremes within a population.
- Favours the most **normal**, or **common**, individuals.
- Occurs with unchanging environmental conditions.

Directional selection
- Favours individuals at the **extreme** in a range of variation.
- Changes characteristics of a population.
- Occurs due to a change in the environment.

Genetic drift
- The **random** change in allele frequency in a population.
- Some alleles are passed on and some disappear.
- Some phenotypes become more common and others more rare.

Genetic bottleneck
- A chance event causes a dramatic reduction in the size of a population and the gene pool.
- A small bottleneck event can have a big effect on allele frequency.

Founder effect
- The loss of genetic variation due to the establishment of a new population by a very small number of individuals from a much larger population.
- Sometimes after a genetic bottleneck event.

Speciation

Speciation is the evolution of a new species from an existing one.

There are two types of isolation that can lead to speciation:

Sympatric speciation – speciation from reproductive isolation mechanisms with no physical barrier.

Examples include:
- A change in courting behaviour of a subset of a species which is not recognised by the rest of the species.
- Polyploidy (a mutation affecting whole sets of chromosomes), particularly in plants.
- Hybrid sterility, a species formed from a mating of two species is reproductively isolated if it is sterile. For example, when a donkey is mated with a zebra the resulting zonkey is sterile, which prevents the two species merging into a single zonkey species.

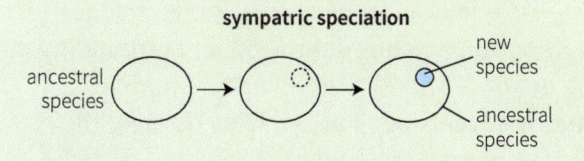

Allopatric speciation – speciation from geographical barriers, such as oceans, rivers, mountains, and deserts.

- When two populations of the same species are separated (isolated) for a time they may experience different environmental conditions.
- This will lead to the selection of different alleles in the two populations.
- In time, the gene pools may become so different that, if reunited, the two populations would be unable to successfully breed with each other.
- The two populations have become separate species.

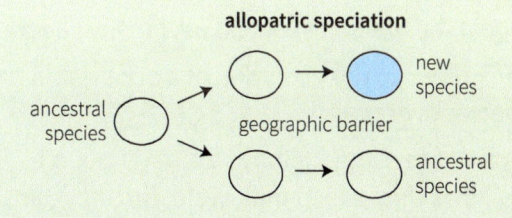

sympatric speciation

allopatric speciation

Chi-squared (χ^2) test

The chi-squared test is used to compare observed results from genetic crosses with the predicted outcomes.

$$\chi^2 = \Sigma \frac{(O - E)^2}{E}$$

Where: O = observed value, E = expected value

Once chi-squared has been calculated, the value can then be looked up on a distribution table. If the value of chi-squared is **smaller** than the critical value, then the difference between the observed and expected data is not statistically significant.

Degrees of freedom	Number of classes	χ^2							
1	2	0.00	0.10	0.45	1.32	2.71	3.84	5.41	6.64
2	3	0.02	0.58	1.39	2.77	4.61	5.99	7.82	9.21
3	4	0.12	1.21	2.37	4.11	6.25	7.82	9.84	11.34
4	5	0.30	1.92	3.36	5.39	7.78	9.49	11.67	13.28
5	6	0.55	2.67	4.35	6.63	9.24	11.07	13.39	15.09
probability that deviation is due to chance alone		0.99 (99%)	0.75 (75%)	0.50 (50%)	0.25 (25%)	0.10 (10%)	0.05 (5%)	0.02 (2%)	0.01 (1%)

← accept null hypothesis | critical value | reject null hypothesis – any difference is not due to chance and is significant

The Hardy–Weinberg principle

The Hardy–Weinberg principle can be used to calculate dominant and recessive allele frequencies in populations if the following assumptions are made:

- the population is very large
- mating within the population is random
- there is no mutation, genetic drift, or migration
- there is no selective advantage for any genotype.

The frequency of alleles, genotypes, and phenotypes in a population can be calculated using the Hardy–Weinberg equation:

$$p^2 + 2pq + q^2 = 1$$
$$p + q = 1$$

where:
- p = the frequency of dominant allele (A)
- q = the frequency of the recessive allele (a)
- pq = the frequency of heterozytotes (Aa)

Artificial selection

In **artificial selection**, humans:
1. select organisms with the desired characteristics and allow them to breed together
2. repeat the breeding process over many generations
3. can influence the evolution of a population or species over time.

Selective breeding includes animals, such as dairy cows (increased milk yield, docility), and plants, such as wheat (increased yield, disease resistance).

It is important to maintain a resource of genetic material for use in selective breeding, including wild types, especially as growing conditions change. It is also important to consider the ethics surrounding more extreme selective breeding to 'improve' domestic species, such as breeding dogs for their looks rather than their physical health.

22

Using a genetic diagram to show a genetic cross

What would be the F₁ generation (offspring) of a cross between two heterozygous brown fruit flies?

1. Assign a **single** letter for the alleles, ideally one that relates to the feature (i.e., B/b for brown).

   Dominant allele = capital letter
   Recessive allele = lower case letter

2. Write the parents' phenotypes, their diploid genotypes, and single gametes.

   Parents:
   Phenotype: brown   ×   brown
   Genotype: Bb   ×   Bb
   Gametes: B b   B b

   B = brown
   b = black

3. Draw a Punnett square and fill it in:

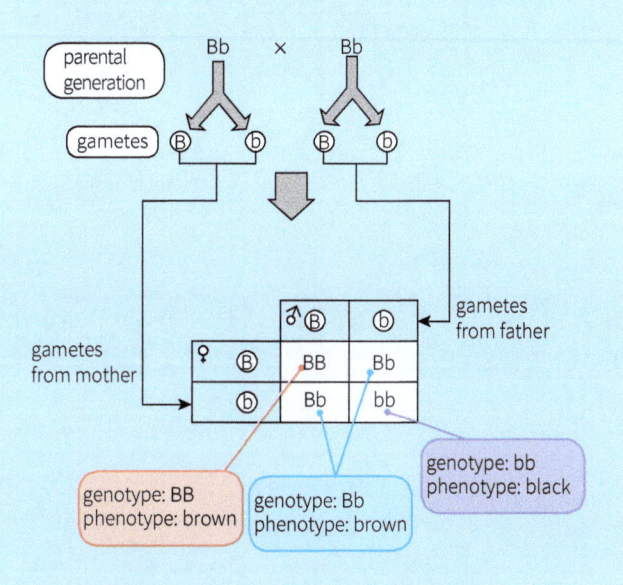

	B	b
B	BB	Bb
b	Bb	bb

   - genotype: BB, phenotype: brown
   - genotype: Bb, phenotype: brown
   - genotype: bb, phenotype: black

4. The last step is to describe the genotypic and phenotypic ratios from the cross.
   From the fruit fly cross, the ratios are as follows:
   Genotypes: 1 BB : 2 Bb : 1 bb
   Phenotypes: 3 brown : 1 black or 75:25
   The outcomes of genetic crosses are predictable.

Monogenic crosses

Monogenic crosses investigate the inheritance of alleles of a **single** gene. There is a single gene for pod colour in peas: green (G) or yellow (g).

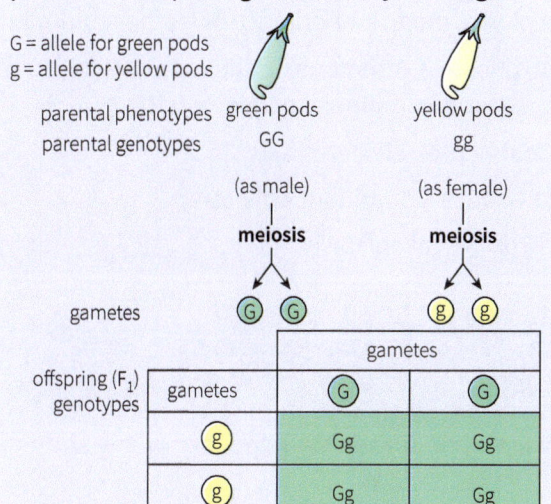

G = allele for green pods
g = allele for yellow pods

parental phenotypes: green pods / yellow pods
parental genotypes: GG (as male) / gg (as female)

meiosis → gametes: G G / g g

offspring (F₁) genotypes:

	G	G
g	Gg	Gg
g	Gg	Gg

F₁ outcomes:
Genotype = 100% Gg   Phenotype = 100% green

Dihybrid crosses

Dihybrid crosses investigate the inheritance of two separate genes on different chromosomes, for example, pea seed colour and pea seed shape. If the parents are both heterozygotes, the ratio of phenotypes will be 9:3:3:1.

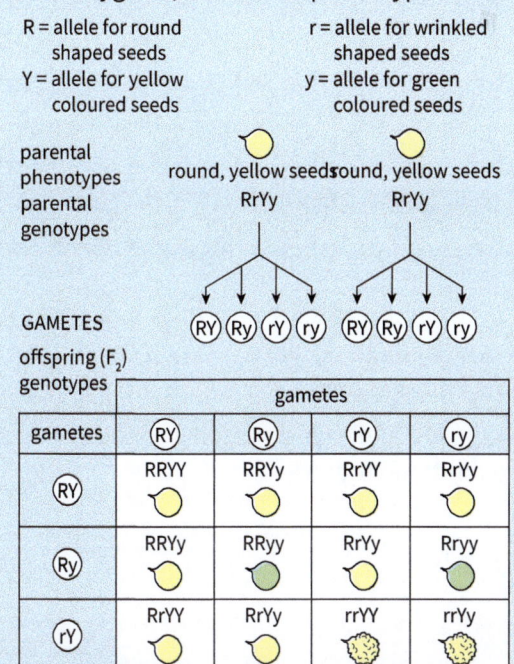

R = allele for round shaped seeds
r = allele for wrinkled shaped seeds
Y = allele for yellow coloured seeds
y = allele for green coloured seeds

parental phenotypes: round, yellow seeds / round, yellow seeds
parental genotypes: RrYy / RrYy

GAMETES: RY Ry rY ry   /   RY Ry rY ry

offspring (F₂) genotypes:

	RY	Ry	rY	ry
RY	RRYY	RRYy	RrYY	RrYy
Ry	RRYy	RRyy	RrYy	Rryy
rY	RrYY	RrYy	rrYY	rrYy
ry	RrYy	Rryy	rrYy	rryy

offspring (F₂) phenotypes:
9 round, yellow seeds   3 wrinkled, yellow seeds
3 round, green seeds   1 wrinkled, green seed

For answers and more practice questions visit www.oxfordrevise.com/scienceanswers

Even more practice and interactive revision quizzes are available on **kerboodle**

22 Knowledge

Epistasis

There are cases where genes at one locus interact with genes at another locus by masking or suppressing their expression. This is called **epistasis**. Examples of epistasis include the inheritance of flower colour in *Salvia* plants and the inheritance of feather colour in chickens.

Epistatic ratios are variations on the normal 9:3:3:1 ratio from dihybrid inheritance for two unlinked genes:

1. **9:7 / 9:3:4** - recessive epistasis
2. **12:3:1** or **13:3** – dominant epistasis
3. **15:1** – reciprocal epistasis

Linkage

Linkage occurs when genes for different characteristics, found at different loci on the same chromosome, are linked (inherited) together.

There are two forms of linkage – **sex linkage** and **autosomal linkage**.

Sex linkage

Sex linkage occurs when the genes are on the sex chromosomes, X and Y.

These chromosomes are homologous, but the smaller Y chromosome has a section missing, and so contains fewer genes. Therefore, males have only one allele of certain genes, and this alone will be expressed in the phenotype.

If the only allele inherited from the mother (the **carrier**) is recessive, the male offspring will suffer from certain conditions that are only or predominantly found in males (i.e., **sex-linked**).

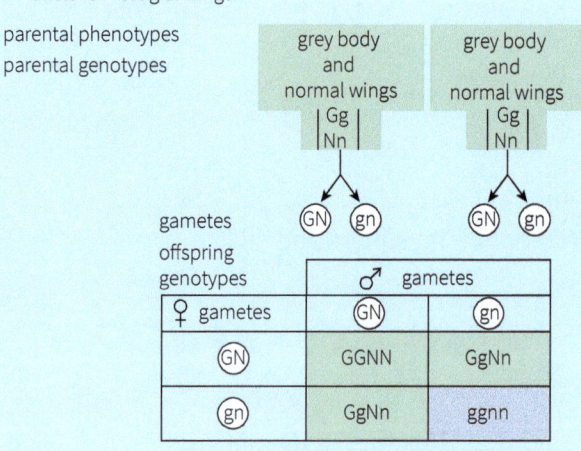

G = allele for grey body
g = allele for black body
N = allele for normal wings
n = allele for vestigial wings

parental phenotypes: grey body and normal wings / grey body and normal wings
parental genotypes: Gg Nn | Gg Nn

gametes: GN gn | GN gn

offspring genotypes:

♀ gametes \ ♂ gametes	GN	gn
GN	GGNN	GgNn
gn	GgNn	ggnn

offspring phenotypes:
3 fruit flies with grey bodies and normal wings
1 fruit fly with black body and vestigial wings

Autosomal linkage

Non-sex chromosomes are known as **autosomes**. **Autosomal linkage** occurs when two genes are on the same chromosome.

The two linked alleles are passed into the gamete and are inherited together.

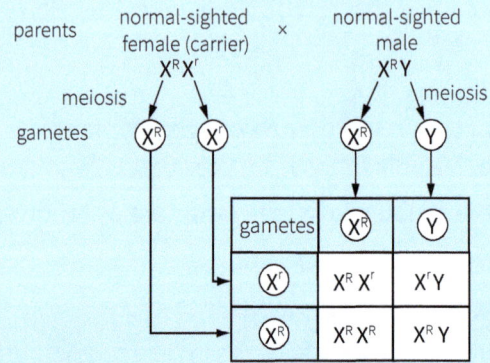

R = allele resulting in normal sight
r = allele resulting in colour-blindness

parents: normal-sighted female (carrier) $X^R X^r$ × normal-sighted male $X^R Y$

meiosis
gametes: X^R X^r | X^R Y

gametes	X^R	Y
X^r	$X^R X^r$	$X^r Y$
X^R	$X^R X^R$	$X^R Y$

F_1 ratio:
1 normal-sighted female : 1 normal sighted female (carrier) :
1 normal-sighted male : 1 colour-blind male

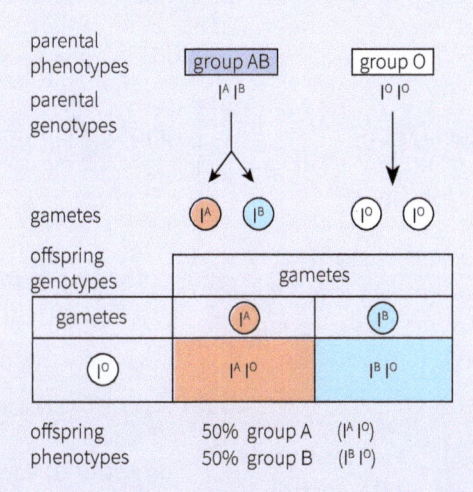

Codominance

Sometimes both alleles are expressed in a phenotype of a heterozygote. This is **codominance**.

For example, snapdragon plants can be homozygous with red flowers or homozygous with white flowers, but the heterozygotes have pink flowers.

In the image on the right, C represents the gene, and R and W represent the alleles. So, the C gene can have either the R allele, coding for red flowers, or the W allele, coding for white flower.

Because genes are represented on both chromosomes, there are two genes. If each has a different allele, and these alleles are codominant, it can result in a mix of both alleles being expressed. In this example, a flower with an R allele and a W allele on each copy of the C gene will have pink flowers.

parental phenotypes: pink flowers $C^R C^W$ × pink flowers $C^R C^W$

offspring genotypes:

gametes	C^R	C^W
C^R	$C^R C^R$	$C^R C^W$
C^W	$C^R C^W$	$C^W C^W$

offspring phenotypes:
50% pink flowers ($C^R C^W$)
25% red flowers ($C^R C^R$)
25% white flowers ($C^W C^W$)

Multiple alleles

Some genes have more than two alleles (e.g., blood groups, or fur colour in rabbits). Although there may be more than two alleles for a gene, only two can be presented at any one time. The alleles may be recessive, dominant, or codominant.

In blood groups there are three alleles:

I^A : dominant over I^O leading to the production of antigen A; codominant with I^B resulting in the production of both A and B antigens

I^B : dominant over I^O leading to the production of antigen B; codominant with I^A resulting in the production of both A and B antigens

I^O : recessive, does not lead to the production of an antigen

There are four blood groups:

A: $I^A I^A$, $I^A I^O$ AB: $I^A I^B$
B: $I^B I^B$, $I^B I^O$ O: $I^O I^O$

parental phenotypes: group AB ($I^A I^B$) × group O ($I^O I^O$)

offspring genotypes:

gametes	I^A	I^B
I^O	$I^A I^O$	$I^B I^O$

offspring phenotypes:
50% group A ($I^A I^O$)
50% group B ($I^B I^O$)

Retrieval

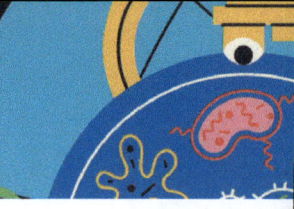

Learn the answers to the questions below, then cover the answers column with a piece of paper and write as many as you can. Check and repeat.

Questions | Answers

#	Question	Answer
1	Phenotypic variation is caused by which types of factors?	environmental and genetic
2	What is phenotypic variation?	variation in the observable characteristics of organisms
3	What is a gene?	a section of DNA that codes for a polypeptide or protein in an organism
4	What is an allele?	one of multiple different forms of a gene
5	Write a definition for discontinuous variation with an example.	qualitative differences between phenotypes that have distinctive groups (e.g., blood group)
6	Write a definition for continuous variation with an example.	variation in a characteristic where there is a range between two extremes (e.g., height, body mass, leaf length)
7	How many genes are involved in discontinuous variation and continuous variation?	Discontinuous variation: usually one gene Continuous variation: many genes, polygenic
8	List two concerns with artificial selection.	1 loss of wild type alleles that may confer a benefit in the future 2 increase of homozygous recessives with detrimental phenotypes (due to inbreeding depression or loss of hybrid vigour)
9	What do we use the chi-squared test for in genetics?	to see if the difference between the observed value and the expected value is significant or not
10	How is a dominant allele represented in a genetic diagram?	with a capital letter
11	Why does autosomal linkage reduce variation?	pairs of alleles are inherited together
12	What is speciation?	the evolution of a new species from an existing one
13	What are the two types of speciation?	allopatric and sympatric
14	Write out the two equations for the Hardy–Weinberg principle.	$p^2 + 2pq + q^2 = 1$ $p + q = 1$
15	List three assumptions made when calculating the Hardy–Weinberg principle.	• the population is very large • mating within the population is random • there is no mutation, genetic drift, or migration • there is no selective advantage for any genotype
16	Is antibiotic resistance in bacteria an example of stabilising selection or directional selection?	directional selection

Maths skills

Practise your maths skills using the worked example and practice questions below.

Calculating chi-squared

If you are required to calculate chi-squared from genetic cross data, you will always be given the equation:

$$\chi^2 = \sum \frac{(O - E)^2}{E}$$

Where:
E = expected value O = observed value

Once you have your chi-squared value, you can use a degrees of freedom table to determine if your results are statistically significant.

Typically, your results are statistically significant when your chi-squared value is less than the number given in the table for $p = 0.05$. This means that there was a less than 5% chance that your results were generated randomly.

Worked example

Question
An F_2 dihybrid genetic cross experiment yielded these phenotypic results in pea plants:

Yellow and round = 85   Green and round = 28
Yellow and wrinkled = 24   Green and wrinkled = 8

Our null hypothesis states that there is no significant difference between our observed results and the expected results. Can you reject the null hypothesis?

Answer
Total number of plants = 145

You would expect the ratio of offspring phenotypes to be 9:3:3:1 (total = 16). you can work out what proportion of plants would be expected (E) to have each phenotype using the following equation:

$$\frac{\text{expected}}{16} \times 145$$

Therefore the expected numbers for the offspring phenotypes are:

$\frac{9}{16} \times 145 = 82$ $\frac{3}{16} \times 145 = 27$ $\frac{1}{16} \times 145 = 9$

Class	Observed (O)	Expected (E)	$O - E$	$(O - E)^2$	$\frac{(O - E)^2}{E}$
yellow round	85	82	3	9	0.11
green round	28	27	1	1	0.04
yellow wrinkled	24	27	−3	9	0.33
green wrinkled	8	9	−1	1	0.11
				χ^2	**0.59**

There were four classes, which gives three degrees of freedom. If you look up 0.59 on a distribution table (see page 256) you see that the value falls between 0.00 and 0.10, which is below the critical value at $p = 0.05$.

Therefore, the difference between the observed and expected data is not significant and you cannot reject the null hypothesis.

Practice

A geneticist carried out a test cross to determine the genotype of a plant with yellow, round seeds.
The offspring of this cross were as follows:

Green round = 47   Green wrinkled = 53
Yellow round = 51   Yellow wrinkled = 45

1 Using the chi-squared test, evaluate whether there is a significant difference between the observed and the expected results.

2 The null hypothesis of this experiment is that there would be no significant difference between the observed and expected results. State whether your results accept or reject the null hypothesis.

Practice

Exam-style questions

1. Marfan syndrome is a genetic disorder that affects connective tissue. People with Marfan syndrome tend to be thin, tall, and have flexible joints.

    Figure 1.1 shows the inheritance of Marfan syndrome in a family.

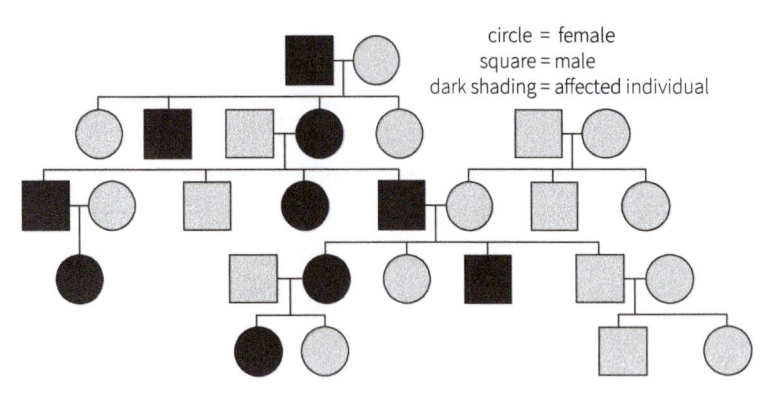

    circle = female
    square = male
    dark shading = affected individual

    Figure 1.1

    (a) (i) Outline the conclusions you can draw about the location and nature of the allele responsible for causing Marfan syndrome. Explain your conclusions.

    ....
    ....
    ....
    ....
    ....
    ....
    .... [4]

    (ii) Explain whether Marfan syndrome shows continuous or discontinuous variation within populations.

    ....
    ....
    ....
    .... [2]

    > **Exam tip**
    >
    > Traits that show discontinuous variation tend to be controlled by one or two genes and are uninfluenced by the environment. Many genetic disorders show discontinuous variation.

2. Fur colour in mice is determined by two genes.

    The allele **A** codes for agouti fur. **A** is dominant to the recessive allele **a**, which codes for black fur.

    Mice that are **cc** homozygous recessive for another gene have white fur, regardless of their genotype for the **Aa** gene. The presence of the dominant allele **C** allows the **A** or **a** alleles to be expressed.

    (a) (i) State the name of this form of gene interaction.

    .... [1]

262 22 Patterns of inheritance

(ii) Suggest an explanation for this gene interaction.

....

....

.... [2]

(iii) The expected offspring phenotypic ratio for two parents that are both heterozygous for both genes (**AaCc**) is shown below.

9 agouti : 3 black : 4 white

When no gene interactions occur, a dihybrid cross between parents that are heterozygous for two genes would normally produce a different phenotypic ratio.

Calculate the expected offspring phenotypic ratio for a dihybrid cross between parents that are heterozygous for two genes that do not interact.

> **Exam tip**
>
> You will not be expected to produce genetic diagrams to show inheritance patterns that involve gene interactions.

.... [3]

3 The colour and texture of pea plant seeds are determined by the following alleles:

R = round, which is dominant to **r** (wrinkled)

G = yellow, which is dominant to **g** (green)

Two pea plants were bred together to produce 200 offspring. A scientist expected 50 offspring that produced round, yellow seeds, 50 that produced round, green seeds, 50 that produced wrinkled, yellow seeds, and 50 that produced wrinkled, green seeds.

The actual offspring phenotypes are shown in **Table 3.1**.

Phenotype	Observed number of offspring
round and yellow	46
round and green	55
wrinkled and yellow	45
wrinkled and green	54

Table 3.1

(a) (i) Use a chi-squared test to calculate whether the scientist's predictions about the inheritance pattern can be supported.

The formula for the chi-squared test is:

$$\chi^2 = \sum \frac{(O - E)^2}{E}$$

The critical value of chi-squared at the 0.05 p level for these data is 7.815.

> **Exam tip**
>
> Your calculated chi-squared value needs to be above the critical value for the null hypothesis to be rejected. This gives us confidence that there is a significant difference between the expected and observed results.

.... [4]

(ii) Predict the likely genotypes of the two parent plants.

> **Exam tip**
>
> Most sex-linked genes are on the X chromosome rather than the Y chromosome. This is because the X chromosome is larger and contains many more genes.

.... [1]

4 Fragile X syndrome is a sex-linked condition with symptoms that include learning disabilities.

The condition is caused by a dominant allele on the X chromosome.

(a) (i) Calculate the expected offspring phenotype ratios for a father with fragile X syndrome and a healthy mother. [2]

(ii) Suggest why females tend to have a milder form of fragile X syndrome than males. [2]

(b) A different form of genetic linkage is autosomal linkage.

Outline how autosomal linkage affects inheritance patterns. [3]

> **Exam tip**
>
> Women will rarely have genetic disorders that are caused by a recessive allele on the X chromosome. This is because they would need to inherit two recessive alleles to have the condition.

5 The alleles of some genes are codominant.

(a) State the meaning of the term codominant alleles. [2]

(b) The ABO blood group gene (I) is an example of a gene with multiple alleles.

I^A and I^B are codominant alleles. Both I^A and I^B are dominant to I^O.

Four blood group phenotypes exist: A, B, AB, and O.

(i) Calculate the expected offspring blood group phenotypic ratios for parents that are blood groups AB and O. [2]

(ii) Give a pair of parental genotypes that would have a 50% probability of producing offspring with blood group O. [1]

> **Synoptic links**
>
> 2.1.1g   4.1.1.h

(iii) The ABO blood group alleles code for different glycoproteins on the cell surface membrane of red blood cells.

Name the two organelles in which these glycoproteins would be synthesised. [2]

(iv) A person who is blood group A will produce an immune response when they are transfused with blood from a person who is blood group B.

Explain why an immune response occurs. [2]

(c) The flower colour of the plant *Mirabilis jalapa* is controlled by two codominant alleles – C^R, which produces red flowers, and C^W, which produces white flowers. Heterozygous genotypes produce pink flowers.

(i) Calculate the expected offspring phenotypic ratio of two plants with heterozygous genotypes. [2]

(ii) State a pair of parental genotypes that would produce only offspring with pink flowers. [1]

> **Exam tip**
> Codominant alleles should be represented as different superscripts on a common capitalised letter. Codominant alleles for black fur and yellow fur in an animal could be represented as F^B and F^Y (or C^B and C^Y), for example.

6 Ellis-van Creveld (EVC) syndrome is a genetic disorder that produces symptoms such as extra fingers and dwarfism.

The allele that causes EVC is recessive.

In a population of Amish people, 1 in 250 people have EVC.

(a) (i) Calculate the percentage of the Amish population that are heterozygous for EVC.

Give your answer to 2 significant figures.

Use the formulae: $p + q = 1$ and $p^2 + 2pq + q^2 = 1$ [4]

(ii) Worldwide, 99.2% of people do not have a recessive allele for EVC.

Calculate the percentage of the worldwide population that are heterozygous for EVC.

Give your answer to 2 significant figures. [4]

(iii) Calculate the percentage of the worldwide population that have EVC syndrome.

Give your answer to 2 significant figures. [3]

(iv) Suggest why the frequency of EVC in the Amish population and the worldwide population is so different. [2]

> **Exam tip**
> Where you know the proportion of one allele, use $p + q = 1$ to find the values for $p^2 + 2pq + q^2 = 1$.

> **Exam tip**
> 'Random assortment' is often called 'independent assortment' – either term is acceptable in an exam.

7 Describe and explain how sexual reproduction can produce genetic variation in a species. [6]

> **Synoptic links**
> 6.1.3f 6.1.3g

8 Compare the procedural and ethical difficulties associated with the use of artificial selection and genetic engineering. [6]

> **Exam tip**
> In your answer to question **8**, you should consider the ethics of both processes and their effectiveness in producing the desired organisms.

Knowledge

23 Manipulating genomes

Genetic engineering

Genetic engineering involves the transfer of genes from one organism, or species, to another. Since the genetic code, transcription, and translation are universal, the transferred DNA is used to make mRNA which is translated within cells of the recipient (**transgenic**) organism.

The gene must first be isolated from one organism and then transferred into another organism using a suitable vector.

Issues surrounding genetic manipulation of organisms

Examples of genetic engineering include:
- introducing the toxin Bt (from bacteria) to give insect resistance in genetically modified soya
- 'pharming' – using genetically modified animals to produce pharmaceuticals.

Positive aspects
- Medicines such as insulin
- Gene therapy to prevent diseases
- Production of drought/disease resistant crops

Concerns
- Social – are there long-term health risks?
- Financial – can poor countries afford GM crops?
- Ethical – can someone ever 'own' an organisms's DNA?
- Environmental – does GM technology affect wild populations?

Gene therapy

Somatic cell gene therapy is a technology where a functioning allele of a gene is introduced into a differentiated body cell that has faulty alleles, so that functioning polypeptides are made by the cells. The treated cells retain the faulty alleles so any offspring of a person treated with somatic cell gene therapy will still inherit the faulty gene.

Germline cell gene therapy involves engineering a gene in a sperm cell, an ovum, or a zygote so that every cell in the growing individual has a non-faulty copy of the gene. The new gene may be inherited by any offspring.

Most gene therapies have yet to be very effective, for example, the effect may be short lived. In addition, gene therapy can only be used to treat genetic disorders caused by recessive alleles of a single gene (e.g., cystic fibrosis).

23

Gene sequencing

A large number of genomes from different organisms have been mapped. The **gene sequences** have allowed:

1. genome-wide comparisons between individuals and between species to aid the study of **evolutionary relationships**
2. sequences of amino acids in polypeptides to be predicted to aid genotype–phenotype relationships
3. the development of **synthetic biology** – a new field of biology designing / constructing new biological molecules or redesigning existing ones.

Examples include genetically modifying organisms and designing new alleles to replace faulty ones.

These advances have also involved **bioinformatics** and **computational biology**.

Bioinformatics – the development of software that allows biologists to organise and analyse raw biological data.

Computational biology – using the data to build theoretical models to predict what will happen in unknown circumstances.

The process of genetically modifying a bacterium

The desired gene is transferred to the host (recipient) cell using a vector (e.g., a bacterial plasmid).

1. The ends of the desired gene are cut using a **restriction** enzyme which breaks the DNA at specific base sequences to leave complementary 'sticky ends' on the gene. The plasmid is also cut open using the same restriction enzyme.

    The plasmid may be labelled by having marker genes (e.g., antibiotic resistance genes, an enzyme gene, or fluorescence genes) inserted into it so that it can be detected after modification.

2. **Ligase** enzymes 'glue' the sticky ends of the plasmid and the gene together with a phosphodiester bond to seal the sugar phosphate backbone, thus forming **recombinant DNA**.

3. Large quantities of the plasmid are incubated with the host bacteria to ensure the bacteria take up some of the recombinant DNA.

    Electroporation (an electric shock) may be used to increase cell membrane permeability to plasmid uptake.

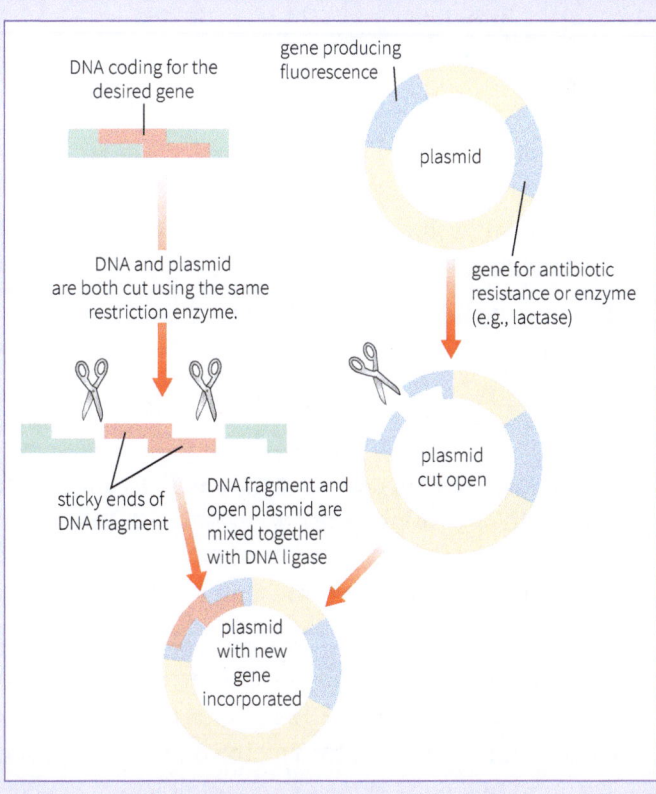

23 Knowledge 267

PCR

The **polymerase chain reaction (PCR)** is a method of amplifying DNA.

There are three main steps to PCR:

1. **Strand separation** – the target DNA is heated to **95 °C** for five minutes to separate the two strands, in a mixture of excess bases, primers, and thermostable DNA polymerase.
2. **Primer binding** – the mixture is rapidly cooled to **55 °C** so primers can bind to complementary sites on the target DNA,
3. **Strand synthesis** – the mixture is heated to **72 °C** and the thermostable DNA polymerase copies both strands of the target DNA.

This process is repeated, and the amount of DNA doubles with each cycle.

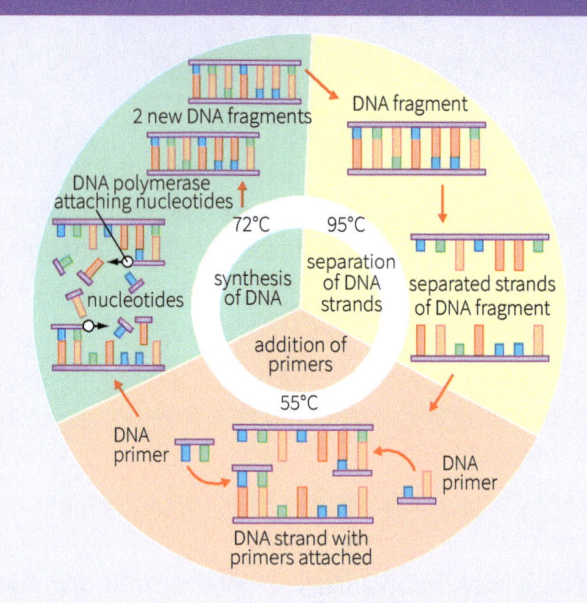

DNA sequencing

DNA sequencing is finding out the precise order of nucleotides.

When DNA sequencing began, it was a slow process. However, fully automated **high-throughput** sequencing has rapidly increased the process speed. In 1995, scientists took 18 months to sequence a bacterial genome.

Today, a genome can be sequenced in less than 24 hours!

The process of DNA sequencing is similar to PCR:

1. The DNA fragment to be sequenced is mixed with excess adenine, thymine, cytosine, guanine, thermostable DNA polymerase, short primers, and special terminator nucleotides of the four bases.
2. The mixture is heated to 95 °C to separate the DNA strands.
3. It is cooled to 50 °C for the primers to anneal (bind) to the DNA.
4. The mixture is then heated to 60 °C so DNA polymerase can synthesise complementary strands of DNA. If a terminator nucleotide is incorporated into the strand, DNA polymerase will be thrown off and the DNA strand will be truncated.
5. The DNA sequence is read by ordering the fragments by size (the same way as DNA strands move in electrophoresis) and recording the terminator nucleotide. The modified nucleotide is fluorescently tagged with a nucleotide-specific colour.

Stages 1–2: DNA strand chopped up, mixed with primer, bases, DNA polymerase and terminator bases

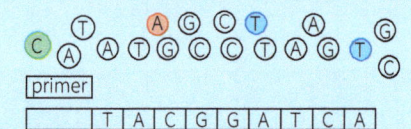

Stage 3: each time a terminator base is added, a strand terminates until all possible chains produced

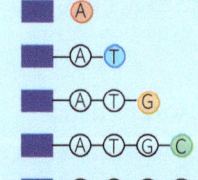

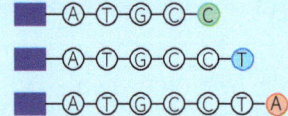

Stage 4: readout from capillary tubes: DNA fragments separated by electrophoresis in capillary tubes by mass, and lasers detect the colours and the sequence

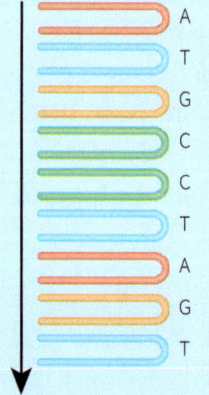

Stage 5: computer analysis of all data to give original DNA sequence

23 Manipulating genomes

Gel electrophoresis

Gel electrophoresis is a technique used to separate nucleic acid fragments (and proteins) based on their mass.

The electric current pulls the negatively charged DNA fragments towards the positive end of the gel. The smallest fragments move the furthest.

The process is accurate enough to separate fragments that differ in length by only one base.

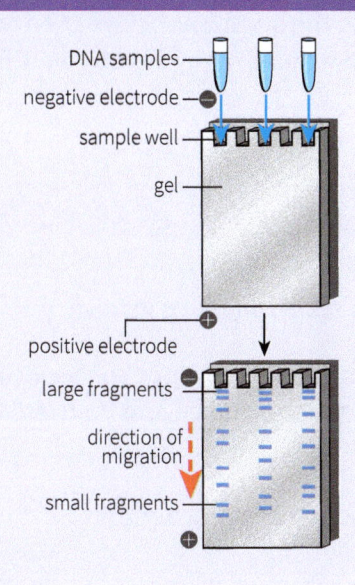

DNA profiling

An organism's genome contains many variable number tandem repeats (VNTRs), which are repeating sequences of nucleotides that appear next to each other (in tandem).

The probability of two individuals having the same VNTRs is very low. This allows **DNA profiling** or genetic fingerprinting to determine genetic relationships and the genetic variability within a population. Genetic fingerprinting analyses DNA fragments that have been cloned by **PCR**.

DNA profiling is used in the following areas:

- Forensic science – to determine if someone was present at a crime scene.
- Medical diagnosis – diagnosis of inherited genetic diseases (e.g., Huntington's disease).
- Animal and plant breeding – to prevent unwanted inbreeding in captive breeding programmes, to identify a desirable characteristic in a crop plant, or to determine parentage of pedigree animals.

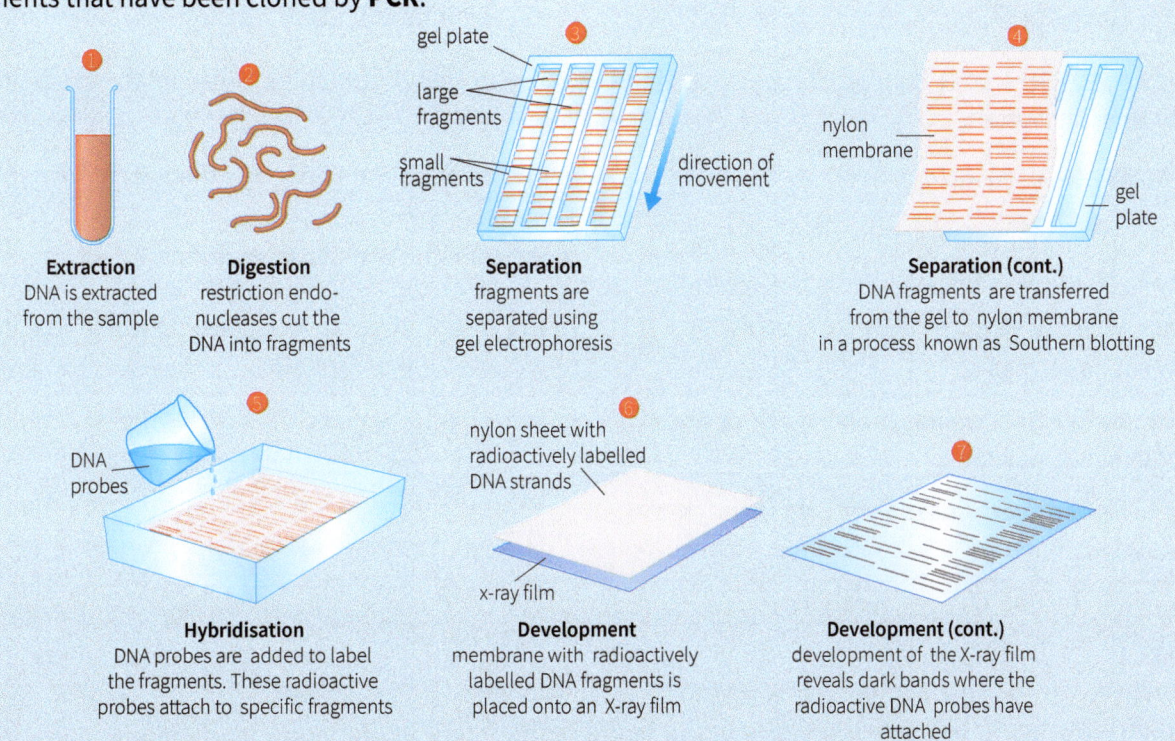

1. Extraction
DNA is extracted from the sample

2. Digestion
restriction endo-nucleases cut the DNA into fragments

3. Separation
fragments are separated using gel electrophoresis

4. Separation (cont.)
DNA fragments are transferred from the gel to nylon membrane in a process known as Southern blotting

5. Hybridisation
DNA probes are added to label the fragments. These radioactive probes attach to specific fragments

6. Development
membrane with radioactively labelled DNA fragments is placed onto an X-ray film

7. Development (cont.)
development of the X-ray film reveals dark bands where the radioactive DNA probes have attached

Retrieval

Learn the answers to the questions below, then cover the answers column with a piece of paper and write as many as you can. Check and repeat.

Questions / Answers

#	Question	Answer
1	What does genetic engineering involve?	the transfer of fragments of DNA from one organism / species to another
2	How is it possible that a gene from one species can be transferred to another, and translated and transcribed?	the genetic code, transcription, and translation are universal
3	What is a restriction endonuclease?	an enzyme that cuts DNA at specific sequences, leaving sticky ends
4	What is ligase?	an enzyme that glues sticky ends together by forming phosphodiester bonds
5	Why is electroporation used in genetic engineering of bacteria?	to increase the permeability of the bacterial cell membrane to increase the chance of plasmid uptake
6	What does PCR stand for?	polymerase chain reaction
7	After each cycle of PCR what happens to the amount of DNA?	it doubles
8	In addition to the DNA template (or target) what other substances are required for PCR?	the four DNA nucleotides, thermostable DNA polymerase, primers
9	List the three stages in PCR and the temperatures involved.	1 strand separation: 95 °C, 2 primer binding: 55 °C, 3 strand synthesis: 72 °C
10	What are VNTRs?	variable number tandem repeats
11	How do VNTRs enable DNA profiling to identify individuals?	the probability of two people having the same VNTRs is very low
12	What is DNA sequencing?	finding the exact sequence of nucleotide bases in DNA
13	During DNA sequencing, why is the mixture heated to 95 °C at the beginning of a cycle?	to separate the DNA double strands
14	Why are terminator nucleotides used in DNA sequencing?	so the DNA strands are truncated, to make the DNA fragments different lengths
15	How are the DNA strands produced through sequencing separated?	by gel electrophoresis
16	Does electrophoresis separate DNA fragments by size or charge?	by size
17	How are the fragments separated by gel electrophoresis?	by an electric current pulling the charged fragments through the gel
18	What charge do DNA fragments carry and to which terminal of the gel are they pulled?	negatively charged, pulled towards the positive terminal of the gel

23 Manipulating genomes

23

Maths skills

Practise your maths skills using the worked example and practice questions below.

Reading the genetic code

The genetic code is very simple: just four nucleotide bases, arranged in triplets. But this code is able to arrange twenty amino acids into a large number of different proteins – the human genome codes for approximately 20 000 proteins!

The ability to decipher the genetic code is an important skill.

Remember: in DNA there are four nucleotides – adenine, thymine, cytosine, and guanine.

Adenine forms a complementary pair with thymine, cytosine with guanine.

However, in both mRNA and tRNA, the base thymine is replaced with uracil.

Worked example

A strand of template DNA that codes for an exon has a base sequence:

A C A T G A T A C C C A

Question
What would the sequences of bases be on a complementary strand of pre-mRNA?

Answer
The best method is to work out what the complementary DNA sequence would be, then substitute uracil for thymine.

The complementary DNA strand would be:

T G T A C T A T G G G T

So, the pre-mRNA would be:

U G U A C U A U G G G U

Question
What would the anticodons be on molecules of complementary tRNA?

Answer
You know that an anticodon codes for one amino acid, and that one amino acid is three bases long, so just split the code every 3 bases:

A C A, U G A, U A C, C C A

Practice

A template strand of DNA has the base sequence:

A C T G T C T C A G A G G A G

1. How many amino acids does the sequence code for?
2. What would the sequences be on a complementary strand of mRNA?
3. What would the anticodons be on complementary molecules of tRNA?
4. Why does a strand of mRNA have fewer bases than the original DNA template?
5. Insulin is a small protein consisting of two polypeptide chains, one containing 21 amino acids and the other containing 30.

   What is the minimum number of bases that could code for an insulin protein (including the STOP triplets)?

Practice

Exam-style questions

1   DNA profiles are produced for various reasons.

   (a) State two uses of DNA profiling.

   ....

   .... [2]

   (b) The production of a DNA profile involves several stages and the use of different techniques.

   (i) Complete **Table 1.1** to outline the stages and techniques used in DNA profiling.

Stage of DNA profiling	How is this achieved?
amplification of DNA	
	the use of restriction enzymes
	electrophoresis
visualisation of banding patterns	

   Table 1.1

   [4]

   (ii) A student described a method for conducting electrophoresis:
   - Prepare a buffer solution for the electrophoresis gel plate.
   - Place DNA fragments in wells at the anode.
   - Pass an electric current through the electrophoresis plate.
   - Switch off the current after 2 hours.
   - Transfer the fragments to a nylon membrane.

   State and explain two errors in the student's method.

   ....
   ....
   ....
   ....
   .... [4]

   (iii) DNA profiles are usually formed from sections of DNA known as variable number tandem repeats (VNTRs).

   Suggest why DNA VNTRs rather than amino acid sequences are used to produce profiles in forensic analysis.

   ....
   ....
   .... [2]

> **Synoptic links**
> 2.1.3g   6.1.1b

> **Exam tip**
> Sometimes you will be asked to 'state' (or 'describe') *and* 'explain'. For this question, you need to identify each error but also explain why they are errors.

(c) Describe the difference between the terms DNA profiling and DNA sequencing.

....
....
....
....
....
....
.... [2]

2 The polymerase chain reaction (PCR) is used to amplify DNA.

(a) Complete the passage below, using the most appropriate words or terms, to outline the process of PCR.

A DNA sample is placed in a thermocycler. A temperature of 95 °C breaks .... bonds in the DNA. The temperature is lowered to .... to enable primers to bond to the separated DNA strands. The temperature is raised to 72 °C to enable Taq DNA polymerase to join .... to each strand.

[3]

(b) (i) Complete **Table 2.1** to show the number of DNA fragments that would be expected after different numbers of PCR cycles. Assume that a single DNA fragment was present at the start of the process.

Number of cycles	Number of fragments
4	
	2^6
	256
	$10^{3.3113}$

Table 2.1

> **Exam tip**
>
> 2^n (2 to the power of another number) tells you how many times you need to multiply by two in your calculation. For example, $2^5 = 2 \times 2 \times 2 \times 2 \times 2 = 32$. PCR is the most likely context for this type of calculation.

[4]

(ii) Suggest two reasons why the theoretical numbers of DNA fragments shown in the table are unlikely to be achieved.

....
....
....
....
....
.... [2]

3 Many advances in DNA sequencing technology have occurred since the original methods were developed in the 1970s.

(a) One method for sequencing DNA is called pyrosequencing, which has the following features:
- Single-stranded DNA is obtained.
- A complementary strand is synthesised through the addition of free nucleotides.
- Two enzymes, sulfurylase and luciferase, catalyse the production of light when a nucleotide is incorporated into the complementary strand.
- The light is detected to determine the order of bases in the DNA sequence.

(i) State one other enzyme that would be used in pyrosequencing.

.... [1]

(ii) One important aspect of the pyrosequencing method has not been described above. This aspect of the method is needed to allow a base sequence to be determined.

Suggest the additional aspect that would be needed to allow the determination of a base sequence.

....

.... [1]

(iii) The enzyme luciferase breaks down a molecule called luciferin to produce light.

Describe the mechanism by which luciferase catalyses this reaction.

....

....

....

....

.... [4]

(b) Describe how bioinformatics and computational biology allow scientists to apply their knowledge of DNA sequences.

....

....

....

....

.... [2]

> **Synoptic link**
> 2.1.4c

> **Exam tip**
> You do not need to learn the details of new sequencing techniques, such as pyrosequencing. However, you may be provided with information and data, as is the case with this question, which you will be asked to interpret.

> **Exam tip**
> The general mechanism of enzyme catalysis that you have learned (including key ideas and terms: substrate, active site, induced fit, and enzyme–substrate complexes) can be applied to unfamiliar examples, such as luciferase.

4 (a) Female mosquitoes can transmit diseases such as yellow fever to humans through biting. Scientists have created genetically modified (GM) *A. aegypti* mosquitoes in an attempt to reduce the spread of these vector-borne diseases.

Two genes were added to the *A. aegypti* genome:
- tTav, which codes for a protein that stops the expression of genes that are crucial to mosquito development
- a gene that codes for a fluorescent protein product

GM *A. aegypti* mosquitoes are unable to survive beyond the larval stage to develop into adults. However, a chemical called tetracycline can stop the action of the tTav protein.

Male GM *A. aegypti* mosquitoes were released into the wild to breed with females. Their offspring would have the tTAV and fluorescent genes.

(i) State the name of the enzyme that would be used to insert the tTAV gene into the DNA sequence of *A. aegypti*.

.... [1]

(ii) Explain why a gene coding for a fluorescent product was added to the genome of *A. aegypti*.

.... [1]

(iii) Suggest how the tTav protein stops the expression of genes that control mosquito development.

....
.... [2]

(iv) Explain why only male GM mosquitoes were released into the wild.

....
.... [1]

(v) Suggest why GM mosquito larvae in laboratories were exposed to tetracycline.

....
.... [1]

(b) Genetic engineering requires genes to be transferred to target cells using suitable techniques, including the use of vectors.

Complete **Table 4.1** to show the methods of gene transfer for different organisms.

Method of vector transfer	Organisms for which this method can be used
	animals
	bacteria
A. tumefaciens infection	

Table 4.1

[3]

Synoptic links
2.1.3g 6.1.1b

Exam tip
'State' implies a brief answer, usually containing less detail than that required when you are asked to 'describe'. When asked to 'state', often your answer will be a single word or a brief term.

5 Sickle cell anaemia is a genetic disease in which abnormal haemoglobin is produced because of a mutated *HBB* gene.

Several groups of scientists are attempting to develop gene therapies to treat sickle cell anaemia.

> **Synoptic links**
> 2.1.6j   2.1.6m

(a) One approach is to remove haematopoietic stem cells from a patient's body. Haematopoietic stem cells can divide to form white blood cells and red blood cells.

The mutated *HBB* gene is replaced in the haematopoietic stem cells, which are transplanted back into the patient.

(i) Explain why scientists target a patient's haemopoietic stem cells for gene therapy.

....
....
....
....
....
.... [2]

(ii) State one advantage of using gene therapy for sickle cell anaemia rather than using bone marrow transplants from donors.

....
.... [1]

(iii) Explain why gene therapy for diseases such as sickle cell anaemia is currently not permitted in embryos.

....
....
....
....
....
.... [2]

(b) Place a tick (✓) in each relevant box in **Table 5.1** to show the features of somatic cell gene therapy and germline gene therapy.

> **Exam tip**
> Remember that multipotent and pluripotent stem cells are found in adults.

Therapy type	somatic cell therapy	germline therapy
May require repeat treatments		
May target stem cells		
Is currently being applied to develop treatments for diseases		

Table 5.1

[3]

276   23 Manipulating genomes

6   Many methods for sequencing genomes have been developed.
    Table 6.1 compares the characteristics of some of these DNA sequencing methods.

Characteristic	Sequencing method			
	Illumina HiSeq 2500	Illumina NextSeq 500	Roche 454 GS FLX+	Pacific Biosciences RS II
cost of the equipment ($)	650,000	250,000	500,000	750,000
sequencing time (hours per run)	60	30	24	4
maximum length of sequence (base pairs)	2×250	2×150	700	40,000
number of bases read per run (gigabases per run)	250–300	100–120	0.7	0.5–1.0
error rate (%)	0.1	0.1	0.2 to 1.0	14

Table 6.1

A student suggested that the Pacific Biosciences RS II method was the best method for DNA sequencing.

Evaluate the student's suggestion.

....
....
....
....
.... [5]

> **Exam tip**
>
> When asked to 'evaluate', your answer should contain arguments that are for and against the conclusion or suggestion. However, there may be more general, contextual points that you can make. An example of this is the first marking point in the mark scheme for this question.

7   Outline the differences between semi-conservative replication of DNA and the polymerase chain reaction (PCR).

....
....
....
....
....
.... [6]

> **Synoptic link**
>
> 2.1.3e

> **Exam tip**
>
> You should concentrate on the most important points when asked to 'outline'. For example, do not describe every detail of the PCR technique in your answer to this question.

8   Describe the use of PCR in forensic analysis of DNA from crime scenes and the use of PCR in DNA sequencing.

....
....
....
....
....
.... [6]

> **Exam tip**
>
> For some level of response questions, you may be tempted to write loads of information. Instead, try to focus on exactly what the question is asking and cover each strand of the question. This question is relatively straightforward – it requires you to recall and describe two related techniques.

Knowledge

24 Cloning and biotechnology

What is a clone?

A **clone** is a genetically identical group of cells or organisms that arise from a single parent through asexual reproduction. Clones can also be created artificially.

Plant clones

Plants produce clones naturally.

These include:

- tubers (e.g., potatoes)
- runners (e.g., strawberry plants)
- bulbs (e.g., daffodils, onions)
- rhizomes (e.g., irises, ginger, turmeric).

Plant clones can also be produced artificially for use in horticulture.

For example:

- taking soft and hard wood cuttings
- tissue culture

Taking a plant cutting

Propagating a plant by taking cuttings is a simple example of cloning.

Taking a cutting:

1. Cut a shoot off a plant just below a node (where leaves grow from).
2. Remove large leaves near the bottom of the cutting, and any buds from the top of the cutting.
3. Dip the cut end of the cutting in hormone powder to encourage the development of roots.
4. Place the cutting in a pot of moist soil or in a jar of water with a clear plastic bag over the leaves to reduce water loss.
5. After a few days, the cutting should start to grow roots.

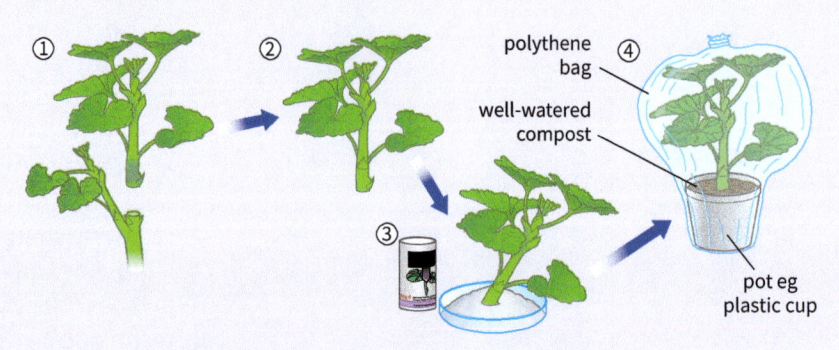

24 Cloning and biotechnology

Production of artificial clones of plants

Plant clones can also be produced through **micropropagation** and **tissue culture**.

Micropropagation is the rapid production of many young cloned plants from stock plant material using plant tissue culture methods.

A simple tissue culture method is as follows:

1 A small amount of plant tissue (often meristematic tissue, such as shoot tips) is removed from the parent and sterilised.
2 The tissue is divided into tiny pieces and placed on a growth medium containing nutrients and plant growth factors.
3 When the tissue samples have started to develop roots and shoots, the plantlets are transferred to a growing medium such as soil or compost.

Farmers and growers exploit 'natural' vegetative propagation and artificial micropropagation in the production of crops.

Advantages include:
- Large numbers of quality, identical plants can be produced quickly.
- Many clones may be raised from GM material.
- Seedless, sterile varieties can be grown to meet consumer taste, such as grapes.
- Rare and endangered plants can be propagated.

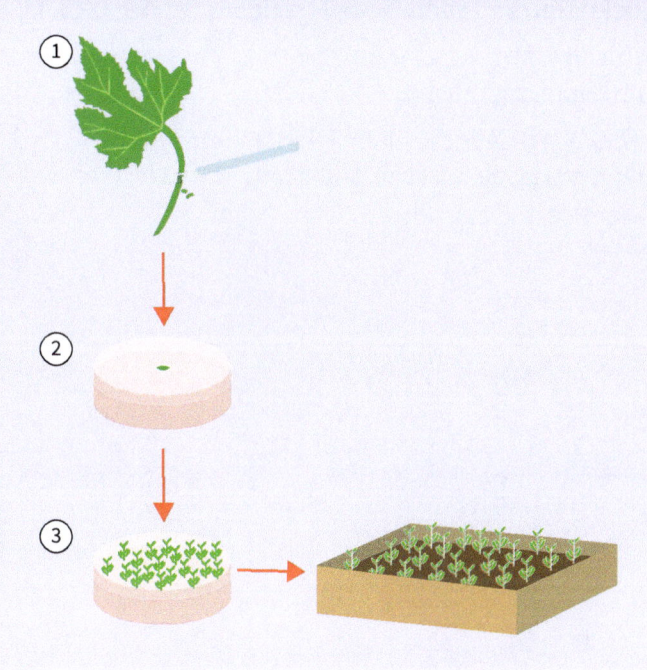

Disadvantages include:
- A monoculture is produced where all clones are susceptible to the same disease.
- Production is expensive.
- Production requires skilled technicians.
- Plants may become infected during production.

Natural clones in animals

Natural clones occur in animals. Examples include:
- Some flatworms (e.g., *Planaria*) can divide by **binary fission** into two genetically identical daughters.
- *Hydra* are able to produce clones by **budding**.
- Some starfish can grow a new body from a detached arm (**fragmentation**).
- **Parthenogenesis** – under some circumstances, unfertilised (diploid) eggs of some amphibians, fish, and insects can develop to form embryos.

Humans, and other mammals, can produce clones when an embryo splits into two to form genetically identical twins.

The process of budding in *Hydra*

Artificial animal clones

Animal clones can be produced artificially through **artificial embryo twinning**, or by **enucleation** and **somatic cell nuclear transfer (SCNT)**.

Artificial embryo twinning
- An ovum is fertilised.
- After a few days the embryo is split into two embryos, which will be genetically identical to each other.

Somatic cell nuclear transfer
- An unfertilised ovum has its nucleus removed (enucleated) and is fused with a somatic (body) cell using an electric shock.
- After a few days' incubation, the resulting embryo is placed in the uterus of a surrogate mother.

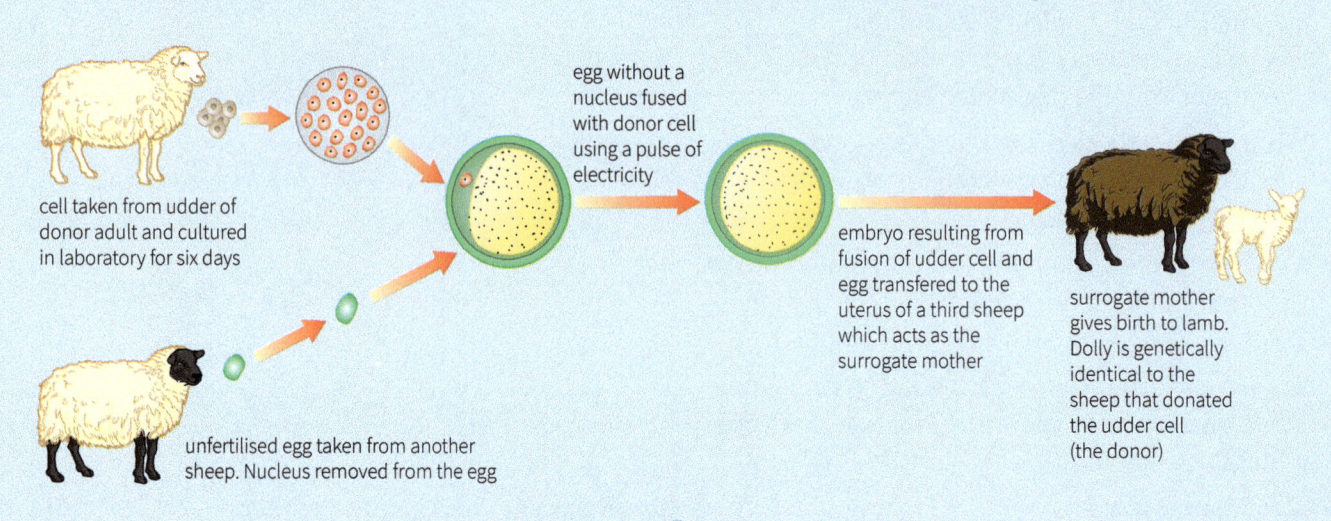

cell taken from udder of donor adult and cultured in laboratory for six days

egg without a nucleus fused with donor cell using a pulse of electricity

embryo resulting from fusion of udder cell and egg transfered to the uterus of a third sheep which acts as the surrogate mother

surrogate mother gives birth to lamb. Dolly is genetically identical to the sheep that donated the udder cell (the donor)

unfertilised egg taken from another sheep. Nucleus removed from the egg

Evaluating animal cloning

Animal cloning could be used in agriculture to produce high quality animals (e.g., cattle) with the certainty of having the desired characteristics.

The process is used in medicine to produce genetically modified animals capable of synthesising useful pharmaceutical products, and genetically identical animals for research purposes (e.g., mice and primates). Goats have been genetically modified to produce milk that contains human anticoagulants (chemicals that reduce blood clotting).

While there are social and economic benefits to creating animal clones using SCNT, there are ethical arguments against artificial cloning in animals.

Arguments for animal cloning:
- SCNT enables genetically modified embryos to be replicated.
- SCNT enables specific animals to be cloned (e.g., pets, successful racehorses).
- SCNT has the potential to produce rare and endangered animals, and even clone extinct animal species.

Arguments against animal cloning:
- The process is very inefficient, with many embryos needed to produce one live birth.
- Many cloned embryos fail to develop, miscarry, or are deformed when born.
- Many cloned animals have a shortened life span.
- Attempts to clone extinct species have been unsuccessful so far.

Biotechnology

Biotechnology is the industrial use of living organisms (or parts of living organisms) to produce food, drugs, or other products.

Microorganisms are widely used in biotechnological processes because they:

- can grow rapidly (generation time of 30 minutes in some cases) at low temperatures
- often produce extracellular chemicals that can be harvested from the growth medium
- can be genetically modified to synthesise useful products (with fewer issues, such as animal welfare)
- can be grown on waste or toxic materials (e.g., waste straw from animal bedding)
- can make products with less contamination than chemical processes
- can be grown anywhere where a fermenter can operate, they are not climate-dependent.

Biotechnological processes that use microorganisms include:

- brewing
- baking
- cheese manufacture
- yoghurt production
- production of antibiotics (e.g., penicillin, and human hormones, such as insulin)
- bioremediation (the use of naturally occurring or introduced microorganisms to clear up pollution).

Using microorganisms to make human food

Microorganisms can be advantageously used to make many types of food.

Advantages include:

- dairy-based foods – yoghurt and cheese (using *Lactobacillus* bacteria)
- vegetarian meat substitutes like the mycoprotein product Quorn (a fungus-based foodstuff)
- yeast- or fungus-fermented soy-based foods such as tofu.

Disadvantages include:

- personal taste (flavour, texture, appearance)
- some people do not like to eat food made by microorganisms or food grown on waste materials.

Culturing microorganisms

Microorganisms are cultured (grown) either in a liquid '**broth**' or on a solid **agar** growth medium. The growth medium contains nutrients ideally suited to microorganisms. However, when culturing microorganisms it is important that **aseptic techniques** are used to reduce contamination from unwanted, and potentially pathogenic, microorganisms.

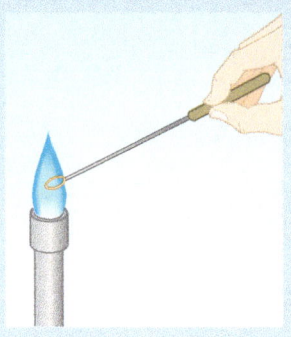

Sterilise the inoculating loop used to transfer microorganisms to the agar by heating it until it is red hot in the flame of a Bunsen and then letting it cool. Do not put the loop down or blow on it as it cools.

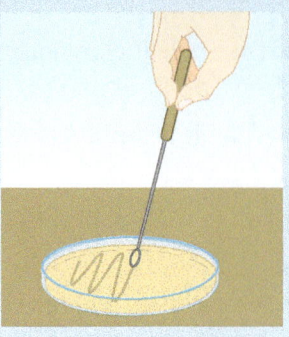

Dip the sterilised loop in a suspension of the bacteria you want to grow and use it to make zigzag streaks across the surface of the agar. Replace the lid on the dish as quickly as possible to avoid contamination.

Seal the lid of the Petri dish with adhesive tape to prevent microorganisms from the air contaminating the culture – or microorganisms from the culture escaping. Do not seal all the way around the edge so oxygen can get into the dish and harmful anaerobic bacteria do not grow.

Immobilised enzymes

Enzymes involved in biotechnology can be **immobilised** so they can be used repeatedly but remain easy to separate from substrate and products. However, the reactions tend to be slow and more expensive to set up.

Enzymes can be immobilised in several ways, using 'supports':

Immobilisation	Method of support	Advantages	Disadvantages
adsorption	bound to clay, resins, or glass beads by non-covalent forces	very high rate of reaction if active site is not obscured	leakage, as weakly bound to support
covalent bonding	covalently linked to an insoluble substance	very little leakage as bonds with support are strong	only a small amount of enzyme can be immobilised
entrapment	trapped in a gel or network of fibres	enzymes are only trapped so active sites are accessible	substrate must diffuse through support so reaction rates can be slow
membrane separation	physically separated from substrate by a partially permeable membrane	active sites are freely accessible	rate depends on diffusion of substrate and products through membrane

Examples of immobilised enzymes include:
- glucose isomerase for the conversion of glucose to fructose
- penicillin acylase for the formation of semi-synthetic penicillins (to which some penicillin-resistant organisms are not resistant)
- lactase for the hydrolysis of lactose to glucose and galactose
- aminoacylase for production of pure samples of L-amino acids
- glucoamylase for the conversion of dextrins to glucose.

24

Growing microorganisms in industry

Microorganisms are cultured on an industrial scale to make food products, medicines, etc. They are grown in large fermenters.

Conditions inside a fermenter are carefully controlled (e.g., temperature, pH, nutrient levels, oxygen, and other gases), to maximise the yield of the required product.

The microbes are grown in two ways:

- **Batch culture**: the microorganisms are placed in the fermenter in a nutrient medium. No other nutrients are added. After a set time period, the fermenter is drained and the products are harvested. Penicillin is produced in this way.
- **Continuous culture**: nutrients are added to the fermenter and products are removed at intervals. Human insulin synthesised by genetically modified bacteria, *E. coli*, is produced in this way.

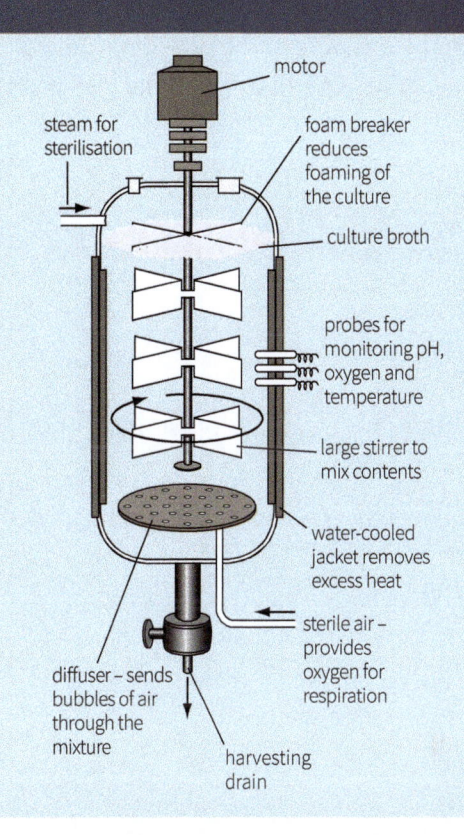

Fermenter diagram labels: motor; steam for sterilisation; foam breaker reduces foaming of the culture; culture broth; probes for monitoring pH, oxygen and temperature; large stirrer to mix contents; water-cooled jacket removes excess heat; sterile air – provides oxygen for respiration; diffuser – sends bubbles of air through the mixture; harvesting drain.

The standard growth curve

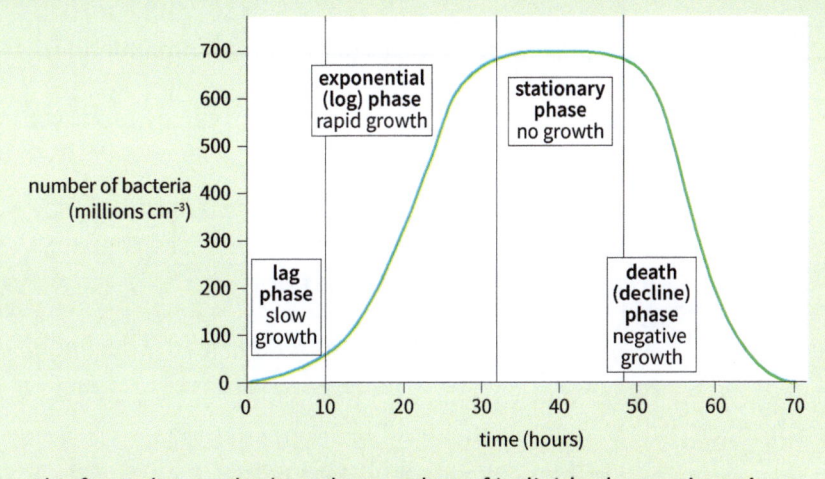

Graph: number of bacteria (millions cm⁻³) vs time (hours), showing lag phase (slow growth), exponential (log) phase (rapid growth), stationary phase (no growth), death (decline) phase (negative growth).

The formula to calculate the number of individual organisms is:

$$N = N_0 \times 2^n$$

Where:
- N = number of organisms
- N_0 = initial number
- n = number of divisions or generations.

The ideal growth conditions for microorganisms can be investigated by culturing them in broth, and counting the microorganisms using serial dilutions.

Stages:

1. Lag phase – microbes are adapting to the conditions, excess nutrients, and space.
2. Exponential (log) phase – rapid growth in population size: each generation doubles the population number.
3. Stationary phase – the death rate equals the rate at which new individuals are produced; waste materials and metabolic products start to build up.
4. Death or decline phase – microorganisms start to die as nutrients are exhausted and levels of waste products and metabolites increase. Eventually all the microorganisms will die.

Retrieval

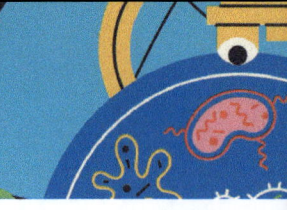

Learn the answers to the questions below, then cover the answers column with a piece of paper and write as many as you can. Check and repeat.

Questions | Answers

#	Questions	Answers
1	What is a clone?	a genetically identical group of cells or organisms that arise from a single parent through asexual reproduction
2	Give four examples of naturally occurring plant clones.	bulbs, rhizomes, runners / stolons, tubers
3	Give two examples of plant cloning techniques used in horticulture.	taking hard or soft wood cuttings, micropropagation
4	When taking a cutting, why do you cut a shoot off just below a node?	roots are able to grow from nodes
5	Why would you dip the cut end in hormone powder?	to encourage the cutting to produce roots
6	What is micropropagation?	rapid production of many young cloned plants from stock plant material using plant tissue culture methods
7	In micropropagation, what should the growing medium contain?	nutrients and plant growth factors
8	Why does the parent tissue need to be surface sterilised?	to prevent the growth of microbial contamination
9	List some of the advantages and disadvantages of cloning plants for horticulture and agriculture.	advantages: many uniform plants can be produced very quickly disadvantages: because the plants are clones they will be susceptible to the same diseases, there will be a reduction in the gene pool
10	List the four stages of a standard growth curve.	lag, exponential (log), stationary, death / decline
11	List the five ways in which animals can produce clones naturally.	binary fission, budding, fragmentation, parthenogenesis, embryo splitting
12	List the two ways in which animals can be cloned artificially.	artificial embryo twinning and somatic cell nuclear transfer (SCNT)
13	What does enucleate mean?	remove the nucleus (from a cell)
14	Why is an electric shock used in SCNT?	to encourage the cells to fuse and divide
15	Why is artificial animal cloning used in agriculture?	to produce high quality animals with the certainty of having the desired characteristics
16	What is biotechnology?	the industrial use of living organisms (or parts of living organisms) to produce food, drugs, or other products

24 Cloning and biotechnology

17	Why must the contents of a fermenter be carefully controlled?	to maximise the yield of the product
18	List the four types of enzyme immobilisation.	adsorption, covalent bonded, entrapment, membrane separation

Maths skills

Practise your maths skills using the worked example and practice questions below.

Calculating pH

Many biological molecules are affected by pH. For example, enzymes have an optimum pH at which they are most efficient. The pH scale is based on the concentration of hydrogen ions in a solution.

The pH of a solution can be calculated when the concentration of hydrogen ions in the solution is known.

The following equation is used (you can use the 'log' button on your calculator to do this):

$$pH = -\log_{10}[H^+]$$

To convert pH back into H^+ ion concentration, remember that:

$$x = \log_b y$$

can be rearranged to:

$$y = b^x$$

Therefore:

$$pH = -\log_{10}[H^+]$$

can be rearranged to:

$$[H^+] = 10^{-[pH]}$$

Note that the minus moved to join the power when rearranging this equation. If you don't do this, you will end up with a very big number!

Worked example

Question
Hydrogen ion concentration of a solution is $0.05 \, mol \, dm^3$.
What is the pH of the solution?

Answer
To convert the concentration, simply substitute the H^+ concentration into the question:

$$pH = -\log_{10}[H^+]$$

So, using a calculator:

$$pH = -\log_{10}[0.05]$$
$$pH = 1.3$$

Question
A solution has a pH of 4.6. What is the H^+ ion concentration of the solution?

Give your answer in standard form to 3 significant figures.

Answer
Here, you know the pH but not the concentration.

$$4.6 = -\log_{10}[H^+]$$

So, you need to rearrange this equation to:

$$[H^+] = 10^{-4.6}$$

So your answer is:

$$[H^+] = 2.51 \times 10^{-5} \, mol \, dm^3$$

Practice

Calculate the pH of the following three solutions:

1. Hydrogen ion concentration is $0.1 \, mol \, dm^3$.
2. H^+ concentration is $0.5 \, mol \, dm^3$.
3. Hydrogen ion concentration is $0.0025 \, mol \, dm^3$.

Calculate the H^+ ion concentrations of these pHs. Give your answers in standard form to 3 significant figures.

4. 2.2
5. 8.71
6. 5.8

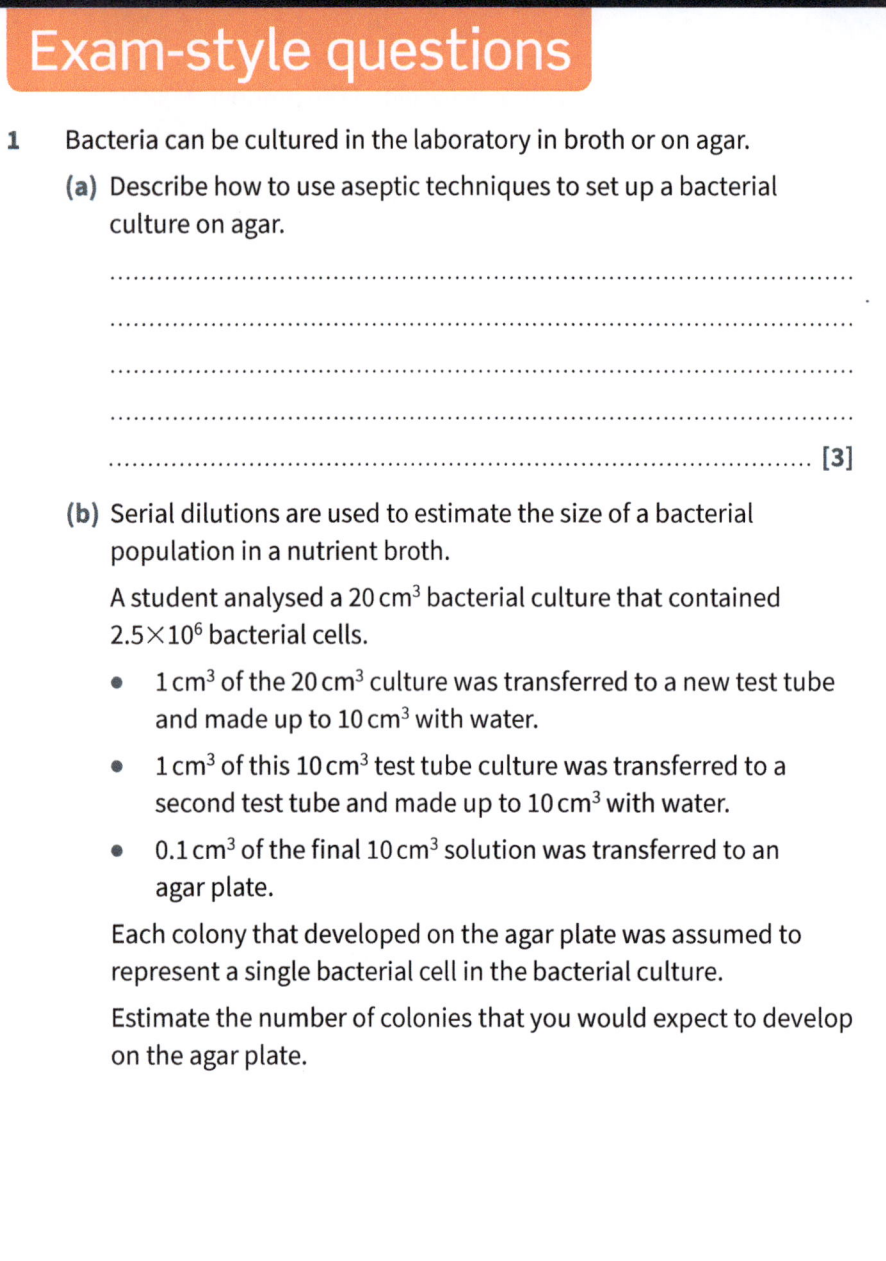

Practice

Exam-style questions

1. Bacteria can be cultured in the laboratory in broth or on agar.

   (a) Describe how to use aseptic techniques to set up a bacterial culture on agar.

   ....
   ....
   ....
   ....
   .... [3]

   (b) Serial dilutions are used to estimate the size of a bacterial population in a nutrient broth.

   A student analysed a 20 cm³ bacterial culture that contained 2.5×10^6 bacterial cells.

   - 1 cm³ of the 20 cm³ culture was transferred to a new test tube and made up to 10 cm³ with water.
   - 1 cm³ of this 10 cm³ test tube culture was transferred to a second test tube and made up to 10 cm³ with water.
   - 0.1 cm³ of the final 10 cm³ solution was transferred to an agar plate.

   Each colony that developed on the agar plate was assumed to represent a single bacterial cell in the bacterial culture.

   Estimate the number of colonies that you would expect to develop on the agar plate.

   > **Exam tip**
   >
   > When you are asked to calculate the number of bacteria present after a serial dilution, you will need to divide the original number of bacteria several times. For example, divide by 10 if you remove and dilute 1 cm³ of a 10 cm³ suspension.

   .... [3]

   (c) Microorganisms can be cultured on an industrial scale in vessels called bioreactors.

   Describe the differences between batch culture and continuous culture in bioreactors.

   ....
   ....
   ....
   ....
   ....
   ....
   ....
   .... [6]

24 Cloning and biotechnology

2   Many factors affect the growth of microorganisms.

(a) **Figure 2.1** shows the standard growth curve of a bacterial population in a closed culture.

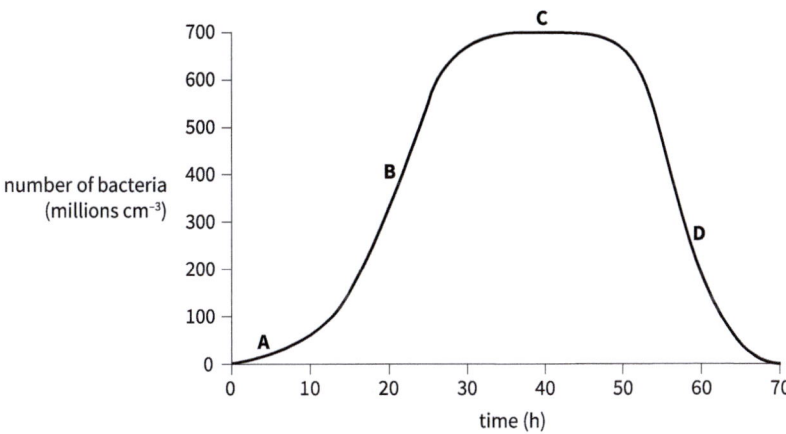

Figure 2.1

Name the growth phases **A** to **D** and explain the pattern of growth shown in each phase.

Name of phase **A**: ....

Explanation of phase **A**: ....
....

Name of phase **B**: ....

Explanation of phase **B**: ....
....

Name of phase **C**: ....

Explanation of phase **C**: ....
....

Name of phase **D**: ....

Explanation of phase **D**: ....
.... [8]

> **Exam tip**
>
> When analysing graphs or tables of data, check the wording of the question. It may be tempting here to describe the patterns of population growth (e.g., '**B** shows the fastest growth rate'). However, the question asks you to give *reasons* for the growth in the four phases.

(b) Students investigated the effect of carbohydrate substrate on the population growth of *E. coli* bacteria.

The students measured the growth of *E. coli* populations when grown with glucose, mannose, and xylose.

(i) State two control variables that the students should include in their experimental method.

....
....
....
.... [2]

(ii) The students estimated the number of *E. coli* cells in one of their broths.

They carried out the following two dilutions:
- 1 cm³ of the original 25 cm³ broth was mixed with 9 cm³ of nutrient solution to make suspension 2.
- 1 cm³ of suspension 2 was mixed with 9 cm³ of nutrient solution to make suspension 3.

The students transferred 0.1 cm³ of suspension 3 onto an agar plate. A total of 18 separate colonies grew on the plate.

Each colony that developed on the agar plate was assumed to represent a single bacterial cell in the original bacterial culture.

Calculate the number of bacterial cells in the original 25 cm³ broth.

Give your answer in standard form.

.... [4]

(iii) The students cultured *E. coli* in a mixture of glucose and xylose.

They obtained the growth curve shown in **Figure 2.2**.

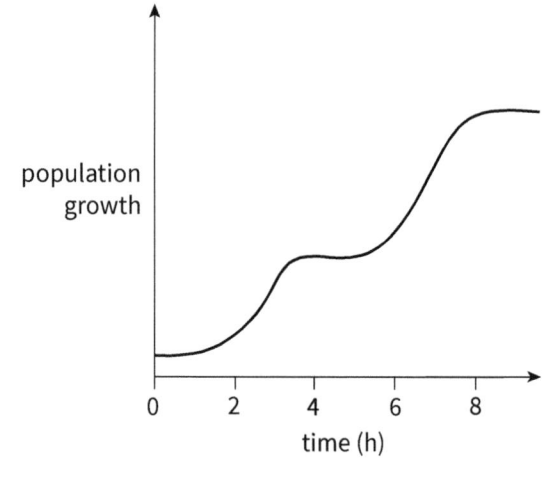

Figure 2.2

Suggest explanations for the shape of the growth curve.

....
....
....
....
....
.... [3]

3   Animals can be artificially cloned through embryo splitting or somatic cell nuclear transfer.

(a) Complete **Table 3.1** below by placing ticks (✓) in the relevant boxes to outline the features of embryo splitting and somatic cell nuclear transfer.

Feature	Embryo splitting	Somatic cell nuclear transfer
Offspring are clones of body cells		
Embryos can be implanted into a surrogate mother		
Uses *in vitro* fertilisation		
Uses enucleated eggs		

Table 3.1

[4]

(b) Evaluate the arguments for and against artificial cloning in animals.

[6]

> **Exam tip**
> This is not a typical evaluation question. The arguments for animal cloning will centre on its practical uses, both current and potential. The arguments against cloning are largely ethical.

(c) Describe how natural clones form in animals.

[2]

4 Plants can form natural clones.

(a) (i) Complete the following passage, which describes natural cloning in plants, using the most appropriate words.

Plants form clones in nature through a process called vegetative .... One example of this occurs in strawberry plants, which produce stems that grow sideways along the ground from the parent plant. These lateral stems are known as .... In potato plants, underground stems called .... swell with stored food. Buds on this storage organ develop and produce new shoots. **[3]**

> **Synoptic links**
> 2.1.6e 2.1.6j

(ii) Natural clones develop from meristem cells.

Suggest three characteristics of meristem cells that enable whole plants to develop from them.

....
....
....
....
.... **[3]**

> **Exam tip**
> 'Suggest' questions tend to tap into your knowledge of the specification in a novel context. The phrase '... enable whole plants to develop ...' should prompt you to think of stem cells.

(iii) Explain whether plant reproduction by cloning involves mitosis or meiosis.

....
....
.... **[2]**

5 Humans clone plants using cuttings or micropropagation.

(a) (i) Suggest one plant hormone that could be applied to encourage root growth in a plant cutting.

.... **[1]**

> **Synoptic link**
> 5.1.5b

(ii) Plant cuttings are watered thoroughly and covered with a plastic bag for several days.

Suggest why the cutting is covered with a plastic bag.

.... **[1]**

> **Exam tip**
> The effect of some plant hormones is dependent on concentration, but question **5(a)(i)** does not require such detail. You need only identify the relevant hormone.

(b) Place the events, **A** to **F**, in the correct order in the boxes below to describe the process of micropropagation.

A the explant is sterilised

B individual cells from the callus are transferred to a new culture medium

C the plantlet is transferred to soil

D the explant divides to form a callus

E the explant is placed in a culture medium

F a sample of meristem tissue is collected from the shoot tips

☐ ☐ ☐ ☐ ☐ ☐   **[3]**

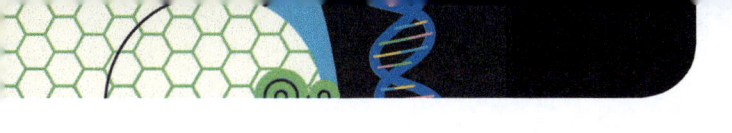

6   Immobilised enzymes are used in the production of foods.

(a) (i) Explain why pH and temperature need to be carefully controlled when using immobilised enzymes.

....

....

....

....

....

....

....

.... [3]

Synoptic link

2.1.4di

(ii) Complete **Table 6.1** to outline the methods of enzyme immobilisation.

Method of immobilisation	What is done?
	enzymes form weak attachments to alginate beads, silica, or another inert material
covalent bonding	
entrapment	

Table 6.1

[3]

(iii) State one use of immobilised enzymes in food production.

.... [1]

(b) Outline the benefits of using microorganisms in food production.

....

....

....

....

....

....

....

.... [3]

Exam tip

This question requires only an outline of the benefits. You will not need to explain the benefits or provide many details.

Knowledge

25 Ecosystems, populations, and sustainability

Ecosystems

In ecosystems, non-living (abiotic factors) and living (biotic factors) parts interact in the same space. Ecosystems are dynamic and can vary in size.

Examples:	Rock pool	Playing field	Large tree
abiotic conditions	water temperature, pH, variation in water depth, sunlight	rainfall, temperature, light intensity (shade), soil type, mineral ions, mowing, trampling	light intensity and quality, water supply, soil type, mineral ions
biotic conditions	plankton food webs, seaweeds, internal consumers (crabs), external predators (seabirds)	competition between plants; pollinators and pest populations	invertebrates and vertebrates that inhabit the tree; surrounding trees

Biomass transfers

In any ecosystem, plants synthesise organic compounds from atmospheric or aquatic carbon dioxide.

Biomass transfers are never 100% efficient; each stage transfers energy to the environment as heat via respiration.

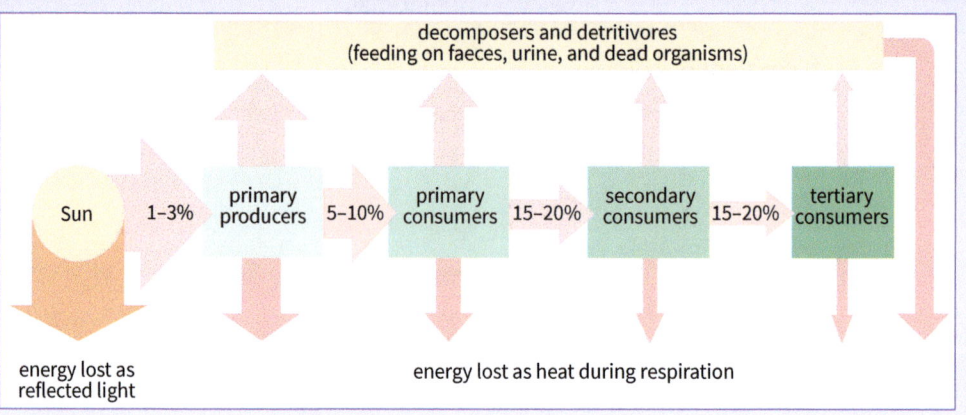

Sun → 1–3% → primary producers → 5–10% → primary consumers → 15–20% → secondary consumers → 15–20% → tertiary consumers

decomposers and detritivores (feeding on faeces, urine, and dead organisms)

energy lost as reflected light

energy lost as heat during respiration

Farming practices and energy efficiency

In farming, energy can be wasted in several ways between trophic levels, which can be expensive to maintain. To make sure farms are as efficient as possible, farmers must find ways to reduce these wasteful energy transfers, and maximise the amount of energy transferred between trophic levels.

Animals
Reduce waste through respiratory energy by:
- reducing movement, which can be controversial (e.g., battery farming)
- heating enclosures.

Plants
Reduce energy waste by:
- simplifying food webs by use of pesticides
- reducing competition by removing weeds
- using fertilisers to keep the soil nutrient rich.

Calculating efficiency
Energy efficiency can be calculated using the following equation:

$$\text{percentage efficiency} = \frac{\text{energy in higher trophic level}}{\text{energy in lower trophic level}} \times 100$$

25

Nitrogen cycle

Nitrogen (N) is present in biological molecules such as amino acids, proteins, and nucleic acids.

In its inorganic form, nitrogen is present as nitrogen gas in the atmosphere (N_2), ammonia (NH_3), ammonium ions (NH_4^+), nitrates (NO_3^-), and nitrites (NO_2^-).

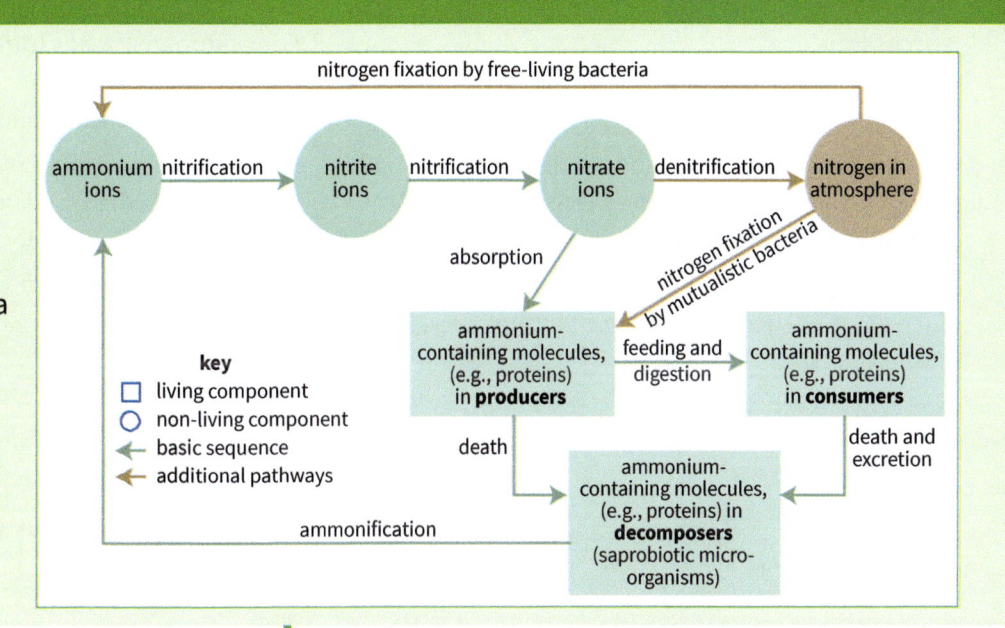

Microorganisms in nutrient cycles

Fungi – **mycorrhizae** facilitate the uptake of water and inorganic ions in plants.

Nitrogen-fixing bacteria – two types
- **ammonification** by free-living bacteria in soil (e.g., *Azotobacter*)
- mutualistic with plants (e.g., *Rhizobium* is the bacteria associated with legumes)

Both reduce N_2 to ammonia.

Nitrifying bacteria – oxidise ammonium ions to nitrites in the soil (e.g., *Nitrosomonas*) and nitrites to nitrates (e.g., *Nitrobacter*).

Denitrifying bacteria – anaerobically reduce nitrates and release nitrogen gas (e.g., *Pseudomonas denitrificans*).

Carbon cycle

The carbon cycle recycles organic compounds in an ecosystem via:
- **decomposition** of dead animals and plants by bacteria and fungi to release carbon dioxide
- **respiration** by plants and animals, which releases carbon dioxide from organic compounds
- **photosynthesis** by plants absorbs carbon dioxide from the atmosphere
- **combustion** of plants and fossil fuels releases carbon dioxide into the atmosphere.

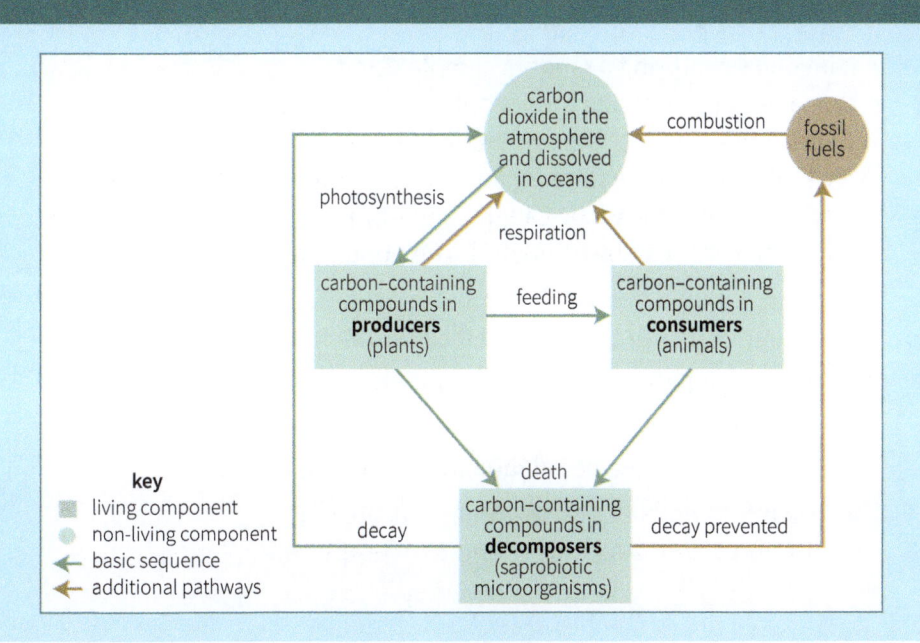

For answers and more practice questions visit www.oxfordrevise.com/scienceanswers

Even more practice and interactive revision quizzes are available on kerboodle

Succession

Communities change over time by **ecological succession**.

Primary succession occurs on barren land, which is first **colonised** by **pioneer species**. Over the years, grasses and perennials colonise, followed by small trees and shrubs (scrub), then larger trees until a **climax community** stabilises on the land.

Changes in biodiversity

Each stage of succession allows certain species to be more successful. That success can lead to changes in the environment, so another species can dominate. For example, grasses form tussocks which trap soil particles around their roots, allowing a layer of soil to develop for shrubs and small trees to grow.

Management of succession

Deflected succession – to maintain a range of habitats and biodiversity, succession has to be managed. This is the basis of **conservation**.

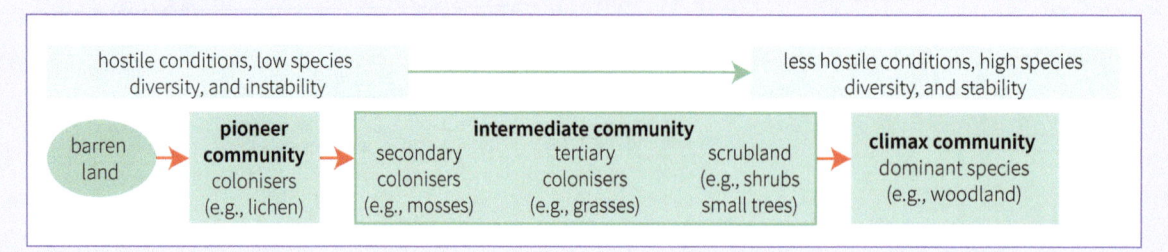

hostile conditions, low species diversity, and instability → less hostile conditions, high species diversity, and stability

barren land → pioneer community coloniers (e.g., lichen) → intermediate community [secondary colonisers (e.g., mosses) | tertiary colonisers (e.g., grasses) | scrubland (e.g., shrubs small trees)] → climax community dominant species (e.g., woodland)

Estimating population size

Slow-moving and sessile (non-motile) organisms
Quadrats can be used to sample a habitat and estimate the population size of a species or compare populations of species.

Quadrats can be placed **randomly** over a given area or along a **belt transect**. A belt transect is used between two points usually along a gradient in a habitat, such as up a rocky shore.

Motile organisms
Mark-release-recapture methods are used for organisms that move around.

It involves capturing a random sample using humane traps, marking those captured, releasing them to mix with the population, then some time later setting the traps again. A proportion of marked organisms will be caught, and from this the population size can be estimated. The population can be estimated using the Lincoln Index.

The assumptions of this method include:

- The population is closed. No migration in or out and no births or deaths.
- All members of the population mix randomly.
- The marks do not harm the organism, are not lost and do not affect the chances of recapture.

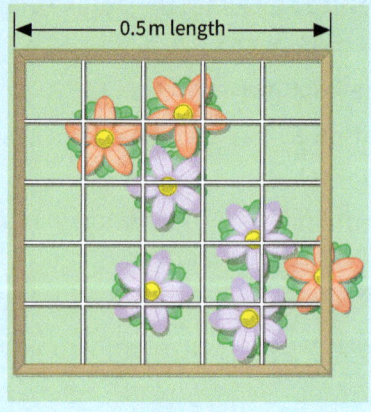

quadrats

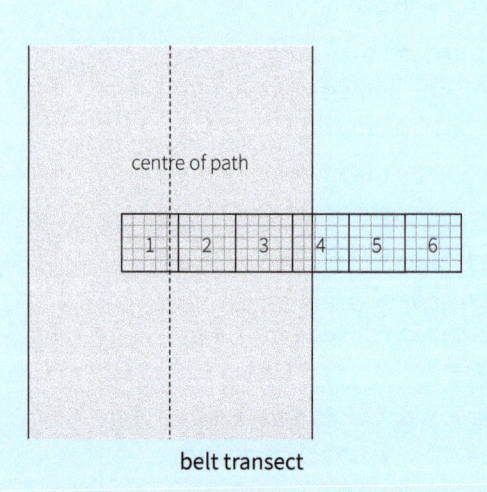

belt transect

25 Ecosystems, populations, and sustainability

Factors determining population size

Carrying capacity is the size of a population an ecosystem can support, due to **abiotic** (non-living) factors (e.g., temperature and weather) and **biotic** (living) factors.

Biotic factors can be split into 3 groups:

- **Interspecific competition** – organisms from different species compete for the same resources, such as red and grey squirrels competing for the same habitats and food.
- **Intraspecific competition** – organisms of the same species compete for the same resources, such as competing for mates, food, and territories.
- **Predation** – the number of predators will determine the number of prey and vice versa, causing predator-prey cycles. For example, lynx populations will increase if there are enough hare to catch. This reduces the hare population, which means fewer lynx will be able to catch hares to survive.

Conservation and preservation

Conservation
Conservation is maintaining biodiversity (of species, and genetic diversity within species) and maintaining ecosystems and habitats through active intervention.

Preservation
Preservation is minimising human impact on an ecosystem or habitat by maintaining them in their present state.

Reasons for conservation and preservation can be split into three groups:

Economic
- Natural spaces often attract tourism.
- Many natural resources come from sensitive ecosystems (e.g., rainforests). By conserving them they can be used sustainably.

Social
- Ecosystems are not fully understood and there is still a lot to discover.
- Natural spaces are important for well-being.
- People can rely on these ecosystems to live.

Ethical
- We have a duty to protect species in unique ecosystems and maintain biodiversity.
- We have a moral duty to preserve ecosystems for future generations to use and benefit from.

Ecological terms

Population – all the organisms of a particular species living in a specific area.

Community – all the populations of different species living and interacting in an area at the same time.

Ecosystem – a self-contained unit where the community interacts with the abiotic and biotic environments.

Habitat – the area where a specific organism or group of organisms live.

Niche – the role a species has in an ecosystem, which includes all the interactions with the abiotic and biotic conditions of the environment.

Net primary production

Net primary production (NPP) is the chemical energy store in plant biomass after respiratory losses to the environment have been taken into account:

$$NPP = GPP - R$$

Where:
- GPP = gross primary production
- R = the respiratory losses to the environment

NPP can be used for plant growth, and is available to other trophic levels in the ecosystem, such as decomposers.

Ecosystem management for sustainability

Human population growth increases the demand for natural resources. In response, humans have to manage ecosystems sustainably.

Managing timber	Managing fish stocks
As timber is removed, it can be replaced by saplings. Forest management techniques: • Coppicing cuts trees close to the ground, so that new stems or 'poles' grow. Coppicing can be done on rotation. • Pollarding cuts trees near the top, promoting the growth of a dense head of foliage. It also prevents animals eating the developing leaves. coppice stool pollard tree	• To prevent overfishing, destructive methods can be banned (e.g., bottom trawling involves the destruction of the seabed to catch fish). • Fishing quotas can be agreed between countries and fishing groups. • Only fish of a particular size can be harvested, younger fish have to be returned to maintain the breeding population. • Fish can be farmed either within the natural setting or separately on fish farms.

Effects of human activities on populations

Sensitive ecosystems have to have protective measures in place to limit the negative effects of human activities on the animal and plant populations. Here are four examples:

Ecosystem	Galapagos islands	Antarctic	Lake District	Snowdonia National Park
Description	A series of islands off the coast of Ecuador that have mostly endemic species (unique to those islands).	A large unique landmass that is unpopulated by humans. It hosts unique organisms and marine ecosystems.	A mountain range with a series of lakes in Cumbria, England, are examples of unique ecosystems.	A large region concentrated around mountains and lakes in Wales. It is made up of varied habitats and hosts unique species.
Protective measures in place	• Has international and local protection. • Limited number of visitors and tourists. • Giving endangered species legal protection.	• Permits required for all visitors. • All organisms are legally protected. • International treaties and agreements to prevent mining and drilling for oil.	• Designated as a National Park and has protection from any developments. • Uses sustainable tourism strategies to fund the management and conservation of the area.	• Designated as a National Park and has protection from any developments. • Uses sustainable tourism strategies to fund the management and conservation of the area.

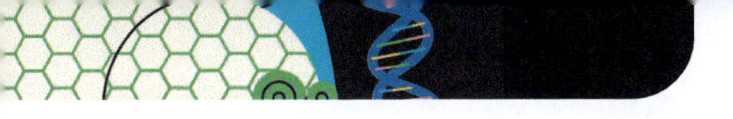

Balancing conservation and human needs

The Masai Mara in Kenya contains several ecosystems (e.g., rivers, woodlands, grasslands) and unique or rare species such as lions, elephants, giraffes, and leopards, and thousands of plant species.

Conflicts
- Many animals are under threat from poaching.
- The land is under threat from agriculture and housing.
- The land needs to be actively conserved to prevent succession of woodland communities.

Solutions
- Ecotourism is used to provide income for conservation initiatives.
- Illegal poaching still happens here, so some areas have tried making controlled hunting legal and to finance conservation.
- Safari parks provide protection and preserve habitats, with active conservation.

Terai region Nepal

This is a subtropical wetland ecosystem at the foot of the Himalayas. Inhabitants include rare animals such as the sloth bear, Bengal tiger, and Indian rhinoceros.

Conflicts
- The land is very fertile and is used for producing many crops. Agriculture is gradually encroaching on the land. Farmers have been draining it, which leads to erosion and then flooding occurs.
- Poverty and corruption means that unregulated logging, hunting, and agriculture are taking place.

Solutions
- Several national parks have been designated within the ecosystem to provide space for conservation and preservation.
- National parks and tourism provide income for local people, deterring unauthorised use of the land.

Peat bogs

Peat bogs are sensitive habitats as they take hundreds to thousands of years to form. They are formed from decaying plant matter in very wet, acidic conditions. Many varieties of moss and small plants, and a rich invertebrate population, grow in this habitat.

Peat bogs are also a significant store of carbon, and their destruction increases atmospheric carbon dioxide.

Conflict
- Peat used to be a source of fuel, until alternatives were used.
- Peat is in high demand by gardeners to improve their garden soil. This sparked a renewed industry in peat removal and distribution.

Solutions
- Alternative fuels to peat are now used.
- Peat bogs have been protected, preserved, and actively conserved.
- Education programmes have made gardeners aware of the impact of using peat in their compost and sustainable alternatives have been developed.

Retrieval

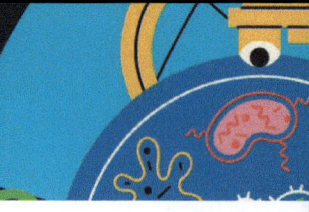

Learn the answers to the questions below, then cover the answers column with a piece of paper and write as many as you can. Check and repeat.

	Questions	Answers
1	What are abiotic factors? Give some examples.	all the non-living factors in an ecosystem (e.g., rainfall, pH, light intensity, temperature)
2	What are biotic factors? Give examples.	all the living factors in an ecosystem (e.g., the plants and animals that live there, predator and prey dynamics)
3	Why are biomass transfers through ecosystems never 100% efficient?	each stage transfers energy to the environment as heat via respiration
4	How do humans improve efficiency in ecosystems?	farming animals – reduce respiratory losses by reducing movement and heating enclosures farming plants – remove weeds, use pesticides
5	What are the inorganic forms of nitrogen in the environment?	in the atmosphere (N_2), ammonium ions (NH_4^+), nitrates (NO_3^-), nitrites (NO_2^-)
6	Which processes recycle nitrogen in the environment?	feeding, digestion, excretion, death, decomposition, nitrogen fixation (by bacteria, plants, and lightning) and by microbial activity through nitrification, denitrification, and ammonification
7	What are the two types of nitrogen fixing bacteria?	free-living in soil mutualistic with plants
8	What do nitrifying bacteria do?	they oxidise ammonium ions to nitrites, and nitrites to nitrates
9	What are the main processes in the carbon cycle?	respiration, photosynthesis, decomposition
10	In which two ways can quadrats be used?	random sampling of an area (abundance) or as a belt transect (distribution)
11	What is the mark-release-recapture technique used for?	estimating populations of motile organisms
12	Where is carbon stored in the ecosystem?	in animal and plant tissue, the atmosphere as carbon dioxide, in fossil fuel reserves, dissolved in water in oceans, as calcium carbonate in limestone
13	What is primary succession?	when species start to colonise a bare piece of land
14	What is a climax community?	the stable community at the end of a period of succession
15	What is deflected succession?	when succession is managed by conservation
16	In general terms, how do pioneer communities and climax communities compare?	pioneer communities are in hostile conditions, have low species diversity, and low stability climax communities are in hospitable conditions, have high species diversity, and high stability

17 What is meant by the term community in ecology?

all the populations of different species living and interacting in a place at the same time

18 Define the term population.

a group of organisms of the same species occupying a particular space at a particular time that can potentially interbreed

Practical skills

Practise your practical skills using the worked example and practice questions below.

Planning an investigation – variables

Planning a scientific method to test a hypothesis is an important skill.

Your investigation will have an **independent variable**, which is the variable you are going to alter, and a **dependent variable**, which will show the consequential change.

However, you must also be able to identify the **control variables**. These are the factors that must be kept constant so they do not affect the dependent variable. You must identify and then plan to keep the control variables constant.

Examples of control variables include:
- pH – use a buffer to maintain a constant pH
- Enzyme concentration – use the same stock solution throughout the investigation
- Substrate concentration – use the same stock solution throughout the investigation.

Worked example

Question
How might you plan an investigation to determine the effect of temperature on the activity of amylase?

Answer
The first thing to do is identify what you're measuring and what you're testing, then identify what variables you need to control so they don't affect your results:

Independent variable: temperature (20, 30, 40, 50, 60 and 70 °C).

Dependent variable: activity of amylase, measured as time taken for iodine to stop turning blue/black.

Control variables: concentrations and volumes of enzyme, substrate, and buffer used.

Then, identify how you will control those variables:

Use a thermostatically controlled water bath and a thermometer to check the temperature to ensure temperatures are accurate and constant

Allow substrate solution to equilibrate in water bath before starting the investigation

Practice

In the investigations below, identify possible control variables, and how they might be kept constant.
IV = independent variable; DV = dependent variable.

1 To determine the effect of pH on the activity of pectinase.

IV: pH

DV: activity of pectinase by measuring the volume (cm^3) of apple juice (sap released from lysed cells)

2 To determine the effect of bile salts on the activity of lipase on milk.

IV: presence and absence of bile salts

DV: activity of lipase as measured by the time taken for a colour change from pink (pH 10) to colourless (pH 8.4) in the indicator phenolphthalein as triglycerides are broken down into fatty acids and glycerol

Practice

Exam-style questions

1 Nitrogen and carbon are recycled within ecosystems. A diagram of the nitrogen cycle is shown in **Figure 1.1**.

Synoptic links

2.1.2p   5.1.2bi
5.2.1e   5.2.2c–e

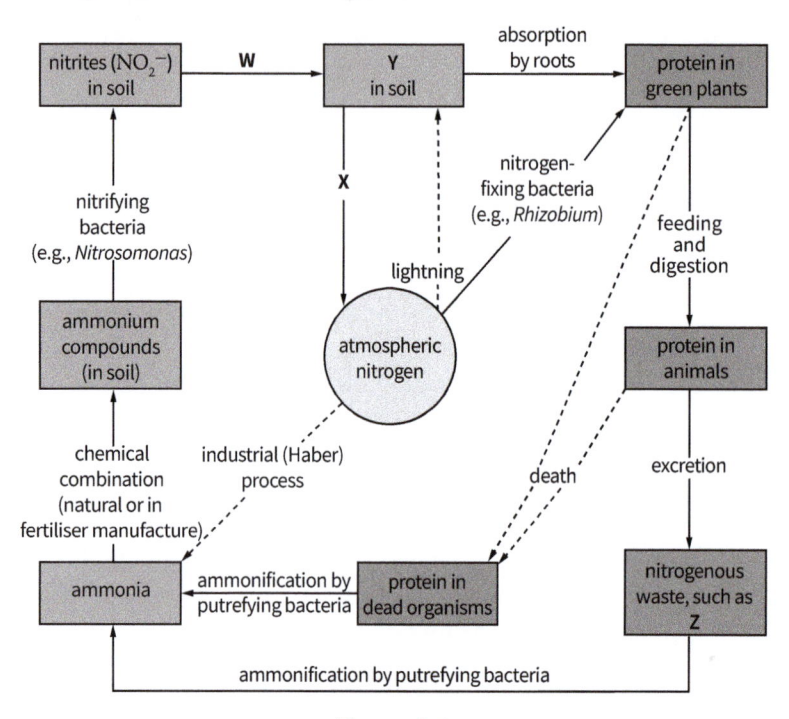

Figure 1.1

(a) (i) State the names of the bacteria represented by **W** and **X** in **Figure 1.1**.

W ....

X .... [2]

(ii) State the formula of the substance labelled **Y**.

.... [1]

(iii) State the substance in mammals represented by **Z**.

.... [1]

(iv) Describe how **Z** is formed in mammals.

....
....
....
....
....
.... [3]

(b) Describe the role of plants in the carbon cycle, including relevant biochemical details.

....
....
....
....
....
....
....
....
....
.... [6]

> **Exam tip**
>
> For this level of response question, you should include relevant details of the reactions in respiration and photosynthesis that involve carbon. Therefore, the light-dependent reaction would not be relevant here.

2 Ecosystems can be protected through either preservation or conservation.

(a) Two examples of ecosystems being protected are outlined in **M** and **N** below.

M – in a peat bog, natural sphagnum mosses were reintroduced. A ditch running alongside the bog was reduced in size.

N – members of the public were banned from entering a rainforest habitat.

Explain whether **M** and **N** are examples of conservation or preservation.

....
....
....
....
....
.... [2]

(b) Describe the conservation methods used to protect a named ecosystem, other than peat bogs and rainforests.

....
....
....
....
....
....
....
....
....
.... [6]

> **Exam tip**
>
> Seven specific examples of ecosystem management are mentioned in the specification. You do not need to know all these case studies in detail. However, learning about a couple of them in greater detail will help you answer questions such as **2(b)**.

(c) Ecological sustainability is the exploitation of natural resources without damaging biodiversity or the ability to meet future requirements.

Use the most appropriate words or phrases to complete the passage below, which outlines sustainable practices in timber production and the fishing industry.

Small-scale production of timber often uses ...., which involves trees being cut close to the ground. On a larger scale, only the .... trees are cut each year.

Sustainability in the fishing industry can be improved by introducing ...., which limit the number of fish that can be caught. The consumption of fish that are lower down in the .... is also promoted. **[4]**

3 Competition is one of the factors that affect the size of a population.

(a) Name one density-independent factor and one biotic density-dependent factor, other than competition, that can affect the size of a population.

Density-independent factor: ....

Biotic density-dependent factor: .... **[2]**

(b) Allelopathy is the release of toxic chemicals by plants to improve their ability to compete with other plants.

(i) One example of allelopathy is the release of chemicals that inhibit chlorophyll production.

Explain how this form of allelopathy would affect plants.

....
....
....
.... **[2]**

(ii) One mechanism of allelopathy is for plants to store toxic chemicals in their leaves.

Suggest how the storage of toxic chemicals in leaves can lead to allelopathy against other plants.

....
....
....
.... **[1]**

(iii) Suggest why the allelopathic properties of an area's natural species need to be assessed when choosing land to use for agriculture.

....
....
....
.... **[1]**

> **Synoptic links**
>
> 5.1.5b   5.2.1ci   5.2.1d

> **Exam tip**
>
> Note the inclusion of 'biotic' in the second part of this question. The density of a population can affect water availability and light intensity, but they are abiotic factors.

25 Ecosystems, populations, and sustainability

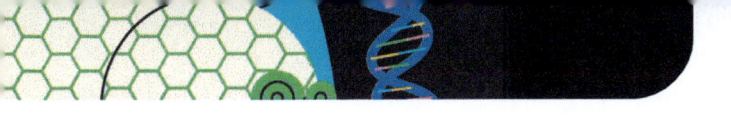

4 Net primary production (NPP) is the amount of energy that enters an ecosystem each year through the production of stored biomass in producers.

(a) Over three years, a farmer grew 180 kg of a crop in a 600 m² field.

Calculate the net primary production of this crop in g m⁻² yr⁻¹. [3]

.... g m⁻² yr⁻¹ [3]

(b) The efficiency of energy transfer between trophic levels can be calculated.

The net primary production in a grassland ecosystem was measured as 42 g m⁻² yr⁻¹.

In one year, a buffalo consumed the equivalent of all the grass in a 88 000 m² area of the grassland.

A total of 570 kg of grass was converted into biomass in the buffalo.

Calculate the percentage efficiency of the energy transfer between the grass and the buffalo.

Exam tip

Check that you are using the correct units for efficiency calculations. Remember to divide by 1000 to convert grams to kilograms.

.... % [3]

(c) Humans can modify their farming practices to maximise primary production in crop plants and increase the efficiency of energy transfer to primary consumers.

(i) Explain the advantage to farmers of growing crop plants in greenhouses at an optimal temperature.

....
....
....
.... [2]

(ii) Explain the advantage to farmers of restricting the movement of farm animals.

....
....
....
.... [1]

5 A group of students studied the organisms living in a grass field.

(a) The students wanted to estimate the population size of a plant species in the field.

Describe a method the students could have used to accurately estimate the population size.

....
....
....
....
....
....
....
....
....
.... [5]

> **Synoptic links**
> 4.2.1b

> **Exam tip**
> In exam questions about sampling populations, you should recall a few key principles: maximise sample sizes, avoid bias, and remember that sampling can only produce an *estimate* of a population size.

(b) Outline how the students could have estimated the plant biomass in the field.

....
....
....
....
....
.... [3]

(c) The students estimated the population size of a particular earthworm species in the field by using the mark–release–recapture method and the formula:

$$\text{population size} = \frac{\text{individuals in sample 1} \times \text{individuals in sample 2}}{\text{number of recaptured individuals}}$$

The students captured and marked 26 earthworms.

Five days later they captured 32 earthworms. Two of these earthworms were marked.

Estimate the population size of the earthworm species in the field.

.... [2]

25 Ecosystems, populations, and sustainability

6   The composition of an ecosystem changes over time through a process called succession.

(a) (i) Place the events, **A** to **F**, in the correct order in the boxes below to outline the process of succession.

A rock erodes to produce a basic soil
B secondary colonisers enter the ecosystem
C a climax community forms
D pioneer species colonise bare rock
E new species establish themselves and outcompete the pioneers and secondary colonisers
F decomposition of pioneer organisms adds nutrients to the soil

☐ ☐ ☐ ☐ ☐ ☐

[3]

(ii) Suggest one anatomical adaptation and one physiological adaptation of a pioneer species.

Anatomical: ....

....

Physiological: ....

.... [2]

(b) A group of students studied a shoreline ecosystem.

The students observed evidence of succession as they walked inland from the sea.

Outline how the students could measure the changes in biodiversity from the edge of the sea to 100 m inland.

....
....
....
....
....
....
....
....
....
.... [4]

Synoptic links
4.2.1b 4.2.1d 4.2.2g

Exam tip
In your exams, you may be asked to name anatomical, physiological, or behavioural adaptations. Remember: physiological adaptations include biochemical and molecular adaptations.

Knowledge

26 Unifying concepts

What is synoptic assessment?

A synoptic question is one where you need to draw links between different topics in Biology and apply your knowledge of them to answer it. The focus in this type of assessment is on seeing the bigger picture based on the various topics you have learnt, to develop a deeper understanding of Biology.

There are many types of synoptic questions, such as short-answer, practical, and extended-response questions, which cover different combinations of topics across the subject. Therefore, it is important that you can identify these connections between topics and apply your knowledge and understanding.

How do we identify and approach synoptic questions?

It is important to think flexibly to stretch your thought process to include various topics, when tackling a question. Apart from extended response questions, many synoptic questions appear as sub-parts within a big question. Here are some tips:

- When you read through the question, think about what topic(s) it is referring to.
- Look for keywords within the question that may give you an idea.
- Be prepared for the question to switch or link to other topics when reading the other sub-parts within the same question.
- Draw on your knowledge from other topics and consider which bits are relevant to answer the question – be careful not to include irrelevant information. This could cost you exam time, and marks.
- Practise more exam questions; you will gain an idea of the topics typically linked together in a synoptic question.
- Develop an awareness of synoptic links by actively looking for links when you revise. If you come across some knowledge that you have gained in previous chapters, that is a synoptic link. One example is osmosis in animal and plant cells, from **Chapter 6** *Biological membranes*. Plant cells do not burst in solutions with high water potential as they have cellulose cell walls to help them withstand the water pressure, which is covered in **Chapter 2** *Cell structure*.
- 'Free-goal Venn diagrams' can help to identify similarities and differences between biological concepts. For example, a three-way Venn diagram for photosynthesis, and aeorbic and anaerobic respiration have lots of overlapping concepts. These 'overlaps' are synoptic links.

Examples of synoptic themes

- Biochemistry of biological molecules – the structures of proteins, lipids and carbohydrates link closely to their individual roles within living organisms.

Extracellular proteins can become enzymes, hormones, and neurotransmitters for cell communication and homeostasis. Intracellular proteins can be involved in cell division, protein synthesis etc. Lipids can act as storage, but also form the basis of membranes around and within cells, which relates to cell communication and recognition.

Different forms of carbohydrates have various functions, forming many different links, from photosynthesis and respiration to translocation in plants.

- Cell signalling – link to local signalling such as histamine, cell recognition, hormones, and neurotransmitters. It can also be linked to the structure of glycoproteins and glycolipids on the cell surface membrane.
- Proteins and genetics – the DNA base sequence affects protein structure, which affects their functions. Proteins have many links to various topics, such as enzyme action in photosynthesis and respiration, cell recognition and signalling.

26

Worked example of a synoptic question

1. All living beings carry out cellular respiration, producing ATP.

   (a) Explain the importance of cellular respiration in living organisms. [2]

Answer to part a:
- ✓ Skeletal muscle contractions or movement via a cytoskeleton
- ✓ Active transport

   (b) The final stage of aerobic respiration is oxidative phosphorylation, which produces most of the ATP molecules in the whole reaction.

   Outline what happens in this stage. [6]

Answer to part b (max 6):
- ✓ Hydrogen is released by reduced NAD and FAD at the cristae, and split into protons and electrons
- ✓ Which pass through electron transport chain, releasing energy from redox reactions
- ✓ The energy is used to pump protons from the matrix into the intermembrane space
- ✓ Increase proton concentration in intermembrane space
- ✓ Chemiosmosis occurs
- ✓ Protons diffuse back into matrix, down electrochemical concentration gradient
- ✓ Through ATP synthase (which makes ATP)

   (c) Apart from oxidative phosphorylation, state two other ways that a plant cell can produce ATP.
   Include the site of these reactions. [4]

Answer to part c:
- ✓ Cyclic/non-cyclic photophosphorylation
- ✓ In thylakoid membrane
- ✓ Substrate-level phosphorylation
- ✓ In cytoplasm AND matrix

   (d) Protons are moved across the cristae by different mechanisms for ATP synthesis. Protons are first moved across the membrane against its concentration gradient by process **A**. They then move back through the ATP synthase down the concentration gradient by process **B**, which drives ATP production.
   Name processes **A** and **B**. [2]

Answer to part d:
- ✓ **A:** Active transport
- ✓ **B:** Chemiosmosis / Facilitated diffusion

! Exam tip
Remind yourself of what respiration provides to help living beings function, with reference to ATP in **2.1.3 Nucleotides and nucleic acids**.

! Exam tip
For short answer questions, be clear and unambiguous in your answer.

! Exam tip
The process of oxidative phosphorylation is covered in **5.2.2 Respiration**. You will also need your knowledge on the structure of mitochondria.

! Exam tip
Make sure to give at least the same number of clear points as the number of marks in the question.

! Exam tip
You should consider what other reactions within a cell can also produce ATP molecules, with reference to **5.2.1 Photosynthesis**, glycolysis and the Krebs cycle in **5.2.2 Respiration**.

! Exam tip
This links to the different mechanisms regarding moving molecules down or against the concentration gradients, specifically in **2.1.5 Biological membranes** about diffusion and active transport. There are also links to **5.2.1 Photosynthesis** and oxidative phosphorylation in **5.2.2 Respiration**.

For answers and more practice questions visit www.oxfordrevise.com/scienceanswers

Even more practice and interactive revision quizzes are available on kerboodle

26 Knowledge 307

Practice

27 Multiple-choice questions

1. Which of the following groups of organelles, **A** to **D**, are responsible for protein synthesis and transport?

    A Nucleus, rough endoplasmic reticulum, and smooth endoplasmic reticulum

    B Nucleus, ribosomes, and mitochondria

    C Nucleolus, Golgi apparatus, and transport vesicles

    D Nucleus, rough endoplasmic reticulum, and Golgi apparatus

    Your answer ☐ [1]

2. Which of the following statements, **A** to **D**, is incorrect?

    A Both plant cells and some prokaryotic cells can do photosynthesis

    B Both animals and plants have centrioles to form spindle fibres

    C The nucleolus in animal and plant cells is responsible for making ribosomes

    D Prokaryotes do not contain membrane-bound organelles

    Your answer ☐ [1]

3. Which of the options, **A** to **D**, states the monosaccharides produced from the hydrolysis of lactose?

    A Two glucose molecules

    B Two galactose molecules

    C One glucose and one galactose molecule

    D One fructose and one galactose molecule

    Your answer ☐ [1]

4 Which of the statements, **A** to **D**, is a typical property of a fibrous protein?

- **A** Compact and spherical shape
- **B** Conjugation with prosthetic groups
- **C** A wide range of amino acids
- **D** Hydrophobic R groups on the outside

Your answer ☐ [1]

5 A DNA base sequence is shown below.

ATTACGGAA

Which three anticodons, **A** to **D**, of tRNA molecules would be needed in the translation of this base sequence?

- **A** UAA UGC CUU
- **B** AUU ACG GAA
- **C** TAA TGC CTT
- **D** ATT ACG GAA

Your answer ☐ [1]

6 Which two nucleotide bases, **A** to **D**, are pyrimidines?

- **A** Cytosine and uracil
- **B** Guanine and thymine
- **C** Guanine and uracil
- **D** Thymine and adenine

Your answer ☐ [1]

7 Which of the statements, **A** to **D**, is true of competitive inhibitors?

- **A** Their effects are always irreversible
- **B** They alter the tertiary structure of an enzyme
- **C** They do not always prevent the maximum rate of reaction from being reached
- **D** They bind to allosteric sites

Your answer ☐ [1]

8   Which concentration, **A** to **D**, would be produced by conducting two ten-fold dilutions of a 1% stock solution of the enzyme catalase?

    A   0.01%

    B   0.1%

    C   10%

    D   100%

    Your answer [ ]   [1]

9   **Figure 9.1** shows the setup of an experiment to investigate osmosis.

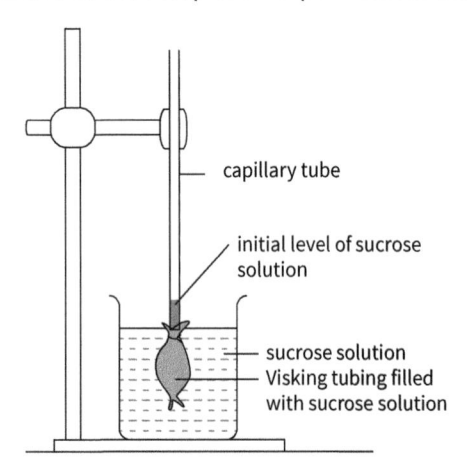

    Figure 9.1

    After 10 minutes, the level of sucrose solution inside the capillary tube has risen. Which of the following statements, **A** to **D**, is the best explanation for this result?

    A   The concentration of sucrose solution in the beaker is higher than that in the Visking tubing, therefore sucrose moves into the Visking tubing by diffusion.

    B   The water potential of the sucrose solution in the Visking tubing is higher than the surrounding solution, therefore sucrose moves into the Visking tubing by osmosis.

    C   The concentration of sucrose solution is higher in the Visking tubing than the surrounding solution, therefore water moves into the Visking tubing by osmosis.

    D   The water potential of the sucrose solution in the beaker is higher than that in the Visking tubing, therefore water moves into the Visking tubing by diffusion.

    Your answer [ ]   [1]

10 Halophiles are extremophiles that thrive in high salt concentrations. Which of the following statements, **A** to **D**, is the best suggestion for a difference between the cell surface membranes of halophiles and those of eukaryotes?

    A   Halophiles have more glycoproteins

    B   Halophiles have more potassium ion channels

    C   Halophiles have more cholesterol

    D   Halophiles have more extrinsic proteins

Your answer [ ]   **[1]**

11 Cells need to go through checkpoints to ensure they are replicated correctly. Which of the following, **A** to **D**, is not checked in the G_1 checkpoint?

    A   The DNA has not been damaged

    B   The centromeres have correctly attached to spindle fibres

    C   The correct number of mitochondria

    D   The correct cell size

Your answer [ ]   **[1]**

12 Which of the following statements, **A** to **D**, is true for meiosis?

    A   Meiosis occurs only in animal cells and not in plant cells

    B   Centromeres are split in anaphase I

    C   The sister chromatids are no longer genetically identical since prophase I

    D   The nuclear envelope only reforms at the end of telophase II

Your answer [ ]   **[1]**

13 Which of the following statements, **A** to **D**, correctly explains a feature of an efficient gaseous exchange surface?

    A   There is a decreased surface area to volume ratio.

    B   There is a poor blood supply to reach equilibrium as quickly as possible.

    C   Ventilation occurs to decrease the concentration gradient of dissolved oxygen and carbon dioxide.

    D   The layers are thin for a short diffusion distance.

Your answer [ ]   **[1]**

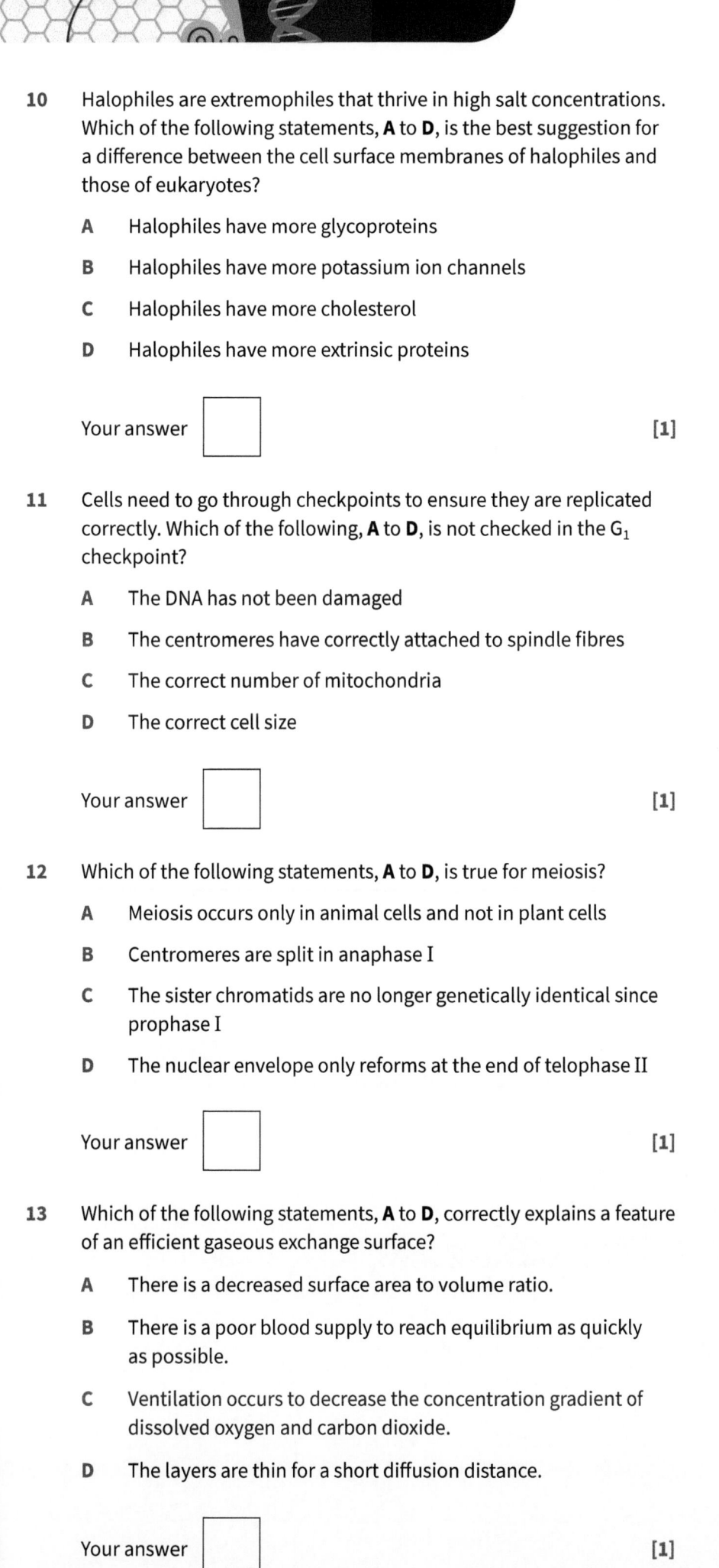

14 Which of the following, **A** to **D**, is the correct name for the protective covering of the gills on a fish?

   A   Buccal cavity

   B   Operculum

   C   Lamellae

   D   Gill plates

   Your answer ☐   [1]

15 Which of the statements, **A** to **D**, explains why the heart beat originates in the cardiac muscle?

   A   AVN receives impulses from the Purkyne fibres

   B   Cardiac muscle repolarises after being stimulated

   C   Cardiac muscle is myogenic

   D   The aorta can maintain the pressure generated by the left ventricle

   Your answer ☐   [1]

16 Which of the ratios, **A** to **D**, is the surface area to volume ratio for a horse which has a volume of 2.24 m^3 and a surface area of 18.26 m^2?

   A   8.15 : 1

   B   0.120 : 1

   C   40.9 : 1

   D   16.0 : 1

   Your answer ☐   [1]

17 Which row, **A** to **D**, of **Table 17.1** shows all of the correct substances transported in phloem tissue and xylem vessels?

Option	Phloem	Xylem
A	water	assimilates and water
B	mineral ions and water	water
C	assimilates and water	mineral ions and water
D	assimilates	mineral ions and water

Table 17.1

   Your answer ☐   [1]

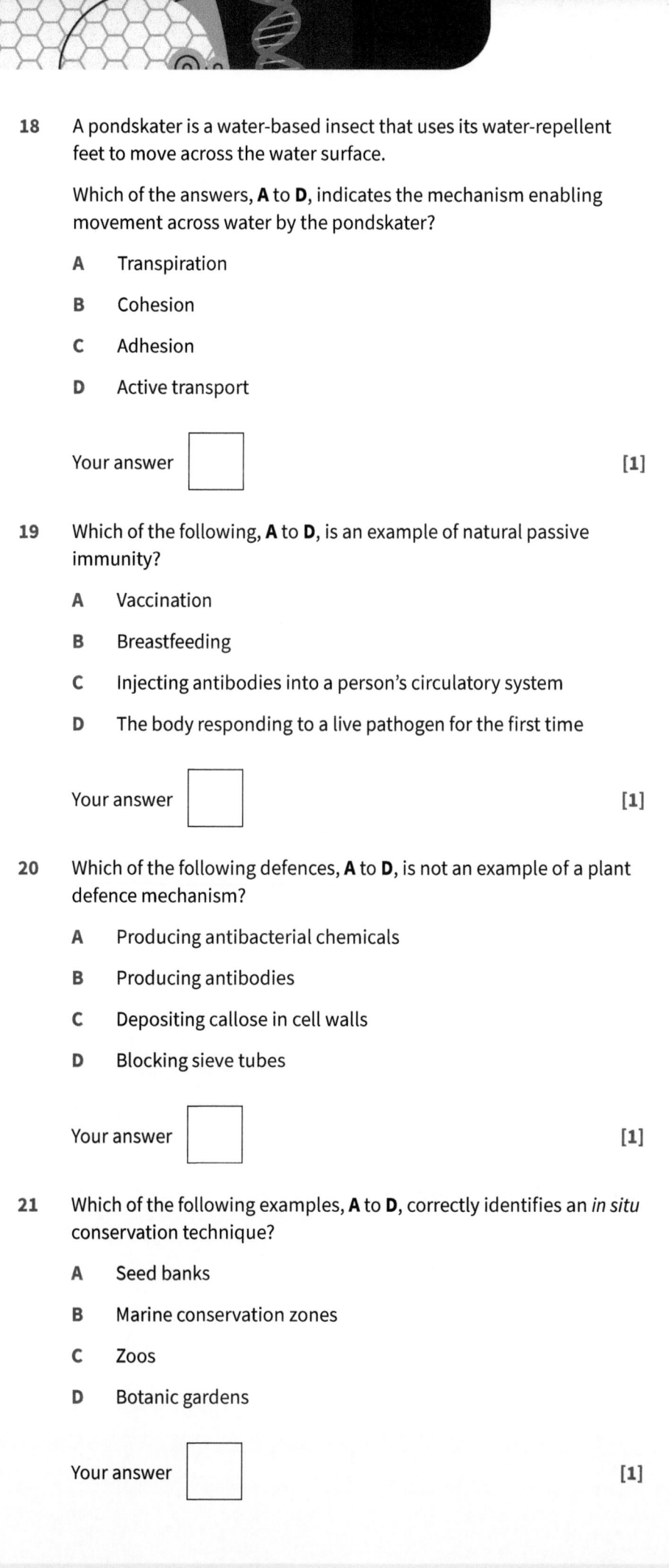

18 A pondskater is a water-based insect that uses its water-repellent feet to move across the water surface.

Which of the answers, **A** to **D**, indicates the mechanism enabling movement across water by the pondskater?

- A Transpiration
- B Cohesion
- C Adhesion
- D Active transport

Your answer ☐ [1]

19 Which of the following, **A** to **D**, is an example of natural passive immunity?

- A Vaccination
- B Breastfeeding
- C Injecting antibodies into a person's circulatory system
- D The body responding to a live pathogen for the first time

Your answer ☐ [1]

20 Which of the following defences, **A** to **D**, is not an example of a plant defence mechanism?

- A Producing antibacterial chemicals
- B Producing antibodies
- C Depositing callose in cell walls
- D Blocking sieve tubes

Your answer ☐ [1]

21 Which of the following examples, **A** to **D**, correctly identifies an *in situ* conservation technique?

- A Seed banks
- B Marine conservation zones
- C Zoos
- D Botanic gardens

Your answer ☐ [1]

22 Which of the following pieces of equipment, **A** to **D**, is the most appropriate to collect butterflies?

   A   Quadrat frame

   B   Sweep net

   C   Pitfall trap

   D   Pooter

   Your answer [ ]   [1]

23 Which of the following kingdoms, **A** to **D**, is not within the eukarya domain?

   A   Fungi

   B   Prokaryotae

   C   Plantae

   D   Animalia

   Your answer [ ]   [1]

24 Which of the following examples of variation, **A** to **D**, is intraspecific?

   A   Rate of growth of a purple cone spruce tree, *Picea purpurea*, in 2018 and in 2019

   B   Mean cranial capacities of the hominins *Homo neanderthalis* and *Homo heidelbergensis*

   C   Heights of mature *Helianthus giganteus* sunflowers in a test plantation

   D   The potency of toxins released from various species of bacteria

   Your answer [ ]   [1]

25 Which physiological response, **A** to **D**, would cause a decrease in body temperature?

   A   Vasoconstriction

   B   Reduced sweating

   C   Hairs lying flat on the skin

   D   Shivering

   Your answer [ ]   [1]

26 Which of the options, **A** to **D**, is an example of an effector?

   A   Pacinian corpuscle

   B   Osmoreceptor

   C   Hypothalamus

   D   Sweat gland

   Your answer [ ]   [1]

27 Which of the vessels, **A** to **D**, carries substances away from the liver?

   A   Hepatic portal vein

   B   Bile duct

   C   Hepatic artery

   D   Sinusoid

   Your answer [ ]   [1]

28 Which statement, **A** to **D**, is true of ultrafiltration in the kidney?

   A   Pressure is increased in the glomerulus because the afferent arteriole is narrower than the efferent arteriole

   B   Small molecules can pass through fenestrations between the epithelial cells of glomerular capillaries

   C   Podocytes are endothelial cells in the glomerulus that enable small molecules to pass into the Bowman's capsule

   D   The basement membrane is a mesh of collagen and glycoproteins that prevents large molecules from passing into the Bowman's capsule

   Your answer [ ]   [1]

29 Which row, **A** to **D**, in **Table 29.1** shows the correct order of events in an action potential?

Option	First	Second	Third	Fourth
A	voltage-gated Na⁺ channels open	depolarisation	voltage-gated K⁺ channels open	repolarisation
B	voltage-gated Na⁺ channels open	polarisation	voltage-gated K⁺ channels open	depolarisation
C	voltage-gated K⁺ channels open	depolarisation	voltage-gated Na⁺ channels open	repolarisation
D	voltage-gated K⁺ channels open	polarisation	voltage-gated Na⁺ channels open	depolarisation

Table 29.1

Your answer [ ] [1]

30 Which of the changes, **A** to **D**, would decrease the speed of nerve impulse conduction in a neurone?

A   An increase in axon diameter

B   An increase in temperature to 80 °C

C   Fewer synapses

D   Myelination

Your answer [ ] [1]

31 Which of the effects in liver cells, **A** to **D**, is caused by insulin?

A   Glycogenolysis

B   Gluconeogenesis

C   Decrease in glucose uptake

D   Glycogenesis

Your answer [ ] [1]

32 Which statement, **A** to **D**, is true of the adrenal medulla?

A   It secretes non-steroid hormones

B   It is located on the outside of an adrenal gland

C   It secretes glucocorticoids

D   It secretes steroid hormones

Your answer [ ] [1]

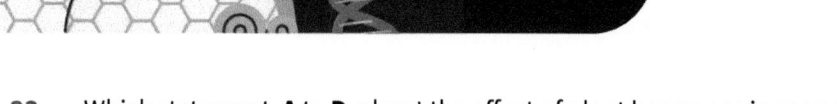

33 Which statement, **A** to **D**, about the effect of plant hormones is correct?

    A   Gibberellins reduce stem elongation

    B   Auxins prevent apical dominance

    C   Gibberellins promote seed germination

    D   Auxins promote the growth of lateral buds

Your answer ☐ [1]

34 Which function, **A** to **D**, is a role of the hypothalamus?

    A   Control of posture

    B   Voluntary responses

    C   Control of heart rate

    D   Temperature regulation

Your answer ☐ [1]

35 Thin layer chromatography is used to separate the photosynthetic pigments in a plant extract. A drop of extract was placed at the bottom of the chromatography paper, which was then placed in a beaker of solvent to separate the pigments.

Table 35.1 shows the retention (R_f) value of each pigment.

Pigment	R_f value
carotene	0.94
phaeophytin	0.64
chlorophyll *a*	0.54
chlorophyll *b*	0.38
carotenoid	0.10

Table 35.1

Figure 35.1 shows the chromatogram of an extract taken from thylakoid membranes from some leaves.

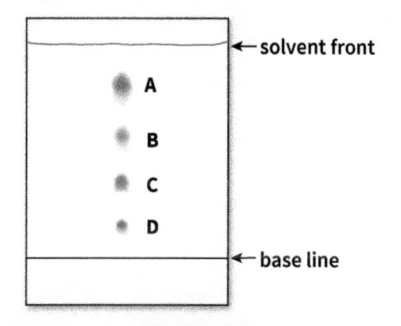

Figure 35.1

Which of the dots, **A** to **D**, is chlorophyll *b*?

Your answer ☐ [1]

36 Which of the following statements, **A** to **D**, is incorrect for photosynthesis?

- **A** Chemiosmosis only occurs in the light-dependent stage and not in the light-independent stage
- **B** Reduced NADP is used to convert triose phosphate to glycerate phosphate
- **C** The enzyme RuBisCo is competitively inhibited by oxygen
- **D** Glycerate-3-phosphate molecules can produce amino acids and fatty acids

Your answer ☐ [1]

37 ATP can be made through substrate-level phosphorylation. Which of the options, **A** to **D**, is the source of energy for this reaction?

- **A** Kinetic energy of protons diffusing across ATP synthase
- **B** Kinetic energy of protons diffusing across the mitochondrial membrane
- **C** Bond energy released during glycolysis and the Krebs cycle
- **D** Bond energy released during the light-independent stage of photosynthesis

Your answer ☐ [1]

38 Which of the following combinations, **A** to **D**, in **Table 38.1** is correct?

Option	Location of electron transport chain	Location of coenzyme A	Location with the highest concentration of protons	Location of lactate formation
A	cristae	intermembrane space	matrix	cytoplasm
B	mitochondrial inner membrane	matrix	intermembrane space	cytoplasm
C	mitochondrial outer membrane	cytoplasm	intermembrane space	matrix
D	cristae	intermembrane space	cytoplasm	matrix

Table 35.1

Your answer ☐ [1]

27 Multiple-choice questions

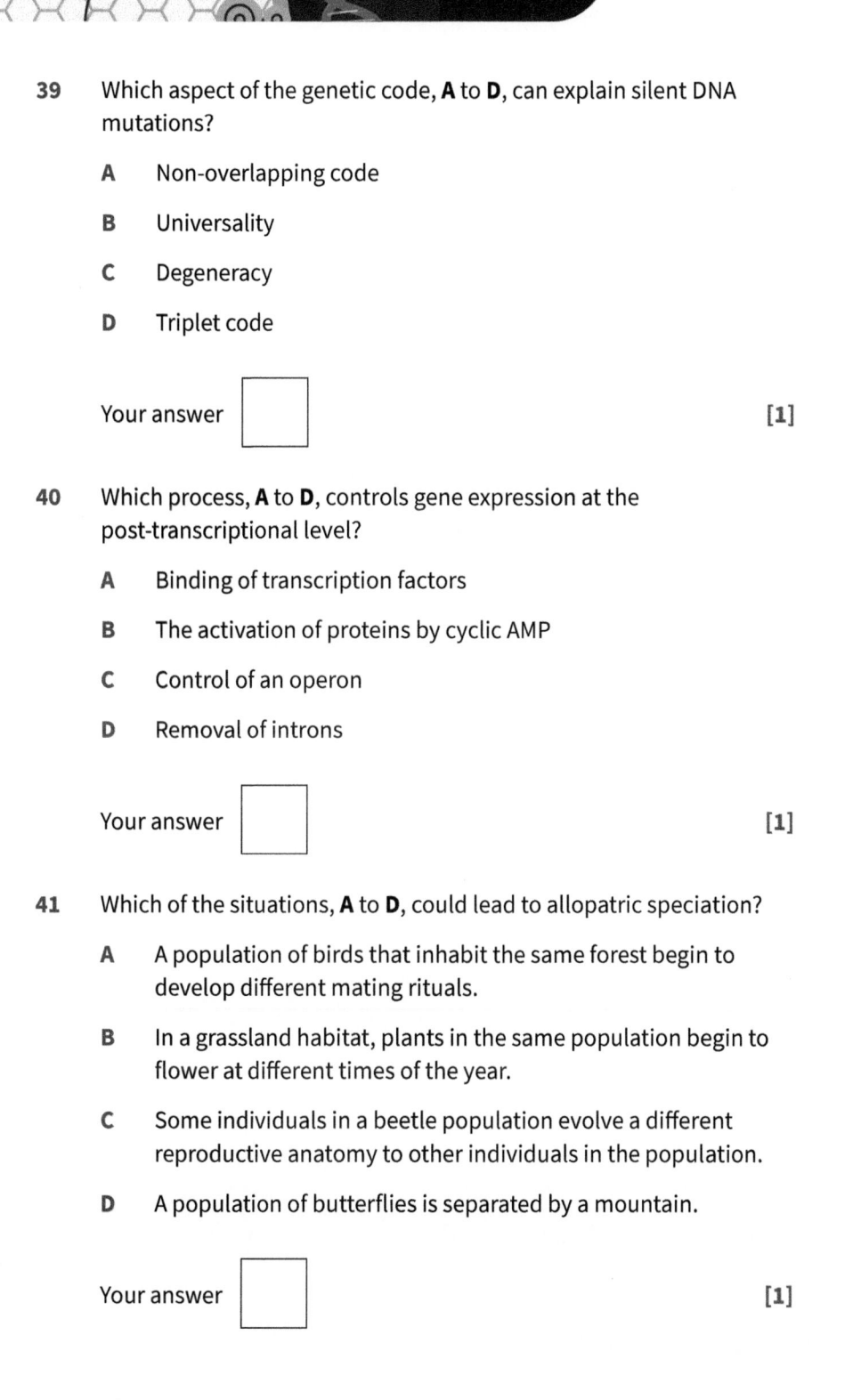

39 Which aspect of the genetic code, **A** to **D**, can explain silent DNA mutations?

    A   Non-overlapping code

    B   Universality

    C   Degeneracy

    D   Triplet code

Your answer [ ] [1]

40 Which process, **A** to **D**, controls gene expression at the post-transcriptional level?

    A   Binding of transcription factors

    B   The activation of proteins by cyclic AMP

    C   Control of an operon

    D   Removal of introns

Your answer [ ] [1]

41 Which of the situations, **A** to **D**, could lead to allopatric speciation?

    A   A population of birds that inhabit the same forest begin to develop different mating rituals.

    B   In a grassland habitat, plants in the same population begin to flower at different times of the year.

    C   Some individuals in a beetle population evolve a different reproductive anatomy to other individuals in the population.

    D   A population of butterflies is separated by a mountain.

Your answer [ ] [1]

42 Which of the following statements, **A** to **D**, is an assumption of the Hardy-Weinberg equations?

　A　The population is small

　B　There is no migration

　C　Mating is non-random

　D　Natural selection is occurring

Your answer ☐ [1]

43 Which option, **A** to **D**, shows the theoretical maximum number of DNA fragments produced after nine cycles of PCR? Assume the first cycle starts with one fragment.

　A　256

　B　$10^{2.4}$

　C　$10^{2.7}$

　D　10^{24}

Your answer ☐ [1]

44 Which enzyme, **A** to **D**, is used to form recombinant DNA by joining a gene to a plasmid?

　A　DNA ligase

　B　Restriction enzyme

　C　Reverse transcriptase

　D　DNA polymerase

Your answer ☐ [1]

45 Which method of enzyme immobilisation, **A** to **D**, uses a cellulose matrix?

　A　Surface immobilisation

　B　Entrapment

　C　Adsorption

　D　Covalent cross-linking

Your answer ☐ [1]

46 Students estimated the number of *E. coli* cells in a nutrient broth.

They carried out these two dilutions:

- $1 \, cm^3$ of the original $20 \, cm^3$ broth was mixed with $9 \, cm^3$ of nutrient solution to make suspension
- $1 \, cm^3$ of suspension 2 was mixed with $9 \, cm^3$ of nutrient solution to make suspension 3.

The students transferred $0.1 \, cm^3$ of suspension 3 onto an agar plate. A total of 22 colonies grew on the plate. Each colony that developed on the agar plate was assumed to represent a single bacterial cell in the original bacterial culture.

Which value, **A** to **D**, represents the most accurate estimate of the number of bacterial cells in the broth?

A 22 000

B 44 000

C 418 000

D 440 000

Your answer ☐ [1]

47 Which of these reactions, **A** to **D**, is carried out by *Azotobacter* in the nitrogen cycle?

A N_2 converted to NH_4^+

B NO_3^- converted to N_2

C NO_2^- converted to NO_3^-

D NH_4^+ converted to NO_2^-

Your answer ☐ [1]

48 Which option, **A** to **D**, shows an appropriate unit for measuring biomass production in an ecosystem?

A $g \, m^{-2} \, s^{-1}$

B $g \, m^2 \, s^{-1}$

C $g \, m^{-2} \, yr^{-1}$

D $g \, m^2 \, yr^{-1}$

Your answer ☐ [1]

Index

A
abiotic conditions 292, 295
abscicic acid 202
acetylcholine (ACh) 183
actin 207
   'power stroke' 207
action potentials 181, 182, 183
activation energy 50, 51
active immunity 123
active transport 63, 111
adaptations 149
adenine 38
adenylyl cyclase 205
adherence 112
adrenal glands 192
adrenaline 205
   first messenger 205
aerobic respiration 230
   summary of aerobic respiration 234
agar culture 282
algae 13
alkaloids 202
all or nothing response 182
alleles, multiple 259
allopatric speciation 255
alpha cells 194
alveoli 85
   features of the alveolus 85
Alzheimer's disease 77
amino acids 26
   specific amino acids 41
   structure of amino acids 26
ammonification 293
amylopectin 24
amylose 24
anaerobic respiration 231
anaphase 53
anatomical adaptations 149
animals 12, 13, 96, 292
   animal responses 204–7
   artificial cloning 280
   natural cloning 279
   nerve impulses in mammals 182
   non-specific defences against pathogens 124
   transport in animals 96–101
antibiotics 123
antibodies 125
   structure and function of antibodies 126
antidiuretic hormone (ADH) 171
antigen-presenting cells (APCs) 124, 125
aorta 96, 98
apical dominance 203
apoplast pathway 112
apoptosis 247
   apoptosis in hand development 247
   effect of alcohol on prenatal mitosis and apoptosis 247
arteries 96, 97, 168
arterioles 97
artificial immunity 123
artificial selection 256
aseptic techniques 282
asexual reproduction 73
ATP (adenosine triphosphate) 38
   structure of ATP 38
atria 98
atrio-ventricular node (AVN) 100
autoimmune diseases 127
autosomal linkage 258
auxins 202
   experimental evidence for the roles of plant hormones 203

B
B lymphocytes 125
B memory cells 125, 127
bacteria 13, 293
   bacterial resistance 123
   genetically modified bacteria 193
   process of genetically modifying a bacterium 266
batch culture 283
behavioural adaptations 149
behavioural responses 158, 159
belt transects 294
Benedict's reagent 25
beta cells 194
binary fission 279
binomials 146
biodiversity 136
   biodiversity and variation 136
   calculating biodiversity 137
   calculating genetic diversity 137
   changes in biodiversity 294
   ecological, economic and aesthetic reasons for maintaining biodiversity 136
   factors affecting biodiversity 139
   in situ and ex situ methods of maintaining biodiversity 139
   legislation to protect biodiversity 139
   sampling 138
   species evenness and species richness 137
bioinformatics 267
biological species 147
biomass transfers 292
biotechnology 281
   culturing microorganisms 282
   growing microorganisms in industry 283
   immobilised enzymes 282
   using microorganisms to make human food 281
biotic conditions 292, 295
Biuret test 25
blood 96, 99, 192
   blood clotting 124
   blood vessels 97
blood glucose levels 194
   decreased blood glucose 194
   increased blood glucose 194
   role of the liver 195
Bohr effect 101
Bowman's capsule 169
brain, human 204
   structure and function 204
breathing rate 86
bronchi 85
bronchioles 85
broth culture 282
buccal cavity 87
budding 279

C
C-shaped cartilage 85
calcium ions 183
   calcium ion channels 195
callose 122
Calvin cycle 216
capillaries 97
carbon-based compounds 23
carbon cycle 293
carbon dioxide 217
   carbon dioxide transport 99
cardiac cycle 98
cardiac (myogenic) muscle 100, 206
carrier proteins 62, 63
carriers 258
carrying capacity 295
cartilage 85
catalysts 50
cell cycle 72
   erythrocytes and neutrophils 74
   meiosis 74, 75, 148
   mitosis 73, 75
   regulation of the cell cycle 72
   variations in cell mass and DNA mass during the cell cycle 72

cell signalling 125, 205
    comparing neuronal and hormonal cell signalling 156
cell structure 12–13
    additional organelles 13
    cell wall 13
    cytoskeleton 12
    organelles common to plant and animal cells 12, 13
    organelles in animal cells 12, 13
    organelles in plant cells 12, 13
    protein production in plant and animal cells 13
cell surface membranes 84
cells 72–4, 85, 99, 111, 112, 124, 168, 192, 194, 195
    genetically unique cells 75
    organisation of cells 75
    specialised cells 76
    stem cells 77, 193
    xylem and phloem 77
cellular control 244
    control of gene expression at post-transcriptional level 247
    control of gene expression at post-translational level 245
    control of gene expression at transcriptional level 246
    gene mutation 244
    homeobox genes 245
    mitosis and apoptosis 247
    regulation of gene expression 246
    transcription factors 246
cellular respiration 235
cellulose 23, 24
centrioles 13
cerebrum 204
chain of reactions 53
channel proteins 62
checkpoints 72
chemical defences 124
chemical systems 156
chemiosmotic theory 233, 234
chemotherapy 53
chi-squared test 256
chloride shift 99
chlorophylls 219
    chlorophyll a 219
    chlorophyll b 219
chloroplasts 13
    structure of a chloroplast 216
cholesterol 25
cholinergic synapses 183
cilia 13
ciliated epithelial cells 76, 85

circulatory systems 96
    human circulatory system 96–101
classification 146
    features and evidence used in classification 147
climax communities 294
clonal selection and expansion 126
clones 278
    artificial animal clones 280
    evaluating animal cloning 280
    natural clones in animals 279
    plant clones 278–9
closed circulatory systems 96
co-enzymes 51, 235
codominance 259
cofactors 51
cohesion 22
cohesion-tension theory 112
collagen 26
collecting ducts 171
colonisation 294
combustion 293
common ancestor 146
communicable diseases 122–7
communication systems in organisms 156–59
communities 295
    succession 294
companion cells 111
competition 295
competitive inhibitors 53
compounds 23
    useful organic compounds 217
computational biology 267
concentration 52, 63
    concentration gradients 84
condensation reactions 23, 26, 39
conservation 139, 295
continuous culture 283
continuous variation 148, 254
Convention on International Trade in Endangered Species (CITES) 139
convergent evolution 148
cortex (adrenal glands) 192
countercurrent system 87
crossing over 75
cyclic AMP (cAMP) 205, 245
    second messenger 205
cytokines 124, 125
cytokinesis 72
cytoskeleton 12
    aiding transport 12
    enabling cell movement 12
    mechanical strength 12

D
Darwin, Charles 147
deamination 168
decomposition 293
defence mechanisms 202
deflected succession 294
denaturing 52
denitrifying bacteria 293
density 22
depolarisation 182, 183
detection 192
detoxification 168
developmental biology 77
diabetes mellitus 193
    potential treatments 193
dialysis 170
differential membrane permeability 182
diffusion 62, 84, 86, 183
dihybrid crosses 257
dipeptide molecules 26
directional selection 255
disaccharides 24
discontinuous variation 148, 254
disease transmission 122
    antibodies 125, 126
    defences 124–5
    direct and indirect transmission 122
    immunity 123, 125, 126, 127
    possible sources of medicines 123
    using antibiotics to manage bacterial infection 123
    vaccinations 127
    vectors 122
dissociation 101
disulfide bonds 27
DNA (deoxyribonucleic acid) 38
    anti-parallel strands 38
    DNA and RNA 39
    DNA evidence in species determination 147
    DNA helicase 39, 40
    DNA polymerase 39
    DNA profiling 269
    DNA replication 39
    DNA sequencing 268
    genetic code 41
    protein synthesis 40
    purification 40
    recombinant DNA technology 266
    semi-conservative DNA replication 39
    transcription 40, 246–7
    translation 41, 245

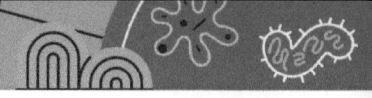

variation in cell and DNA mass
during the cell cycle 72
domains 146
three domains 146
double closed circulatory systems 96

E

ecosystems 292, 295
biomass transfers 292
carbon cycle 293
conservation and preservation 295
ecological succession 294
ecological terms 295
economic, social and ethical reasons for conservation and preservation 295
microorganisms in nutrient cycles 293
net primary production (NPP) 295
nitrogen cycle 293
populations 294–5
ectotherms 158
effectors 157
elastic tissue 85
elastin 26
electrical systems 156
electrocardiograms (ECGs) 100
electrochemical gradient 182
electron transport chain (ETC) 230, 233
electron acceptors 233
electroporation 266
embryo twinning 280
emulsion test 25
endocrine system 192
adrenal glands 192
endocrine glands 192
endocrine response 205
pancreas 193
endocytosis 62
endotherms 158
energy 25
energy efficiency 292
calculating efficiency 292
enucleation 280
environment 148
environmental variation 254
enzymes 50, 194, 266
activation energy 50, 51
active site 50
co-enzymes, cofactors and prosthetic groups 51
enzyme concentration 52
enzyme-substrate complexes 50, 52
enzymes in metabolic pathways 53
immobilised enzymes 282
inactive precursors 51

induced-fit model 50
inhibitors 53
investigating the effects of variables on enzyme activity 51
lock-and-key model 50
pH 52
specific enzymes 50
substrate concentration 52
temperature 52
epistasis 258
epithelial cells 76, 85
erythrocytes 74, 76
ester bonds 25
esterification 25
ethene 202, 204
evaporation 112
evolution 147
adaptations 149
convergent evolution 148
evolutionary relationships 267
factors affecting the evolution of a species 255
natural selection 147
speciation 149, 255
variation 148
ex situ and in situ conservation 139
exchange surfaces 84–7
excitatory inputs 181
excretion 168
kidneys 169–70
liver 168
exocytosis 62
exons 247
expulsion reflexes 124
extracellular reactions 50

F

facilitated diffusion 62
farming practices and energy efficiency 292
fatty acids 24
feedback systems 157
fibrous proteins 26
fight or flight response 205
fish 87, 96
flagella 13
fluid-mosaic model 60
fossil record 147
founder effect 255
fragmentation 279
fruit ripening 204
functional proteins 26
fungi 13, 293

G

gametes 148

gas exchange systems 84
adaptations of gills 87
concentration gradients 84
gas exchange in insects 86
increased surface areas 84
structure of the human gas exchange system 85–6
thin layers 84
gel 181
gel electrophoresis 269
gene expression 246
control of gene expression at post-transcriptional level 247
control of gene expression at post-translational level 245
control of gene expression at transcriptional level 246
gene mutations 148, 244
harmful, neutral and beneficial effects 244
types of mutation 244
generation of impulses 182
genes 41, 245
gene sequencing 267
gene therapy 267
genetic bottlenecks 255
genetic code 41
triplets 41
universal, non-overlapping and degenerate 41
genetic crosses 257
genetic diversity 137
genetic drift 255
genetic engineering 266
DNA sequencing 268
gel electrophoresis 269
gene sequencing 267
gene therapy 267
issues surrounding genetic manipulation of organisms 266
PCR 268
process of genetically modifying a bacterium 266
genetic variation 147, 148, 254
genetic variation through sexual reproduction 254
genus 146
germline cell gene therapy 267
gibberellins 202
experimental evidence for the roles of plant hormones 203
gills 87
countercurrent system 87
gill lamellae 87
glands 157, 171, 192
globular proteins 26

glomerular filtration rate (GFR) 170
glomerulus 169
glucagon 194
glucose 24
    gluconeogenesis 194, 195
    glucose isomers 23
glycerate 3-phosphate 217
glycogen 23, 24, 168
    glycogenesis 194, 195
    glycogenolysis 194, 195
glycolysis 230, 232
glycosidic bonds 24
goblet cells 85
Golgi apparatus and vesicles 13
gradients 84, 182
growth 73
guard cells 76

H
habitats 295
haemodialysis 170
haemoglobin 26, 96
    oxygen binding affinity 101
haploid cells 75
Hardy–Weinberg principle 256
heart 98
    control of heart action 100
    effects of hormones and nervous mechanisms on heart rate 205
    electrocardiograms (ECGs) 100
    pressure and volume changes during the cardiac cycle 98
heat capacity 22
hepatic artery 168
hepatic vein 168
hepatocytes 168, 195
hexose monosaccharides 23
hierarchy 146
high-throughput DNA sequencing 268
homeobox genes 245
homeostasis 156
    cell signalling 156
    control of blood glucose levels 194
    negative and positive feedback 157
    receptors and effectors in the nervous system 157
    temperature control 158–9
homologous chromosomes 75
hormonal cell signalling 156
hormones 171
    effects of hormones and nervous mechanisms on heart rate 205
    endocrine system 192–5
    plant hormones 202–4
Hox clusters 245
human circulatory system 96

Bohr effect 101
carbon dioxide transport 99
comparing blood, tissue fluid, and lymph 96
haemoglobin and oxygen transport 99
oxygen dissociation curve 101
pressure and volume changes during the cardiac cycle 98
structure of blood vessels 97
structure of the heart 98
tissue fluid formation 97
human gas exchange system 85
    breathing rate and oxygen uptake 86
    features of the alveolus 85
    human ventilation 86
    trachea lining 85
hydrogen bonds 27
hydrolysis 23, 39, 183
hydrophilic properties 60
hydrophobic properties 25, 60
hydrophytes 112
hydrostatic pressure 97
hypothalamus 159, 171

I
immobilised enzymes 282
immunity 123
    autoimmune diseases 127
    cell-mediated immunity 126
    humoral response 127
    structure and roles of B and T lymphocytes 125
in situ and ex situ conservation 139
inactive precursors 51
independent assortment 75
inflammation 124
inheritance 254–5
    artificial selection 256
    autosomal linkage 258
    chi-squared test 256
    codominance 259
    dihybrid crosses 257
    epistasis 258
    Hardy–Weinberg principle 256
    linkage 258
    monogenic crosses 257
    multiple alleles 259
    sex linkage 258
    using a genetic diagram to show a genetic cross 257
inhibitors 53
    inhibitors as metabolic poisons 53
    medicinal use of enzyme inhibitors 53
inhibitory inputs 181

insects 86, 97
insulin 26, 194
    control of insulin secretion 195
    diabetes mellitus 193
integration 181
interleukins 125
interphase 72
    G1 72
    G2 72
    S 72
interspecific competition 295
interspecific variation 148
intracellular reactions 50
intraspecific competition 295
intraspecific variation 148
introns 247
involuntary (smooth) muscle 85, 206
iodine solution 25
ionic bonds 27
ions 181, 182, 183, 195
    inorganic ions 22
irreversible binding 53
isomers 23
IUCN (International Union of the Conservation of Nature) Red List 139

K
keratin 26
kidneys 168, 169, 192
    effects of kidney failure and its potential treatments 170
    production of urine 170
    reabsorption of water by the collecting ducts 171
    structure of a nephron 169
kingdoms 146
Krebs cycle 230, 233

L
lac operon 246
latent heat of vaporization 22
leaf fall in deciduous plants 202
legislation to protect biodiversity 139
ligases 266
light-dependent reactions 216, 218
light-independent reactions 216, 217
limiting factors 219
link reaction 230, 232
linkage 258
lipids 25
    properties and functions of lipids 25
liver 168
    liver cells 195
    role in controlling blood glucose concentration 195
loop of Henle 169

lungs 85–6, 168
lupus erythematosus 127
lymph 96
lymphocytes 125
lysosomes 13, 124

M

macrophages 124
mark-release-recapture 294
mass flow 111
medicines 123
medulla (adrenal glands) 192
meiosis 74
   crossing over 75, 148
   independent assortment 75, 148
   significance of meiosis in life cycles 75
membrane structure 60
   active transport 63
   endocytosis 62
   exocytosis 62
   facilitated diffusion 62
   factors affecting membrane structure and permeability 61
   membrane components 61
   osmosis 63
   simple diffusion 62
   types of membrane transport 60
messenger RNA (mRNA) 40
metabolic pathways 53
metabolites 22
metaphase 53
microorganisms
   culturing microorganisms 282
   growing microorganisms in industry 283
   microorganisms in nutrient cycles 293
   standard growth curve 283
   using microorganisms to make human food 281
micropropagation 279
mitochondria (mitochondrion) 12, 235
mitosis 73
   effect of alcohol on prenatal mitosis and apoptosis 247
   main stages in mitosis 73
   mitosis and apoptosis 247
   significance of mitosis in life cycles 73
   viewing mitosis 75
molecules 22–7, 183
   chemical tests for biological molecules 25
   double-stranded molecules 38
   molecular evidence in species determination 147
   single-stranded molecules 38
moles, marsupial and placental 148
monogenic crosses 257
monomers 23, 26
monosaccharides 23
motile organisms 294
motor neurones 180
MRSA (methicillin-resistant Staphylococcus aureus) 123
mucous membranes 124
mucus 85
multicellular organisms 156
multiple sclerosis 127
multipotent cells 77
muscles 85, 100, 157
   mammalian muscles 206
   neuromuscular junctions 207
   sliding filament model of muscular contraction 207
mutations see gene mutations
mycorrhizae 293
myelination 180
myogenic (cardiac) muscle 100, 206
myosin 207
   'power stroke' 207

N

natural immunity 123
natural selection 147, 255
negative feedback 157, 194
nephrons 169
   structure of a nephron 169
nervous system 157
   effects of hormones and nervous mechanisms on heart rate 205
   endocrine response 205
   nerve impulses in mammals 182
   organisation of the mammalian nervous system 205
net primary production (NPP) 295
neuromuscular junctions 207
   sliding filament model of muscular contraction 207
neuronal cell signalling 156
neuronal communication 181
   advantages of synapses 181
   cholinergic synapses 183
   myelination 180
   nerve impulses in mammals 182
   receptors 181
   structure and function of a synapse 183
   structure and function of neurones 180
neurones 180, 181, 182

neurotransmitter molecules 183
neutrophils 74, 76, 124
niches 295
nitrifying bacteria 293
nitrogen cycle 293
   nitrogen-fixing bacteria 293
non-competitive inhibitors 53
non-permanent binding 53
non-random sampling 138
nucleic acids 38–41
nucleotides 38
   DNA nucleotide 38
   RNA nucleotide 38
   structure of ATP 38
nucleus 12
nutrient cycles 293

O

oncotic pressure 97
open circulatory systems 96
operculum 87
opportunistic sampling 138
opsonins 124
optimum pH 52
optimum temperature 52
organic substances 23
organisms 156, 266, 294
organs 75
   organ systems 75
ornithine cycle 168
osmoregulation 171
   osmoreceptors 171
   reabsorption of water by the collecting ducts 171
osmosis 63, 112
   osmosis in different concentrations of solution 63
oxidative phosphorylation 234
oxygen 99, 101
   electron transport chain (ETC) 233
   oxygen dissociation 101
   oxygen loading 101
   oxygen uptake 86

P

Pacinian corpuscles 181
palisade cells 76
pancreas 193
pandemics 127
Parkinson's disease 77
parthenogenesis 279
passive immunity 123
pathogens 122
   humoral response 127
   phagocytes 124
   plant defences against

pathogens 122
plant defences against pathogens 122
primary non-specific defences in animals 124
transmission of pathogens 122
PCR (polymerase chain reaction) 268, 269
    primer binding 268
    strand separation 268
    strand synthesis 268
pentose monosaccharides 23
pepsin 26
peptides 26
peripheral temperature receptors 159
peritoneal dialysis 170
permanent binding 53
personalised medicine 123
pH 52
phagocytes 124
    phagocytosis 124
    phagosomes 124
phagocytosis 62
pheromones 202
phloem 77, 110
    loading and unloading of sucrose in the phloem 111
    structure and function of phloem 111
phosphate groups 38
phosphodiester bonds 39
phospholipids 25
    phospholipid bilayers 60
phosphorylation 234
photosynthesis 216, 293
    Calvin cycle 216
    factors affecting rate of photosynthesis 219
    flow chart of photosynthesis 216
    light-dependent reactions 216, 218
    light-independent reactions 216, 217
    photosynthetic pigments 219
    structure of a chloroplast 216
    uses of triose phosphate 217
photosystems 219
phylogenetic trees 146
    phylogenetic species definition 147
physiological adaptations 149
physiological responses 158, 159
pinocytosis 62
pioneer species 294
placenta 101
plants 12, 13, 292
    adaptations of plants living in extremes 112

commercial use of plant hormones 204
experimental evidence for the roles of plant hormones 203
leaf fall in deciduous plants 202
plant clones 278
plant defences against pathogens 122
plant hormones 202
plant responses 202
production of artificial clones of plants 279
seed germination 202
sources and sinks 111
stomatal closure 202
taking plant cuttings 278
transport in plants 110–13
vascular system 110
plasma membrane 12
plasmodesmata 111
pluripotent cells 77
poisons 53
polymers 23
polymorphism 137
polypeptides 26
polysaccharides 24
    structure and function of polysaccharides 24
populations 295
    estimating population size 294
    factors determining population size 295
positive feedback 157, 182
posterior pituitary gland 171
postsynaptic neurones 183
potassium ion channels 195
potometers 112
practical assessment 2–3
    chromatography or electrophoresis 6
    colorimeter or potometer 6
    dissection 4
    investigation into the measurement of plant or animal responses 9
    investigation using a data logger or computer modelling 8
    microbiological techniques 7
    microscopy 4
    qualitative testing 8
    rates of enzyme-controlled reactions 5
    research skills 9
    sampling techniques 5
    transport in and out of cells 7
predation 295
preservation 295

presynaptic neurones 183
primary immune response 127
primary succession 294
prophase 53
prosthetic groups 27, 51
proteins 26, 62, 63, 99
    protein production in plant and animal cells 13
    protein structures 27
proximal convoluted tubules (PCTs) 169
pulmonary artery 96
pulmonary vein 96
pumps 63
Purkyne tissue 100

Q
quadrats 294
quaternary structures 99

R
R groups 27
random fertilisation of gametes 148
random sampling 138, 148, 294
reabsorption 169, 183
    reabsorption of water by the collecting ducts 171
reagent test strips 25
receptors 157, 159, 171, 181, 194
recombinant DNA technology 266
red blood cells 99
reflex actions 206
refractory period 182
relay neurones 180
repolarisation 182
reproductive success 147
respiration 230, 293
    aerobic respiration 230, 234
    anaerobic respiration 231
    chemiosmotic theory 233, 234
    electron transport chain (ETC) 230, 233
    glycolysis 230, 232
    importance of co-enzymes in cellular respiration 235
    Krebs cycle 230, 233
    link reaction 230, 232
    mitochondria 235
    respiratory quotient 231
    respiratory substrates 231
    substrate-level phosphorylation vs. oxidative phosphorylation 234
responses 127, 158, 159, 182, 194
    animal responses 204–7
    plant responses 202–4
resting state 182
restriction enzymes 266

reversible binding 53
rheumatoid arthritis 127
ribose 38
    ribose sugars 23
ribosomes 13
ribulose bisphosphate 217
Rio Convention on Biological Diversity (CBD) 139
RNA (ribonucleic acid) 38
    RNA polymerase 40
root hair cells 76
rooting powders 204
rough endoplasmic reticulum (RER) 40
routine vaccinations 127
rubisco 217

S
sampling 138
    sampling techniques 138
saturated fats 24
saturation point 219
secondary immune response 127
secretion 192
seed germination 202
selection pressures 147, 255
selective reabsorption 169
semilunar valves 98
sensory neurones 180
sensory receptors 181
sessile and slow-moving organisms 294
sex linkage 258
    sex-linked inherited conditions 258
sexual reproduction 254
sieve tube elements 111
simple diffusion 62, 84
single closed circulatory systems 96
sino-atrial node (SAN) 100
skeletal (voluntary or striated) muscle 206
skin 124
smooth (involuntary) muscle 85, 206
smooth endoplasmic reticulum (SER) 13
sodium ions 181, 182, 183
solvents 22
somatic cell gene therapy 267
somatic cell nuclear transfer (SCNT) 280
sources and sinks 111
spatial summation 181
Spearman's rank correlation coefficient (rs) 149
specialised cells 76
species 146, 147
    adaptations to environment 149
    factors affecting the evolution of a species 255
    investigating variation in a

species 148
    speciation 149, 255
    species evenness 137
    species richness 137
sperm cells 76
spiracles 86
spirometers 86
squamous epithelial cells 76
stabilising selection 255
starch 23, 24
stem cells 77, 193
    potential uses of stem cells in research and medicine 77
stomatal closure 202
stratified sampling 138
stretch-mediated sodium ion channels 181
striated muscle (voluntary or skeletal) 206
substrates 50, 52, 231
    substrate-level phosphorylation 234
succession 294
    management of succession 294
sucrose 111
summation 181
surface area 62, 84
    surface area to volume ratio 84, 110
sympatric speciation 255
symplast pathway 112
synapses 181
    cholinergic synapses 183
    structure and function of a synapse 183
    synaptic knob 183
synthetic biology 123
synthetic biology 267
systematic sampling 138

T
T helper cells 125, 127
T lymphocytes 125
tannins 202
target cells 192, 194, 195
taxonomy 146
telophase 53
temperature 52, 62
    temperature coefficient 52
temperature control in organisms 158
    behavioural responses 158
    ectotherms 158
    endotherms 159
    increasing body temperature 159
    physiological responses 158, 159
    reducing body temperature 159
temporal summation 181
tertiary structures 50

thin layer chromatography (TLC) 219
threshold potentials 182, 183
tidal volume 86
tissue 75, 85, 100, 192
    layers of tissue 181
    tissue culture 279
    tissue fluid 96, 97
    tissue repair 73, 77, 124
totipotent cells 77
toxic metabolic waste 168
trachea 85
    trachea lining 85
tracheae (insects) 86
    tracheal fluid 86
    tracheoles 86
transcription 40, 246–7
    transcription factors 246
transducers 181
transfer RNA (tRNA) 40
translation 41, 245
translocation from sources to sinks 111
    loading and unloading of sucrose in the phloem 111
transmission of impulses 182
    unidirectional transmission 183
transpiration, investigating 112
transplants 170
transport 12
    active transport 63
    transport in animals 96–101
    types of membrane transport 60
transport in plants 110
    adaptations of plants living in extremes 112
    investigating transpiration 112
    loading and unloading of sucrose in the phloem 111
    structure and function of phloem 111
    structure and function of xylem 112
    supply of nutrients 110
    transport systems 110
    transport vessels 110
triglycerides 25
triose phosphate 217
triplets (codons) 41
tropisms 202

U
ultrafiltration 169
unsaturated fats 24
uracil 40
urea 169
urine 169, 170
    using urine for medical diagnosis 171

V

vaccinations 127
vacuolar pathway 112
vacuoles, permanent 13
valves 98
variation 72, 136, 254
    causes of variation 148
    different types of variation 148
    genetic variation 147, 254
    investigating variation in a species 148
    Spearman's rank correlation coefficient (rs) 149
vascular bundles 110
vectors 122
veins 96, 97, 168
vena cava 96
ventricles 98
venules 97
vital capacity 86
voluntary muscle (skeletal or striated) 206

W

Wallace, Alfred Russel 147
water 110
    osmoregulation 171
    pathways in plants 112
    properties of water 22
    water potential 63, 169, 171
weed killers 204
wound repair 124

X

xerophytes 112
xylem 77, 110
    dead lignified cells 112
    structure and function of xylem 112

OXFORD
UNIVERSITY PRESS

Great Clarendon Street, Oxford, OX2 6DP, United Kingdom

Oxford University Press is a department of the University of Oxford.

It furthers the University's objective of excellence in research, scholarship, and education by publishing worldwide. Oxford is a registered trade mark of Oxford University Press in the UK and in certain other countries

© Oxford University Press 2020

The moral rights of the authors have been asserted

First published in 2020

All rights reserved. No part of this publication may be reproduced, stored in a retrieval system, or transmitted, in any form or by any means, without the prior permission in writing of Oxford University Press, or as expressly permitted by law, by licence or under terms agreed with the appropriate reprographics rights organization. Enquiries concerning reproduction outside the scope of the above should be sent to the Rights Department, Oxford University Press, at the address above.

You must not circulate this work in any other form and you must impose this same condition on any acquirer

British Library Cataloguing in Publication Data

Data available

978-1-38-200863-1

10 9 8 7 6 5 4 3

Paper used in the production of this book is a natural, recyclable product made from wood grown in sustainable forests.

The manufacturing process conforms to the environmental regulations of the country of origin.

Printed and bound by CPI Group (UK) Ltd, Croydon, CR0 4YY

Acknowledgements

Cover artwork by John Devolle.

p10l: John Durham/Science Photo Library; **p10r**: Science History Images/Alamy Stock Photo; **p75**: Rattiya Thongdumhyu/Shutterstock; **p90**: SRattiya Thongdumhyu/Shutterstock; **p104**: Shengyong Li/Shutterstock; **p118**: Henry Thomson/Science Photo Library; **p119**: Garry Delong/Science Photo Library; **p121**: SB7/Shutterstock; **p136**: Alex Mustard/Nature Picture Library/Science Photo Library; **p139**: James King-Holmes/Science Photo Library; **p155**: Gerarda Beatriz/Shutterstock; **p169**: Jose Luis Calvo/Shutterstock; **p174t**: Ikelos Gmbh/Dr. Christopher B. Jackson/Science Photo Library; **p174b**: Science Photo Library Medimage / Science Photo Library; **p176**: Kevin Mackenzie/University of Aberdeen/Science Photo Library; **p199**: Ed Reschke/Stone/Getty Images; **p211**: Biology Media/Science Photo Library; **p223**: OUP; **p278**: Fedorov Ivan Sergeevich/Shutterstock.

All other artwork by QBS Learning

Every effort has been made to contact copyright holders of material reproduced in this book. Any omissions will be rectified in subsequent printings if notice is given to the publisher.

Be maths confident in science

Practical support for the mathematical elements of A Level science

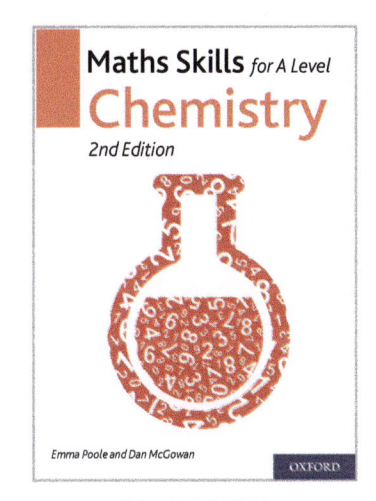

Maths Skills for A Level **Chemistry** 2nd Edition
Emma Poole and Dan McGowan
OXFORD
978 019 842897 8

★★★★★

Plenty of practice questions. Worked examples and model answers for revision and exam preparation. Very good to increase maths skills and to get top grades.

Amazon review for Maths Skills for A Level Chemistry (previous edition)

★★★★★

Fantastic. I finally understand the maths.

Amazon review for Maths Skills for A Level Chemistry (previous edition)

Maths Skills for A Level **Biology** 2nd Edition
James Penny and Philip Leftwich
OXFORD
978 019 842899 2

Maths Skills for A Level **Physics** 2nd Edition
Carol Tear
OXFORD
978 019 842898 5

Available to order from Amazon and other retailers

www.oxfordsecondary.com/mathsskillsforscience

OXFORD